AFTER BUSH

The foreign policy of the George W. Bush administration has won few admirers, and many anticipate that his successor will repudiate the actions of the past eight years. In their provocative account, Lynch and Singh argue that Bush's policy should be placed within the mainstream of the American foreign policy tradition. Further, they suggest that there will, and should, be continuity in US foreign policy from his presidency to those of his successors. Providing a positive audit of the war on terror (which they contend should be understood as a Second Cold War), they maintain that the Bush Doctrine has been consistent with past policy at times of war and that the key elements of Bush's grand strategy will continue to shape America's approach in the future. Above all, they predict that his successors will pursue the war against Islamist terror with similar dedication.

Timothy J. Lynch is Lecturer in American Foreign Policy in the Institute for the Study of the Americas at the University of London.

Robert S. Singh is Professor of Politics in the School of Politics & Sociology at Birkbeck College, University of London.

After Bush

THE CASE FOR CONTINUITY
IN AMERICAN FOREIGN POLICY

Timothy J. Lynch and Robert S. Singh

CAMBRIDGE
UNIVERSITY PRESS

CAMBRIDGE UNIVERSITY PRESS

Cambridge, New York, Melbourne, Madrid, Cape Town, Singapore, São Paulo, Delhi

Cambridge University Press
The Edinburgh Building, Cambridge CB2 8RU, UK

Published in the United States of America by Cambridge University Press, New York

www.cambridge.org
Information on this title: www.cambridge.org/9780521880046

First published 2008

Printed in the United States of America

A catalogue record for this publication is available from the British Library

ISBN 978-0-521-88004-6 hardback

Tim Lynch dedicates this book to his mother, Elizabeth Lynch

Rob Singh dedicates this book to his father, Shiv Singh

Contents

viii Contents

List of figures

Acknowledgments

This is a better book than it might otherwise have been because of the input, support (and occasional distractions) of the following people: Shereen Colvin, Marty Cupp, Toby Dodge, John Haslam, Paul Hughes, Marc Landy, Heather, Michael, and Peerson Lynch, Robert McGeehan, Iwan Morgan, Jim Pfiffner, Alison Powell, and David Watson. Several anonymous readers provided very helpful feedback. Ashley Prime, our research assistant for the book, went beyond the call of duty in proofing and other tasks; we are indebted to Gary L. McDowell and the University of Richmond for facilitating her work with us.

We are grateful to the following institutions for facilitating writing and research, and for hosting lectures, seminars, and papers where we were able to discuss aspects of the arguments we make in the book: All Souls College, Oxford; the American Foreign Policy Section of the British International Studies Association; the American Politics Group of the Political Science Association of the UK; Cumberland Lodge; the Department of Political Science and Fondren Library at Southern Methodist University; the Eccles Centre for American Studies at the British Library; the US Foreign Policy Section of the European Consortium for Political Research; the Institute for the

Study of the Americas, School of Advanced Study, University of London; the Oxford Senior Research Seminar in American Politics; the Rothermere American Institute; the Royal United Services Institute for Defence Studies; the Sandhurst Defence Forum; the International Institute for Strategic Studies; and the United States Discussion Group at Chatham House.

Our students at Birkbeck and ISA, with whom we debated our ideas, also have our thanks.

Errors of fact, interpretation, and futurology remain exclusively our own.

A change of leaders is the joy of fools.
Romanian proverb

Introduction:
Winning the Second Cold War

My fellow Americans, I speak to you tonight with the heaviest of hearts. One hour ago, at 8.30 p.m. East Coast time, pursuant to my constitutional authority as Commander-in-Chief and in accordance with the laws of war, I authorized strikes by the United States military on the principal cities of the state of Iran, including the capital, Tehran. These attacks were nuclear in nature. They achieved their objectives in full. You will recall that, three years ago at my inauguration, I stated clearly and unequivocally that it would be the policy of the United States to regard any attack on its territory with weapons of mass destruction as an act of war and that my administration would not hesitate to hold those responsible to full, direct and draconian account. I made clear then, as I make clear again now, that whether attacks on the United States be committed by an outlaw state or by a terrorist group to whom the weapons had been supplied or sold by such a state, I would hold all relevant parties accountable. As you know, these past four weeks have seen the agencies of the federal government seek to deal with the emergency response to the vicious and unprovoked attacks in Washington, Los Angeles, and New York. During that time we received credible intelligence that the nuclear devices exploded in those cities originated from the Iranian arsenal and that officials in the Iranian nuclear and intelligence agencies actively assisted their delivery to the suicide operatives who detonated the weapons. That intelligence was confirmed by the CIA and the NSA, who have closely been monitoring communications between the operatives and the Iranian authorities. The United States therefore acted accordingly tonight. Our actions were taken after full and lengthy consultation with the members of the National Security Council and key members of the congressional leadership. I deeply regret having to act in this manner. But I state again to all those who seek to harm the people of the United States and our allies: We will not tolerate attacks on our citizens. We will not accept threats to our free way of life, our values and the institutions we hold dear. We will not hesitate to visit full and appropriate retaliation on you should you succeed in your evil intent to harm us. We will prevail in this war. May God bless the United States of America.

The President of the United States, 19 June 2016

Eight years after entering office, the president departed the White House under a cloud. With his nation seemingly mired in an unwinnable and intractable war in a faraway land of which most Americans knew little and cared less, the president's political reputation lay in tatters both at home and abroad. His partisan rivals seized the opportunity of a rare national electoral triumph, while critics within his own party pondered with a mixture of bafflement and despondency how a momentous opportunity for a generational partisan advantage could have been squandered by their leader.

If this tale seems familiar, so it should. For it is that of Harry S. Truman, not George W. Bush. Or, more accurately, it is the tale of both Truman and Bush. Truman, like Bush, entered the Oval Office with low expectations, as a moderately successful US senator and machine politician. Like Bush, Truman possessed modest foreign policy credentials, having forged his Senate career on domestic concerns, and with only four months as vice-president to Franklin D. Roosevelt prior to his succeeding to the White House upon FDR's death. Even though he soon brought the Second World War to a dramatic and successful conclusion, American voters replaced a Democratic Congress with a Republican one at the 1946 elections, much as the defection of Senator James Jeffords gave control of the Senate to the Democrats in June 2001. Of most consequence, just as the terrorist attacks of September 11, 2001 transformed the presidency of Bush, so the onset of the First Cold War ended the brief moment of demobilization and peace that the Second World War's decisive end had promised America. Instead, the Truman Doctrine of containment of communism committed the United States to a generational conflict, one at once military, ideological, political, diplomatic, cultural, and covert in character. Its first substantive military test, in Korea, was one that, after an initially dramatic success for America, became deadlocked. Following the 'loss' of China, allegations of communist subversion at home, and seemingly intractable domestic problems, Truman left Washington in January 1953 with his standing lower than it had ever been. Few then would have greeted the notion that Truman would come to be regarded as a 'near great' president with anything other than derision, much less that the Republican Party – whose 1952 platform excoriated containment as an 'immoral,' ineffective, and cowardly policy against Soviet communism – would subsequently enshrine that approach as the cornerstone of US foreign policy for the next thirty-eight years.

In this book, we explain why, like the Truman Doctrine before it, the Bush Doctrine will outlast the president whose name it bears – and why it must. The case for continuity in American foreign policy after Bush rests on the central proposition that, for reasons deriving from both the international system and domestic American politics, the key axioms of the Bush Doctrine – however contentious they remain currently and however much a return to 'realism' may seem the order of the day – will not ultimately be foresworn by mainstream Americans of both parties. Moreover, the Doctrine's fundamental tenets will continue to exert a forceful hold upon foreign policy analysts and practitioners alike in a dangerously anarchic and threatening world in which American power remains the pivotal force against the twenty-first century's new totalitarians.

On January 20, 2009 a new American president will be inaugurated, the victor of the 2008 presidential election. After two tumultuous terms in which his approval ratings soared to the heights of 90 percent only to plummet to the low thirties after his re-election in 2004, President Bush will depart Washington, DC, no doubt for his beloved ranch at Crawford, Texas. A global sigh of relief will find its powerful echoes within the United States among millions of Americans who always loathed, or came to disapprove of, the Texan. Hopes and expectations of Bush's successor heralding a 'kinder, gentler' nation will be widespread, with millions eager to welcome back the 'return' of an America that addresses the world in softer tones and disavows precipitate military action – perhaps not entirely, but certainly without broad international support.

But are those hopes and expectations realistic? If this book's opening address cannot be made by a president named George W. Bush in 2016, is it inconceivable that a future occupant of the Oval Office could be obliged to make such a declaration to a people scared by Islamist terror and scarred by a new and unprecedented national calamity? And if it *is* conceivable, might this suggest that the forces of continuity shaping American foreign policy before, during, and after the Bush presidency are more profound and deeply rooted than is commonly appreciated? In short, rather than Washington's recent course being an aberrant departure from the norm, might American foreign policy after Bush more resemble than contradict that of the 2001–9 years? In this book we argue that it will – and that it should.

The case for continuity

As Shakespearian tragedies, the intertwined fates of American foreign policy and the presidency fare well. Invariably they offer a rich series of compelling characters, complex rivalries and unexpected plot turns. American history repeatedly furnishes us with tales of triumph and disaster that brook few fictional rivals. A president succeeds to office under a cloud of legitimacy, for example, lacking the mandate of having won the White House through a majority of the popular vote. A notoriously incurious and relatively provincial man, especially when contrasted with his self-consciously urbane and cosmopolitan predecessor, the new president's focus is his familiar terrain of domestic politics. His party soon loses control of one house of Congress. More dramatically, a new international security crisis signals the magnitude and lethality of an enemy threat that requires decisive global action by the United States across a number of fronts. The president responds by issuing a sweeping vision of the international system and the multiple threats it contains that Washington must confront, essentially dividing the world into those who are with or against America. The doctrine that bears his name then provides the basis for a reinvigoration of America's grand strategy and world role, supported by a far-reaching reorganization of the federal government itself.

Notwithstanding their obvious dissimilarities, the parallels between the Truman and Bush presidencies are instructive. The Bush presidency was the most important and controversial in American foreign policy since Truman. But the demise of the Bush presidency marks not the repudiation of an aberrant or even revolutionary disjuncture in foreign policy but the beginning of the end of the first phase in a Second Cold War against jihadist Islam. The past is, in this respect at least, truly prologue, even as this particular prologue has now passed. Just as Truman left office with his popularity at its lowest ebb, his party charged with a succession of foreign policy failures, and the nation mired in a seemingly unwinnable war, so Bush ends his tenure with relatively few commentators either within or outside America mourning his exit. But, like Truman before him, Bush's imprint on American grand strategy, his joining a global war on Islamist terror and establishment of policies at home and abroad to see America prevail in that war will remain substantially intact under his successors. The central premises and prescriptions of the National Security Strategy (NSS) documents of 2002 and 2006 will continue to shape American foreign policy in the new administration of 2009–13 and beyond.

At the outset, even to entertain the notion of continuity as an accurate description, much less a confident prescription, for American statecraft might appear perverse. 'Failure' has featured more frequently than 'success' in the titles and sub-titles of books on American foreign policy for several decades, indicative more of the political affinities of those authoring such analyses than the acuity of their assessments. Expert international opinion – distilled from counsels such as the *New York Times* and *Washington Post*, the Council on Foreign Relations, the British Broadcasting Corporation, and al-Jazeera – treats as axiomatic the failure of the Bush foreign policy not only in Iraq but in the broader war on terror, from Latin America to Southeast Asia, and in the volatility enveloping the developing world. The desirability of a new strategic course being charted for America after the 2008 presidential election seems incontestable. This is what hundreds of learned volumes and tens of thousands of column inches have urged on Washington for several years, their sage advice vindicated – in their own eyes at least – by the worsening state of international order, the failure of the war on terror to pacify Muslim lands from Algeria to Malaysia, and the seemingly inexorable increase in global anti-Americanism. In style and substance, after the excessive militarism, secrecy, and hubris of Bush, a return to old-style realism, if not quite to the liberal institutionalism and cosmopolitanism so beloved of most western intellectuals, is surely merited. Now is the time when all Americans of goodwill reject unilateralism, 'coalitions of the willing,' and preventive war, and instead rally to the United Nations, international law, multilateralism, and peace. In the fevered speculations inside the Washington beltway, amid the pundits experienced in the horse races of partisan conflict and electoral calculation, few find any presidential candidates promising 'more Bush.' Is this not the clearest indication that the failed policies of an unloved administration will soon be put decisively to rest?

Our answer is emphatically not. To anticipate such a future is to wait for Godot as surely as it is to invite continuing irresolution and irresponsibility by Washington in the face of grave and growing international threats. America, that mercifully 'dangerous nation,' has periodically experienced brief moments of Hamlet-like intro-spection and self-doubt.[1] But rarely has its irresolution or irresponsi-bility in the face of international disorder lasted for long. In this book, we not only challenge the notion that foreign policy under Bush departed from the American foreign policy tradition, arguing instead that it fitted within and extended that tradition. We also advance the case that, after Bush, there will exist few compelling reasons to expect or want America's fundamental approach to inter-national affairs to alter substantially from that outlined in the NSS of 2002. Continuity, not discontinuity, will remain the hallmark of foreign policy. American primacy, as a means and end, will not be rejected. Preventive and preemptive action, as important supple-ments to traditional strategies of containment, will not be aban-doned. The belief that the political character, internal configuration and the avowed intentions of national regimes matter as much as their capabilities will not disappear. A belief in the desirability and justness of a liberal democratic peace will stay firm. Whatever the temporary appeal of the siren calls of narrow realists, liberal interna-tionalists, and isolationists alike to abandon a confident and assertive American foreign policy, the gravity of the threats that America faces, the intractable interdependence of US fortunes with the rest of the world, and the enduringly distinctive nature of American interests, ideals, and identity together preclude an extended disen-gagement from an increasingly dangerous world.

Moreover, the alternative grand strategies on offer for the US provide little cause for optimism that rejecting a distinctly American internationalism will serve America well. Change there will be in foreign policy, as always, in elements of successive administrations' style, tone, personnel, policy priorities, theoretical justifications, strategic adjustments, and tactical emphases. But history teaches that such changes invariably occur at the margins of established policy, not in its central precepts. We live in a time of severe and increasing danger, comparable to that at the outset of the Second World War. As such, there will be no repudiation by mainstream Republicans or Democrats of the necessary option of 'coalitions of the willing,' nor will there be a newly emphatic embrace of multilateralism and the UN, a downsizing of the defense budget, a retardation of national and theater ballistic missile defense, or a U-turn on treaties such as the International Criminal Court. For all their recent acrimony, Democrats and Republicans have more in common with each other on foreign policy than they do even with their closest allies in Europe and Asia. Americans remain a patriotic but nationalistic people, eager for peace but prone, more than they may appreciate, to war. Focusing our eyes on the particular controversies of the moment should not blind us to the strong and extensive continuities that exert a more profound influence on America's world role and influence.

Few scholarly enterprises, admittedly, are so fraught with pitfalls as predicting future directions in US foreign policy in the midst of a highly contentious present. Public intellectuals in general, and political scientists in particular, have a poor record of accurate prophecy.[2] Moreover, even realism – the dominant school in international relations theory – has failed to account for some of the most momentous of developments in world affairs, not least the collapse of the Soviet Union. When conventional wisdoms are tacking strongly in another direction, too, the most prudent course might appear to be to bend with the prevailing wind. But, whilst being mindful of the many failures of prediction to which our profession is guilty as charged, and Bush's deep unpopularity, it is imperative to depersonalize US foreign policy and engage in a serious analysis of the dilemmas facing American decision-makers. Indeed, it may well be only several years hence (whether another Republican or a Democrat takes the helm) that will provide the full corrective to the view that the Bush era was an aberration.

But the case for an essential continuity in the operation of US foreign policy after Bush rests on strong foundations. As recent years have demonstrated, America remains, for better and worse, the primary and central actor on the world stage. Washington operates in a world of imperfect information, political and policy trade-offs, a limited menu of available options, and circumscribed time lines and mechanisms for exerting influence. How new policy-makers fare in confronting the deeply embedded problems that they face will determine whether the type of declaration imagined at the outset of this chapter (one that could as plausibly address an Islamist Pakistan as Iran), and the humanitarian tragedy it represents, can be avoided through a successful execution of the next phase of the Second Cold War.

The Second Cold War

Since the collapse of the Soviet Union and America's emergence as the sole world superpower, scholars have labored to describe and predict the nature of global affairs. After the attacks on New York and Washington of 9/11, this task assumed an even greater urgency. Some cast their prognoses in terms of competing ideas that emerged in the decade that spanned the end of one era and the onset of another. Concepts such as the 'End of History,' the 'Clash of Civilizations,' and 'globalization' became enlisted in attempts to assess the post-1991 and then the post-9/11 world order.[3] Some analysts searched for clues in the concept of 'empire' and whether America, for good or ill, was such a thing.[4] Still others sought either to confirm or challenge the appropriateness of the 'war on terrorism' declared by President Bush. A few, following the tradition of international relations scholar John Mearsheimer, even suggested we might 'soon miss the Cold War.'[5]

These concepts have contributed valuable lenses by which current conflicts can be viewed. In this book, however, we argue that an additional approach can be added. It is one that seeks to locate the variety of competing arguments on world order into a broader and, perhaps, more useful notion. Our central thesis here is a simple one: we are in the early stages of a Second Cold War. This sequel, for all its differences from its predecessor, nonetheless has many marked similarities with it, ones whose nature and reach have been obscured partly by our proximity to that conflict and partly through our own failures of imagination. Moreover, if the Second Cold War is ultimately to be won, understanding the parallels between the two Cold Wars is a fundamental prerequisite in informing the statecraft, strategies, and tactics that may eventually secure that victory.[6]

It is necessary to engage in a suspension of disbelief in order to approach the Second Cold War with dispassion. Of course, certain key elements of the First Cold War are not apparent in the Second. The United States occupies a singular unrivalled military supremacy in the international system. That system is not bipolar. Rather, according to your chosen paradigm, it is unipolar, multipolar or apolar. Communism, as an ideology employed and exported by revolutionaries to challenge liberal democratic market capitalism, has exhausted its influence and appeal (though Islamism, equally inspiring to some, has not). The 'hard' security threats of the First Cold War – the mutually assured destruction of a nuclear exchange – have evolved into the challenges posed by the spread of weapons of mass destruction, 'rogue states,' and catastrophic 'superterrorism' by non- or sub-state organizations such as al Qaeda – as determined as the West's enemy in the First Cold War but uncontained by the West's deterrents.

These differences, however, should not blind us to the powerful continuities and parallels that exist between the First and Second

Cold Wars. The First and Second World Wars differed in their underlying causes, in the character of the participants, and in the nature
of the fighting. Similarly, the two Cold Wars differ in terms of their
causes, protagonists, and battles but otherwise share many key features. Most notably, as we will argue throughout this book, debates
about the First and Second Cold Wars exhibit:

i.   *Disagreement about the appropriate historical point at which they
     commenced.* In the case of the First Cold War, it is conventional
     to date the conflict as having begun at, or shortly after, the end
     of the Second World War, with the rapid breakdown in relations
     between the western allies on the one side and the Soviet Union
     on the other. Some, however, mark the Bolshevik Revolution of
     1917 as the beginning of the First Cold War, an ideological con-
     flict interrupted by the outbreak of a second 'European civil
     war.'[7] Similarly, while many commentators mark either 1989 or
     9/11 as having initiated a new era in international relations,
     others point to the Iranian Revolution of 1979 as having marked
     the crucial beginning of conflict between 'radical' or 'political'
     Islam and the West.[8]

ii. *Disagreement over the duration of the conflict.* If it is conventional
     to locate the First Cold War's origins in 1945, it is equally
     conventional to date its ending at 1989 – with the peaceful rev-
     olutions in Eastern Europe and the clear abandonment of expan-
     sionist communism by Moscow that these signaled – or at 1991,
     with the USSR's collapse. But, in charting the course of the First
     Cold War, scholars have emphasized the quite distinct time
     frames that existed from 1945 to 1991, and the markedly differ-
     ent nature of superpower relations between and within these.
     Equally, wherever one cares to identify the precise date of the
     beginning of the Second Cold War, our expectations should be
     of a dynamic rather than static conflict – a war likely to embody
     markedly different historical moments before the fighting is
     finally exhausted.

iii. *Disagreement about the nature of the conflict.* If a lack of consensus
     still characterizes discussions over when the First Cold War
     began and ended, there is also disagreement on what the conflict
     was about. For some, it was an essentially ideological conflict
     between two rival social systems whose long-term viability
     depended upon the defeat and transformation of the other. For
     others, the conflict was not about ideology *per se* but about
     Moscow's expansionism and its exportation of revolution. With
     the arrival of Mikhail Gorbachev in 1985, and the fruition of
     Ronald Reagan's hardline approach, the conflict was essentially
     over, even though it took six more years until the USSR was for-
     mally wound up.[9] For others, however, the First Cold War was
     less about ideology than about traditional 'great power' rivalry
     and the nature of a bipolar international system from 1945 to
     1991. Equally, 'responsibility' for the First Cold War's onset has
     been laid variously at the feet of the Soviet and American
     leaders. Similarly, the Second Cold War has not yet seen the
     development of consensus about either what it is centrally
     about – terrorism, radical Islam, Islam, American imperialism –
     or who or what bears the responsibility for its onset – George
     W. Bush, neoconservatives, Washington, al Qaeda, jihadists,
     Islamism. The very fact that, in the West at least, intellectuals,
     analysts, and policy-makers alike have proven unable to settle on
     a common term for characterizing the current predicament – war
     on terrorism?, the long war?, World War III?, World War IV?, the
     war on radical Islam? – is powerfully suggestive of the dissensus
     that bedeviled participants in the First Cold War.[10]
iv. *Global conflagration.* Although critics regard the argument of
     John Lewis Gaddis that the Cold War might appropriately be
     retermed the 'Long Peace' as typically inattentive to 'third world'
     conflict, he hit on something profound yet simple: there was no
     direct 'hot' war between the USA and the USSR.[11] The central
     theater in which it was played out was Europe – where, in

contrast to 1914–18 and 1939–45, very few people died – with extremely bloody but peripheral campaigns across the other continents.[12] The Second Cold War differs from its predecessor in important respects in this regard. Its central theater is the Middle East, even though its scope is global. The Second Cold War has already seen the US involved in direct conflict with its principal (but not only) enemy – in Afghanistan – and in a second 'hot' war in Iraq. But the conflict is not likely to be characterized by constant 'hot' wars. Like the First, the Second Cold War will be generational in length and waged by multiple strategic and tactical means, of which direct military engagement is but one – exceptional – element.

v. *Divisions.* One of the most important features of the First Cold War was the internally divided nature of the communist threat. What western planners saw as a monolith was, with the benefit of hindsight and archival access, splintered and filled with internal distrust. To a lesser extent, divisions among America's allies have been underplayed but were occasionally fierce. What much of post-First Cold War research has revealed is the extent to which we still do not know how and why events occurred as they did but also the troubling level of mistaken beliefs and erroneous assumptions held at the time by key actors, about themselves and about their enemies. Divisions over how best to secure overall objectives were a constant of the First Cold War. So, too, was the situation in which the behavior of the apparent 'superpowers' could become hostage to clients and allies. Nations had to prioritize and to select options in many instances where no good options existed. Given the stakes, this was hardly surprising. Nor is it surprising that such divisions also strongly characterize the Second Cold War. Consensus on matters from the appropriate identification of the 'enemy,' through the urgency of the conflict, to the definition of what might constitute victory and the relative emphasis to be accorded military, economic, diplomatic, and cultural instruments to achieve this end, is a distant and dim prospect. Just as in the First Cold War, Washington had of necessity to ally with toxic regimes in order to defeat a more serious and immediate enemy, so it remains in the Second.

vi. *Agency*. The 'great man' school of history overplays individual agency in world history. Historical determinism underplays it. Skillful leaders can, as in the First Cold War, analyze situations shrewdly, articulate policies clearly, and craft the most efficient fitting of means to ends to realize their goals. That is, leaders can act – or emerge – as statesmen as well as politicians. Equally, their calculations can prove catastrophic.[13] But beyond the political and intellectual elites of particular societies, the mass of individuals who – whether consciously or otherwise – form participants in the Second Cold War can act in ways to prolong or inhibit its duration. In the First Cold War, millions of Americans were active foot soldiers in the struggle against communism, from the men and women in the US armed forces to the workers in defense industries, analysts in the think tanks and members of federal agencies charged with implementing containment. More broadly, by paying the taxes that funded the federal government's instruments of containment – from the Marshall Plan to SDI research – and by maintaining the domestic conditions that underpinned America's superpower status, the American public shaped an era that ultimately yielded the defeat of their most potent adversary. Yet millions of individuals in communist regimes refused to imbibe the oppressive doctrine under which they were forced to labor. It was ultimately the pressure from this genuinely popular movement that saw the inevitable defeat of communism. By analogy, the vanquishing of Islamic terrorism in the Second Cold War cannot occur solely through the efforts of non-Islamic forces, however carefully calibrated their statecraft. It rests, centrally, upon the ability and willingness of millions of Muslims – not merely within the Middle East, Asia, and Africa but globally – to reject jihadism and effect an Islamic Reformation that marries the protections of political liberalism to the values of Islam.

There is a military maxim that fighting a current war with the strategy of the last is doomed to fail. The First and Second Cold Wars are an exception to this rule. As we will argue throughout this book, the current struggle against Islamic fundamentalism shares too many similarities with the last great war of ideology to sacrifice its strategic lessons. In scale, scope, duration, internal divisions, agency, and, happily, result, the First Cold War offers a roadmap for the Second – one which no American administration after Bush will reject.

Plan of the book

In the pages that follow, we advance the case for continuity in an assertive American foreign policy as the surest route to winning the Second Cold War. The next chapter argues for the place of the Bush Doctrine within the American foreign policy tradition. Bush's foreign policy was not apart from but, rather, remarkably consistent with past practice.

Chapter 2 takes this argument a stage further by looking at how the post-9/11 response has utilized – not undercut – the US Constitution.

Chapters 3 and 4 then evaluate contrasting interim audits of the Second Cold War, contending that, on balance, it has achieved considerable success. As such, and although it has a long way to go, it is unlikely to suffer significant substantive revision through the 2010s.

Chapter 5 examines the controversial place of the Iraq War and occupation within the longer-term goals of the Second Cold War. Viewing this campaign as mismanaged but not misconceived, we find analogies not so much to Vietnam but to the Korean conflict of the First Cold War as a more helpful guide to the likely course of Iraq policy into the future.

Chapter 6 then considers the broader Middle East, contending that the Bush approach will continue to shape that of his successors in this crucial region. Compared to the situation in 1979, US policy in the Middle East has been positively transformed, to the extent that no serious American statesman or stateswoman will seek, or be able, to change the fundamental terms of the new engagement.

Chapter 7 argues that, *contra* much realist sniping, America will continue to enjoy unparalleled international primacy with little or no attempt to balance against it. Rather, we argue that alliances are more likely to be conditioned by an acceptance of the indispensability of American power in the face of a new global enemy. The remaking of an English-speaking alliance – which includes India – is posited in our assessment of America's emerging friends and foes.

Chapter 8 establishes the domestic terrain of modern foreign policy, arguing that the Second Cold War, like the First, has commanded, and will continue to command, a broad domestic consensus.

Our concluding chapter, rather than attempting long-range prophecy, argues on the basis of where we have come from and where we are likely to go after Bush: toward an America and a world order in which US power is accepted not for its moral purity but for its constant utility in a deeply dangerous world.

I

Bush and the American foreign policy tradition

War is God's way of teaching Americans geography
                                        Ambrose Bierce, c. 1900

In this chapter we argue that the war on terror – the Second Cold War – is better understood as a revision rather than a rejection of the dominant American foreign policy tradition. Indeed, the war's durability as a strategy, and the prospects for its ultimate success, flow from its unification of the different strands of that tradition. These are enumerated below and the Bush foreign policy weighed against them. In what follows we place the Second Cold War on a wide historical canvas. In the next chapter we consider in more detail Bush's use of the American 'national security constitution.' Continuity, not change, is the hallmark of each.

Is there a US foreign policy tradition?

'Tradition,' as a concept, is difficult to define with precision. It smacks of what international relations theorists term 'unit-level variables': national character and custom, particularity and idiosyncrasy, history and experience. Identifying a distinctive foreign policy tradition inevitably involves the scholar in this often fuzzy realm of analysis. Attempts at definition are invariably normative. That is, scholars define a foreign policy tradition that is consonant with their generalized view of American conduct. Walter Russell Mead, for example, observes 'a special providence' in the history of US foreign policy that accounts for its utility – 'American foreign policy works,' he says.[1] Noam Chomsky also observes a tradition but one much more ruthless in its coherency and intent: 'the major [foreign] policy goal of the US has been to maximize repression and suffering.'[2] Mead highlights a 'pragmatic and results driven' world view.[3] Chomsky fulminates against a doctrinaire American imperialism. To identify a tradition or persistent pattern one clearly does not have to be sympathetic to America's international ambitions. And yet the language of tradition, its definition and deployment, is often (though not exclusively) the preserve of those who recognize some exceptional, even virtuous, and consistent quality to US designs. Tradition is a loaded term.

Several factors – some the product of luck, others of conscious design or clash of designs – form the contours of the American foreign policy tradition. Inescapably, the physical situation of the United States, especially at its birth, conditioned how its government navigated the external world. The structure, character, and reach of that government, in turn, affected its foreign policy. Historians and political scientists continue to dispute the explanatory power of each. At the risk of oversimplification we will paint the two significant strands of the tradition and then suggest how and why Bush worked within rather than against them.

The tradition take one: geography and ideology

Assertions of an exceptional lineage in American foreign policy history have a long pedigree but increasingly are not academically fashionable. The notion of any nation state, let alone that of the United States, being exceptional contradicts the cultural relativism of modern university teaching. It is not unusual for student scorn to greet the claim that America, of all places, enjoys a special providence.[4] The argument from exceptionalism rests on the interplay and tension between two American persuasions: insularity (born of geography) and expansionism (born of ideology).

Geography as destiny

Customarily, when Alexis de Tocqueville's *Democracy in America* (1835) is abridged his first chapter is sacrificed.[5] This is a shame since 'The external configuration of North America,' its title, suggests that geography is a significant part of the American story. In this neglected chapter, Tocqueville wonders at the remarkable physical bounty of the United States. 'The valley of the Mississippi,' he contended, was 'the most magnificent dwelling that God has ever prepared for the habitation of man . . . . [and the whole] continent the still-empty cradle of a great nation.'[6] Geography did not merely separate America from Europe but set the stage for a wholly new society:

> It was there that civilized men were to try to build a society on new foundations, and applying for the first time theories until then unknown or reputed inapplicable, they were going to give the world a spectacle for which the history of the past had not prepared it.[7]

The geography of the United States made its exceptional experiment possible. The Puritans, it should be recalled, were on an 'errand into the *wilderness*.'[8] The French Revolution was similarly, grandly experimental but bounded by its geographic limits. The new post-1789 France was still encircled by an old Europe. Revolutionary or not, the new regime still had to be mindful of its neighborhood. Indeed, the Revolution's greatest progeny, Napoleon Bonaparte, was so attuned to France's security situation that his solution to it – aggressive expansion – marks out the substantial legacy of 1789; the proclaimers of the Declaration of the Rights of Man ended up killing very many men, women and children indeed (including several of Tocqueville's relatives).[9]

It has become common in textbooks to observe that the newly united American states, post-1787, faced the opposite situation. Americans enjoyed unparalleled oceanic protection to their east and west while to their north lay a 'relatively weak "hostage" state,' and beyond that a largely frozen ocean.[10] 'The Americans have had no neighbours and consequently,' noted Tocqueville, 'no great wars.'[11] For the first several decades of its life the US faced a serious European threat, including war on its own soil (against the British, 1812–14) and a more sporadic Mexican threat, but otherwise its eastern coast (at least until 2001) and southern border have been policeable and secure. The indigenous people within the new nation – quickly and tragically laid waste by disease and expropriation – 'vanished like a sound without an echo.'[12]

This remarkably fortuitous geography has afforded, according to this version of the foreign policy tradition, what has been called a 'free security.'[13] As the label implies, security was purchased at little cost, especially compared to that incurred by European nations. America, according to this understanding, has not had to fight for its security so much as avoid the fights of others – many miles away – whose security is anything but free. The US can (or could) afford to isolate itself from old world struggles because its security was only tangentially linked to their outcome. As John Adams, the second president, acknowledged:

> There is a Balance of Power in Europe. Nature has formed it. Practice and Habit have confirmed it, and it must exist forever . . . It never could be our interest to unite with France in the destruction of England . . . On the other hand, it could never be our duty to unite with Britain in too great a humiliation of France.[14]

An accident of geography accounts for the United States' relative immunity to foreign invasion; there is really no American equivalent to the state-on-state attacks that punctuate European history. Indeed, a third of what constitutes the present-day contiguous USA was *purchased*, not seized, from France in 1803, a fact to which we shall return later. Isolationism, the concept that America's security is proportional to the absence of its formal ties with foreign nations (fewer ties equals more security), thus presents itself as an important strand of the US foreign policy tradition. And it has never really gone away. 'The external politics of the United States,' wrote Tocqueville, 'consists much more in abstaining than in doing.'[15]

American foreign relations can be mapped by the ebb and flow of this isolationist impulse. For example:

Introvert	Extrovert
1776–98	1798–1824
1824–44	1844–71
1871–91	1891–1918
1918–40	1940–66/7
1966/7–80	1980–ongoing

Arthur Schlesinger Jr. called it part of the 'cycles of American history,' in which the 'conduct of [foreign] policy is subject to cyclical fluctuations of withdrawal and return.'[16] Isolationists have some choice sources on which to draw. In arguably the most important foreign policy prescription ever offered, the Republic's first president implored his countrymen to leave the world alone:

> [H]istory and experience prove that foreign influence is one of the most baneful foes of republican government . . . Hence, therefore, it must be unwise in us to implicate ourselves by artificial ties in the ordinary vicissitudes of her politics, or the ordinary combinations and collisions of her friendships or enmities.[17]

In the 1830s, Tocqueville commended the freedom of action offered by Washington's parting advice:

He succeeded in keeping his country at peace when all the rest of the universe was at war, and he established as a point of departure that the self-interest well understood of Americans was never to take part in the internal quarrels of Europe.[18]

'No foreign entanglements' was not an ideological premise but good realism. Robert Kagan, more recently, despite a staunch defense of the basic decency inherent in US foreign policy, concedes that it is not ideology but situation – geographic and historical – that determines a nation's foreign policy. A young, emerging state has a pressing need to cut deals, to duck and weave in order to remain secure. Since alliances must necessarily be decided by their practical utility rather than their political purity, 'we may safely trust to temporary alliances for extraordinary emergencies,' George Washington advised.[19] A nation without great economic and military power – nineteenth-century America – had to find ways of advancing its position that did not require the application of such power. Nations with troops and money – nineteenth-century Europe – enjoyed the luxury, and consequences, of their deployment.[20]

The most influential geography-as-destiny thesis was offered by Frederick Jackson Turner in 1893. It is not just distance from the 'old world' that allows for American isolationism and selective engagement but the physical scale and nature of the American nation itself. It is its own pressure valve – or at least it was during the frontier expansion of the nineteenth century. Until 1890, announced Turner, 'The existence of an area of free land, its continuous recession, and the advance of American settlement westward, explain American development.'[21] The environmental hostility of the border zone, 'the meeting point between savagery and civilization,' necessitated a westward mindset, antithetical to foreign concerns. 'The frontier is the line of the most rapid and effective Americanization.' What Germans were – the land they came *from* – in Turner's example, was irrelevant when set against the frontier they went *to*:

> The wilderness masters the colonist. It finds him a European in dress, industries, tools, modes of travel, and thought. It takes him from the railroad car and puts him in the birch canoe.[22]

According to this version of the tradition, the security situation facing the frontiersman and the character of the regime shaped by him was – after a sprinkling of Lockean individualism – almost entirely endogenous.

The legacy of this atomistic social freedom is often forgotten or ignored by contemporary non-American (especially European) commentators. The frontier experience is dismissed as too anachronistic to explain an extant US world view or is revisited to remind us that it was a period of suffering – even genocide – for Native Americans and African-Americans and/or created an unhealthy and enduring love of guns.[23] A less noticed, but no less significant, legacy of the frontier was the relative obscurity of nearly all American politicians, particularly of presidents. European geography has always been conducive to travel. European statesmen have recurrently asserted a right – by violence, consent, or, more recently, public apathy – to involvement in the politics of their near neighbors. The notion of a European statesman having no experience of foreign affairs is unthinkable. Not so American presidents. Pre-White House exposure to international politics is the exception rather than the rule of presidential biographies. Indeed, rather ironically, formal experience of the outside world has been inversely proportionate to the ability to travel to it.[24]

Does American geography explain Bush foreign policy? In part, yes. If anything, Bush entered the White House with considerable 'foreign' policy experience by virtue of being governor of Texas, 1995–2001 – an executive post that necessarily demands interaction with Mexico; the Texas–Mexico border is the longest under the quasi-jurisdiction of a single American state.[25] And yet this was a man who was either, to his detractors, ignorant of world affairs – 'I don't have the foggiest idea about what I think about international, foreign policy'[26] – or, more generously, motivated to render American foreign policy more humble, his presidential campaign theme in 2000.[27]

If geography has been so important where does this lead us? Does US foreign policy follow a pattern that its exceptional security situation lays down?[28] The US is more secure than other aspiring hegemons and so can afford to allow its domestic character to inform its external posture. France has historically been unable to do this. It has had to worry about its neighbors. French values have had a far more limited impact on French imperial and foreign policy, which is cynical and cunning (and occasionally effective as a result) because that is what guarantees the nation's domestic security. China presents a similar case: a nation surrounded by potential and actual aggressors. Chinese foreign policy has inescapably reflected this security situation. US foreign policy, in contrast, can be and has been expansive and moralistic because its geographic situation allows it such indulgences – a freedom of action denied to former great powers (whose antipathy toward the United States has grown in proportion to their cognizance of this quirk of fate). Fate allows America to be exceptional; it is no accident that Tocqueville opens his famous book the way he does.

Ideology as destiny

Alongside the oddity of geography is the ideology made possible by it. This ideology has been defined in several ways. The concept of an ideology is problematic in itself, occupying 'a complicated realm where conceptual confusion often reigns.'[29] Latin America, similarly geographically distant from Europe, developed very differently to the United States. Australia, more distant still, is better known for its prized isolation than any expansionist mission. On its own, geography is rarely destiny. Likewise, if we glance at the history of the greatest powers of the last century we observe how ideology has often been subservient to enduring geo-strategic interests. Adolf Hitler exploited the longstanding German concept of *Lebensraum* but he did not invent it. Stalin's creation of a buffer zone in Eastern Europe after Hitler's defeat was certainly clothed in socialist rhetoric but is better explained as a response to recurrent invasions from the west, several pre-dating the USSR.[30] The great historian of American politics Richard Hofstadter pondered how 'It has been our fate as a nation, not to have ideologies but to be one.'[31] America was made by an ideology. France and Russia existed before their revolutions; the United States did not. The ideology of the United States – unlike that of France, Germany, and Russia – trumped the geography that made it possible. Also, unlike these nations, America's constitutional project stuck, allowing it to enjoy 'an ideological continuity in the realm of foreign policy.'[32] This tension between a geography inviting inversion and an enduring ideology demanding expansion is central to the American foreign policy tradition and it is one George W. Bush captures rather well.

The United States was not dedicated to insularity but rather to a proposition that all people have rights – given not by government but by God. These rights were 'unalienable' and universal. The particularity of geography necessarily gave way to the universalism of ideology. Indeed, with America's nationalism defined in civic, not ethnic or religious, terms, the nation was rendered especially attractive as a destination for immigrants from around the world. Abraham Lincoln, the greatest president and rhetorician in American history, understood the special attraction and obligation of his nation:

> [The authors of the Declaration of Independence] set up a standard maxim for free society, which should be familiar to all, and revered by all; constantly looked to, constantly labored for, and even though never perfectly attained, constantly approximated, and thereby constantly spreading and deepening its influence, and augmenting the happiness and value of life to all peoples of all colors everywhere.[33]

The consistency of Bush's rhetoric lies in the rearticulating of this universalistic compulsion – Bush as statesman – one which is in

tension, both before and after 9/11, with his isolationist impulses –
Bush the Midland rancher. Thus an 'exemplarism,' born of separate-
ness and physical distance, exists in tension with a 'vindicationism,'
born of universalist principles.[34] The former justifies a disdain for
foreigners – let them follow us if they want – which has allowed
America to withdraw from them: 'Strait is the gate and narrow is the
way that leads to liberty,' wrote John Adams, 'and few nations, if any,
have found it.'[35] The latter demands an active mission to spread the
American way of life abroad: 'We have it in our power,' wrote
Thomas Paine, 'to begin the world all over again.'[36] After 9/11, there
has been more Paine and Lincoln than Adams in the Bush foreign
policy.

Some of the greatest writing on America wrestles with this
ineluctable tension. Tocqueville observed an insular nation, separated
by geography, wedded to a 'fated . . . irresistible and universal' democratic ideology.[37] He puzzled over a people far from the vicissitudes of
European politics who were nevertheless obsessed – 'insatiable for
praise' – with how Europeans perceived them. 'One cannot imagine a
more disagreeable and talkative patriotism. It fatigues even whose who
honor it.'[38] Louis Hartz, now much derided by the American academic
left,[39] wrote influentially of the American 'national liberal spirit' and
an 'absolute national morality' which was 'inspired either to withdraw
from "alien" things or to transform them: it cannot live in comfort
constantly by their side':

> American conceptions of foreign policy respond to the old argument
> between experiment and destiny – between the United States per-
> ceived as one nation among many, liable like all others to angelic
> impulses and predatory lusts; and the United States perceived as a
> chosen nation appointed by Providence to redeem the fallen world . . .
> Its messianism is the polar counterpart of its isolationism . . .[40]

This tension is basic to American foreign policy and has endured
for more than two centuries. The Monroe Doctrine of 1823 and the

Bush Doctrine of 2002 both capture it. James Monroe asserted his
nation's right to interfere in the Americas and to deny that right
to Europeans. He claimed the right to expand and to remain isolated. 'Most Americans saw no contradiction between the principle of isolationism and hemispheric hegemony.'[41] George W. Bush
demanded a right to act in isolation, if necessary, to realize US security by securing the universal rights of foreigners. Bush, elected in
part to make America's external posture more humble (isolationist
impulse), initiated a bold reformation of the Middle East (expansionist impulse).

The attempt to simultaneously maximize influence and minimize
interference is an odd but enduring feature of how America has dealt
with the outside world. In pursuing such a grand Middle Eastern
plan, the chosen instruments were hedged and limited – regime
change (expansionist impulse) via lean, quick, in-and-out military
force (isolationist impulse). Some have claimed this duality answers
a domestic imperative: to be idealist in ends but realistic in means.
Colin Dueck believes this results in foreign policy on the cheap –
high ambitions (usually articulated by presidents) with low responsibility (embraced by a risk-averse Congress). It certainly recurs with
remarkable regularity. Woodrow Wilson's League of Nations plan
died on the Senate floor in 1920. Harry Truman's early efforts to
contain a staunch ideological opponent, 1947–50, relied on too few
US troops. The same observation can be made of Bush's on-going
Iraq occupation, especially at its beginning.[42] Certain factors compel
intervention – the demands of trade and security have inescapably
forced the United States to play global politics – while others factors
induce withdrawal – the desire to make trade the sole purpose of
foreign entanglements, for example. Thus trade, for scholars of
several persuasions, becomes a motive that explains both engagement *and* withdrawal. Likewise, in broader terms, the ideology of the
United States is schizophrenic: warning against the costs of intervention whilst simultaneously demanding it.

The tradition take two: security and trade

The concept of a 'free security' afforded by geography – and the theories of introversion and extroversion it invites – is open to challenge on several fronts. American security has not been a constant and it has never been cost-free. Americans, even at the nation's birth, as Walter LaFeber points out, 'did not live in any splendid isolation, far from the turmoil and corruption of Europe. They instead had to live in settlements that were surrounded by great and ambitious European powers.'[43] Security changed in focus rather than degree as the Republic matured. Its greatest bloodletting took place in 1861–5 – an internal war, certainly, but one which was hardly isolated from international politics.[44] Conceptions of national *in*security would continue to be various, dependent on the people holding them, from frontiersmen to freedom riders.[45]

Critics of US foreign policy have recurrently chastised its makers for demanding a limitless power to realize a perfect security. This critical perspective has been in vogue since the early years of the First Cold War – communism was never the threat Washington made it out to be and thus all anti-communism was paranoia – but has been especially apparent in the war on terror/Second Cold War – wherein, the critics charge, threats have been exaggerated to facilitate executive tyranny and military expansion.[46]

Even a cursory analysis reveals a history scarred by surprise foreign attack. Americans have had many reasons to demand *better* security. The war of 1812, the Alamo, Fort Sumter, Pearl Harbor, 9/11 – none of these assaults violated a perfect security. They did lead to quite justifiable demands to improve the nation's security at significant cost. The burden of realizing a free, let alone a perfect, security is not what separates the American statesman from his European counterpart. As we shall discuss in a moment, George W. Bush can hardly be chastised for seeking a pristine security. Consistent with his forebears, he set about finding *enough* security by eliminating foreign structural forces that threatened that security.

It is also worth noting how patterns of congressional activism in foreign policy correlate remarkably well with perceptions of national security. For example, 1850–1900, an era of more limited foreign policy threat, is regarded as the age of 'congressional government.'[47] The rise of foreign threat thereafter, in broad terms, demanded the rise of presidential prerogative in foreign policy and a matching deference from Congress to the White House – what we term in the next chapter the national security constitution. FDR did not come to Capitol Hill to lobby for a declaration of war on Japan. He asked that a state of war be recognized, knowing the legislature's answer before he rose to speak. Threat has a way of focusing the minds of politicians in ways that more pacific periods do not.[48] Tocqueville observed this in 1831 and George W. Bush was illustrative of the trend.[49] The 1990s were marked by significant assertions of congressional authority in foreign affairs – arguably at the expense of necessary presidential counterterrorism strategy.[50] This interregnum has deservedly earned a reputation not as the 'end of history' but, rather, as a derelict holiday from it.[51] After al Qaeda attacked in 2001, history returned with a vengeance, and presidential activism was demanded, not merely acquiesced in or appeased, by Congress.

The fundamental point is that security has had a marked impact on how the American government organizes its foreign policy. Different institutions rise and fall dependent on the security situation in which the nation finds itself. This is a long way from asserting that an unreasonable demand for a free/perfect security leads to overextension abroad and/or repression at home. The American foreign policy tradition has been shaped by threat because threats – potential and actual – are basic and recurrent phenomena in US history. Tocqueville was right: 'Accidental causes can increase the influence of the executive power.'[52] They always have and they still do, a theme to which we shall return at length in the next chapter.

Trade as the American foreign policy ideology

The linking of America's trading prowess with its search for security is a fundamental part of a foreign policy tradition that Bush articulated very well. Much of the rest of this book goes on to support the means and ends of Bush foreign policy. We do so in part because he synchronized the quest for security with the mechanism of trade. To grasp this argument it is necessary to understand the ideology of American foreign policy as one substantially rooted in material (and thus in economic and trade) terms.

Rather than being pulled in two directions, American foreign policy responds to economic stimulus because its ideology is aspirational in material terms; the Declaration of Independence asserts an unalienable right to *the pursuit* of happiness. Changed from 'property' late in its drafting, Jefferson's preamble captures a core component of the American ideology: the attribution of positive moral value to the quest for economic wealth and the 'domestic Tranquility' (posited in the Constitution's preamble) it ensures. A tranquil nation is comprised of citizens active in the pursuit of independence from centralized power. Such independence strengthens the bonds of kinship between citizens and nations that trade with one another. The morality of trade is not a discrete one – few moralities are. Indeed, it depends on its active propagation abroad – this is where the markets that facilitate the pursuit of happiness are to be found. Other ideologies have sought to foster rival moralities. Communism was predicated on the immorality and 'scientific' unsustainability of capitalism. One can of course dispute the morality of the American system but not its remarkable success, especially compared to the record of its many ideological competitors who have fallen by the wayside.

American foreign policy seeks markets. To establish them, policymakers must foster security and stability abroad to complement tranquility at home. They might occasionally, of course, prize turmoil and transformation but only so as to affect new orders conducive to American capitalism. Without order markets cannot flourish. With no market there is only the dead hand of the state to impose national meaning – such states have rarely lasted long and in the twentieth century were decisively superseded and (in the case of the Soviet Union and China) eclipsed by the American model. The remarkable success of the American ideology became evident in the middle-to-late nineteenth century, reaching its fruition in the next. While Europeans played class politics at home and power politics abroad – with a creeping welfare dependency and much war – Americans got rich.[53] Whereas in Europe trade unionism helped to retard economic innovation, in the United States free labor, mass immigration and property rights set the nation on a course of unparalleled economic growth.[54] By 1955, it was the US dollar that accounted for a semblance of civilization in Europe and offered the only viable hope for its continued survival.[55] Even today, regions of the world not penetrated by US capital remain, in material terms, desperate places to live.[56]

American entrepreneurialism and the rapid industrialization it advanced, far outpacing domestic needs, demanded overseas expansion. (On this point Lenin was right.) The language of business consequently became basic to the style and substance of US foreign policy. The greatest geographic expansion in American history was not an invasion but a *purchase*; President Jefferson's real estate deal with France in 1803 doubled the size of the United States and cost a mere seven cents a hectare.[57] The single largest American state was similarly the result of a real estate deal – with Russia.[58] Some of the most decisive American interventions in world politics have been decisive because they have been economic: the Marshall Plan, the Bretton Woods agreement, the World Trade Organization, and World Bank. The US Federal Reserve is arguably (along with the Pentagon) the most powerful tool of foreign policy – and shaper of the foreign policy of other nations – in history. Consider that one of the most

reviled think tanks in contemporary international relations is the
American *Enterprise* Institute and that Bush's international development agenda was run via the Millennium Challenge *Account*.[59] In
9/11's wake, New York Mayor Rudy Giuliani urged an especially
American response: 'Show you're not afraid . . . Go shopping.'[60]

Moralism-legalism

Lawyers proliferate in the United States not only because the nation
is the product of a text that requires interpretation but because property, a legal construct, figures so prominently in its ideology. There is
a concomitant American preference for legal structures in international affairs, as in the domestic realm, for the same reason: they
secure rights on which the American ideology is built internally and
exported. The League of Nations and the United Nations were
American creations. Both were dedicated to the protection of rights
(national and individual) and were engineered to empower each
institution with their enforcement by 'arbitration or judicial settlement.'[61] In a direct and deliberate echo of the US Constitution's preamble, the 1945 UN Charter begins 'We the people of the United
Nations determine . . .'

George F. Kennan, the inventor of the most influential, beautifully
written, if prescriptively imprecise, grand strategy in American
history – First Cold War containment – warned of what he called the
'legalistic-moralistic approach to international problems.'[62] This
naïve if noble approach – 'that it should be possible to suppress the
chaotic and dangerous aspirations of governments in the international field by the acceptance of some system of legal rules and
restraints' – is best reserved, he said, for the private conduct of
'Anglo-Saxon' people.[63] Mechanisms that bring stability in domestic politics do not translate well into international relations, argued
Kennan. Moral aspirations are a dubious basis for foreign policy.[64]
Better, he suggested, to use tools and strategies that advance a moral
agenda by coincidence rather than by design. His famous 'Long

Telegram' from Moscow on February 22, 1946 argued that America's allies and adversaries would respond better not to moralistic lectures but to the example set by American 'health and vigor.' Such 'self-confidence' derived, according to Kennan, more from economic robustness than from military might. Such US self-confidence would firstly confound the Soviet analysis 'that capitalism contains the seeds of its own destruction' and, secondly, invite nations to join the American experiment. Security for Kennan – without which there could be no morality, private or public – would naturally augment as American markets spread. The answer to an overly moral-legal approach – which had ruined Woodrow Wilson after the First World War – was to adopt, after the Second, a more helpful, hopeful and practical reliance on what America was very good at: building markets and creating international organizations that facilitated them. The Soviet Union's inability to do likewise, argued Kennan, with considerable prescience, would cause its collapse without the recourse to war.[65]

Security = markets

This trade emphasis is important because it helps explain why so much of the US response to physical attack was grounded in the massive subvention of vanquished powers with US dollars and, as Kennan argued in 1946–7, the subsequent creation of capitalist markets.[66] The long-term solution to Japanese aggression at Pearl Harbor was to turn that island nation into America's chief economic competitor – from occupation and martial law to Marshall Plan and motors cars in the space of a generation. The tradition's detractors scoff at the cynicism of naming an oil tanker after a future national security advisor – Chevron's *Condoleezza Rice* – but the symbiotic relationship of commerce and foreign policy is of long standing and hardly constitutes a conspiracy.[67] The prominence given to trade is not the preserve of business-leaning Republican administrations. Bill Clinton may have spoken of a foreign policy that draws 'more generously from American

democratic experience and ideals, and lights fires in the hearts of millions of freedom-loving people around the world' but the fuel would
be commerce and markets.[68] Clinton's first substantial bureaucratic
innovation was the creation of a National Economic Council (NEC)
to complement (and one day, he envisaged, replace) the National
Security Council, created in 1947.[69] The Arkansan's greatest economic legacy – if not his greatest legacy full stop – was the creation of
the North American Free Trade Area (NAFTA).[70]

George W. Bush was the first president to hold an MBA (from
Harvard).[71] Despite a checkered business career thereafter – from relative failure in oil to fame in baseball – he was nothing if not in tune
with the commercial disposition of US foreign policy. His belief in
the political utility of capitalism is a basic feature of his international
strategy, as it will be for his successors. Like his predecessors, he
responded to foreign attack with bloody war and, like them, followed
up with a massive economic reconstruction package.[72] We consider
the Iraq War in detail in chapter 5. At this juncture it is worth
remembering what great trust was put in oil wealth as the balm for
post-invasion Iraq, and also how uncontroversial the strong role of
American private enterprise in Iraq was for the Bush team. Allowing
entrepreneurs to risk their capital and lives for material reward was
an entirely natural decision for Bush. Halliburton's financial outlay
in and return from Iraq was in accord with a foreign policy tradition
which has consistently prized commercial risk and the social benefits
that follow in its wake.[73] 'The US is the only country,' notes Robert
M. Perito, 'that uses commercial contractors to staff its police con-
tingents in UN peace operations.'[74] The inability of the new Iraq to
create an order conducive to capitalism highlighted a lack of fore-
sight and planning on behalf of the Bush administration. It does not,
however, disprove the thesis that trade shapes US foreign policy.

Some western university students – rarely schooled in economics –
are still capable of marching against American imperialism on a
Saturday afternoon. Some of their professors continue to recycle the

Marxism that, as students themselves, led them onto the streets, in greater numbers but with no greater wisdom, a generation ago. The prism through which we view the history of empires is the history of failed European ones. In reality, American 'imperialism' has consistently 'differed from the classic European form in that it did not seek administrative control over markets and peoples, but principally access to markets.'[75] Bush was a good example of this. He did not want to control Iraqi oil, he wanted to buy it. The physical and political control of this resource is an infinitely more expensive proposition than its purchase at market; trading with Saddam Hussein was a good deal cheaper than overthrowing him. It is dogmatic economic determinism to argue that America seeks hegemony rather than sales.

Much debate surrounds the consequences of an ideology driven by a pursuit of material prosperity. Some continue to argue that American capitalism destroys authentic, non-free-market cultures.[76] Others suggest that an economic ideology risks American overextension and is thus damaging to US interests and any accompanying moral mission. The work of William Appleman Williams, through the 1960s and still read today, does not dispute the role of the economic 'open door' in shaping post-Second World War US diplomacy. He *does* argue that it is ruinous of American security.[77] For Williams, US foreign policy had degenerated into an 'imperialism of idealism,' recurrently leading America 'to overplay its hand.' Imperialisms of any sort, said Williams, always invite a counterresponse. In claiming an 'omnipotence' for America's imperialism, its makers began 'The terrifying momentum toward disaster.'[78]

There are any number of approaches building on the Williams argument.[79] Rather than offering an exhaustive critique of each we cite them collectively in support of our conception of the American foreign policy tradition as substantially materialistic in its means and aims. The pragmatism of the tradition has had a remarkably positive impact on the coherence and utility of US strategy over time. The aspirational

ideology that animates American foreign policy causes it to be necessarily sensitive to, and robust in the face of, ideological opponents.

'A decent respect to the opinions of mankind'?

An emphasis on material happiness is one reason why US foreign
policy, in contrast to the rigidity of European forms, has been
pragmatic. American policy-makers have tended to value foreign
alliances for their utility rather than their ideological purity. In a
'world community' that holds multilateral action as a moral value
(the more multilateral, the more moral) the American resort to unilateralism is heresy. Much ink has been expended condemning Bush
for this post-9/11 turn away from multilateralism. This assertion of
what supposedly motivated American presidents before Bush ignores
Washington's farewell address (discussed earlier in this chapter) and
America's long record of using alliances and international institutions when it suited their interest and rejecting them when they did
not. Even Woodrow Wilson, the great League of Nations multilateralist, recognized the limitations of filial obligation in international
politics. In 1919 he warned the British government to abandon the
expectation of preferential treatment on the basis of kinship.[80]

The argument that American foreign policy is better characterized
as multilateral before Bush rests on one of two mutually exclusive
interpretations of its history. The first one, heard often from
American Democrats, sees in American political development an
evolving understanding of the United States as an 'indispensable
nation,' a concept popularized by its first female secretary of state – a
Democrat.[81] As its power increases and Europe's declines there is an
attendant moral obligation – understood by presidents like Wilson,
FDR and Clinton – to use this power to build permanent alliances of
peace. In these, great power competition is replaced by concerns with
human rights, human progress and prosperity and the world thus
made 'safer for our children and grandchildren, and for *those people
around the world who follow the rules.*'[82]

The second interpretation argues that the United States understood the Westphalia settlement of 1648 – which gave birth to the
modern state system – differently from the nations that were party to
it, and still does. For the European powers, Westphalia set the stage
for an era of balancing in which security took precedence over
expansion. Wars broke out to restore the security balance. Alliances
were conditioned by interests. The United States, when it entered
this system – then approaching its height in the late eighteenth and
early nineteenth centuries – operated to a different standard. Its universal claims made it resistant to alliances grounded in Realpolitik,
and its geography made them less vital. Americans would transcend
such amoral diplomacy, expecting, rather, 'that the appearance of
their country on the diplomatic scene would be instrumental in
effecting a new departure in international relations and would usher
in a new, a better world.'[83]

This bracing if naïve approach persists. The US has rarely held
multilateralism as a moral imperative. Contrary to many who view
the Declaration of Independence's injunction, wherein America
pledged 'a decent respect to the opinions of mankind,' this was not
about abiding by other nations' wishes. Rather, it was that a decent
respect 'requires that they should declare the causes which impel
them to the separation.' In other words, such respect compelled
Americans to spell out the reasons for their actions. International
communitarianism cannot have a morality greater than the self-
evident truths that animate the American Declaration.[84] If unilateralism advances them, good; if concerted action does the same, good.
This is quite different from how European governments navigate the
world. We have seen in recent American-led wars a European compulsion to portray them as morally suspect if they are not sufficiently
multilateral. Iraq (2003) is the most obvious example of this, but
reservations over 'American unilateralism' also informed the EU's
response to Bosnia (1994–5) and Kosovo (1999), instances where
America's own national security was not immediately or directly

threatened. Just how multilateral does multilateralism have to be? Or, as Robert Kagan asked of the French foreign minister, Dominique de Villepin:

> Is there a certain, magic number of supporting nations that bestows legitimacy? Or is it the quality of one's allies that matters more than the quantity when defining 'multilateralism'? Is France worth more than Spain?[85]

This inquiry was renewed by Peter Wehner, a Bush speechwriter, who articulated a position few American policy-makers of the post-Second World War era would reject:

> Should nations be paralyzed from acting unless they receive the support of the Security Council? How many nations need to support an action before it is considered sufficiently multilateral and therefore justifiable? Ten? Fifty? One hundred and fifty? And what happens if a nation, perhaps for reasons of corruption or bad motivation, seeks to prevent a particular action from being taken?[86]

Reservations over America's can-do attitude in several post-First Cold War interventions have turned to barely concealed revulsion, among some commentators, over US rejection of more 'ethically pure' treaties such as the International Criminal Court, the Comprehensive (Nuclear) Test Ban and Kyoto.[87]

Consistent with the purported moral sanctity of multilateralism is the belief that it is more effective practically than the unilateralism of any one state. This is open to dispute on a number of fronts. If anything, the lesson of post-1991 international crises is that if the US government does not act the EU is unlikely to so do. US ambivalence over the Rwandan genocide (1994) goes some way to explaining – even if it does not excuse – European inaction. It seems reasonable to argue that, without an American willingness to take on Serbia in 1994–6 and 1999, EU leaders, as Alija Izetbegović, the president of Bosnia-Herzegovina, is alleged to have said, 'would have talked and talked until we are all dead.'[88] Sometimes the multilateral imperative (which of its very nature requires an illusive consensus) leads to a lethal inaction.[89]

In questioning the utility of multilateralism, the Bush administration has met with both praise and blame. Those who praise its flexible unilateralism or selective multilateralism argue that this has been a consistent theme of US foreign policy, both before and after the creation of the United Nations in 1945.[90] Its detractors argue that Bush has betrayed the multilateral turn that America took during the Second World War. Sympathizers see the continuation of a pragmatic tradition, while critics chastise the administration for rupturing that tradition. Iraq is currently central to this debate. For his opponents, Bush's removal of Saddam was illegal because it was not sanctioned by an explicit UN resolution, despite Saddam being in violation of at least sixteen such resolutions during the previous twelve years. According to Bush's critics, the higher morality of multilateralism, which he had violated, was not balanced by the widely recognized morality of regime change. Fidelity to a policy process matters more now than what the policy brings about. We will consider this argument more fully in chapter 3.[91]

Robert W. Tucker and David C. Hendrickson argue that Bush has broken the post-1945 US foreign policy tradition:

> The 18 months since the launch of the Iraq war have left the country's hard-earned respect and credibility in tatters. In going to war without a legal basis or the backing of traditional US allies, the Bush administration brazenly undermined Washington's long-held commitment to international law, its acceptance of consensual decision-making, its reputation for moderation, and its identification with the preservation of peace. The road back will be a long and hard one.[92]

America, the writers contend, had waged a First Cold War consistent with international law: 'US leaders generally made every effort to square their actions with international law. And despite some transgressions, the overall fidelity of the United States to internationalist norms contributed strongly to the legitimacy of US power.'[93] Their key example is NATO. This formal alliance enjoyed legitimacy not because it was a vehicle for US power, say Tucker and Hendrickson, but because it derived its legitimacy from the UN Charter that proscribed state-on-state aggression. 'Had NATO been constituted on any other basis it would not have gained the support it did.' Informal proxy warfare against the Soviet Union and its allies – war waged without recourse to international law and international institutions – invariably weakened American legitimacy, they argue.[94] These authors perpetuate the now routine association of Vietnam with Iraq – wars fought outside of NATO and without UN approval. 'The United States' isolation in international society in the late 1960s . . . represented the lowest ebb of US legitimacy in the post-World War II era.'

The claim that Vietnam is proof (and Iraq proof positive) that America cannot operate successfully outside a formal international legal framework is dubious. 'Failure' in each war was a product not of their illegitimacy but of military mistakes that led a 'defeat-phobic' American public to turn against the war. Poor tactics lose wars. The bombing of Serbia in 1999 – in which not one US soldier died at the hands of the enemy – was similarly unmoored in international law since it commanded no UN resolution and yet was militarily a stunning success. As we move into an era of even greater American military superiority the notion that the efficacy of this power is directly proportional to the formal international approval it can secure is increasingly untenable. One of the least successful wars was waged under a UN flag (Korea, 1950–3), while one of the most successful under a UN flag (the Gulf, 1991) was still opposed by many of the same individuals who opposed the 2003 Iraq campaign. Obedience to international law may please Brussels, Paris and Bonn but it is no guarantee of military success or of American security. This is why Bush was prepared, like his predecessors, to act outside its remit.[95] It is an approach that we anticipate his successors will also be constrained by reality to take.

Consider the argument of Lawrence Kaplan:

> Notwithstanding critics who insist Iraq proves the folly of thwarting the will of the United Nations, the Bush doctrine's reservations about 'submitting to the objections of a few' hardly set it apart from its predecessors. Every US president since the UN's establishment has acted at one time or another without its approval. Given the institution's congenital indecision, every future president will do so as well. Being little more than the sum of its parts, even today the UN quietly tolerates Iran and Sudan's flouting of its own resolutions.[96]

Robert Kagan has adopted a similar line and added to it a volume on pre-twentieth-century foreign policy, which highlights the enduring strands of American international strategy and its foreign reception as a 'dangerous nation.'

In response to Tucker and Hendrickson's assertions of a multilateralism betrayed, Kagan observes that US foreign policy in the First Cold War was rarely fixated on the moral superiority of international law or of formally concerted war-making. Rather, American presidents have used all means calculated to meet US security ends. Indeed, says Kagan, 'security, not law, established American legitimacy' in those predominantly Western European nations that sought it.[97] US power in the First Cold War was embraced not because it was constrained by international organizations and their laws but because it was effective in protecting against a less wholesome power. It is the nature of power, not the formal constraints under which it must operate, which has determined its legitimacy. The UN Charter – the human rights guarantees of which remain unimplemented by the majority of its signatories – hardly saved Western Europe from communist takeover. It was American military power and economic subvention that allowed Europe to survive and the EU to flourish.

This is not to argue, of course, that the American foreign policy tradition necessarily induces skepticism toward international law and multilateralism. As Kennan argued, there is an almost unhealthy American need to run the world according to moral-legal codes (observe Versailles 1919). Multilateralism is also a large part of the American story. The Republic would likely have been still-born had not a rather effective alliance with France not tipped the odds decisively in its favor. Recurrent American administrations have always looked for friends when in pursuit of trade or of enemies. Bush and Rumsfeld wanted *coalitions* of willing nations, not a splendid isolation. The American foreign policy tradition is not a willful loneliness, as Bush explained in the National Security Strategy of 2002:

> We are . . . guided by the conviction that no nation can build a safer, better world alone. Alliances and multilateral institutions can multiply the strength of freedom-loving nations. The United States is committed to lasting institutions like the United Nations, the World Trade Organization, the Organization of American States, and NATO as well as other longstanding alliances. Coalitions of the willing can augment these permanent institutions. In all cases, international obligations are to be taken seriously. They are not to be undertaken symbolically to rally support for an ideal without furthering its attainment.[98]

Isolation on the world stage negates the utility of any state's foreign policy. Ideology, whilst it provides an interpretative thread to American foreign policy behavior, has not always been the nation's chief foreign policy tool. The Second World War and the ensuing First Cold War – ideological in their ends – were substantially marked by an American willingness to swallow hard and join up with some of the least ideologically sound political systems in modern times. If FDR could ally with the Soviet Union from 1941 to 1945, his successors could certainly accommodate, without too much agonizing, Mao's China, Pinochet's Chile, Musharraf's Pakistan or Karimov's Uzbekistan. These were/are alliances of utility, forged in the expectation of victory over a more dangerous ideological foe and in the hope of the eventual democratic conversion of the morally suspect ally. (We will rejoin this argument in chapter 4.)

This *à la carte* multilateralism and flexible friendship has a far longer history than more recent equations of American legitimacy with international consent. In any foreign venture, American administrations have sought to broaden the quality and quantity of their allies. On-going US policy toward North Korea has relied heavily on the interaction of *six* nations. Indeed, it can be argued that Pyongyang's resistance to international demands is fueled by the multilateral character of those demands. Being threatened by the 'international community' is not nearly so frightening and behavior modifying as confronting the righteous anger of a powerful state unconstrained by the need to please its friends. The Sudanese government has rarely quaked in the face of threats from the UN. Saddam Hussein came to rely on western multilateralism negating American ambitions to topple him. Did not the UN resolutions that legitimated his expulsion from Kuwait also prevent the march on Baghdad in 1991? American foreign policy relies on friends when it can but will act without them when it must. 'There is a difference,' Bush said, 'between leading a coalition of many nations, and submitting to the objections of a few. America will never seek a permission slip to defend the security of our country.'[99] Barack Obama has said much the same: 'No President should ever hesitate to use force – unilaterally if necessary – to protect ourselves and our vital interests when we are attacked or imminently threatened.'[100]

Conclusion

From both genuine belief and professional self-interest, academic analysts and partisan politicians often depict American foreign policy as a series of dramatic choices and far-reaching alternatives. But the more we study history the more we are forced to admit that American administrations actually differ very little when it comes to foreign policy and especially to national security; they tend to observe the behavioral patterns of their predecessors. George W. Bush reacted in much the same way as Woodrow Wilson and Franklin Roosevelt did, and as Al Gore would likely have done, when faced by an attack on US citizens: wage war then attempt to reintegrate their foe into a capitalistic, institutionalized world order.

The US government recurrently declares domestic 'wars' – against trusts, poverty, drugs, terror, even banks – and fights both hot and cold wars abroad, against a variety of nation states, small and large, and terrorists, religious and secular. George W. Bush's declaration of a 'crusade' on September 16, 2001 was only superficially controversial: crusades are basic and regularized phenomena in American public policy – foreign and domestic.[101] The First Cold War was a crusade, literally so, against an atheistic communist empire.[102] Not to have spoken in similar terms after the Twin Towers fell would have been extraordinary. We reject, therefore, the fallacy of immediacy, of 'presentism' – that what is now is necessarily and always new.[103]

A better question would be to ask why American public policy is so often construed in such Manichean terms. Our answer goes to the heart of the paradox of the American foreign policy tradition, one that Bush captures very well. To understand why the United States has been so successful in international relations we must grasp the pragmatic and ideological nature of its approach. It is pragmatic insofar as it is not wedded to pre-existing conceptions of international legitimacy. This affords Washington considerable room for maneuver. It rarely acts on imperatives that are not pragmatic. Its trade policy relies on the flexibility of market calculation rather than dogma – it uses what works. However, since trade is a primary means to perpetuate a right to pursue happiness, America has a tendency to construe those that challenge this right as morally beyond the pale, as enemies rather than merely opponents or competitors. This denies American policy-makers room for maneuver. Their domestic and foreign policies are punctuated by wars against sometimes nebulous enemies at home and abroad – drugs, crime, poverty, tyranny and terror – for these are the forces that set themselves against not just the American state and its territorial security but the eternal truths on which it is founded.

We did not expect Bush to abandon this traditional approach; nor do we expect his successors to do so. The enduring American willingness to confront ideological opponents ideologically perplexes more self-consciously cosmopolitan (but no more secure) polities like those in Europe. That continent's history in the last century conditioned its governments and peoples against ideological warfare. It taught them to live with threats, to regard them as problems to be managed rather than resolved, and, prompted by moral relativism and post-imperial guilt, to tolerate their enemies.

The United States has an alternative history. It has fought fierce ideological wars that have preserved, enhanced, and spread fundamental freedoms. The War of Independence removed British tyranny. The Civil War destroyed slavery, the Second World War Nazism, the First Cold War communism abroad (whilst extending civil rights at home). When presidents have confronted ideological opponents they have invariably beaten them. To not so dedicate to fight would be to call into question American national identity and the ideological premise of the United States itself. To conduct a discrete North American experiment in the capacity of people for self-government would be to deny the experiment's universal applicability. Amoral foreign policies do not sit well in the US tradition and tend to have a short shelf life – observe Kissinger's détente. Moral campaigns, on the other hand, stick. For this reason Bush's war on terror is better understood as falling squarely within, and extending, the US foreign policy tradition. So, too, is the constitutional propriety of the war Bush joined, a subject to which we turn in the next chapter.

2

The constitution of American national security

A feeble executive is but another phrase for a bad execution . . . whatever it may be in theory, must be, in practice, a bad government.

Alexander Hamilton, *Federalist* 70

The next thing I knew, the discussion was onto the subject of fascism in America. Everybody was talking about police repression and the anxiety and paranoia as good folks waited for the knock on the door and the descent of the knout on the nape of the neck. I couldn't make any sense out of it . . . one of the great unexplained phenomena of modern astronomy: namely, that the dark night of fascism is always descending in the United States and yet lands only in Europe.

Tom Wolfe[1]

To its critics, the Bush administration post-9/11 responses were anything but carefully calibrated or constitutionally sound.[2] The charge list is invariably a long one: from warrantless wiretapping and the monitoring of international banking transactions by the National Security Agency, through military tribunals, the use of presidential 'signing statements' and the invocation of executive privilege at home to instances of prisoner abuse, coercive interrogation and extraordinary renditions abroad, the administration strained not only every sinew to wage its war on terror but also stretched the meaning of the US Constitution to breaking point. If America had finally revealed its imperial pretensions after September 11, then the president had likewise emerged as a more imperial figure in his studied neglect of constitutional convention and barely concealed contempt for international law.[3]

In this chapter we challenge such wisdom as more conventional than wise and extend further our argument that, in terms of the sweep of American history, more continuity than change characterized the Bush foreign policy. *Ceteris paribus*, the types of controversy that have recently dominated discussion of American foreign policy – in terms not only of its substance but also the constitutional legitimacy and political efficacy of its methods – are likely to remain a markedly familiar presence in the post-Bush years. This is not to deny that innovative departures that tested established constitutional understandings and generated marked academic and popular dissensus occurred under Bush. The terrorist attacks of 9/11 rightly occasioned new policies, initiatives, and programs by the executive and legislative branches of the federal government to meet the asymmetrical and acephalous challenge to American – and global – security posed by jihadist Islam. These occurred, however, in the context of a presidential primacy in foreign affairs whose constitutionality was politically settled, theoretically well grounded and historically long established.

Absent from too many critical commentaries was a recognition of what we term the 'national security constitution' that has, since at least 1950, steadily but dramatically conditioned the practice of the federal government in its international relations. Just as the Constitution has accommodated the transformation of domestic American life without significant formal revision since 1787, so the apparently rigid and changeless document has facilitated and legitimated the radical alteration of the nation's engagement with the world that was demanded by its rise to globalism during and since the Second World War. This evolving constitutional settlement has not

abrogated the Founding Fathers' prescriptions for shared responsibility in the shaping of the democratic republic's 'foreign entanglements.' But it has allowed and, with few, but important, exceptions,
sustained a presidential primacy in matters of American national
security that successive presidents of both parties have inherited,
preserved, and expanded – and in which both the US Congress and
the federal judiciary have (with few, but significant, exceptions)
acquiesced.

That this evolution in the constitutionally sanctioned practice of
foreign affairs has received relatively limited critical examination is
a function of the preoccupation of constitutional scholars with
domestic political questions, the relative reluctance of the judiciary
to intrude on executive–legislative relations as they apply 'beyond
the water's edge,' and the comparative popular inattention traditionally accorded the reciprocal role of the United States in the
world and the world's impact upon domestic American life. But the
post-9/11 actions of the Bush administration drew on and strengthened the constitutional, legal and political primacy of the presidency
in international affairs, evident since the 1950s. An adequate understanding of American foreign policy after Bush, as well as a precondition of assessing accurately Bush's foreign policy, therefore entails
an appreciation of how the evolving national security constitution
pre-dated and will long outlast the Bush administration, shaping not
only America's international relations but also the complex interac-
tions of the White House, Capitol Hill and federal judiciary for years
to come.

Our analysis of the national security constitution therefore
addresses four key elements that have conditioned, and will continue
to dominate, the making of American foreign policy into the 2010s
and beyond:

• the intimate relationship of war and the Constitution;
• the primacy of the presidency in the post-1950 constitutional
  settlement;

- the efficacy of the new balance as it pertains to foreign affairs;
- the location of the Bush administration within, rather than outside, this distinctive national security constitution.

Katznelson and Shefter are entirely correct to emphasize how American political development has been consistently 'shaped by war and trade' from the Republic's founding to the present.[4] Despite being a nation that prizes peace and prosperity, America has frequently and reluctantly found herself at war, a pattern that is likely to continue rather than cease in the foreseeable future. As such, and despite the fears and apprehensions of civil libertarians that range from the reasonable and judicious to the fevered and irrational, the trade-offs between American security and individual liberty that have been a constant since 1787 will remain an integral and irrevocable feature of American life well beyond 2009.[5] In advancing this case, we explain how and why the original understanding of the Framers has been parsed into a constitutional practice in which the Bush administration was – and its successors will remain – firmly located. We also seek to provide a firm justification for the national security constitution that demonstrates how strong America's constitutional democracy remains, in contrast to the fragile system so commonly depicted in conventional critiques of the war on terror.

War and the Constitution

The Constitution of the United States was forged in, by, and for war. From the Declaration of Independence and the rejection of the weaker Articles of Confederation through the preamble to the Constitution's pledge to 'secure the common defense' to the National Security Strategy documents of 2002 and 2006, war and the threat of war has been an integral, constant, and powerful force in American political development.

Since gaining its independence, America has fought eleven major wars and dozens more 'limited' wars, although Congress has only formally issued a declaration of war on five occasions.[6] Across the more than two centuries since the Republic's founding, the United States has defended itself from conquest by the British, extended its continental boundaries on the battlefield against Native Americans and its neighbors north and south, preserved the Union through a momentous and bloody Civil War, acquired territories outside the mainland from the Philippines to Cuba, participated to crucial effect in two world wars, waged a third global conflict against Soviet-led communism, fought twice on the Asian peninsula for a duration of fifteen years, and twice sent tens of thousands of Americans to the Middle East to defeat the military of Saddam Hussein. While Samuel Huntington has argued that Americans will respond with unanimity to foreign foes only when both American national security and values are under threat[7] – conditions that, pre-9/11, he held only applied to the Second World War – the perennial lack of unanimity among the American public over war has not substantially impeded Americans taking to the battlefield to protect or advance the nation's vital interests.[8]

Questions of war have also exerted a profound and lasting effect on American home life. Whilst, prior to 1945, the federal government typically disbanded its armed militias after the cessation of military hostilities as rapidly as it had previously assembled them for specific conflicts, America's political, economic, and social transformation is in large part an artifact of war. The 1787 Constitution granted new tax-raising powers to federal authorities, which they used to establish a militia of 7,000 men by 1801 (compared to the eighty left at the end of the Revolutionary War). After the Civil War, the federal government retained sufficient troops to occupy the South and fight Native Americans without regular militia support. Pressures of defense spending during and after the Civil War led the federal authorities to levy an income tax (repealed in 1872), institute duties on imports, and, in 1913, make permanent an income tax through the Sixteenth Amendment to the Constitution. The

Second World War saw the American economy and population transformed, with 56 percent of eligible American men mobilized for war. With that global war superseded by another anti-totalitarian war, however, the initial post-Second World War demobilization was rapidly reversed. By 1949, the new Department of Defense (the successor to the Department of War) was charged with maintaining a massive and permanent standing military that by 1961 numbered some 2.5 million men in uniform. Defense spending reached 14.3 percent of Gross Domestic Product by 1953 and 9.1 percent by 1961, ultimately declining to 3 percent by the 1990s but still, in the context of a remarkably successful national economy, yielding direct defense expenditures in excess of $300 billion ten years after the First Cold War's end. Even during the 'peace and prosperity' years of the 1990s, some 10 percent of all employment in America was estimated to be related, directly or indirectly, to defense and, with the $48 billion increases that quickly followed the 9/11 attacks, defense spending was a substantial contributor – as it had been in the 1980s – to America's massive federal debt. The evolution of the American party system has in turn been shaped and reshaped by the positions that the parties have assumed on the salient national security issues of their day – a pattern that, after a brief hiatus during the 1990s, when national security no longer figured in national elections, is echoed in contemporary partisan competition.

If America's past and present at home and abroad is more closely linked to questions of war than many Americans typically imagine, so too is the historic focal point of American government and politics – and the central construct (with the Declaration of Independence) underpinning the civic nationalism integral to American national identity. The marriage of constitutional design and national security has been complex in its nature, robust in the face of internal and external challenge, and resilient in its adaptation to new and demanding conditions. That the nexus between the Constitution and the security of the continental United States should be a matter for relatively limited attention in America is an ironic but powerful tribute to the success of the former in assuring the latter. Indeed, the academic and popular controversies surrounding America's response to 9/11 illustrated how intertwined the relationship between constitutionality and security remains. There was no debate in America after September 11 among Democrats, Republicans or independents, progressives or conservatives, over *whether* a Constitution designed in and for the eighteenth century could meet the new security threats of the twenty-first, only *how* best it would do so. Caught between the Scylla of terrorist threats to public safety and the Charybdis of eroding civil liberties the latter debate, nonetheless, has been vociferous and contentious – so much so that Cass Sunstein has ventured that 'it would not be a surprise if these conflicts ultimately become the most important in all of constitutional law.'[9]

Such universal American faith in the Constitution's provisions in the first decade of the twenty-first century might appear anachronistic and inattentive to the dramatically changed security environment facing the United States. Even those presidents who served during the First Cold War's height, much less the Framers of the Constitution, could hardly have envisaged the new security era. But in its adaptation to the demands of national security, the Constitution has accommodated transformations in America's external environment at least as momentous as those of its domestic setting. Six distinct but related aspects of a dramatically changed security nexus combine to make unique the environment in which America now operates.

First, the end of the First Cold War, the collapse of the Soviet Union, and the inability or unwillingness of other major powers to spend substantially on defense have left the international system in a state of sustained unipolarity. After 1991, in terms of global force projection, Washington was left as (and remains) the only player able to mobilize rapidly its peerless armed forces and deploy them around the globe. Whether to deter aggression against sovereign states, combat ethnic cleansing, or provide a meaningful security guarantee as an 'offshore balancer' of consequence,[10] America occupies a unique position as – in the words of Madeleine Albright – the 'indispensable nation.'[11]

Second, even though it was neither formally nor legally declared to be a war, the war on Islamist terrorism joined by Washington after 9/11 ensured that America was now committed to a generational struggle against jihadism on a series of fronts focused on, but not limited to, the Middle East. The question of war thereby gained a degree of temporal protractedness, if not permanence, that has compounded America's strategic pre-eminence in the global conflict.

Third, the traditional factors making for the superiority of the executive branch over its competitors in foreign policy in general, and security in particular, accorded the White House a clear and decisive (albeit not uncontested) primacy in crafting American grand strategy. Although hardly infallible, the informational, intelligence, diplomatic, and organizational advantages of the executive – and the comparative deficiencies of the legislative and judicial branches – increased wartime presidential power significantly.[12]

Fourth, even prior to 9/11, the tendency of a relatively insular American public to 'rally round the flag' on matters of security lent the White House significant potential sources of support for a vigorous defense of the homeland, a defense that necessarily entailed going on the offense abroad. As several scholars have documented, in the 1990s an isolationist or defeatist American public, one resistant to US military interventions abroad and supine in the face of military fatalities, did not rise.[13] Rather than being 'casualty-phobic,' Americans are reliably 'defeat-phobic.'[14] Public support for deployments invariably depends on the particular objectives of the mission and its prospects for success. Even where a mission's goals were not widely accepted, the prospect of success would invariably yield public support. As such, not only did 9/11 plausibly lower the bar

for popular support for military action but the increasing sophistication of US technology and accompanying decline in relative fatalities in war likely increased the confidence of the public in the
prospect of low-cost interventions abroad.[15]

Advanced technology also weighed heavily in the fifth and sixth
factors in the new security environment. In the former, new technology such as missile-equipped unmanned predator drones meant
that the scope and nature of US military action was of an altogether
different order than previously. Attacks on terrorists crossing deserts
in Yemen by Unmanned Aerial Vehicles (UAVs), authorized from
Central Command in Tampa, Florida, were no longer the realm of
science fiction but of military fact. In terms of the latter, the very
sophistication of US military forces meant that effective multilateral
military action, however desirable, was decreasingly feasible. In
terms of 'interoperability,' not even America's closest allies, such as
the United Kingdom, could now consistently engage in comprehensive joint actions, a problem we will return to in chapter 8. It was not
just the scale of the US defense budget but the logistical scope and
technological sophistication of its results that multiplied the precision, reach and lethality of American force. As such, in military
terms, a unilateralism of necessity rather than choice was imposed on
Washington's military deliberations after the First Cold War's end.

After 9/11, while many commentators addressed the strategic and
tactical dimensions of the campaigns, academic critics of the military
interventions in Afghanistan and Iraq also focused on the relative
war powers of the presidency and Congress. For many, the invocation of an expansive war on terror and the manner by which the
Bush administration waged it violated the appropriate constitutional
balance between the two ends of Pennsylvania Avenue. On this
reading, war-making had become a tool of presidential policy rather
than an instrument of last resort. In effect, the issue of waging war
was now an executive prerogative rather than a matter to be shared
with, and even reserved to, Congress. Moreover, despite legislative

attempts to rein in executive war powers (most notably, the War Powers Act of 1973), the White House remained dangerously unanchored by effective constitutional constraints. As Karl Schonberg described it:

> The problem that confronts American foreign policy at the opening of the twenty-first century is that the system has fallen out of balance; the presidency has attained greater sway over the power to make war than the Founders ever would have accepted.[16]

That the Iraq War was a preventive 'war of choice' rather than necessity, on this view, compounded the constitutional malaise, with America committed to a deployment lacking a compelling rationale, international legality or effective constitutional sanction.[17] Or, as Senator Robert Byrd (D-WV) put it:

> The nature of the threats posed by a sudden attack on the United States may have changed dramatically since the time when the Constitution was drafted, but the reasons for limiting the war powers of the president have not changed at all.[18]

Is, then, the constitutional regime on national security in general, and war powers in particular, so unbalanced as to effectively cede monarchical power to the president it originally denied? Did Bush cynically exploit a climate of fear to advance a profoundly illiberal attack on constitutional precedents? And, if so, why has the response of the American public and elites alike to such constitutional violence been relatively muted? To address these questions it is necessary to contextualize the war powers issue, to reintroduce politics to the excessively formal, legalistic and ahistorical framework that most analysts have brought to the question, and to outline the place of war powers within the national security constitution. When this is done, the Bush approach can be treated with a more sanguine and judicious assessment, one that treats Bush's wartime actions as neither revolutionary nor unconstitutional. Indeed, we argue that the robust health of America's constitutional arrangements – in terms both of relations between the branches and between order and liberty – is very much in accordance with political and legal pragmatism.

War powers

The conventional scholarly case here is one that appears – contrary to the vagueness, ambiguity and competing interpretations in which most constitutional discussions are shrouded – unusually clear and confident. In terms of the Framers' intent, the general model of a separated system of government sharing powers across its branches, each with a mutual veto over the other, is clear. Thus, Article I, Section VIII grants Congress the power:

> 'to declare war . . .,' 'to lay and collect taxes . . .,' 'to provide for the common defense . . .,' 'to raise and support armies . . .,' 'to provide and maintain a navy . . .,' 'to make rules for the regulation for the land and naval forces . . .,' to 'provide for calling forth the militia to execute the laws of the Union, suppress insurrections and repel invasions . . .,' to 'provide for organizing, arming, and disciplining the militia . . .,' to 'make all laws necessary and proper for carrying into execution the foregoing powers, and all powers vested by this Constitution in the Government of the United States.'

Congress is also accorded exclusive power over the purse: 'No money shall be drawn from the Treasury but in consequence of appropriations made by law.'

By contrast, the sole war power granted to the executive branch is in Article II, Section II: 'The President shall be the Commander-in-Chief of the Army and Navy of the United States, and of the Militia of the several States, when called into actual service of the United States.' According to scholars such as Louis Fisher, Michael Glennon, and Harold Koh, the Framers intended this power to allow the president to repel sudden attacks on America, American lives and property but not to launch offensive military operations.[19] The original proposal to give Congress the power to 'make' war was altered to that of 'declare' precisely so the president could defend the nation from attack in conditions where congressional assent was difficult to achieve (not least since the assembling of members of Congress would take several weeks). Crucial to this conventional understanding, then, is the notion that the European model of war-making had been decisively rejected by the Framers in favor of a shared model of collective judgment. The decision to initiate war was given to Congress, with the president retaining the unilateral authority only to repel attacks. The engine of war thus required two keys, not one, to start. As Thomas Jefferson wrote to James Madison in 1789: 'We have already given in example one effectual check to the dog of war by transferring the power of letting him loose from the executive to the legislative body, from those who are to spend to those who are to pay.' Four years later, in 1793, Madison reiterated this understanding, noting that:

> the Constitution supposes what the history of all government demonstrates, that the executive is the branch of power most interested in war, and most prone to it. It has accordingly, with studied care, vested the question of war in the legislature . . . Those who are to conduct a war cannot in the nature of things be the proper or safe judges whether a war ought to be commenced, continued or concluded.[20]

Proponents of this 'original understanding' of the distribution of war powers typically draw a straightforward historical sequence from the founding to the present.[21] During the first period, from the founding through the nineteenth century, the original division was broadly adhered to and reinforced by precedent. In the *Prize Cases* (1863), for example, the Supreme Court declared that the president 'has no power to initiate or declare a war either against a foreign nation or a domestic State.' In the second period, from 1900 to 1945, a partial collapse of the original understanding occurred, with the declaration of the 'Roosevelt Corollary' to the 1823 Monroe Doctrine to justify

American military intervention not just to protect American lives
and property but also to promote foreign policy goals. The decisive
collapse of the foundational principles, however, took place from
1950 to the present, an era of presidential usurpations, ineffective
congressional response, and supine judicial acquiescence. From
Truman's deployment of American forces under a United Nations
mandate but without a congressional declaration of war to Korea in
1950, through the undeclared war in Vietnam, to the attempt to
rescue the American hostages in Iran in 1980, the invasion of
Grenada in 1983 and air strikes on Libya in 1986, the invasion of
Panama in 1989, the first Gulf War in 1991, the bombing of Serbia
in 1995 and 1999, and the Iraq War of 2003, successive presidents
sent American forces around the world to wage wars not declared by
Congress. Such actions amounted to a series of constitutional *coups
d'état*, threatening to morph America's constitutional system into a
banana republic where presidential whim dictated war. Or, as
Glennon argued in relation to the first Gulf War:

> Starting from President Bush's unilateral commitment to defend Saudi
> Arabia and proceeding to Congress' jury-rigged approval, the episode
> represented a textbook example of how an audacious executive,
> acquiescent legislature and deferential judiciary have pushed the
> Constitution backwards toward the monopolistic system of King
> George III.[22]

But the notion that American chief executives have been engaged
in such a process of constitutional time travel, however striking, is
simply wrong. In foreign affairs, the Constitution remains what
Corwin famously termed 'an invitation to struggle for the privilege
of directing foreign policy,' one that the elected branches have rarely
refused.[23] What is remarkable in this regard, however, is the relative
paucity of attention dedicated to war powers by constitutional scholars. Commentators from across the spectrum have barely mentioned
war powers in otherwise extensive works on constitutional theory, a

function partly of the far more extensive jurisprudence on domestic questions and the courts' recognition of the essentially political nature of the issue.[24]

Three arguments challenge the case that the modern practice of going to war violates constitutional propriety: the structural thesis; the 'Living Constitution' case; and the functionality argument. Taken together, the post-1950 practice of chief executives receives formidable constitutional, legal, and political support. Let us deal with each in turn.

Structural thesis

The most prominent and strong support for the structural thesis can be located in the arguments of John Yoo in *The Powers of War and Peace* and is echoed in the dissenting opinions of Justices Scalia, Thomas, and Alito in the war powers decisions of the Rehnquist and Roberts Courts.[25] Yoo's case emphasizes the Framers' original understanding 'to create a political system in which each branch could use its own constitutional powers to develop foreign policy.'[26] On his reading, which stresses not subjective intention but the plain meaning of the structure and text, the notion that prior congressional declarations of war are required is unsupported. 'Declaration' as understood at the time meant not authorizing subsequent actions but a legal recognition of a pre-existing state of affairs. Other provisions in the Constitution (such as prohibiting states from waging war 'without the consent of Congress' and specifying where and how presidents needed to act with the 'advice and consent' of the Senate, such as appointments and treaty-making) support the notion that, had the Framers wished to preclude 'presidential wars,' they could and would have devised language to this end. What they did, however, was to vest Congress with the legislative authority, in particular over funding and regulating the armed forces, that would ensure that – if sufficient political will existed – presidential aggrandizement could be resisted. The structure and text of the Constitution, by dividing the executive and commander-in-chief roles from those of declaring and funding war, did not provide for a system in which wars required prior authorization by Congress. But Congress could nonetheless preclude or terminate wars it opposed through its power of the purse and other legislative mechanisms. As Yoo notes:

> Even today, after the end of the Cold War, Congress continues to authorize standing armed forces capable of conducting large-scale military operations around the world. It funds weapons systems that allow the United States to engage in a wide variety of interventions, from quick, surgical cruise missile strikes to power projection by carrier groups to invasions by heavy armored forces. By providing long-term funding for a permanent military capable of such operations, Congress has given the executive the means to send troops immediately into combat overseas. By not taking the step of placing conditions on their use, as is often done with domestic spending programs, Congress has implicitly allowed their deployment.[27]

As Thomas's dissent, joined by Scalia and Alito, in *Hamdan v. Rumsfeld* (2006) notes, Congress has a 'substantial and essential role in both foreign affairs and national security.' But the fact that 'Congress has provided the President with broad authorities does not imply – and the Judicial Branch should not infer – that Congress intended to deprive him of particular powers not specifically enumerated.'[28] Presidential decisions on national security are entitled to a 'heavy measure of deference' since this is where executive power is at its zenith and judicial power its nadir. The history of modern American wars has seen no formal declarations, some authorizations (serving as the functional equivalent of declarations), and, in the case of Kosovo, one war that had no prior congressional authorization. But the unwillingness of Congress to constrain the executive is a political matter, not a constitutional derogation. As Yoo observes, 'We should not, however, mistake a failure of political will for a violation of the Constitution . . . Recent wars show only that Congress has refused to exercise the ample powers at its disposal, not that there has been an alarming breakdown in the constitutional structure.'[29]

Yoo's case provides powerful endorsement of an expansive reading of presidential war powers. In emphasizing the structure and text of the constitutional provisions at the expense of the Framers' intentions, it raises substantial doubts as to established interpretations that treat congressional primacy in war powers as axiomatic. If his arguments do not negate the case that constitutional power over the decisions to initiate and carry out war are shared, they nonetheless offer credence to the notion that the presidency derives vital powers not only from the structure and text of the Constitution but also from constitutional practice through the ages. In this respect, the 'Living Constitution' case supplements the structural argument.

The 'Living Constitution'

The marked irony in the case advanced by proponents of congressional primacy is that they advocate a fidelity to the constitutional text and its 'original understanding' that they rarely endorse on any other constitutional question, from the death penalty to gay rights. Most progressives since the Warren Court (1953–69) have favored a permissive approach to constitutional interpretation that vests the document with a substantial elasticity. The Constitution's clauses should be read broadly rather than narrowly, and the judicial branch should be willing to overturn rather than to defer to the decisions of the elected branches. The Constitution should not be read either in terms of the 'plain meaning' of its provisions or the understanding accorded those provisions at the time they were drafted or ratified. To do so would not only freeze the Constitution in an eighteenth-century time warp but would also yield results repugnant to liberal sensibilities. In interpreting the document in a more creative and flexible fashion, supplemented by the history and legislative intent underpinning disputed laws, the courts are thereby able to adapt the Constitution to the demands of a changing America. As such, policies from desegregation to reproductive rights have not only been accorded constitutional legitimacy and protection but have also been effectively initiated by the courts in the face of executive and legislative deadlock or opposition. Their defenders tend to concur with the rationale – if not the outcome – of *Trop v. Dulles* (1958), that the interpretation of constitutional clauses (in this case, the Eighth Amendment) must draw their 'meaning from the evolving standards of decency that mark the progress of a maturing society.'

There is a curious anomaly in the emphatic denial by advocates of a 'Living Constitution' that any such elasticity attends the life-and-death questions of national security. As Justice Robert Jackson famously observed, in weighing security and liberty concerns:

> The choice is not between order and liberty. It is between liberty with order and anarchy without either. There is a danger that, if the Court does not temper its doctrinaire logic with a little practical wisdom, it will convert the constitutional Bill of Rights into a suicide pact.[30]

There are, of course, sound reasons as to why an insistence on faithfulness to original intent, assuming this can be conclusively ascertained, might be appropriate. War is a vital matter and, even if the actual fighting extends only to the less than 1 percent of the American population that now wears the uniform, its effects on the nation can be dramatic and traumatic. Recognizing this reality, it clearly was the intent of the Framers to check unconstrained executive power on such a momentous question and to share that power between the elected branches of the federal government.

But this case not only neglects the evolution of executive–legislative relations on foreign policy since 1950 but also exaggerates the degree to which the Constitution's provisions have been usurped. Whatever the merits of the congressional and presidential primacy schools in terms of an original understanding of war powers, on separation of powers questions it is self-evident that the evolution of historical practices has been highly relevant to constitutional interpretation. The case for presidential primacy does not reject the shared powers written into the constitutional structure and text but views the interpretation of key constitutional provisions as having accommodated to an altered modern reality. If, as even the conservative Justice Felix Frankfurter noted, 'It is an inadmissibly narrow conception of American constitutional law to confine it to the words of the Constitution and to disregard the gloss which life has written upon them,' that injunction should apply with equal force to foreign as domestic policy. Indeed, as Stephen Holmes has observed, 'Neglect of historical context as an all-important shaper of constitutional law has always been intellectually unwise. After "historical context" crashed into our lives two months ago (that is, on September 11, 2001), ignoring it has become politically impossible.'[31] If the Constitution is to be construed as more than a noble piece of paper and not a suicide pact, it is important to locate the war powers debate within the broader development of the national security state and its accompanying national security constitution.

Presidential primacy in the national security constitution: history, form, and functionality

Even an avowed constitutional 'minimalist' such as Sunstein concedes that an understanding of the historical 'gloss' that life has afforded the words of the Constitution on foreign affairs 'greatly favors the President':

> There can be no doubt that for questions of national security, the President has assumed authority that the text alone might not sanction. The power to make war is a leading example; Presidents have often engaged in military actions without the kind of legislative authorization that Article I appears to require.

Historical practice makes it 'plausible' that the president has acquired more constitutional authority than the text alone seems to contemplate in the realm of national security. Yet Sunstein then denies that such an understanding means that, even when the nation is at risk, the president must be 'in charge of the apparatus of government.' To affirm this is to 'reject a constitutional accommodation that, by tradition no less than text, unambiguously retains Congress's role as the nation's lawmaker' and, thereby, to be guilty of 'National Security Fundamentalism.'[32]

But while the United States is a nation of laws, it is first a nation. One need not minimize the congressional role as law-maker to affirm that national security is the first and most fundamental priority for government. Consonant with the Constitution's provisions according the presidency 'all' executive powers, the presidency now bears the primary (but not the exclusive) responsibility for assuring this. To deny this is to ignore or repudiate the accumulated historical practices of an entire half-century and to neglect the key role of executive orders, agreements, proclamations, appointments, and other non-legislative mechanisms for crafting public policy in America. One can reasonably go further, to observe that far from being an aberration in American constitutional history, the dominant pattern of the use of war powers has been one of presidential initiative (frequently absent advance or explicit legislative authorization) followed by congressional approval or acquiescence. This pattern was discernible in the early days of the Civil War, when Lincoln took dramatic action between the fall of Fort Sumter and the convening of Congress in special session on July 4, 1861, during two world wars prior to their official declarations, through the 'limited wars' of the First Cold War and down to the Clinton deployments in Haiti, Bosnia, and Kosovo.

As such, unless one rejects the case that America has been at war since 2001, there is little that is revolutionary or suspect in recent presidential exercises of executive power. If there is a noteworthy change in recent years, it resides more in the interventions of the federal judiciary on war powers. Historically, the main themes that emerged in terms of judicial determinations of the legality of presidential actions were a marked reticence to interfere with the major policies of the elected branches and the laying down of limits after the fact in a few select cases.[33] From the founding until the middle of the twentieth century, the need for the elected branches to cooperate as the Framers intended was reinforced by this judicial restraint, along with the resistance of Americans to maintaining a standing army in peacetime and the reluctance of American leaders to enter into 'entangling alliances.' The need of both branches to persuade each other of the merits of military action had to occur anew in each case of likely or looming conflict, whilst relatively small or 'limited' engagements did not demand major military mobilizations and often were conducted after congressional consultation but without prolonged public debate.

The origins of the transformation of the national security constitution can be located in the policies and actions of the Truman administration (1945–53). While the evolution of the new constitutional settlement drew directly and indirectly on prior presidential initiatives, and while the settlement would, subsequently, progress through steady and incremental stages, its key contours were established by Truman. The Truman administration negotiated, and the US Senate ratified, a series of mutual defense treaties and other agreements (most notably the setting up of NATO) under which the United States committed to join with other nations in resisting outside (communist) aggression. Some of these stated explicitly that an attack on one ally would be deemed an attack on all and that each would respond under its own constitutional procedures – which could, in America's case, entail the president's ability to repel a sudden attack. The development of a massive military establishment, allied to a nuclear arsenal whose potential use demanded the control of an entity capable of acting speedily (the presidency), was a matter on which both White House and Congress agreed.

In the reorganization of the executive branch, the congressional support for an executive-led and assertive international role, and the judicial legitimating of the national security state, the Truman administration recalibrated not only America's relations with the rest of the world but also the internal governance of foreign policy-making. Moreover, this recalibration and its central mechanisms (executive orders, executive agreements, White House declarations, a professional military under the civilian control of the Pentagon, and the establishment of an array of federal departments and agencies from the CIA and the NSC to the NSA) outlasted the global conflict for which they were designed, setting the parameters by which not only the First Cold War but also the Second would be waged.

Inevitably, the balance of constitutional war powers was steadily shifted in, and by, this new era. Rather than the president and congressional leaders seeking support for a mobilization of armed forces to meet a specific threat on each separate occasion, those forces were permanently ready to meet particular exigencies of the on-going Soviet threat. In meeting specific communist threats during the First Cold War, the authorization already existed in many, but not all, cases in the form of the treaties and agreements that had been entered into by Washington. While the Supreme Court's ruling in US v. Curtiss-Wright Export Corporation (1936) that the president 'acts as the sole organ of the federal government in the field of international relations' has attracted reasonable critical ire, the notion that the presidency is the prime organ of the federal government in international relations has substantially more to sustain it. America's rise as a major world power strongly abetted the New Deal-era expansion of federal power at home to benefit the presidency as an institution. The demands of a global war strongly reinforced the constitutional authority and resource advantages that the executive branch possessed. The president's status as the only nationally elected figure in American government, the head of state as well as the head of the government, and the commander-in-chief at wartime were similarly compounded by the rise of national mass media and instant communications.

Moreover, an extensive array of instruments supplemented and made effective the constitutional and legal authority of the national security presidency. By issuing executive agreements, presidents bypassed the formal treaty-making process, circumventing the need for Senate approval. By issuing executive orders, presidents determined policies outside the formal legislative process and, between 1920 and 1998, no less than 10,203 executive orders (roughly 130 annually) were issued.[34] If presidents wished to circumvent the reporting requirements often laid down by Congress for such orders, these could be repackaged as executive memoranda, determinations, administrative directives or proclamations. Key foreign policy appointments such as the national security advisor did not require Senate approval, while even those that did could be made as recess appointments (such as John Bolton's appointment as UN ambassador in August 2005). And by issuing national security directives, which neither Congress nor the public has an opportunity to review, presidents could keep their decisions entirely secret. (It was not legislation but NSC 68 that effectively codified First Cold War containment policy as 'involving the fulfillment or destruction not only of this Republic but of civilization.') As William Howell rightly emphasizes, the Constitution does not explicitly recognize most of these policy vehicles but, via an expansive reading of Article II powers shared by Democratic and Republican administrations alike, these have:

> radically impacted how public policy is made in America today. The president's powers of unilateral action exert just as much influence over public policy, and in some cases more, than the formal powers that presidency scholars have examined so carefully over the past several decades.[35]

This has been especially so in foreign policy, where three crucial actors also played critical roles in the development of the new constitutional compact privileging the national security presidency.

First, the two main political parties supported both the goals of
containment during the First Cold War and the institutional primacy
of the presidency. Just as post-9/11 partisan conflicts have been
intense while taking place within the context of broad agreement
on the key strategic elements of the war on terror, so during the
early First Cold War years partisanship was aggressive, harsh, and
unabated. Republican attacks on Truman for 'losing' China and
miring the US in an unwinnable war in Korea were at least as fierce
as Democratic attacks on Bush for the Iraq War after 2003. But, just
as the Iraq controversy has obscured the extent to which the Second
Cold War – the war on terror – retains broad bipartisan support, so
the consensus on the First Cold War was far more widespread than
an observer in 1952 might have imagined from the partisan rhetoric.
Particularly after Eisenhower's defeat of Robert Taft for the GOP
presidential nomination in 1952, Republicans and Democrats
viewed the world and the institutional context of foreign policy-
making in broadly similar terms. Vietnam ultimately produced a
breakdown in that bipartisan consensus that continued until 9/11,
with partisan conflicts encompassing specific regions and issues
(Central America, Africa, China, arms control) and the respective
roles of the two branches – a tension aggravated by the post-1968
norm of divided party control of the White House and Congress.
Nonetheless, despite attempts by Congress to reassert its constitutional prerogatives, the principal features of the new relationship
between the presidency and Congress, the expansive executive role
in crafting and implementing foreign policy, and the extensive executive branch apparatus were enduring features of the post-1950 era.
Presidential primacy did not translate into presidential dominance,
but the lead role for the White House remained a fulcrum of national
security policy.

Second, Congress played a role that at times actively facilitated
and endorsed, and at other points passively acquiesced in, an
expanded executive role in foreign policy. This was partially the

result of a broad partisan consensus overlaying the institutional divide between the White House and Capitol Hill. The institutional machinery for the new era was expressly approved by Congress in authorizations, the resources allocated in appropriations and, with varying degrees of success, oversight exercised. Far from being pre-empted as the nation's law-maker, that role was continually performed by the House and Senate, albeit to divergent reactions from the executive branch. In this regard, the notion of presidential 'usurpation' of congressional prerogatives fails to appreciate precisely what critics of presidential primacy typically emphasize: the two branches' co-equality. To castigate the executive branch for acting without factoring in the legislature's role provides not only a partial picture of the separated system of government but also ignores both the political agency and responsibility of Congress.

As Howell has argued, an excessive concentration on the legislative presidency – on how successful presidents are in persuading Congress to enact desired, or to resist undesirable, statute laws – provides a misleading picture of constitutional powers. The president, by acting first, can frequently exercise 'power without persuasion.' There is no constitutional impropriety to such actions. But the president is advantaged here by the respective limitations on the other branches of government. Congress has the authority and capacity to overturn presidential actions. Its will to do so, however, is often constrained by the difficulties in assembling legislative majorities in the two houses, the super-majoritarian requirements to overcome the filibuster in the Senate and the need to overcome a presidential veto. In the contemporary era of heightened partisanship and relatively cohesive congressional parties, the likelihood of decisive congressional action is as modest as Congress's propensity to gridlock and indecision is strong. In cases of foreign policy, in particular, the presidency is thus accorded a functional (but no less constitutional for that) head start.

Third, the federal courts in general, and the Supreme Court in particular, have rarely intruded on foreign policy. The courts, which could strike down executive actions as being unconstitutional, possess no electorally derived legitimacy or policy expertise so to do. Traditionally, the judiciary had responsibility for certain matters touching on national security, such as cases affecting ambassadors and consuls, admiralty and maritime jurisdiction, and cases alleging treason. But the more conventional role of the courts has been to determine whether each elected branch has performed its proper constitutional role in the initiation and conduct of military conflict. In these cases the Court has typically deferred to the political process.

Even on matters of civil liberties, claims of national security have exerted a strong force, particularly in wartime. During the First World War, for example, almost 1,000 persons were convicted under laws Congress passed making it a crime to circulate false statements intended to interfere with military success or to utter or publish words intended to bring into contempt the government, Constitution or flag of the United States. The Supreme Court, using the 'clear and present danger' test, upheld these convictions in *Schenck v. US* (1919). In *Dennis v. United States* (1951), the Court upheld convictions of Communist Party leaders for deliberately conspiring to teach and advocate the overthrow of the government by force and violence. Even in the landmark case of *US v. Nixon* (1974), the Court implied that had Nixon's claim of executive privilege been grounded on the 'need to protect military, diplomatic, or sensitive national security secrets' it might have been successful. In *DaCosta v. Laird* (1973), a case challenging the government's power to draft citizens to fight an undeclared war, and in *Holtzman v. Schlesinger* (1973), a suit where members of Congress directly challenged the president's power to wage war without a declaration, the courts refused to intervene, noting, *inter alia*, that:

- former presidents had, on more than 200 occasions, sent military forces into combat without a formal declaration of war;
- control over the use of military forces was committed by the Constitution to the political branches; and that

- Congress possessed many ways of resisting a president's policy if it so chose.

As Howell argues, 'When presidents unilaterally set policies that do not require any positive congressional action, they enjoy tremendous discretion; *non-action on the part of Congress and the courts is functionally equivalent to support.*'[36]

The War Powers Resolution

Nowhere is the relative merit of the separation of powers in foreign policy better illustrated than in the War Powers Resolution of 1973. Passed over Nixon's veto, the law required the president to consult with Congress about possible troop deployments and limited the use of troops to sixty days without specific legislative authorization. Yet the measure effectively ceded to presidents the legal authority to wage war for ninety days without congressional consent and unconstitutionally delegated the legislative war power to the executive. Presidents of both parties have rejected the measure's constitutionality (which has never been resolved by the courts) and mostly ignored its provisions, following the injunction of 'act now, inform later.' Lawsuits seeking to enforce the resolution have invariably failed. In *Crockett v. Reagan* (1982), *Lowry v. Reagan* (1987), *Dellums v. Bush* (1990), *Campbell v. Clinton* (1999) and *Doe v. Bolton* (2003), federal courts have rejected suits against executive military competences on various grounds:

- that the issue is a 'political question' beyond judicial competence;
- that the facts are ambiguous; and that
- the Congress could make the War Powers Resolution effective if it wished to act to that end.

This last argument claims that the resolution of the conflict between the branches should best be pursued by congressional majorities, acting through legislation, rather than by individuals or groups of law-makers bringing suit.

Thus, self-enforcement having failed, only the political will to make the measure apply will suffice. But the political will has never existed in Congress to enforce the resolution or to strengthen it. Most law-makers are risk-averse and reluctant to vote against the president on war powers, especially once the military is already deployed. With the exception of the two Gulf Wars, presidents since Vietnam have also tended to use the US military in relatively short conflicts that have avoided large-scale deployment of ground forces. The resolution's declared intent to ensure 'that the collective judgment of both the Congress and the president will apply to the introduction of US armed forced into hostilities' has failed because a substantial proportion of law-makers are unwilling to take the responsibility that attends such an introduction, being content to leave the possible fallout from a military failure to the president.

Given the controversies since 9/11, it is important to recall that none of the uses of force during the Clinton presidency was explicitly authorized by Congress. In the 1994 threatened deployment to Haiti, Clinton based his action on sufficient authority under Article II as commander-in-chief. In the Balkans in 1994–5, Clinton ordered the participation of US forces in bombing Serbia (and subsequently the dispatch of 20,000 US troops as part of IFOR) 'pursuant to my constitutional authority to conduct US foreign relations and as Commander-in-Chief' and on the basis of the 'authorization' provided by 'UN Security Council resolutions and in full compliance with NATO procedures.' The continued air flights and occasional bombing of Iraq were justified using precisely the same reasoning as Bush was later to invoke, namely, on the basis of the continued applicability of the January 14, 1991 congressional authorization to use force. Clinton interpreted this as conferring broad authority on the president to implement UN resolutions to 'restore international peace and security in the region' and 'uphold and implement resolution 660 (1990) and all subsequent resolutions.' The Kosovo campaign, lasting seventy-nine days, was the first presidential war and the first major use of force in American history to be conducted in the face of the explicit refusal of the Congress to authorize it. On April 28, 1999, the House voted to prohibit the president from using appropriated funds to send ground forces into Kosovo without congressional approval and voted against a formal declaration of war (by 427–2, the first war declaration that Congress had voted on since 1941). But the House also voted by 290–139 against a resolution that proposed to end the war by invoking the WPR and rejected (by a 213–213 tie) a resolution supporting the on-going air campaign. These machinations prompted White House press secretary Joe Lockhart to note wryly that the House had voted 'no on going forward, no on going back, and they tied on standing still.'[37] Subsequently, Congress later approved appropriations for the war at twice the level requested by the Clinton administration.

Railing against the Iraq War, Senator Byrd wrote in 2003 that 'The power of Congress to declare war is a political check on the president's ability to arbitrarily commit the United States to military action.'[38] Yet, as the above instances graphically reveal, it is no such thing, nor has it been for several decades. This does not, however, mean that America has reverted to a monarchical model. Recognizing that presidents under specific political circumstances will act unilaterally does not mean that sustained tyranny has arisen. If congressional majorities and large segments of the American public respond vigorously and negatively to specific presidential actions, political pressures will minimize the duration and the impact of such actions. Conversely, if Congress and large segments of the public go along, formal legal restrictions will have few decisive effects. The primary function and value of legal restrictions is to raise the political costs of unilateral executive actions – a condition as applicable to the Bush era as to that of his immediate predecessor. In this respect it is vital to refer not solely to formal constitutional texts but to the real-world politics that inevitably, and rightly, conditions their interpretation. As Howell records:

presidents have always made law without the explicit consent of Congress, sometimes by acting upon general powers delegated to them by different congresses, past and present, and other times by reading new executive authorities into the Constitution itself.[39]

The Bush experience chimes strongly with, not against, traditional American currents.

Bush and the national security constitution

The Bush administration's response to the 9/11 attacks was to announce that America was at war. That sentiment was shared across America and, on September 14, both houses of Congress passed a resolution (by 98 votes to 0 in the Senate, and 420 to 1 in the House) giving the president latitude to:

> use all necessary and appropriate force against those nations, organizations, or persons he determines planned, authorized, committed, or aided the terrorist attacks that occurred on September 11, 2001, or harbored such organizations or persons, in order to prevent any future acts of international terrorism against the United States by such nations, organizations, or persons.

Opinion polls on September 13 had found majorities ranging from 66 to 81 percent of Americans willing to approve a formal declaration of war. A raft of measures followed, from the PATRIOT Act to the creation of the Department of Homeland Security, that echoed the institutional reorganization of the Truman years and that were intended to reduce the likelihood of a repetition of the attacks (the success of which is assessed in chapter 4). Most observers noted that the presidency had also received a wartime 'khaki' mandate that substantially strengthened the president's authority, power, and popularity.

The question of whether America is at war has received much commentary and is central to other aspects of the critique of Bush, such as the legality of military tribunals detaining 'enemy combatants.' But the relevant question, as Posner notes, is not whether the 9/11 attacks were acts of war in a formalistic legal sense but whether politically they should be deemed acts of war.[40] Posner contends that this judgment, in turn, rests on the likely consequences of the determination, which is sound enough. But it also turns on what we understand by war. One difficulty here is that the concept of war, while still fatally real to dozens of nations, has fallen into *desuetude* among liberal democracies. The issuance of formal declarations of 'total' war is not inconceivable today. But it is largely an historic relic.[41] A range of commentators have argued that, whether on principle or as an instrumental tactic to frustrate jihadists, mass casualty terrorism should be treated as a crime, the province of law enforcement authorities.

But the case for war has nonetheless been compelling. There can be no question that, had a national government authored the 9/11 attacks, a state of war would have been deemed to have existed between it and the US. Whatever the proximate political ends of al Qaeda and its affiliates, there can be no question that it seeks to kill as many Americans as its capacities will allow. Unlike terrorist groups such as the IRA or ETA, the jihadist network has no sensitivity to the loss of lives. Nor is there any meaningful political negotiation that can realize its goals through concessions and compromise. According to the 2006 Quadrennial Defense Review:

> The US is a nation engaged in what will be a long war . . . Since the attacks of September 11, 2001, our Nation has fought a global war against violent extremists who use terrorism as their weapon of choice, and who seek to destroy our free way of life. Our enemies seek WMD and, if they are successful, will likely attempt to use them in their conflict with free people everywhere. Currently, the struggle is centered in Iraq and Afghanistan, but we will need to be prepared and to arrange to successfully defend our Nation and its interests around the globe for years to come.

In granting extensive authority to the president to wage the war on terror as he determined it, Congress explicitly accorded the executive autonomy of action – but that was nonetheless subject to future congressional scrutiny and revision.

Much the same logic applied to the Iraq War. In the summer of 2002, Alberto Gonzalez, the president's chief legal counsel, had argued that Bush already possessed sufficient authority to go to war with Iraq, based on his constitutional prerogatives as commander-in-chief, the 1991 congressional authorization for the Persian Gulf War, and the resolution of September 14, 2001. But the White House ultimately sought congressional approval, which was given on October 10, 2002. The Senate voted 77–23 in favor of the Iraq resolution, with 48 Republicans supporting it and 1 in opposition. The Democrats were divided, 29 in favor, 21 against. In the House, which voted 296–133 in support, a minority (81) of Democrats voted in favor of the resolution, with the majority 126 voting against. 215 Republicans supported the president's request, while 6 voted against.[42] The resolution stated that the president was:

> authorized to use the Armed Forces of the US as he determines to be necessary and appropriate to (1) defend the security of the US against the continuing threat posed by Iraq and (2) enforce all relevant Security Council Resolutions regarding Iraq.

These, then, were – in line with prior precedents – not instances of authoritarian presidential coups but express congressional empowerments. Yet Fisher, the most emphatic critic of the modern war powers balance, contrasted the two Iraq Wars thus:

> In the end, Congress had two models to choose from. It could have acted after the election, as it did in 1990–91. It could have acted in the middle of an election, as in 1964. The first maintained the integrity of the legislative institution by minimizing partisan tactics and scheduling legislative debate after the Security Council voted. The second placed Congress in a position of voting hurriedly without

the information it needed, and with information it did receive (the two 'attacks' in the Tonkin Gulf) of dubious quality. In 2002, Congress picked the Tonkin Gulf model. There may be times when Congress might have to authorize war in the middle of an election. The year 2002 was not one.[43]

Such criticisms appear perverse. As most political scientists concur, elections tend to be retrospective evaluations of the incumbent. To debate a matter as momentous as war prior to such a popular evaluation appears entirely reasonable. To await the verdict of the Security Council would seem irrelevant in terms of the crucial constitutional issue of who authorizes war. Indeed, elsewhere Fisher criticizes excessive reliance on UN resolutions by presidents as precisely one of the elements most problematic in post-1950 constitutional practice.[44] Moreover, the vote prior to the 1991 authorization was quite close in the Senate (52–47). Had three Senators switched sides, Washington would have been left in a position where the UNSC had approved the use of force, the president believed he had the authority to use force, and one house of Congress had refused to authorize such force while the other house had approved. Such a position could well have resulted in a constitutional crisis and humiliating irresolution in the Gulf. Even Glennon, a critic of presidential war primacy who castigated Bush Sr. in 1991, conceded that maneuverings over the 2002 resolution represented 'political misjudgments, not constitutional violations.'[45]

Despite the distinctive character of the attacks and the ensuing war, the Bush response to 9/11 featured patterns very familiar to prior wartime presidencies, patterns entirely consonant with the original understanding of war powers, the national security constitution and presidential primacy. Moreover, it largely conformed to the prescription of Justice Jackson, that the president's power is maximal when he is acting under an authorization from Congress, minimal when the exercise of power is 'incompatible with the expressed or implied will of Congress' and in the middle when Congress is silent.[46] In the

cases of the Afghanistan and Iraq campaigns, the authorization by
Congress was explicit and broad. Some law-makers may subsequently
have developed misgivings about such authorizations, but the legislative authority to revoke, revise, or reformulate such grants of
power remains Congress's to make. In the case of the NSA wiretapping and finances programs, while there was no prior express
authorization, the circumstances of 9/11 made such initiatives rational and, at least in principle, defensible under the combination of
Article II authority and implicit grants of existing authorizations. In
the cases of military tribunals and coercive interrogation, the pre-
sumption of presidential war powers authority was at minimum reasonable, however questionable the merits of the particular adopted
policies. 'Prisoner abuses' were aberrations – recurrent in every war –
rather than the logical consequence of the authority under which
Bush acted.

Most critically, the separation of powers is not a one-way street,
and Congress has the capacity to exercise its expansive constitutional authority to rein in the executive where it identifies egregious
constitutional excess or where substantive policy disagreements
exist. Perhaps the most obvious instances of this encompassed those
areas – coercive interrogation, NSA surveillance, and military tribunals – where criticism of the administration was especially strong.
In each case, the administration revisited decisions made in the heat
of the post-9/11 crisis. When the Senate voted in October 2005 to
insert statutory language to ensure that overly abusive and coercive
interrogation techniques could no longer be employed by the military, the White House negotiated acceptable terminology, and the
Pentagon issued new guidelines in September 2006. When the
Supreme Court declared congressional authorization a necessary
requirement for the use of military tribunals, the administration
worked with Congress to fashion new regulations. Whatever the
merits or demerits of the original policies, it is precisely in this kind
of legislative oversight and intervention that the sharing of war

powers, so strongly emphasized by proponents of congressional primacy, consists.

A similar observation can be advanced in regard to the judiciary. The Supreme Court rulings in *Hamdi v. Rumsfeld* (2004), *Rasul v. Bush* (2004), and *Hamdan v. Rumsfeld* (2006) provided a mixed blessing for critics of the war on terror. On the one hand, the fact that the Court did confidently intervene on matters of war powers for the first time since 1952 was an important development, refuting any notion that in America *inter arma silent leges* (amidst war laws are silent). Moreover, its rulings provided partial rebukes of the administration in its conduct of the war. This despite the fact that, in the case of *Hamdan*, the Court majority expressly ignored the statute (the Detainee Treatment Act of 2005) that Congress had passed to end jurisdiction over the habeas applications of Guantanamo detainees. But the very fact that the judiciary intervened made it difficult to sustain the case that an imperial presidency was establishing an autocratic regime defying constitutional muster. The involvement of the Supreme Court on the issue of detainees' rights, which affected two Americans in total, eloquently attested to the robustness rather than the fragility of constitutional democracy. Even on this most crucial of issues (national security and war powers) rights have become so fully institutionalized in America that the judiciary is able to intervene assertively. Far from being a matter for *Schadenfreude* over the Bush 'regime,' the interventions demonstrated strikingly well the self-policing nature of the divided democracy and constitutional system that has served the United States so well for so long.

However, the divided Court offered at least modest reason to anticipate that the argument for expansive presidential power in war powers could yet gain majority support among the justices – a development that should give pause to skeptics of the national security presidency. While the rulings certainly went against the Bush administration, the war powers decisions have strongly echoed traditional themes in war power jurisprudence, not least in emphasizing the importance of the elected branches of the federal government acting together. Beyond this, in their dissenting opinions in these and other separation of powers cases, at least four of the nine justices (Roberts, Scalia, Thomas, and Alito) expressed varying degrees of support for the notion that the Constitution, statute law and precedent together afford an extensive but not unlimited authority to the wartime presidency as commander-in-chief. Given the age and frailty of some of the remaining members of the Court, the future appointment of a justice with similar views on presidential power could plausibly tilt the balance of the Court in a way that upholds rather than strikes down the aggressive assertion of executive prerogatives in wartime.

Although hailing the Court's interventions in these recent war powers cases, civil libertarians nonetheless objected to many of the post-9/11 policies as egregiously cynical overreactions to security threats that threatened sacrosanct liberties (in particular, privacy protections, freedom of the press, the rights of criminal suspects), implying that counterterrorism must accommodate itself to the liberties, not the other way round.[47] But, as Posner argues, such an approach is at best 'unsound':

> The events of September 11 revealed the United States to be in greater jeopardy from international terrorism than had been believed by most people until then – revealed it to be threatened by a diffuse, shadowy, but very dangerous enemy that had to be fought with internal police measures as well as with military force. It stands to reason that such a revelation would lead to our civil liberties being curtailed. A pragmatist would say they *should* be curtailed to the extent that the beneficial consequences for the safety of the nation (which, remember, is a concern of constitutional dignity rather than a concern to be weighed *against* the Constitution) outweigh the adverse impact on liberty.[48]

That even constitutional scholars and progressives such as Bruce Ackerman should concede the necessity of reassessing the liberty–security balance is indicative of the severity of the threat facing

America, even if the particular prescriptions for rebalancing are unconvincing.[49] Thus far, the judgments reached by federal authorities have indeed been pragmatic. The (re)balancing of liberty with security – for example in the PATRIOT Act's provisions and NSA data mining of international phone calls – has occurred with the decisive support of most Americans, a reality that, politically, has been attested to by the support of mainstream Democrats for such policies. The vast swathe of civil liberties and rights for Americans has been *entirely* unaffected by the war on terror, which has preserved comprehensive guarantees for American citizens far more extensive than in comparable liberal democracies such as the UK (where CCTV surveillance, centralized computer records of private details, and limits on freedom of expression are of a scale and nature unheard of in America).

The indictment over historic breaches in respect of liberties needs, though, to be weighed against the pragmatic security questions of the time and at the time. Measures that may be latterly deemed unnecessary and excessive may appear at the time warranted and compelling. Moreover, as Posner notes, the 'lessons of history' beloved of civil libertarian critics of the war on terror are doubly inaccurate. For one thing, the 'lesson' of American history is not that US public officials habitually exaggerate dangers to the nation's security but rather the opposite, that they underestimate them: from the danger of secession in the Civil War, Japanese attack in the Second World War, through Soviet spying, to Soviet missiles in Cuba, the Iranian revolution and 9/11 itself. A second historical claim, that the erosion of wartime liberties will remain in place after the war or emergency's cessation, is similarly unsupported. The curtailments of liberty that took place in the Civil War, the two World Wars, and the First Cold War did not outlast the emergencies, whether real or (in the case of the First World War and the 'Red Scare') imagined. Civil liberties were not only restored but enlarged after the wars ended, and, in the case of the First Cold War, civil liberties and rights were far greater in scope and deeper in foundation by its end (in part, precisely because of the pressures of wartime conflict over four decades, not least to end segregation, than at its outset; and, as we now know, many of the charges of subversion and espionage leveled in that era were accurate).

In the case of the protracted war against terror, it is difficult to maintain that the tilt of the balance between safety and liberty has been either egregious in its own right or remotely comparable to the abandonment of *habeas corpus* during the Civil War or the internment of Japanese and Japanese-Americans during the Second World War. The question of how long the threat will remain – and what evolving balance between liberty and public safety is prudent to meet the threat – is impossible to estimate. As such, the types of constitutional conflicts that punctuated the Bush years are unlikely to diminish in future presidencies.

Conclusion

Presidential primacy is the central feature of the constitution of American national security. The functionality of executive primacy, combined with the institutional and political problems attending concerted congressional action and judicial entry into the 'political thicket' of war, powerfully magnify the constitutional powers ascribed to the presidency by the Framers. Because of his unique position within the system of separated government and separated powers, the president enjoys numerous opportunities to take independent action, with or without the express consent of Congress or the courts and, thereby, effectively to set public policy on his own. This does not mean that the American Republic has embraced a quasi-monarchy, that Congress has been marginalized in the foreign policy-making process, or that wartime contingencies have silenced the rule of law. But the possession of a series of resource advantages, the imperatives shaping prompt and decisive action by Washington in the international arena, and the comparatively poor positions of the Congress (in mobilizing collective action) and the courts (in political legitimacy) underpin the authority and power of the chief executive. The unprecedented threat posed by jihadist terror has amplified the venerable debate over war powers and illustrated the relative neglect accorded that question by constitutional scholars. But the Bush administration's use of war powers has occurred in accordance with, not as a departure from or challenge to, America's national security constitution. As Yoo observes, 'The president always must act pursuant to some authority either directly granted by the Constitution or delegated to him by Congress.'[50]

The wartime conditions that followed the attacks of 9/11 confirmed the centrality of the national security presidency, and Bush's successors, similarly, will both benefit and suffer from the particular political focus and heavy burden that war accords the White House. The presidency remains, as JFK once observed, an office of extraordinary power operating under extraordinary limitations. Even in wartime, war is not synonymous with foreign policy, and the constitutional and political constraints on the 'imperial' presidency are much broader than merely the war power alone. Presidential power remains, in this sense, contingent rather than unconstrained even where it is at its most potent. As successive presidents have demonstrated, moreover, reticence rather than eagerness is a much more common characteristic of the White House where matters of war are concerned.

3

The Second Cold War on Islamist terror: negative audits

My own suspicion is that many Americans have enjoyed Bush's 'terror war' more than they wish to admit. Feeling scared can be oddly pleasurable, like participating in a real-life action thriller, when one is allied in imagined combat with a united country of brave patriots. The plot line is simple – good guys against satanic forces – and pushes aside doubts and ambiguities, like why exactly these people are out to get us. Does our own behavior in the world have anything to do with it? No, they resent us because we are so virtuous – kind, free, wealthy, democratic. The contest, as framed by Bush, invites Americans to indulge in a luxurious sense of self-pity – poor, powerful America, so innocent and yet so misunderstood. America's exaggerated fear of unknown 'others' is perhaps an unconscious inversion of its exaggerated claims of power.

William Greider[1]

The pseudo-left has too great an investment in anti-Americanism to admit that there can be a reason for evil independent of Washington's control.

Clive James[2]

This notion that inside every human being is the burning desire for freedom and liberty, much less democracy, is probably not the case. I don't think anyone knows what burns inside others. Food, shelter, security, stability. Have you read Erich Fromm, 'Escape from Freedom'? I don't agree with him, but some people don't really want to be free.

Brent Scowcroft[3]

The statesman, unlike the academic, cannot wait for international relations theory to work itself out. He must have a policy that addresses the perceived power distribution in the world.

Fareed Zakaria[4]

Negative assessments of the war on terror are prolific. Here we divide them into three large but broadly cohesive camps:

- the conservative/realist;
- the left-liberal; and
- the 'old' European.

They are not mutually exclusive. Our argument here is that they capture neither the success of that war nor do they offer, singularly or in combination, a workable plan for the post-Bush years. By default, Bush foreign policy is likely to endure because there is nothing viable with which to replace it. There is nothing viable because the Second Cold War is working – imperfectly perhaps but, like containment in the First, working nonetheless.

Our argument in this chapter is drawn from the lessons of that First Cold War. This conflict provides a firmer historical context within which to assess the war on terror than is allowed for in the present apparent polarization. Debates over how to confront communism were many and various throughout the First Cold War but they belonged to a broad consensus. Today, debates over how to confront terrorism in the Second Cold War look similarly various. Both were/are debates within a consensus position. They were/are arguments over tactics, not strategy. The positions assessed below have failed to weaken that consensus. As we will see, their faulty auditing of the war on terror has won few converts.

The conservative/realist audit

One of the most distinctive features of the foreign policy debate
since 9/11 has been its rightward orientation. An increasingly self-
doubting liberal-left has found it difficult to break into a debate,
over the appropriate moral character of US foreign policy, that it
once led. Instead, the contending voices now emanate from the
pages of conservative journals and think tanks.[5] We can find no
left-wing counter-example to that set by Vice-President Cheney in
making the neoconservative *Weekly Standard* required reading for
all White House staff. In 1996, Robert Kagan and William Kristol
bemoaned a foreign policy conservatism 'adrift' and 'confused'.[6]
Today, the poverty of the left's contribution is symbolized in an
increasingly shrill anti-Bushism which has gone not much further
than support for Cindy Sheehan, the Dixie Chicks and the doomed
senatorial candidacy of Ned Lamont.[7] The auditing of the war on
terror is vital and lively in their opponents' camp. It is here that a
clash between optimism and pessimism, between hope and expectation is joined.

For realists, there are two main arguments against what we call the
Second Cold War. The first indicts the strategy's seemingly limitless
ambitions. The second, by conflating American popularity abroad
with security at home, argues that because the war is unpopular with
foreigners, leading them to balance against the United States, it must
be revised.

Power as limits, balance as inevitable?

As a theory of international relations, realism has not much time for
hope.[8] War is a recurrent feature of human affairs. *Igitur qui desiderat
pacem, praeparet bellum* ('If you want peace, prepare for war'). Despite
a fatalism that contends for the permanence of war, prominent realists have come out against this one. John Mearsheimer has deployed
the godfather of classical realism against the Bush strategy. Hans

Morgenthau, he says, would have opposed the war on terror.[9] Realism, says Mearsheimer – says Morgenthau – offers a better strategy for navigating international relations than neoconservatism – which he holds as the organizing theory behind the war on terror – because it recognizes limits. It appreciates that even great power will ultimately have to be tailored to meet reality. Because the war on terror is premised on a hopeful faith in the perpetuity of American military supremacy it will necessarily over-reach and invite either balancing behavior on the behalf of inferior, insecure, and jealous states or quagmires, as in Iraq.[10] Realism is more realistic, argues Mearsheimer, not unsurprisingly. It marries aims to means.

When governments see US belligerency and interventionism they do not join the American bandwagon but balance against it. 'We live in a balancing world,' he tells us. This is the pitfall of the Iraq War specifically and the war on terror generally, says the realist. Rather than winning converts to the cause, Bush generated opposition and balancing coalitions. Weak states like a strong state checked. Like children in a playground, the bully is only as strong as the allies he can intimidate to his cause. His dominance is precarious for this reason and likely to force defections.

The equation of the war on terror with 'imperial overstretch' informs several realist audits. Ever since Paul Kennedy popularized the concept as a guide to 'inevitable' US decline in *The Rise and Fall of the Great Powers* (1988) – which predicted the USA's demise but not that of the USSR which was occurring even as he wrote – realists have searched for its various manifestations.[11] Graham Fuller condemns the war on terror for positing unrealizable ends, a war in which 'fatigue emerges in direct proportion to the ambitiousness of the undertaking. From its early days, this administration adopted a strategic vision and peremptory posture whose implementation would prove exhausting under the best of circumstances.'[12]

Harvard's Stephen Walt has pursued a similar line. In a clear allusion to contemporary American power, his book opens with the

words of the great conservative thinker Edmund Burke, addressing
the pitfalls of British primacy in the late eighteenth century:

> I dread our own power and our own ambition; I dread our being too
> much dreaded . . . We may say that we shall not abuse this astonish-
> ing and hitherto unheard-of power. But every other nation will think
> we shall abuse it. It is impossible but that, sooner or later, this state of
> things must produce a combination against us which may end in our
> ruin.[13]

Realism makes states the basic unit of analysis in international
relations. How states interact determines their performance – which
is measured by how much power and/or security that performance
accumulates. Realists grant very little explanatory power to internal
state character. Democracies and dictatorships navigate an essentially anarchic world in broadly similar ways. Because the imperatives are the same so are the means to achieve them. Consequently,
a foreign policy that seeks international security by achieving democratic regime change is doomed. For the realist, foreign affairs are like
human nature – fixed and immutable. Despite Bush's hopes, creating
more democracies will not alter the fundamental dynamics of world
order. For Mearsheimer, a belief in the transformative power of
democracy is 'hooey.'[14] The international system cannot be transformed. States will not cascade into democracy because America
wills it. They will more likely do the opposite and resist American
political engineering.

The contortions of realism in the face of the war on terror are captured in the oxymoronic title of a book by Anatol Lieven and John
Hulsman: *Ethical Realism*.[15] This is a manifesto in defense of the men
who used to run American foreign policy, including especially those
in the Bush Sr. administration. They are the same officials who, as
George Packer observed, 'abandoned Afghanistan to civil war and al
Qaeda, allowed Saddam to massacre his own people, and concluded
that genocide in the Balkans was none of America's business.'[16] The

authors' 'vision' is a return to realist normalcy. (Several liberals have joined them, which we will discuss shortly.) Ethical realism would abandon the 'spread of freedom and democracy,' i.e., the ethical dimensions of American foreign policy, and replace them, pace Mearsheimer, Fuller, and Walt, with a renewed recognition of 'the limits of American power.'[17] This new approach 'is not cynical' and, unlike classical realism, is not 'attracted to ruthlessness for its own sake.' Rather, 'It is rooted in the commonsensical, everyday morality and generosity of spirit that Americans practice themselves and expect of their neighbors.'[18] Indeed, the authors concede that the neoconservative emphasis on the character of regimes, including America's, is valid. They just refuse to accept the logical corollary that regime change is thus central to American security.

Regime change is not an emphasis unique to the Second Cold War. It has long been central to US foreign policy. Few 'rogue states' have attacked the United States or severely compromised its interests without suffering regime change as a consequence. The Southern Confederacy (1861–5) did not long endure. Japan and Germany both underwent regime change in 1945. We could even cite Latin American examples – Chile 1973 and El Salvador in the 1980s – to highlight the basic recourse to regime change in Washington's national security strategy. True, the US did not engage in such a strategy toward the USSR – it was never explicitly attacked by it – but successive American presidents sought to destabilize the Soviet Union's international proxies – only the Cuban and North Korean grotesqueries proved immune. George Bush Sr. arguably failed to continue this tradition. Arguably, because even this great champion of the ethical realists was prepared to make war on behalf of values. For example, he defended his Somali intervention in 1992 by declaring that 'no one should have to die at Christmas.'[19] As Ivo Daalder and Robert Kagan point out, Bush Sr. 'launched two interventions aimed at purely "humanitarian" purposes (Somalia) or to remove a dictator and effect a change of regime (Panama).'[20]

His over-cautious approach to communist collapse in 1989–90 stands in marked contrast to the subversion of Soviet interests as practiced by every president since Truman. The first Iraq War was also an occasion when the US, under Bush Sr., balked at regime change, and yet 'ethical realists' now laud this hesitancy as wisdom. Abandoning Yugoslavia in 1991–2 was likewise for Bush Sr. and his increasingly nostalgic supporters evidence of judicious statecraft.

It is difficult to envisage how the great realist fear of a balancing coalition would have resulted from a more assertive US policy in these episodes. Russia was not noticeably more friendly toward the United States when Bush and Baker ignored the Serbs in 1991 than it was when the US was bombing them, under Clinton, later in the decade. Arab regimes have no more balanced against US power post-Saddam than they did when he was running Iraq. The explanatory power of balance has been problematic for some time. Realism, of any stripe, has not been able to explain why, when communism collapsed, leaving the US predominant, states did not balance against US power. In fact, they rushed to join its imperium. This obsession with balance – one conditioned by the theoretical rigidities of realism itself – fatally undermines the realist audit of the war on terror. Since balancing is not happening, it does not provide grounds to indict the Bush approach.

As Robert Lieber observes, 'there is considerable evidence that balancing is not really taking place.'[21] We concur here with Michael Mandelbaum: 'If America is a Goliath, it is a benign one. Unlike the case of Goliath, moreover, no David, or group of Davids, has stepped forward to confront the United States.'[22] Several reasons account for the failure of states to balance against the United States. The simple reason is that they can't. The impediments to an anti-US alliance are considerable. Politically and diplomatically there is little love lost between the states that realists, ignoring internal state character, claim should come together. Russia and China are no warmer toward each other because of America's war on terror. Consider that when they were apparent communist soul-mates, 1949–91, they still managed to come to the brink of war in 1969. 'They are traditional rivals,' as Robert Kagan notes, 'and the rise of China inspires at least as much nervousness in Russia as it does in the United States.'[23] The European Union, by the same token, was no more cohesive, no closer to a unified foreign policy, in 2008 than in 2001 – before Bush.

Militarily, the war on terror, and here it is unlike previous global conflicts, has not seen significant rises in the defense spending of other nations. Given the demographic obstacles to such spending it would be unwise to predict anything other than American military pre-eminence for several decades to come. As Mark Haas notes, 'despite much recent discussion in the international relations literature and some policymaking circles about the likelihood of China (and to a lesser extent the European Union) balancing US power in coming decades, the realities of social aging and its economic and military effects make such an outcome unlikely.' Moreover, he argues,

> global aging increases the likelihood of continued peaceful relations between the United States and the other great powers. Studies have shown that the probability of international conflict grows when either the dominant country anticipates a power transition in favor of a rising state or states, or when such a transition actually takes place. By adding substantial support to the continuation of US hegemony, global aging works against either outcome from transpiring. An aging world therefore decreases the probability that either hot or cold wars will develop between the United States and the other great powers.[24]

Whatever the precise cause, the predicted balancing coalitions have certainly not formed. Tariq Ali's depiction of 'an axis of hope' – between Bolivia, Cuba, and Venezuela – challenging American power in its own hemisphere, is fantasy.[25] Franco-German and Sino-Russian concerns over Iraq did not metamorphose into formal treaties amongst these nations. There is no Warsaw Pact equivalent in the Second Cold War and nor is there likely to be. As Walter Laqueur notes, 'There have been few volunteers to act as world policemen – it is admittedly not an attractive job, unpaid, with little gratitude to be earned.'[26] Indeed, in the absence of a rival, America is likely to be more ambitious not less. Here we concur with Ivo Daalder and Robert Kagan, who, bucking a scholarly consensus, argue that:

> The distribution of power in the world since the collapse of the Soviet Union – not very different today, despite the rise of powers such as China and India – *invites military intervention* by a dominant military power unchecked by the deterrent power of any nation or grouping of nations with roughly equal strength.[27]

Realism and the new power of popularity

The failure of balancing activity to occur led realists to find fault in the Bush strategy elsewhere. Somewhat odd, given their prior theoretical concerns, is a new-found realist fear of American unpopularity. The war on terror not only represents an open-ended commitment to an unattainable end but one in which potential allies are turned into enemies, 'the Arab street' into a recruiting ground for terrorists. Realism used to eschew the explanatory power of such nebulous concepts as public opinion. According to Hans Morgenthau, foreign policy should be immune to such currents. The 'conditions under which popular support can be obtained for a foreign policy,' he observed, 'are not necessarily identical with the conditions under which a foreign policy can be successfully pursued.'[28] Henry Kissinger, arguably the most powerful realist statesman in American history, has recurrently chided public opinion for its corrupting influence on the foreign policies of several states, contemporary and historical.[29] Being liked might be a happy consequence of international strategy but it was not its key aim. Now realists argue it is. And because they do, their audit of the war on terror is overwhelmingly negative.

The problems of this approach are evident in John Mearsheimer and Stephen Walt's controversial thesis on the activities of the 'Israel

Lobby.'[30] As realists, pace Morgenthau, they distrust the harmful impact of domestic politicking on the pursuit of the national interest. As war on terror skeptics they have felt obliged to condemn the Bush strategy for its insulation from the popular will, at home and abroad:

> The combination of unwavering support for Israel and the related effort to spread 'democracy' throughout the region has inflamed Arab and Islamic opinion and jeopardised not only US security but that of much of the rest of the world. This situation has no equal in American political history.[31]

The debate this argument generated was fierce and lies outside the scope of this book.[32] What we find interesting is how two of the world's most respected realist scholars have determined to condemn the war on terror on the basis of its foreign reception. Rather than unpopularity being an unfortunate by-product of the pursuit of the national interest, it is now, by definition it appears, a negation of the national interest. Put somewhat crudely, but not inaccurately, what makes Arabs happy fulfills American national interests. By extension, what makes Israelis happy, according to Mearsheimer and Walt, retards those same interests. For liberals to pore over polling data to find empirical evidence of the unpopularity of the war on terror is not unusual. For realists to join them is a denial of the theoretical clarity of realism itself. Indeed, Mearsheimer and Walt share the left-liberal conviction that the failure of the war on terror is down to the influence of Israel and its Washington 'Lobby.'

There is a growing academic literature on anti-Americanism as an international political phenomenon.[33] For decades, the liberal-left has prized anti-Americanism as a mobilizing force among 'victims' of US 'imperialism' and/or understood it as the predictable 'blowback' of American foreign policy.[34] Much of liberal international relations theory asserts that empathy, commonality, and interconnectedness make the world a more pacific place. Such assertions are the bedrock of the democratic peace hypothesis. Today, however, conservatives and realists have joined them. In their conception, the war on terror must be indicted for catalyzing a violent anti-Americanism that led to 9/11 in the first place.[35] Bush supposedly lost Arab 'hearts and minds.'[36] Less acknowledged is the fact that the al Qaeda plot was hatched during the Clinton presidency – even as his air force was attacking Serbian Christians in defense of Kosovar Muslims and as his diplomats were forcing the pace of an Israel–Palestine settlement; 9/11 was born against Clinton not Bush. For Stefan Halper and Jonathan Clarke, two conservative/realist scholars, 'the costs of anti-Americanism' are disproportionately great.[37] But the tangible benefits of America's following a specifically 'pro-Muslim' policy are far from clear.

This determination to evaluate the war on terror on the basis of its foreign, substantially Arab-Muslim, reception is, we suggest, to confuse polling data with strategic efficacy. The war is not a public relations exercise. It is no surprise to find that messy campaigns, like Iraq, within the wider Second Cold War, and ugly features of the war, like Guantanamo Bay and Abu Ghraib, offend the people they are meant to liberate. Saddam, of course, tortured and killed several thousand Muslims (mostly Shiites and Kurds) at Abu Ghraib but achieved less infamy in the Muslim world for doing so than did America's temporary use of the prison.[38]

We do not argue that such aberrations should be ignored and concede that American popularity has been affected by them. What we find more remarkable, however, is not Arab disaffection with US mistakes but heightened jihadist loathing when the United States chooses to wage war on behalf of Muslim populations. If the US can bomb Christians to protect Muslims, as it did in Bosnia in 1994–5 and Serbia in 1999, and yet, as a consequence, augment the fury of Islamists, then there is little any American president can do to be better liked. We concur with the senior Bush administration official who said, 'The idea that the jihadists would all be peaceful, warm, lovable, God-fearing people if it weren't for US policies strikes me as not a valid idea.'[39]

If war fought on behalf of Muslims does not bring Muslim appro-bation, there is little chance peaceful diplomacy will achieve it.[40] As Brendan Simms, the chronicler of Serbian aggression, observes:

> For a long time, I saw the inability of the US to parlay its efforts on behalf of European Muslims – which were in evidence again over Kosovo in 1999 – into credit within the wider Umma as a failure of American public diplomacy. But in the course of my own modest efforts at public meetings, in the newspapers, and the odd appearance on 'Muslim' channels, I quickly realised that I was hitting a brick wall. Most Muslims were simply not interested in hearing that the US gov-ernment had been a staunch supporter of Bosnian Muslims. By the time I added that prominent American Jews – among them Richard Perle and Paul Wolfowitz – were leading protagonists of intervention on behalf of the Bosnian Muslims, they had switched off.[41]

The Islamist world view is essentially immune to US behavior. 'There is no reason to assume,' as Richard Betts notes, 'that terrorist enemies would let America off the hook if it retreated.'[42] As Richard Clarke points out, 'The jihadist terrorists oppose the US not for what it believes or does, but because they see America as a barrier to their creation of theocratic nation-states or caliphates.'[43] Hussein Massawi, former head of Hezbollah, illustrated the futility of western public diplomacy more bluntly. 'We are not fighting so that you will offer us something,' he said. 'We are fighting to eliminate you.'[44]

The left-liberal audit

The response of the political/academic left is significantly compro-mised by Bush choosing a path once advocated by it: the overthrow-ing of dictatorships and their replacement with free governments. A conservative/realist can deride the illusions of such a strategy, a liberal cannot. To deny the imperative of regime change would be to reject a core component of the liberal world view. To compensate, liberal opinion has sought refuge in a moral and cultural relativism.[45] Rather than support the overthrow of tyrants, many on the left reject the American superiority that makes such regime change possible. For several, the war on terror is a clash of equivalent evils, of, according to Tariq Ali, 'fundamentalisms' and therefore not worth the fighting.[46] This equivalence masks an animating anti-Americanism but is couched in terms of opposition to war. The US is opposed by many on the left because it is seen as the last great catalyst of conflict. America is far worse than the opponents it provokes and creates. Ali does not actually contend for moral equivalence in the war on terror. '[T]he most dangerous "fundamentalism" today,' he says, ' "the mother of all fundamentalisms" is American imperialism.'[47] As a now exiled member of the left opined:

> In the last decade or so had this 'anti-war' rabble had its way, we would have seen Kuwait stay part of Iraq, Bosnia and Kosovo cleansed and annexed by 'Greater' Serbia and the Taleban retaining control of Afghanistan. You might think that such a record would lead its adherents to be dismissed as a silly and sinister fringe but instead it is they who pose as the principled radicals and their opponents who are treated with unconcealed disdain in the universities and on the BBC.[48]

To deny the efficacy and morality of war necessarily makes a liberal audit of the war on terror problematic – of what value is the auditing of something illegitimate regardless of how it is fought?

Like realists, left-liberals predict US decline. Unlike realists, they rather want it to happen. A declining America poses less threat. Less threat means less 'global resistance.' Less global resistance means less terrorism. Thus, the liberal audit proceeds on the basis that the war on terror is the most effective means to weaken American hegemony. America, as liberal IR theorist G. John Ikenberry has argued, is inadvertently balancing against itself.[49] The political left has sought alliance – of convenience and ideology and often both – with the war's targets because this is the surest way to retard American power. As Osama Bin Laden pointed out in 2003, 'there is nothing wrong in Muslim interests converging with those of the socialists in the battle against the Crusaders, even if we believe and declare that the socialists are apostates.'[50] The illiberal character of the left's new allies is secondary to their anti-Americanism. 'Why is it,' asks a once proud left-winger, 'that apologies for a militant Islam which stands for everything the liberal-left is against come from the liberal-left?'[51] The war on terror is a primary rallying cry of the left.[52] Mainstream American politics, in contrast, has embraced the war as the better of a rather limited list of viable responses to global jihadist terrorism. The 2004 'Democratic National Platform for America,' for example, emphasized three central concerns of the post-9/11 era: waging a war on terror, retarding WMD proliferation, and extending the zone of democracies.[53] The war as strategy commands consensus. Tactical disputes, as in all wars, remain over the appropriate battles to fight within it. Hence the on-going debate about Iraq.[54]

The left-wing audit argues that America's foes have been emboldened by the war's fighting. The more extreme position – that Republicans created a fantasy enemy in order to compel domestic obedience and foreign expansion – seems to us too detached from reality, too conspiracy-seeking to be worth scrutiny, despite a willingness in some to endow it with academic rigor.[55] There is a more reasonable liberal audit, however. It proceeds from one or both of the following bases.

The first is anchored in a psychological approach to America's place in the world. The US is an imperfect political system. It facilitates the existence, side-by-side, of great wealth and poverty, of economic opportunity and political alienation. Its culture is remarkably fluid and open and yet its media is unquestioning and establishment-serving. Non-whites enjoy high office, but the US is historically and culturally racist. The US Constitution decries established religion, but Christian evangelicalism now dictates the tone and content of

American politics. The United States provides something for everyone to hate, for everyone to love. As Claus Christian Malzahn
observed in *Der Spiegel*:

> For us Germans, the Americans are either too fat or too obsessed with
> exercise, too prudish or too pornographic, too religious or too nihilis-
> tic. In terms of history and foreign policy, the Americans have either
> been too isolationist or too imperialistic. They simply go ahead and
> invade foreign countries (something we Germans, of course, would
> never do) and then abandon them, the way they did in Vietnam and
> will soon do in Iraq.[56]

For liberals, before 9/11, this contradictory character made US
foreign policy problematic but workable. The US could and should
sustain alliances and countenance military force that supports free
peoples or people facing genocide. The Second World War, most obviously, and the First Cold War, less evenly, commanded liberal sympathies because they were struggles against easily identified and
self-identifying enemies. Arthur Schlesinger Jr.'s seminal defense of
liberal anti-communism, *The Vital Center*, animated a generation
of liberals against Soviet communism and made them tolerant of
American imperfections.[57] The dissensus over Vietnam and, at home,
the Great Society ruptured liberalism and made US shortcomings a
fundamental barrier to a moral foreign policy. Many liberals began to
question the equity of a values-based foreign policy – 'who are we to
tell others how to live?'[58]

No comparable 'center' formed after the First Cold War. From
1991 to 2001, American foreign policy drifted in and out of human-
itarianism (Somalia and the Balkans) and do-nothingism (Rwanda
and Congo). A schizophrenia over the value and efficacy of US interventionism precluded the establishment of a coherent doctrine to
rival liberal anti-communism and the containment strategy it
advanced – what was there to be contained? An *ad hocism* married to
a hope that other actors, most notably the European Union and the

United Nations, would step up to the plate left foreign policy liberals skeptical of US power but unsure of what to replace it with. Only after 9/11 did this liberal indecision transmute into a more clearly oppositional response to American foreign policy. The 1960s revisionist literature on US First Cold War strategy excepted, most liberals did not contend that communism was the deliberate creation of Washington DC. After 9/11, in contrast, the enemy came to be understood as the product of American unfairness and hypocrisy, even of American conspiratorial design. Some liberals have been more willing to blame America for the hatred visited upon it than to seek answers in the organic nature of the enemy itself.

The second basis of the liberal response does not necessarily fit the foregoing profile but does tend to support the *it's-our-fault* thesis. Some of the most respectable scholars of international relations fall into this category.[59] Their auditing of the war on terror is almost universally negative.[60] Whilst the criticisms are varied, two distinct objections stand out: the war on terror as 1) a violation of due process, and as 2) the fomenter of instability. We will consider each in turn.

Process over policy (or it's not what you do it's the way that you do it)

The first, a more typically liberal indictment, is the failure to ground the war on terror within recognized legal constraints – national and international. Since, the argument goes, the war is procedurally suspect its outcomes will lack not only efficacy but, and crucial to the liberal thesis, legality. Any number of left-liberal critiques make this argument. In chapter 2 we discussed the exaggerated case made against Bush's handling of civil liberties in the war on terror. For the left, this approach is replicated abroad with what they see as persistent US violations of international law – from the Geneva Conventions to the UN Charter. The liberation of Iraq, to which we turn in chapter 5, is indicted not, primarily, for the bloody mayhem of its aftermath but for its basic illegality – it commanded no UN resolution, for example – irrespective of the good and bad consequences of the invasion itself. Would a perfect transition from Baathism to liberal democracy in Iraq have quieted this liberal fixation with process? We doubt it. For liberals who obsess over legalism, *how* Saddam was removed matters more than the fact of his removal. *How* terrorism is countered, rather than the success or failure of counterterrorism, is a question basic to the liberal analysis. Liberal auditing of the war on terror thus becomes a hunt for erroneous procedure on the behalf of the Bush administration.

Fiat justitia et ruant coeli ('Let justice be done though the heavens fall').[61] As Michael Ignatieff has observed, the contemporary liberal alternative refuses to surrender 'invariance for the sake of effectiveness.'[62] As a consequence, any international action, especially American-led, that does not conform to a preconceived notion of legality, let alone to an international legal process, is suspect. That legality is often derived from a United Nations resolution or some other conception of world opinion. It is such reasoning that imbues the UN with a moral force greater than the sum of its parts. This is because, in the liberal conception, the UN is seen as the world's moral arbiter, its circumvention, even if in defense of a moral claim, is to be chided. The war on terror in theory and practice is thus condemned.

In Britain, for example, Tony Blair was assailed primarily for subverting two legal processes in his 'march to war in Iraq.' The first was his complicity with the Bush administration in waging war without an explicit UNSC resolution. The second was his selective interpretation of legal advice – as proffered by Lord Goldsmith, the British attorney general – which was itself equivocal and inconsistent over the war's legality.[63] These twin 'crimes' were independent of what actually transpired in Iraq. That is, they would have been central to the liberal audit irrespective of their practical consequences. Liberals have been far easier on George Bush Sr. and John Major for obeying the UN by leaving Saddam in place in 1991. Marching on Baghdad, said Bush Sr., 'would have taken us way beyond the imprimatur of international law bestowed by the resolutions of the Security Council.'[64] Liberals applauded his wisdom.[65]

Stability before freedom

If the realist audit has become more liberal (with its new-found fear of American unpopularity), the liberal audit has become more realist (with its new-found love of stability). Each is in the process of co-opting the other. The obsession with process and the legality it supposedly confers was once a peculiarly liberal phenomenon, but now realists embrace it too. 'Stability is all' used to be a realist mantra; now it is liberals who demand its reinstatement. In 2004, John Kerry ran on the supposed superiority of Middle Eastern 'stability' over regime change. In the build-up to the Iraq War Senators Hillary Clinton (D-NY) and Carl Levin (D-MI) supported the invasion on the basis that Saddam was a threat to regional stability. When that stability proved illusive, these Democrats withdrew their support for the Bush strategy.

University and newspaper liberals continue to apostrophize 'the war on terror.' They assert that regime change is good but that instability is bad. Bush is chastised for his idealism rather than his cynicism. Jonathan Freedland, the liberal *Guardian* journalist, admitted that he found foreign policy realism increasingly enticing:

> It's hard to read [the anti-Bush books of Dennis] Ross and [Zbigniew] Brzezinksi [sic] without coming to share their nostalgia for the steady, realistic, and grounded statecraft of George H. W. Bush in contrast with the faith-based pursuit of neoconservative fantasy that has passed for international affairs under his son.[66]

Richard Falk prefers the use of 'order' to stability, but the effect is much the same. In his conception, 'a more humane world order' was maturing 'impressively during the 1990s' until the US reaction to 9/11 'wrecked' it.[67] That putative but promising pre-Bush 'global normative order,' he wrote, consisted of articles of faith long basic to the liberal canon:

> international law, prudent limits of warmaking, the authority of the UN, the promotion of human rights and democracy, as well as other widely endorsed precepts of international morality associated with the alleviation of poverty and other forms of human suffering.[68]

For Falk, each element was interdependent and all were progressing satisfactorily until George W. Bush retarded them. One of his chief crimes, according to Falk, was to 'discredit' America's 'Vietnam syndrome' and thus remove its purported 'discipline of restraint.' Quite how the Vietnam syndrome and 'the authority of the UN' in the 1990s helped achieve the liberal order Falk cherishes is not clear. It is enough in his account to associate an asserted rise in UN authority and fall in US belligerence with a better world. His desire to end human suffering is understandable and laudable. We do not accept, however, that war-making is by definition destructive of this end. As Bush argued with some justification, 'For decades, American policy sought to achieve peace in the Middle East by promoting stability in the Middle East, yet these policies gave us neither.'[69] The 'fetid swamp of stable despotism' is not worth the protection liberals implicitly afford it.[70]

Liberals like Falk are on troubled territory in trying to marry Westphalia with human rights. The inviolability of state sovereignty – the principle that has conditioned international relations since the Treaty of Westphalia of 1648 – makes interfering on behalf of human rights within states extremely fraught. The principle of state sovereignty is in ineluctable tension with freedom and human rights.[71] Bush used the word 'freedom' forty-seven times in NSS 2002 and twenty-seven times in his second inaugural. He mentioned 'stability' only nine times in the first case and not at all in the second. This may be a mere empirical measure but it does reveal a war president committed to a human rights agenda in contrast to liberal and realist demands for stability and order.

The UN faces the same dilemma as Bush's opponents in this regard. Somehow it must balance human rights with states' rights. Which is it obliged to defend first, the rights of people or of their governments? Its charter's preamble wants it both ways – 'to reaffirm faith in fundamental human rights, in the dignity and worth of the human person, in the equal rights of men and women and of nations large and small'[72] – without offering a solution when these rights, of peoples vs. states, come into conflict.

The Bush solution is that offered by all his predecessors. It treats appeals to the UN as contingent on how well UN actions will meet US national security objectives. Once these objectives have been defined as cognate with a quest for human freedom, as they surely were in his second inaugural, but not only here, the Westphalian emphasis – so central to so many who marched against the war on terror – becomes decidedly secondary. Respecting Westphalian notions of stability, for Clinton and Bush, for example, would have meant tolerating Slobodan Milošević and Saddam Hussein rather than removing them.[73]

Michael Mann, the noted UCLA sociologist, is adamant that the US should do less abroad, not more. It should 'leave alone,' 'steer clear,' not chose sides, resist arbitrating impenetrable conflicts, 'Stay away from quagmires!'[74] Above all else, according to Mann, America should seek stability in its foreign relationships rather than pursue 'extraordinary foolhardy militaristic policies' like regime change and democratization.[75] Mann, a significant liberal scholar, audits the war on terror as a realist. Indeed, but for the profusion of exclamation marks in his text, much of his analysis would count as typical realism.

Even Marxists now deride what was once the essential prerequisite for their proletarian revolution: global instability. American foreign and economic policies are indicted by Eric Hobsbawm, the veteran communist professor, as the chief cause of human misery.[76]

Bush made the world more volatile with his terror war, he argues. Unlike Lenin, Hobsbawm does not want conditions to get worse. The ironies of this about-face are manifold. It is now neoconservatives who are prepared to risk turmoil in order to advance social change and the left who attack them for doing so. It is the US war on terror which seeks to topple fascist dictatorships while the left march in their defense. As Nick Cohen, in his youth a devotee of the Hobsbawm vision, comments wryly:

> On 15 February 2003, about a million liberal-minded people marched through London to oppose the overthrow of a fascist regime . . . In Madrid, about 650,000 marched to oppose the overthrow of a fascist regime in the biggest demonstration in Spain since the death of General Francisco Franco in 1975. In Berlin, the call to oppose the overthrow of a fascist regime brought demonstrators from 300 German towns and cities, some of them old enough to remember when Adolf Hitler ruled from the Reich Chancellery . . . The French protests against the overthrow of a fascist regime went off without trouble. Between 100,000 and 200,000 French demonstrators stayed peaceful as they rallied in the Place de la Bastille, where in 1789 Parisian revolutionaries had stormed the dungeons of Louis XVI in the name of the universal rights of man.[77]

Before leaving consideration of the liberal demand for stability (even at the price of fascism) it is worth recalling that US foreign policy has rarely been premised on an exclusive drive for order. The war on terror is not waged to stabilize international relations but, where it counts, to upset those relations. This reasoning has important historical precedent. Neville Chamberlain's chimerical stabilization of Anglo–German relations at Munich in 1938 merely emboldened Adolf Hitler. Stabilizing US–Soviet relations via a series of compromises and quids-pro-quo, known as détente, in the 1970s merely stoked Moscow's adventurism. By the decade's end they had invaded Afghanistan. Dictators invariably see a democracy's willingness to be pragmatic and negotiate as a sign of weakness and as an indication that threats pay. The First Cold War went America's way when it refused to stabilize that conflict. By extension, Arab tyranny will be weakened by denying it the stability necessary for its survival. The Second Cold War on Islamist terror is premised on such logic.

The 'old' European/Venusian audit

Like the liberal audit, the European approach has been to chastise American exaggeration of the 9/11 foe. In some ways, the European audit is a caricature of both right and left critiques. These, at least, acknowledge the nature, even if they dispute the scope, of the threat. Rather than organize to meet a realized and growing danger, European leaders and publics obsess about a predicted one. The *theory* of anthropogenic climate change, rather than the *fact* of man-made terrorism or WMD proliferation, is increasingly the EU's top priority.[78] The Iraq War, of course, never commanded a European consensus, but European politicians now even question the purpose of campaigns, like Afghanistan, once held as legitimate American responses to global terrorism. In February 2007, Germany, France, and Belgium questioned the efficacy of the Afghan War and refused an American request for more NATO soldiers.[79] Where does this rejection of the American analysis come from?

Soon after 9/11, Robert Kagan announced that 'Americans are from Mars and Europeans are from Venus.'[80] He observed a growing and permanent divergence in the world views, and consequent diplomacy, of the United States and of the European Union. The thesis has been much maligned as an oversimplification. Timothy Garton Ash, for example, mocks Kagan's caricature of a Europe where 'values and spines have dissolved in a lukewarm bath of multilateral, transnational, secular, and postmodern fudge.'[81] But Kagan captures some elementary differences in the tolerance of terrorist threats both sides are prepared to accept – for the US, low, for the EU, high.

Inescapably, the war on terror was audited by Europeans through this Venusian prism.

Europe was nearly destroyed by war. If New York had Ground Zero on 9/11, Germany in 1945 represented Year Zero. A thousand years of bloodletting reached its zenith in the Second World War. European leaders resolved 'never again.' Wars fought for the victory of one value-system over another were to be eschewed in favor of a bureaucratic process which would render ideological impulses – and the wars they stoked – impotent.[82] Americans experienced that war differently, and nearly every war they have subsequently fought. For them, wars worked. America won them. More than this, and in profound contradistinction to an exhausted Europe, the US had maintained the material wherewithal to fight them. The legacy of these divergent experiences, and here we concur with Kagan, is a Europe prepared to countenance any response to a security threat except war and a United States prepared to use war when such action looks likely to work. For European leaders, and here we have in mind the recent statecraft of France and Germany, war is invariably the worst possible option. For George Bush, as for his predecessors, including Lincoln, 'In a choice of evils [war] may not always be the worst.'[83]

We are all Americans?

The famous *Le Monde* headline ('*Nous sommes tous américains*') is repeated often to show how Europe identified with the United States after 9/11 (usually accompanied by the assertion that the Bush administration squandered this goodwill with its war on terror).[84] A careful reading of the text beneath the headline reveals a different emphasis: *Now, America, you are just like us. We have experienced terrorism. We have responded by engagement with it. You must do the same.* Northern Ireland is often heralded as evidence that terrorists can be assuaged by building them into a peace process. This analysis conforms to a wider European narrative advanced by the *Le Monde* editorial. This holds that increasingly sophisticated governance, as in the EU, requires similarly sophisticated methods to tackle terrorism. Rather than the blunt stick of Bush's war, European governments, with a much longer history of facing terrorists, advise more conciliatory, cosmopolitan approaches.[85] For the EU, diplomacy is not about wielding big sticks but big carrots. It is about appeasement.

What this peculiarly European approach misses in its appropriation of the Northern Ireland model was the efficacy of war as a means to bring terrorists to the table. It was not so-called Track Two ('quiet') diplomacy that divested the Irish Republican Army of its guns but a bloody, brutal campaign waged against them by the British army, controversially abetted, at times, by pro-British loyalist terrorists, in the decade before the 1994 ceasefire.[86] The futility of armed struggle had to be conceded by the terrorists before they would countenance a political strategy. Somewhere along the line we have forgotten that defeating terrorists militarily is a necessary first step to talking to them. If the Northern Ireland peace process offers any model it is surely this one. The war on terror, through this European prism, necessarily appears too belligerent, too wild-west, to effect a lasting peace. Such a peace, as the EU has learned since 1945, relies on the abandonment of moral absolutes, not, contra-Bush, on their embrace. (We will consider the likely future course of US–EU relations, given their diverging responses to terrorism, in chapter 7.)

According to BBC journalist Peter Taylor, there is a strategic equivalence between the terrorists of Belfast and Baghdad. If the first can be talked into peace so can the second.[87] Since, the theory goes, terrorism is a consequence of western failure, its extremism can be lessened by western penitence and appeasement. The war on terror is, of course, founded on a very different understanding. It is one which accepts little blame for terrorism as a phenomenon. It is skeptical that terrorists can be 'engaged.' And, contrary to the Spanish capitulation after their 3/11, it insists that terrorists are better confronted by strength than by weakness.[88]

For America, the war on terror is fundamentally strategic. It involves a series of campaigns aimed at securing a geo-strategic situation in which terrorism and its WMD capacity is retarded and the prospects of democracy enhanced. In Europe, terrorism is treated as a sociological problem.[89] The attendant diagnosis is that we must counter terrorism by changing the nature of our society. British opinion, despite the 'special' Anglo-American relationship, is particularly susceptible to this line of thinking. Rather pointedly, in his first joint press conference with President Bush, Gordon Brown defined terrorism as 'a crime.'[90] The designation was the obverse of Bush's analysis: terrorism as war. The terrorist, like the criminal, Brown implied, is not autonomous but, rather, a product of what we do to him. He is provoked, as a London-based security expert diagnosed, by 'some sort of unhappiness with the society in which [he] live[s].'[91] He is a natural reaction to institutional racism or to economic deprivation. If we don't wrongly imprison him he won't hate us. Change our behavior and we change his. This gulf in analyses and the divergent policies that flow from them is unlikely to be bridged any time soon.

Conclusion

Little of what passes for prescription from the left and right camps in American politics will actually have much effect on the course of the war on terror. Neither conservatives nor liberals have offered an analysis powerful enough to weaken the consensus on which US foreign policy currently rests. In some cases, there is a splitting within camps. Several prominent liberals, for example, refuse to audit the war on terror on the basis of American failings. In doing so, they contribute to the consensus that will sustain the Bush Doctrine into the next presidential term.[92]

The realist and liberal audits remain mired in nostalgia. Realists, who became the dominant theorists of international relations in the

First Cold War, have tried to apply the lessons of that conflict too rigidly. Because the existential enemy today presents himself from caves and housing estates rather than in foreign capitals and palaces, realists deduce he poses a negligible threat. In the realist view, such non-state actors are peripheral in explaining how international relations unfold. States, for them, remain the basic units of analysis. That states might ally with terrorists or leak WMD to them is a phenomenon with which realists have yet to grapple. They didn't do such things in the First Cold War. The continuity of state behavior, especially the survival instinct, across millennia, suggests, for realists, they won't do so now. As we assess more fully in chapter 5, the realist case against the Iraq War, for example, was dependent on viewing Saddam as rational and containable. The war proceeded on the basis that he was not. Bush and his allies could not trust to the realist assertion that all states are deterrable. The possibility, however slight, that Saddam might endow terrorists with a state-level capacity was sufficient to warrant his removal, against realist objections.

As this book argues, the lessons of the First Cold War for the Second are manifold. But they are not the ones posited by realists. The struggle with communism was like the current one with Islamism in that it demanded an energetic, state-centric strategy. The current war is premised on an explicit First Cold War rationale: communist/jihadists in possession of actual states or in receipt of state sponsorship are/were the most to be feared. To negate this threat, the United States, in both eras, was/is obliged to destabilize and ultimately change regimes, that might harbor the enemy, into democratic governments, that would/will not. The First Cold War was a long game, built on the western side on a substantial and enduring consensus, waged on many fronts, against a seemingly diverse enemy. And so is the Second.

If realists remember too fondly the certainties of state behavior under conditions of bipolarity, too many liberals are nostalgic for a world that never existed. The charge against Bush is that he violated a series of precedents, a charge that the historical record does not sustain. No American president has put the requirements of international law above the demands of national security. No president turned to the UN for the idealism that that organization embodies rather than its limited utility. No president has disavowed democracy and accepted the moral equivalence of rival forms of government. Too many liberals have audited the war on terror against an illusory standard. The appropriate standards for such an audit are the subject of our next chapter.

4

The Second Cold War on Islamist terror:
a positive audit

You may not be interested in war, but war is interested in you.

Leon Trotsky

War is an ugly thing, but it is not the ugliest of things. The decayed
and degraded state of moral and patriotic feeling which thinks that
nothing is worth war is much worse.

John Stuart Mill[1]

If you are a reader of the Harry Potter books, you might describe this
as the war that must not be named.

US Republican aide, 2007[2]

Al-Qa'eda brain surgeons fail to blow up large car full of petrol.

Spoof headline, *Spectator*, July 2007[3]

Is the war on Islamist terror working? In 1952 a similar inquiry was
made of the First Cold War: are we winning? In this chapter we run
an interim audit and argue that declarations of victory, as in the
1950s, are premature but that the United States is winning. At the
very least the war has been instrumental in denying further triumphs
to the enemy. The US has not yet won the war on terror, but the
manner and method of its fighting has made future 9/11s (and worse)

less likely, not more. For this reason of fundamental utility, the next administrations – Democratic or Republican – will tweak but not transform the design George W. Bush put in place. As with the First, the Second Cold War commands a domestic consensus that his successors will work with and within. Iraq notwithstanding, the wider war is set to continue for the simple reason that no serious presidential candidates have been able or willing to formulate an alternative. They have not been able to do so because there is no need – the war is working.

The war on terror as a war on capacity

The aim of the war is to defeat terrorism of 'global reach.' This definition is offered four times in the National Security Strategy of 2002 (NSS 2002), reiterated in the 2006 revision, and features in much Bush administration rhetoric.[4] Nine days after 9/11 Bush dealt in semantics: 'Our war on terror begins with al-Qaeda, but it does not end there. It will not end until every terrorist group of *global* reach has been found, stopped and defeated.'[5] It is the core recommendation of the 9/11 Commission Report: 'What to Do? A Global Strategy' (chapter 12).[6] Despite the rather awkward and unpopular acronym of the global war on terror – GWOT – it succeeds in making the scope of the campaign clear.[7] In a 2007 poll of American professors of international relations, 50 percent identified 'international terrorism' as the 'most important' foreign policy issue facing America; WMD proliferation was a close second (45 percent).[8] The Bush Doctrine, given form and substance in NSS 2002, seeks to curtail the capacity of terrorists to wage coordinated war against the United States with weapons greater than hijacked aircraft and homemade bombs. The African embassy bombings in August 1998 were the initial, portentous example of such coordination, hitting two US embassies simultaneously, 400 miles apart, killing 224 people. The attacks of 9/11 (2,970 dead in less than eighty minutes at four points, three of them hit as planned) were sufficient evidence of global reach to necessitate a qualitatively different response from America to the one obtaining before that day.[9]

The war on terror was not declared in response to a one-off fluke but to an ideologically coherent, if not yet centrally coordinated, campaign which has, up to the time of writing, manifested itself in New York (1993 and 2001), Buenos Aires (1994), Dar es Salaam and Nairobi (1998), Yemen (2000), Washington, DC (2001), Bali (2002), Mombassa (2002), Bombay (2003), Istanbul (2003), Najaf (2003), Jakarta (2004), Madrid (2004), Jerusalem (since 1948), Baghdad (since 2003), London (since 2005), and Glasgow (2007), and will doubtless do so again.[10] The war does not aim to end all terrorism nor extinguish evil but to limit the capacity of both. After 9/11, it was determined that train and plane tickets should remain the absolute limit of the terrorist's arsenal. 'Had the 9/11 hijackers had weapons of mass destruction available to them,' observes Robert Lieber, 'it is reasonable to conclude that they would have had no reservations about using them.'[11] The war is thus better understood as a war against the states that might endow terrorists with an offensive, state-level capacity. Here we argue this strategy has worked. In this chapter we offer an audit of the war on terror which argues for, and predicts, continuity in its fighting.

We take it as axiomatic that global Islamist terrorism poses the greatest extant danger to western security. Indeed, we believe this will remain the consensus view within American politics.[12] Even in American academia, the level of threat, if not always the means to meet it, commands broad agreement.[13] The First Cold War was built on an American consensus against communism. '[T]his battle,' declared President Bush, 'is more than a military conflict. Like the cold war, it's an ideological struggle between two fundamentally different visions of humanity.'[14] The analogy is not perfect, but we think understanding how America met this enemy explains much about how it confronts, and should confront, the current one.

The war on terror has three clear objectives, as laid out in the National Security Strategy of September 2002. First, the war intends to secure the American homeland against catastrophic terrorism specifically and lower-level terrorism generally. Second, the war means to destroy terrorist sanctuaries abroad by removing their root cause – non-democratic governance. Third, it seeks to encourage a coalition of states in these efforts. In this chapter we will evaluate the war at home and abroad before considering its bearable financial costs.

The war at home

Properly understood, the war at home seeks not just to prevent another 9/11 but to forestall something far worse. That neither a repeat nor an attack of even greater magnitude has come to pass – at least not at the time of writing – provides some evidence of the war's effectiveness. Skeptics have argued that it is luck rather than cogency of response that accounts for the absence of a repeat attack, that al Qaeda has not mounted a second strike despite the war on terror not because of it. We acknowledge the problem of having to prove a negative, that the war on terror has prevented events that by definition lie beyond measurement because they did not happen. Here is what we do know.

Institutional reformation is working

In some fundamental ways the federal government failed on 9/11. The heroism that marked that day resides at the personal and local level: brave passengers wrestling with hijackers on United 93; New York fire fighters ascending the steps at the World Trade Center; a city mayor marshaling the emergency response. Contrast this with the impotency of the Bush White House in the initial minutes and hours after the attacks: USAF jets scrambled too late to intercept the hijacked planes; the intelligence failures across the FBI and CIA that allowed terrorists to board those planes. Not every lesson about central government failure on that day has been learned. But many have.

Bush put in place a number of new federal agencies and institutions to counter terrorism at home. The Department of Homeland Security (DHS) represents the single greatest act of bureaucratic invention since the New Deal of the 1930s. The 9/11 Commission Report (pt. 13) argued for 'a different way of organizing government.' The DHS was the substantial response. As the Agricultural Adjustment Act (1933) was for Franklin Roosevelt, the DHS and PATRIOT Act are for George Bush: the substantial institutional innovations on which his domestic record will be judged. Like Roosevelt's AAA, the relevance and utility of the DHS will inform political and scholarly debate for some considerable time.

Has this institutional reformation made America safer? On balance, the answer is a qualified 'yes.' Our answer is equivocal because safety is difficult to measure empirically.[15] A better question would be: has the DHS changed the culture and process of domestic counterterrorism? To this we answer with a more positive 'yes.' The significant failing of US intelligence in the build-up to 9/11 was the absence of coordination between and within departments.

This was compounded by the post-First Cold War 'peace dividend' (1989–2001) that resulted in a 22 percent cut in intelligence staffing.[16] The FBI agent who observed an 'inordinate number of individuals of investigative interest' attending flight schools in Arizona, only to have his fears rebuffed, will stand alongside the radio operator at Kahuku Point, Oahu, who, on the morning of December 7, 1941, spotted a squadron of planes heading toward Pearl Harbor but was told not to worry.[17] When the so-called twentieth 9/11 hijacker, Zacarias Moussaoui, was under arrest for visa violations in August

2001 his case, despite a joint FBI–CIA investigation, was not acted on by the Director of Central Intelligence, George Tenet.[18] In a phrase that became commonplace in the various post-9/11 inquiries, there was a failure to 'connect the dots.'[19]

Until the creation of the DHS in 2002 there existed no central, threat-evaluating department in the US government. Nor was there a dot-connecting tsar. In consequence, different agencies defined 'homeland security' in different ways.[20] National security has been subject to formal, centralized control since 1947, but homeland security has not. Before 2002, 'no one single government agency [had] homeland security as its primary mission. In fact, responsibilities for homeland security [were] dispersed among more than 100 different government organizations.'[21] Significantly, the DHS has now placed the Department of Defense firmly within America's counterterrorism strategy. Bush's restructuring of counterterrorism, after 9/11, as a multifaceted war on terror, rather than as a mere police operation, significantly altered and improved the process by which US officials have acted. The next president will certainly retain many of the innovations established under their predecessor. These include the daily intelligence briefing by the Director of National Intelligence, a dot-joining post established by the Intelligence Reform and Terrorism Prevention Act, signed into law by President Bush in 2004.[22] Similarly, the DHS is likely only to increase its power and budget in the coming years.

Civil liberties hold

It is mistaken to condemn the revisions of domestic policing necessitated by the war on terror as a sinister plot to destroy American civil liberties. As we observed in chapter 2, the war on terror has, like most of America's previous conflicts, meant a rebalancing of civil liberties against the demands of civil security – the PATRIOT Act being the most obvious example of this.

Despite much media hype and academic foreboding, the scope of fundamental freedoms has remained essentially unaltered. Indeed, the war on terror has been fought against a backdrop of intense domestic public scrutiny – to say nothing of foreign opinion – that reveals the robust health of such rights as the freedom of speech, religion, and assembly, rather than their abrogation. In this respect, the opening decade of the twenty-first century more closely resembles that of the 1960s. In both periods an unpopular war was being waged abroad as rights at home flourished. The civil rights movement, criminal rights, feminism, hippies, the counter-culture, Yoko Ono and the Warren Court took root during the First Cold War generally and the Vietnam War years specifically. One could hardly contend that Michael Moore and Bill Moyers have suffered criminal sanction or had their freedom of speech abridged because of their opposition to the war on terror.[23]

Legal sanctions have been mild in the war on terror and where they have not been mild they have been recalibrated by America's separation of powers system. That system, properly understood, means to mix and not just to separate powers. Bush was subject to this mixing as were presidents before him.[24] For example, when Bush administration efforts, public and covert, tried to increase the ease and efficacy of wiretapping, the Roberts Court reined it in and Congress – both before and after the 2006 midterms, i.e., under GOP and Democratic control – threatened hearings. In June 2007, the Senate Judiciary Committee subpoenaed the White House over the issue of wiretapping without warrants; three of the 13–3 majority were Republicans.[25]

Bush's desire to maintain the intelligence-gathering and security function of the US holding facility on Guantanamo Bay was likewise subject to judicial scrutiny and revision. In *Rasul v. Bush* (2004), for example, the Supreme Court ruled that detainees at the rented US base had the right to seek habeas corpus. In *Hamdan v. Rumsfeld* (2006), the Court ruled that 'enemy combatants' were protected by the Geneva Convention.[26] According to a prominent legal scholar,

'We may rightly regard Hamdan as a victory for the principle of checks and balances.'[27] In June 2007, a Virginia federal appeals court ruled that labeling a man an 'enemy combatant' did not mean he could be held indefinitely by the military, as Bush had argued.[28] Even military judges, despite pressure from the Bush administration, have refused to bring war crime charges against such men.[29] This is all by way of arguing that the prevention of a second 9/11 has *not* been purchased at the price of American civil liberties – just as the fight against global communism in the First Cold War ultimately advanced, rather than retarded, rights at home. A more apt question might be: has domestic counterterrorism been weakened by a refusal to enforce greater restrictions on civil liberties? We argue no. The war at home has augmented American safety whilst leaving civil rights essentially unhampered. Polling data generally confirm this conclusion.[30] There is nothing in the record of the current war that equates to the internment of Japanese-Americans after Pearl Harbor, nor with the post-First and Second World War 'red scares.' Polling suggests that Arab-Americans have felt themselves subject to greater scrutiny as a result of US counterterrorism but also that they feel more American than their counterparts feel British, German or Spanish.[31] Indeed, the US remains the destination of choice for Arab/Muslim refugees (see Figure 1), the group more likely than any other to be subject to rights abridgment – an abridgment that has not occurred.[32]

The Second Cold War has not made America a less attractive destination for Arab migrants. Indeed, as the US fought wars on behalf of ethnic Muslim populations in the middle–late 1990s (in Bosnia and Kosovo), Arab immigration declined. During the war on terror it has grown. American foreign policy does not affect the popularity of the United States as a haven.[33]

US vs. UK counterterrorism

Whilst some fairly obvious American counterterrorism policies have been copied by the British government, especially after the July 7,

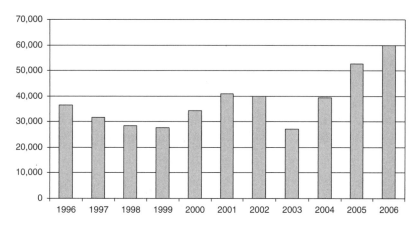

Figure 1 Total number of immigrants to the US from Arabic-speaking countries, 1996–2006

Source: US Department of Homeland Security, *Yearbook of Immigration Statistics 2006*; at www.dhs.gov/ximgtn/statistics/publications/LPR06.shtm (table 3: Persons Obtaining Legal Permanent Resident Status by Region and Country of Birth: Fiscal Years 1997–2006).

2005 attacks in London, there remains a fundamental difference of approach and, importantly, of attitude. As David Davis, the Conservative shadow home secretary, observed, the US and UK governments have responded differently to terrorist attacks.[34] Three formal, reliable (even readable) and generally consensus-building reports have shaped the American war on terror – The National Strategy for Homeland Security, the Joint Inquiry into Intelligence Community Activities Before and After the Terrorist Attacks of September 11, 2001 (both published in 2002), and the 9/11 Commission Report (2004).[35] The Labour government had the Butler and Hutton inquiries – over the Blair government's case for war in Iraq – and aroused, by so doing, more public opprobrium and distrust than it did lessons for counterterrorism.[36] The Bush administration implemented thirty-seven of the thirty-nine recommendations contained in the 9/11 Commission Report. The British government has refused to organize an equivalent official 7/7 public inquiry. As Davis argues convincingly, 'An independent inquiry would have forced us to confront and remedy the flaws in our approach.'[37]

Attitudinal differences also obtain. Whilst America responded to 9/11 with a remarkable upsurge of patriotism – on which the legitimacy of the war on terror has been built – 7/7 led to a less confident British reassertion of multiculturalism and the renewal of the argument that the war on terror, and Iraq specifically, was to blame for jihadist violence in the UK. After the botched attacks on London and Glasgow in June 2007, Gordon Brown insisted that his new government use neither 'Islam' nor 'Islamism' as descriptors for the terrorists – for fear of alienating 'the Muslim community.' 'If "Islamist" is out,' asked one commentator, 'what do we call them?'[38] Ian Blair, Commissioner of the London Metropolitan police, has been criticized for indulging in as much 'diversity' advocacy and pseudo theology as he has counterterrorism.[39] In consequence, while the US has managed to negate organic Islamist rage – at least so far – London has become 'the Star Wars bar scene for Islamic radicals,' as a former counterterrorism official in the Bush and Clinton administrations called it. The city, he said, has attracted 'a polyglot group of intellectuals, preachers, financiers, arms traders, technology specialists, forgers, travel organizers and foot soldiers.'[40]

In any auditing of the war on terror it is worth recalling the legitimacy and consensus on which it rests in America and contrasting it with the skeptical response of European governments and elites, who do not consider that such a war is even possible. Europe, of course, has endured no equivalent of 9/11. But the British reaction to 7/7 and, especially, the Spanish after 3/11 suggest that, should a greater atrocity be committed, European leaders will withdraw even further from the war on terror. Despite the inherent diversity of the American polity, its declared war on terror commands a consensus sufficient to make it the on-going basis of counterterrorism.

The war abroad

In spring 2007, President Bush reminded an audience in Ohio that 'we must aggressively pursue the enemy and defeat them elsewhere so we don't have to face them here.'[41] That strategy has two key prongs. The first seeks to kill or imprison foreign terrorists and relies on the calibrated use of 'hard power.' The second seeks to turn the systems which nurtured them (like Iran and Syria) or repressed them into terrorism (like Saudi Arabia and Egypt) into democracies and, whilst this prong may deploy 'hard' coercive power, calls for the use of 'soft power' – or 'getting others to want what you want' by co-option rather than coercion.[42] The war on terror, to date, provides an already rich history of those twin efforts. Bush sought to win his war by turning his enemies into democrats. In so doing he is pursuing an approach basic to US foreign policy for over 200 years and one his successors will advance even as they campaign against it in 2008.

Hard power and the Rumsfeld metric

In October 2003, Secretary of Defense Donald Rumsfeld puzzled over how to measure the success of the US response to 9/11:

> Today we lack metrics to know if we are winning or losing the global war on terror. Are we capturing, killing, or deterring and dissuading more terrorists every day than the madrassas and the radical clerics are recruiting, training, and deploying against us?
>
> Does the US need to fashion a broad, integrated plan to stop the next generation of terrorists? The US is putting relatively little effort into a long-range plan, but we are putting a great deal of effort into trying to stop terrorists. The cost-benefit ratio is against us! Our cost is billions against the terrorists' costs of millions.
> - Do we need a new organization?
> - How do we stop those who are financing the radical madrassa schools?
> - Is our current situation such that 'the harder we work, the behinder we get'?[43]

Liberal critiques labeled the test the 'Rumsfeld metric' and seized on his lack of certainty as a concession of failure.[44] It was 'hard to avoid the inference,' wrote one scholar, 'that the war has created more terrorists than it has killed.'[45] Read in context, Rumsfeld appears rather more open to arguments than defeatist. But a key auditing problem remains, acknowledged by the former defense secretary, of how to measure the number of terrorists killed or converted as a consequence of the war.[46]

Consider how we might account for the nature of global terrorism after 9/11. Why has there been no second 9/11? If the war on terror has worked, the Rumsfeld metric should provide some kind of measurement. There seem to us to be three basic responses to this question, the first two of which we reject, the third we advance.

Hypothesis 1: 9/11 was a miscalculation on al Qaeda's part

This argument is occasionally raised in objection to an expansive American campaign. Perhaps, the argument proceeds, 9/11 was the worst (or best) al Qaeda could do – an expression of their weakness, not their strength. And in committing this massacre they have permanently damaged their long-term prospects. James Fallows of the *Atlantic Monthly*, and hardly a Bush supporter, has argued this. The US should declare victory. Al Qaeda has been effectively beaten. Move on.[47] Like us, Fallows argues that the jihadist recourse to western public transportation systems reveals their weakness, not their strength. Whilst we do not share his optimism that jihadist terrorism has been beaten we do argue it has been effectively limited by action undertaken by the United States.[48] Without access to WMD, jihadists have been forced to rely on killing tourists and commuters. In the years since 9/11, their capacities have not kept pace with their aspirations.

Variations on this theme have been offered by others. Gilles Kepel, a French scholar of Islam, advances a flickering candle thesis. 9/11, for him, was indicative of Islamist impotence.[49] Francis

Fukuyama argued as long ago as 1992 – the beginning of 'the end of history' – that Islam, let alone Islamism, offered no viable alternative to liberal democracy and was thus doomed to second-rate status. It might launch an occasional attack but so what? The West had won.[50]

There is something in both these arguments. But, again, they are not sufficient to presage a fundamental change in how America is fighting this war. The shadowy nature of the enemy makes estimations of its strength uncomfortably imprecise. As we insist throughout this book, the Second Cold War is not waged against terrorists as individuals, cells or even armies – the strength of which is forever shifting – but against their capacity. 9/11 revealed an intent incongruent with a capacity. They would have done far worse had they had the means. The war aims to deny them those means. We are left with the unsettling but logical conclusion, given their past behavior, that al Qaeda, Hezbollah and other jihadists will continue to seek a doomsday weapon. To operate on any other basis is to court disaster. If 9/11 was indeed a strategic miscalculation it is one that, we should assume, the enemy will seek to put right.[51]

Hypothesis 2: There are no terrorists in the United States and only a few abroad

John Mueller has argued that because there has been no second 9/11, nor any significant terrorist strike on the American homeland since that day, it is reasonable to conclude that there are 'almost no terrorists' in the United States and that 'few have the means or the inclination to strike from abroad.' Rejecting the Department of Homeland Security's fear of a perpetual vulnerability, he asks:

> if it is so easy to pull off an attack and if terrorists are so demonically competent, why have they not done it? Why have they not been sniping at people in shopping centers, collapsing tunnels, poisoning the food supply, cutting electrical lines, derailing trains, blowing up oil pipelines, causing massive traffic jams, or exploiting the countless other vulnerabilities that, according to security experts, could so easily be exploited?[52]

If terrorism indicates the presence of terrorists, fairly obviously, then, using Mueller's logic, no terrorism indicates their absence. Those who assert a terrorist threat is ever-present become Chicken Littles. If threats are not realized, Mueller seems to argue, then they are not real. A resting terrorist is not a terrorist. The obvious rebuff to this argument is that on September 10, 2001 the same argument could have been made. Because there had been no mass-casualty, jihadist terrorism to that point, there were no jihadist terrorists.

For John Mueller, not hearing from terrorists increases the likelihood that they do not exist. For Robert Mueller, FBI director since 2001, not hearing from them increases the likelihood that they are plotting something spectacular. 'I remain very concerned about what we are not seeing,' he said in 2005.[53] Attractive though John Mueller's logic appears, what it actually offers policy-makers is an optimism unmoored in a pragmatic caution. What is the US government to do, if Mueller is right, except abandon the pretense of a global counterterror strategy? What should the DHS do less of? John Mueller does not tell us. There is a saying among seismologists that the further away from the last big earthquake, the nearer you are to the next. Caution surely dictates preparation. Indeed, as Dick Cheney argued, it demands over-preparation: 'we have to treat it as a certainty in terms of our response.'[54] A war against an enemy that might be weaker than he actually appears is a safer bet than something less than a war against an enemy who is more powerful than he appears.

The flipside to John Mueller's logic is that the Second Cold War, and especially Iraq, has increased terrorism. It is unfortunate that those skeptical of the war on terror embrace both mutually exclusive conclusions. That is, skeptics argue the war has made no difference because there are no terrorists (pace John Mueller) *and* that the war has created more terrorists (the central finding of the 2006 National Intelligence Estimate). How can we know which is true? They both surely cannot be. Which proposition is the US counterterrorism official obliged to accept? Robert Kagan has recognized the problem inherent in the NIE analysis:

> did the authors of the NIE calculate the effect of the Sept. 11 attacks on the recruitment of terrorists or the effect of the bombings in Madrid and London? It is certainly possible that these events produced an increase in would-be terrorists by showing the possibility of sensational success. So if there is an overall increase, how much of it was the result of Iraq or the Danish cartoons or other perceived Western offenses against Islam, and how much of it is a continuing response to al-Qaeda's own terrorist successes before, on and after Sept. 11?[55]

Hypothesis 3: The war on terror is working

This hypothesis seems to us the most logical. It provides the only viable basis for the next stage in the Second Cold War. If hypotheses 1 and 2 are wrong but we act on them we tempt calamity. Our logic is not complex. If we cannot be sure about the scope of threat facing the United States and the West, it is better to adopt a worst-case-scenario approach. Hoping for the best has rarely served America well in its previous ideological struggles. The first two hypotheses will be falsified if al Qaeda pulls off a second spectacular attack, the third will survive, though will require recalibration. The first two are hopeful predictions which, if wrong, could spell disaster, the last the only appropriate basis for US counterterrorism for the 2010s.

The three Ts nexus

The bombings of the Madrid (2004) and London (2005) transport systems, killing 243 commuters, rather than showing that the war is not working, demonstrate that terrorist capacity has not advanced beyond public transport tickets and improvised, homemade devices. The failed London bombers on July 21, 2005 used flour and hair bleach, purchased over the counter, as key ingredients.[56] The thankfully hapless attackers of London's West End and Glasgow Airport on

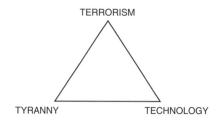

Figure 2 The three Ts of the Bush Doctrine

June 29–30, 2007 used patio gas, petrol and nails as their weapons of choice.[57] In a not insignificant way, such attacks reveal a jihadist capacity fortunately incongruent with their avowed intent. This is a fair measure of the war on terror's success: it has limited attacks to public transportation – a perennially soft target for terrorists of many varieties, from the Irish Republican Army to the Japanese Aum, from ETA to the Tamil Tigers – and night clubs.[58] The war on terror has kept them that way. The London tube and bus attacks of July 7, 2005 suggest the war on terror is working.

This judgment accepts the disconcerting but inescapable logic of the three Ts nexus. See Figure 2. Before 9/11, there was an assumption or hope that any combination of two of the three represented a manageable threat. Any two can be tolerated, all three cannot. For example, terrorists without recourse to a tyranny (a rogue state, for example) would be unlikely to secure a technology matching their aspirations. A tyrant, by the same token, may have such a WMD capacity but without terrorists to deliver it to he poses an acceptable risk – he can be deterred by conventional means. The combination of terrorists and tyrants but lacking a deadly technological capacity can be a worry for the United States but does not present an imperative for action. Afghanistan under the Taliban, for example, united tyranny with terrorists but not both with significant technology. Bin Laden had to rely on American aviation technology and training facilities to pull off his 9/11 attack. This explains, in part, why Clinton's belligerence toward that nation in the 1990s was so circumscribed.[59]

However, when all three come together, the threat crosses a threshold of acceptability. Indeed, the perception of combination demands preemption, not patience. As we argue more fully in chapter 5, Iraq was not invaded because of new evidence of its WMD capacity or its proliferation efforts. Saddam was toppled because of the fear that the United States had *no* new evidence and thus could not be sure of his relationship with terrorists or of his technological capacities. 'Unbalanced dictators with weapons of mass destruction can deliver those weapons or missiles or secretly provide them to terrorist allies . . . The gravest danger to freedom lies at the perilous crossroads of radicalism and technology.'[60] Accordingly, declared Bush, 'I will not wait on events, while dangers gather. I will not stand by, as peril draws closer and closer.'[61]

Rumsfeld did not refer to the three Ts nexus but his 'prism of 9/11' rationale for the Iraq invasion is synonymous with it:

> The coalition did not act in Iraq because we had discovered dramatic new evidence of Iraq's pursuit of WMD; we acted because we saw the existing evidence in a new light – through the prism of our experience on 9/11. On that day, we saw thousands of innocent men, women and children, killed by terrorists. And that experience changed our appreciation of our vulnerability – and the risks the US faces from terrorist states and terrorist networks armed with weapons of mass murder.[62]

The logic of the three Ts nexus privileges best-guess action more than it prizes total accuracy. For example, as Cheney argued, 'if there's a 1% chance that Pakistani scientists are helping al Qaeda build or develop a nuclear weapon, we have to treat it as a certainty in terms of our response. It's not about our analysis,' he said. 'It's about our response.'[63] George Tenet, CIA Director from 1997 to 2004, concurred:

> There was no question in my mind that [Cheney] was absolutely right to insist that when it came to discussing weapons of mass destruction in the hands of terrorists, conventional risk assessments no longer

applied; we must rule out any possibility of terrorists succeeding in their quest to obtain such weapons. We could not afford to be surprised.[64]

The fear of the tyranny-terrorism-technology nexus is not the sole preserve of Bush strategists. This part of his doctrine, perhaps the most important of all, is one widely shared across the American political spectrum.[65] For this reason, the Bush Doctrine is likely to remain in place for some considerable time after its architect leaves office. Consider the following exchange in the first presidential debate in 2004:

> [JIM] LEHRER: . . . So it's correct to say that, if somebody is listening to this, that both of you agree, if you're re-elected, Mr. President, and if you are elected [Mr. Kerry], the single most serious threat you believe, both of you believe, is nuclear proliferation?
> BUSH: In the hands of a terrorist enemy.
> KERRY: Weapons of mass destruction, nuclear proliferation.[66]

Barack Obama reaffirmed this consensus in 2007:

> This century's threats are at least as dangerous as and in some ways more complex than those we have confronted in the past. They come from weapons that can kill on a mass scale . . . They come from rogue states allied to terrorists . . . We must confront the most urgent threat to the security of America and the world – the spread of nuclear weapons, material, and technology and the risk that a nuclear device will fall into the hands of terrorists. The explosion of one such device would bring catastrophe, dwarfing the devastation of 9/11 and shaking every corner of the globe.[67]

The neoconservative military historian Max Boot shares his assessment:

> The proliferation of nuclear weapons has the greatest ability to trump US military hegemony. The atomic bomb is more than sixty years old. It belongs to an age of rotary-dial telephones and fin-winged cars. It is

a miracle that it has not been used by maniac dictators or political radicals since 1945, but that streak won't last forever . . . There is little in
theory to prevent al Qaeda from carrying out its oft-expressed desire to
create an 'American Hiroshima.' In the words of Eugene Habiger, a
retired four-star general who once ran antinuclear terror programs for
the Department of Energy, 'it is not a matter of if; it's a matter of *when*.'[68]

Graham Allison offers the following terrifying scenario of a ten-
kiloton nuclear device exploded on Manhattan Island:

> On a normal workday, more than half a million people crowd the area
> within a half-mile radius of Times Square. A noon detonation in
> midtown Manhattan could kill them all. Hundreds and thousands of
> others would die from collapsing buildings, fire and fallout in the
> ensuing hours. The electromagnetic pulse generated by the blast
> would fry cell phones, radios, and other electronic communications.
> Hospitals, doctors, and emergency services would be overwhelmed by
> the wounded.[69]

The possible proliferation from states to terrorists of weapons of mass
destruction was, said Douglas Feith, undersecretary of defense (2001–
5), the 'principal strategic thought underlying our strategy in the war
on terrorism.'[70] There are very few Democrats who would differ.
Indeed, several important Democrats have argued that the nexus is
being insufficiently addressed by Bush, suggesting that a more vociferous anti-proliferation policy will mark the next Democratic administration.[71] The logic of the three Ts nexus is a deeply unsettling one
but one which unsettles many across the American political spectrum.

Has the three Ts imperative been applied elsewhere than in
Afghanistan and Iraq? Have American efforts at coercive non-
proliferation worked? Given the fear of the nexus we might suppose
that the United States has adopted an overtly aggressive and coercive
posture in order to negate it. On balance, this is not the case. Bush
foreign policy could hardly be characterized as one preemptive action
after another.[72] If anything, the nexus inspired the adaptation of soft

rather than hard power strategies. Hard power was used, certainly, but to prepare the arena for the penetration and perpetuation of American soft power. The greater the fear of proliferation after 9/11 the greater the resort to democratization as the long-term solution.

Democratic enlargement: counterterrorism via soft power

A common misconception is that the war on terror has disavowed soft power in favor of hard. The creator of these labels, Joseph Nye, has continually assailed this imbalance.[73] Certainly, hard power spending has risen since 9/11 – though more slowly than domestic welfare spending (a point to which we shall return shortly). The ability to project military power across some 6,000 miles and to topple two entrenched rogue regimes – in Kabul and Baghdad – in a matter of weeks necessarily entailed greater spending on the US military. Reconstructing Afghanistan and Iraq, similarly, has seen the Defense Department, for some fairly obvious reasons, consume up to 93 percent of all US spending on those nations.[74] Research, as well as historical experience (in Germany, Japan, and South Korea), suggests that 'higher force levels for longer time periods promote successful nation-building.'[75] Whilst we dispute the efficacy of much soft power spending, especially on such dubious projects as public diplomacy among Arabs and 'outreach' to Muslims, we do not deny that Bush spent as much and more on 'soft power' as did his predecessor, Bill Clinton, the champion of liberal internationalism (see Figure 3).

What did this combination of hard and soft power achieve? As we increase our distance from January 30, 2005, the day Iraq held its first democratic national election, we forget just how remarkable an event this was. It was not just American neoconservatives who applauded. Walid Jumblatt, the staunchly anti-American leader of the Lebanese Druze Muslims, called the elections 'the start of a new Arab world . . . The Berlin Wall has fallen.'[76] Elections in neither Afghanistan nor Iraq have returned stable governments but they are

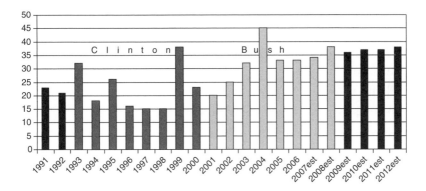

Figure 3 US 'soft power' spending in billions of dollars, 1991–2012

Source: White House, *Historical Tables, Budget of the United States Government, Fiscal Year 2008*, 87–9 (table 5.1: Budget Authority by Function and Subfunction, 1976–2012); at www.whitehouse.gov/omb/budget/fy2008/pdf/hist.pdf. We define soft power here as all federal spending on 'international affairs' (as opposed to national defense or 'hard power') which is comprised of 'international development and assistance'; 'international security assistance'; 'conduct of foreign affairs'; 'foreign information and exchange activities'; and 'international financial programs.' It excludes the amorphous soft power of American culture, which is rather beyond the power of any president to increase or decrease.

indicative of a nascent democracy in nations for whom the very thought would have been a fantasy only a few years ago. The creation of nominal democracies is an improvement over the maintenance of active dictatorships. The Taliban has been replaced by a constitutional system. Baathist tyranny has been rolled back to Syria. The First Cold War was marked by US efforts to contain communism and, where possible, establish democratic governance in nations susceptible to, or already victims of, communist takeover. The Third World was the central focus of this strategy. This basic strategic recourse was continued under George W. Bush, albeit in a different arena and against a different enemy.

It would be wrong to cite everything positive that has occurred since 2001 as evidence of the success of the Bush strategy. Neither, however, would it be quite right to conclude that he had no success.

The 2005 Lebanese revolution, for example, and the subsequent withdrawal of Syrian forces, despite some serious setbacks in the years since, are difficult to dissociate entirely from US-led regime change in Afghanistan and Iraq, as Jumblatt confirmed. Similarly, explicit American agitation on behalf of democratic rights in the Middle East was certainly not a barrier to the experiment in municipal elections (the first ever) in Saudi Arabia in February 2005. That same month, the Egyptian president, Hosni Mubarak, declared he would run against a serious challenger to his office for the first time in the nation's history.[77] In May 2007, he sanctioned the creation of an opposition political party, the Democratic Front.[78] The $815 million in economic assistance (and $1.3 billion in military aid) the US has given each year, on average, since 1979 did not produce democratic reforms until very recently. The efficacy of the assistance is thus open to dispute. It is hard to claim that such cajoling of Cairo has catalyzed these promising but mild moves toward democracy. According to a former US ambassador to the country, 'Aid offers an easy way out for Egypt to avoid reform. They use the money to support antiquated programs and to resist reforms.'[79] Our point here is that an exclusive reliance on only soft forms of power may well compound problems they are meant to solve. Soft power is not a panacea.

'Who "won" Libya?'

The debate between soft and hard power advocates is especially strong over Libya.[80] For some, Muammar Gaddafi's decision to abandon his nuclear ambitions in December 2003 was a vindication of liberal inducements. Tony Blair saw Tripoli's reversal as proof that 'problems of proliferation can, *with good will*, be tackled through discussion and engagement.'[81] Robert Litwak concurs, at least insofar as the reasons given for the policy shift by Libyan officials were those attaching to the promise of western largesse rather than to the threat of American embargoes. According to Gaddafi's son, it was the US security guarantee to Libya in return for its abandoning its nuclear program that made his father switch paths: 'They said we, the West, and international society will be responsible for the protection of Libya . . . Why should we have an army? If Egypt invades Libya, the Americans are going to stop it.'[82] The victory of soft power seemed incontrovertible on the twentieth anniversary of the American bombing of Tripoli. On April 15, 2006, Lionel Richie and José Carreras performed a 'concert for peace' outside Gaddafi's bombed house.[83]

For others, including ourselves, coercive diplomacy played the more decisive role. Neoconservatives argued that the example of regime change in Iraq forced Gaddafi's U-turn – 'Saddam was deposed, eights month ago, on flimsy evidential grounds,' observed the Libyan leader, 'just think what will become of me when the Americans have absolute knowledge of my WMD capacity.'[84] '[F]ive days after we captured Saddam Hussein,' noted Dick Cheney pointedly, 'Qaddafi came forward and announced that he was going to surrender all of his nuclear materials to the United States.'[85] This 'Libyan surrender,' concurred Charles Krauthammer, was the product of 'a clearly enunciated policy – now known as the Bush Doctrine – of targeting, by preemptive war if necessary, hostile regimes engaged in terror and/or refusing to come clean on WMDs . . . Hussein did not get the message and ended up in a hole. Qaddafi got the message.'[86] Ronald Reagan had, after all, bombed Tripoli in April 1986 in reprisal for its sponsorship of terrorism. Precedent therefore tended to support the conclusion, no doubt shared by the Libyan regime, that, through a 9/11-three Ts prism, the US would not balk at doing so again, and more decisively.

The Libyan case is a classic example of liberal internationalists assuming everyone thinks like them. The regime, according to them, responded to inducements to rejoin 'the society of nations' rather than to the fear of American violence. It was not the war on terror that accounted for Gaddafi's conversion but his empathy with, or threatened exclusion from, a liberal project. Bush was more realistic about why Libya changed course. 'Actions by the United States and our allies,' he said, 'have sent an unmistakable message to regimes that seek or possess weapons of mass destruction: Those weapons do not bring influence or prestige. They bring isolation or otherwise unwelcome consequences.'[87] These 'unwelcome consequences' are perennially undervalued, even eschewed, in liberal statecraft when, in reality, they are a form of hard power that makes soft power possible. Neither works in isolation, both are only effective in tandem. As Jentleson and Whytock conclude, 'there is greater potential complementarity between force and diplomacy than more singular advocates of one or the other tend to convey.'[88]

This reasoning is not unique to the Second Cold War. The blending of soft and hard approaches is basic to how America negates foreign threats. The European Union prizes very highly the efficacy of soft power – because that is the only kind of power it possesses.[89] Such power has proved to be eminently resistible. Slobodan Milošević did not respond to threats to deny Yugoslavia EU membership but to US bombs. Soft power counts for little without a willingness to deploy – to intervene with – hard/military power. Clinton understood this approach with some clarity; Bush refined it. Their successors will do likewise.

Has Pyongyang been won?

Like Libya, there is contestation over whether hard or soft power brought the apparent closure of North Korea's uranium enrichment plant in Yongbyon in July 2007.[90] In the short term, the soft power of financial appeasement seems to have worked. Freeing up North Korean bank accounts abroad and supplying subsistence provisions (like fuel oil) to the socialist paradise appear to have worked. But there remains considerable debate over the extent of Pyongyang's commitment to a nuclear-free future. In several respects, the Democratic Peoples Republic of Korea presents a clear test of the

rationale underlying the war on terror: it conforms to most definitions of rogue status and is keen to proliferate for profit.[91] The DPRK
represents the three Ts nexus in stark relief. It was, after all, the third
member of 'an axis of evil' described by Bush in 2002. The regime
needs the financial profits of such proliferation more than most; its
economy has followed the Zimbabwean model into moral and economic destitution.[92]

However, Bush diplomacy toward Pyongyang was *not* much different from that of Clinton. Bush did not seek to test his doctrine in
North Korea. Even his most forceful supporters baulked at using military preemption against the regime. The Pepperdine scholar Robert
Kaufman ('more pro-Bush than Bush himself' according to Colin
Dueck)[93] rather ducks North Korea. Because the regime faces an
'inevitable demise,' Kaufman advocates neither containment nor
preemptive strikes.[94] Neoconservative Norman Podhoretz concedes
that American options are limited when it comes to dealing with
North Korea:

> The only remaining hope is that its neighbors, and especially China,
> will in their own interests force it to disarm by threatening to cut off
> the aid by which the Kim Jong Il regime remains afloat. This is clearly
> what Bush is trying to accomplish, and, thin as the prospect of success
> may be, it is hard to see what else he can do short of risking a nuclear
> war.[95]

In many ways, the Bush approach has out-multilateralized that of
Clinton. Reliance on six-party talks – comprised of China, Japan,
North and South Korea, Russia, and the US – its proponents argue,
has yielded more concessions from Kim Jong Il than have threats.
John Bolton, Bush's penultimate and enduringly controversial UN
ambassador, was increasingly a lone voice in his calls for a harder
line. North Korea is being handled in a determinedly multilateralist/
realist fashion. Bush has been complicit in this approach. It is hard
to imagine any president doing anything much different. Why risk a

nuclear conflagration with a bankrupt regime that can be bought off
with heating oil? Americans may not be able, in Nye's formulation,
to get Kim Jong Il to want what they want but they can get him to
want what America has got.

Who will lose Pakistan?

If the North Korean case study demonstrates how soft power can
appease a tyrant, the limits of soft power diplomacy can be seen in
Pakistan. The Bush administration, like Reagan's, spoke vociferously
about the benefits of democracy but was flexible in demanding it of
its allies. Despite the crucial position of Pakistan – as a nuclear power,
terrorist conduit, and nominal base for al Qaeda and the Taliban –
Bush relied on cajolement and economic incentives to keep the military junta of Pervez Musharraf on-side.[96] This 'hearts and minds'
strategy essentially disavowed military threats or even demands for
democratization. The efficacy of this approach is open to question.
Again, it is evidence of the limits of soft power in creating greater
security for America.[97] The when-you've-got-them-by-the-balls-
their-hearts-and-minds-will-follow approach may be a crude caricature of what US policy toward Pakistan might look like but it does at
least have the virtue of embracing a hard power component. Barack
Obama caused considerable controversy when he suggested he might,
as president, countenance bombing Pakistan.[98] He seemed to share
the analysis that Pakistani compliance in the war on terror was more
in evidence when America was threatening them with 'stone-age'
status than when it trusted to financial donations – though he wanted
to see more of those too.[99]

Critics argue that only a hypocritical nation would urge the
democratization of states like Afghanistan and Iraq whilst sustaining
the military dictatorship of Pakistan, the autocracy of Uzbekistan or
the feudal theocracy of Saudi Arabia.[100] The war on terror is hardly
unique in this regard. The First Cold War was replete with US
alliance-making of dubious moral character. Such an auditing of

both cold wars misses the necessity of nose-holding when facing an existential threat. In her famous *Commentary* article, the late Jeane Kirkpatrick argued that American foreign policy came most unstuck when it was guided by a naïve moral compass. Jimmy Carter was her case study. The fear, for her, was not that friendly dictators would be replaced by liberal internationalists but by 'less friendly autocrats of extremist persuasion.'[101] The logic applied to Iran in 1979 – when a westward-looking dictator was overthrown by anti-American Islamists – applies today in places like Pakistan. American interests are rarely served by abandoning friends on account of their moral turpitude. This enemy-of-my-enemy-is-my-friend approach explains why the US–Soviet wartime alliance of 1941–5 was so effective, despite the less than pristine human rights record of Joseph Stalin, and why, in the First Cold War, supporting Pinochet's junta in Chile was preferable to allowing communist subversion across that continent.[102] Ultimately, as Kirkpatrick predicted, right-wing regimes, like Chile, transitioned into functioning, pro-western democracies. The odds on this happening to Pakistan and Kazakhstan are perhaps long but only possible at all if they remain within the US camp.

How much does the war on terror cost?

Government spending on national defense in the first five years of the war on terror (2002–7) consumed an average of 3.9 percent of America's GDP.[103] Social security, in the same period, consumed an average of 4.3 percent and means-tested entitlements (like Medicare, food stamps, and family support assistance) 2.8 percent.[104] Mandatory spending on welfare programs (including social security and other entitlements) was almost three times that of defense at 11.3 percent of GDP. By 2012, social programs entailing direct transfer payments to individuals (including social security and other entitlements) will consume an estimated 68 percent of the federal budget, defense only 16.8.[105] US Congressmen recurrently stress the issue of costs, but how

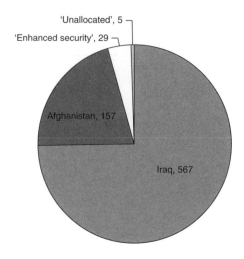

Figure 4 Breakdown of FY 2008 global war on terror request to Congress
(in billions of dollars)

Source: Amy Belasco, 'The Cost of Iraq, Afghanistan, and Other Global War on
Terror Operations since 9/11,' CRS Report (RL33110), June 28, 2007
('summary'); at www.fas.org/sgp/crs/natsec/RL33110.pdf.

expensive is the war? Are we dealing with a situation in which spending rises in direct proportion to a limitless threat? The realist and
liberal audits offered in the previous chapter certainly argue so. The
injustice of overspending on defense in the face of domestic poverty
is a mantra of the political left – despite the considerable advantage
the welfare-spending departments of the American government
enjoy over the Department of Defense. Conservatives and realists, for
different reasons but with invariably the same intent, argue that overspending reduces the effectiveness of government while increasing
its size.

According to a Clinton national security budget official, by the
time you turn this page Iraq will have cost the US between $500k
and $750k, equating to some $611 billion since 2001.[106] If the FY
2008 war requests are approved by Congress, total funding for Iraq
and the war on terror would reach about $758 billion. This is broken
down into its component parts in Figure 4:

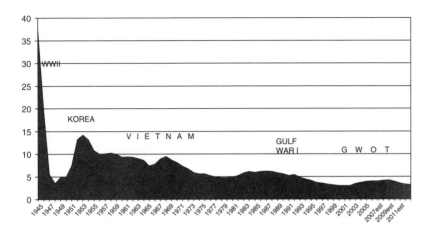

Figure 5 National defense spending as a percentage of GDP, 1945–2012

Source: White House, *Historical Tables, Budget of the United States Government,*
Fiscal Year 2008, 136 (table 8.4); at
www.whitehouse.gov/omb/budget/fy2008/pdf/hist.pdf; and US Office of
Management and Budget, *The Budget for Fiscal Year 2005, Historical Series,* pp. 45–
50. Note: GWOT includes Afghanistan and Iraq war spending.

When the Iraq campaign is excepted the wider war appears sustainable and appropriate. Iraq included, the cost necessarily rises, but the
key question is: compared to what? What is the appropriate cost for a
global war? At what point do the appeals of accountants taken precedence over an existential threat? These questions are not designed to
justify infinite spending regardless of practical effect, nor do we
contend that social welfare spending should be cut to buy the imple-
ments of war.[107] Rather, our argument is that fiscal rectitude rarely
determines the efficacy or justness of American wars. Costly wars can
be successful (the Second World War), cheap ones problematic (Gulf
War I).[108] Certainly, in comparative terms the war on terror is not that
expensive – in either blood or treasure. During the Vietnam War
defense spending consumed over twice the proportion of GDP (9.5
percent in 1968) than it has during Iraq (4.0 in 2006; see Figure 5).[109]
   Also consider that, as a proportion of its GDP, the United States
spends less on Afghanistan and Iraq than several other nations.

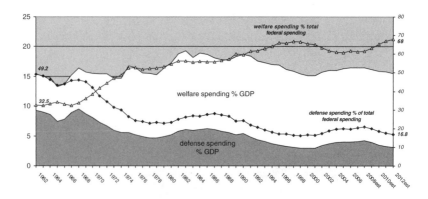

Figure 6 Rising welfare, falling defense

Source: White House, *Historical Tables, Budget of the United States Government,*
Fiscal Year 2008, 322 (table 16.1); at
http://www.whitehouse.gov/omb/budget/fy2008/pdf/hist.pdf. The term 'welfare'
covers all social programs entailing direct transfer payments to individuals
(including social security and other entitlements).

Kuwait, Qatar, UAE, and Saudi Arabia, for example, had all spent
more on Iraqi reconstruction (to 2006), as a percentage of their GDP,
than America.[110]

In 2007, the US government spent 62 per cent more on defense
than in 2001.[111] It should be recalled that the 1990s saw a decline
in defense spending consistent with the lowered threat perception
after the First Cold War, from 5.6 percent of GDP in 1989 to 3
percent in 2000. Not since 1800 had America spent this little of its
wealth on defense. So the starting point for the war on terror was a
historically and remarkably low level of defense spending, especially given America's unipolar status after 1989. No power in
history has possessed such military potential at so little cost to its
domestic prosperity. Some twenty-six countries spend a greater
percentage of their GDP on defense than the United States.[112]
Currently, the United States spends more of its GDP on health
programs than on its military (5 per cent vs. 4; see Figure 6). It is
American welfare not warfare spending that threatens its long-term
financial health.

Anthony Cordesman reasons that a projected 1–2 percent increase in DOD spending would present 'no strain on [the] US economy even by historical standards.'[113] Mackubin Thomas Owens has argued that by spending 4.5 percent of GDP on defense 'America will be able to lead coalitions against terrorists, restore order to unstable regions, do peacemaking in regions of vital interest, deter aggression and win a war if deterrence fails. The benefits of the resulting world order far outweigh the costs.'[114] Lowering defense spending in the 1990s hardly augmented American security, as 9/11 revealed. The quality of spending matters, of course, more than the quantity, but it is difficult to imagine what significant security benefits will accrue from economizing in the face of such an unpredictable enemy. Global military primacy, at such a small percentage of America's wealth, 'remains a bargain.'[115] As Owens concludes:

> One obvious benefit of bearing this burden is the prevention of major war. Four and a half percent of GDP is a small price to pay considering the alternatives. During the peak years of World War II, US defense spending constituted 38.6 to 40 percent of GDP [see Figure 5], not to mention the lives of some 400,000 Americans lost over the course of the war. Clearly the cost of preventing war is far less than the cost of fighting one. And prevention of war is the main objective of primacy.[116]

Figure 7 compares the number of American soldiers killed in the nation's major foreign wars. The Second World War resulted in the death of nearly 0.3 percent of the total US population, Vietnam 0.03 percent. The war on terror (*including* Iraq) has claimed an equivalent 0.001 percent of the US population, some seven times less the number killed on American roads in the same period (about 40,000 per year). The leading cause of death for Americans of fighting age is not foreign war but traffic accidents.[117] Between May 2006 and July 2007 more British troops were being killed per 1,000 personnel-years (8.8) than their American counterparts (7.3).[118] It has been estimated that 25 percent of the US population in 1975 knew a soldier

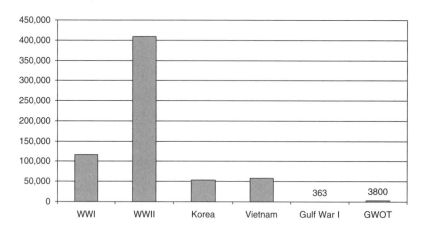

Figure 7 US soldiers killed in major wars, 1917–2007

Source: Department of Defense, Principal Wars Table; at
siadapp.dmdc.osd.mil/personnel/CASUALTY/WCPRINCIPAL.pdf.

killed or injured in Vietnam. 'To reach that scale today, at least
250,000 more US troops would have to die or be wounded' in the war
on terror.[119] America would have to occupy Iraq for a further 285
years, at the current casualty rate, to reach this figure.[120] The
Pentagon has renamed the war on terror the 'Long War' but they
surely do not have nearly three centuries in mind.[121] Critics of the
war often contend that an American has a greater chance of being
killed by lightning or in an accident involving a deer than by a terrorist attack.[122] This is, of course, true but only so long as the capacity of terrorists remains limited and sporadic. An al Qaeda cell
with access to WMD would certainly become more deadly in statistical terms than the weather and the automobile. One nuclear explo-
sion in New York could kill more people than all America's wars
combined.

To reiterate, the war on terror aims not to end all terrorism but to
prevent a doomsday strike. It seeks to deny to 'the world's worst
leaders,' said Bush, 'the world's worst weapons' – not for the fear that
such leaders will use them but that they might provide them to others
prepared to do so.[123] Terrorists, as Christ said of the poor (John 12:8),

will always be with us. Their capacity to harm, however, is contingent on their access to state sponsorship. Thus, the war on terror is a state-level war much like those previously fought and won by the United States.

Does freedom have an accountant?

Ronald Reagan ran up a considerable economic deficit but won the First Cold War. In 1983, the budget deficit was 5.7 percent of American GDP. It has never been as high again. In 2006, despite a global war on terror, the deficit was just 1.9 percent.[124] One does not have to be an eternal optimist to acknowledge a considerable spare capacity in the US economy to wage the current war. America's willingness to incur debt does not guarantee the spread of world freedom, but fiscal rectitude and balanced budgets are no guarantees either. The post-1989 'peace dividend' – which saw Clinton scale back US military spending and, by 1998, bring the federal budget into balance – was, with hindsight, a decade in which the Islamist threat gathered, despite US wars on behalf of Muslim populations (in Kuwait, Somalia, Bosnia and Kosovo). Spending less in the current climate, for reasons of short-term fiscal discipline, is unlikely to ameliorate the threat the US currently faces.

Conclusion

Despite a widespread unhappiness with the war's name – has there ever been a war the title of which went so far to determine the normative responses to it? – we argue that the war on terror is both an appropriate title and style of response given the nature of the enemy. 'Cold War' was surely more metaphorical a label, but few would now insist on using quotation marks around it. Since the 1960s, the United States has waged wars on poverty, drugs, and crime. Like terror, each of these enemies was an abstraction. Like terror they were all, certainly for those on the political left, consequences of state failure. War against these foes was/is regarded as legitimate. But terrorism, despite its manifest genesis within deficient political systems and failed states, is somehow not worth a war. Indeed, unlike poverty, it is something the politically sophisticated are obliged to tolerate. In this chapter we have argued otherwise.

As a title, the war on terror is not simply rhetorical. Like the previous wars that have marked American public policy, domestic and foreign, the war on terror identifies not only the source of the enemy being fought – poor governance – but evokes a qualitatively different institutional response on behalf of the American government. Declaring a war on drugs in the 1980s, for example, extended the jurisdictional lines from the Drug Enforcement Administration to the Department of Defense. It succeeded in grounding American counter-narcotics strategy within a wider hemispheric approach that dealt with external supply rather than just internal demand. Declaring a war made this institutional shift logical, even necessary. Something similar was intended by Bush's war declaration after 9/11. On February 26, 1993, jihadist terrorists attempted to topple one tower of the World Trade Center onto the other. Clinton treated the attack as a crime. The perpetrators became the target of the Department of Justice and US courts. The response to the second, successful attempt, eight and a half years later, went after root causes. It determined not just to police terrorism better but to remove its state-level support and, even more boldly, destroy the political systems against which terrorists had set their stall or from which they pursued a greater lethality. One can, of course, dispute the efficacy of such an approach but not the institutional transformation it brought about. Only a war could do this. The American government is too unwieldy a complex to respond effectively without the imperatives of a war.

Reagan once quipped that liberals fought poverty, and poverty won.[125] It is ironic that his analysis of the failure of Johnson's war on poverty mirrors that proffered by critics of Bush's war on terror: in each case the enemy got worse as a consequence of waging war against it. We think Reagan had a point but that Bush's critics do not. The elephant in the room, or not in the room, at the time of writing, is the absence of a second 9/11. A predicted recurrence was an operating assumption in the first months after the New York and Washington attacks. Many Americans believed 9/11 to be a prelude rather than a denouement. Whilst we do not share an unbounded optimism in the permanent retardation of jihadist terrorism, we do conclude here that the war on terror has played a fundamental role in keeping America safe from that threat. What others attribute to luck or chance, we grant to the Bush strategy.

The French prime minister Georges Clemenceau (1841–1929) defined war as 'a series of catastrophes that results in victory.' Any war, especially a long one, will invariably have its share of setbacks. The war on terror does not embody a perfect balance of force and diplomacy, hard and soft power. It can exaggerate threats because it is in the nature of wars for this to happen. It will, at times, see in the enemy a cohesion that might be illusory. It might prize military effi-cacy over the demands of nation-building. The Second Cold War provides examples of all these. But so did the First. An interim audit of both these global conflicts would, according to the date chosen, yield either gloom or hope. In neither the cold war nor the war on terror (the First and Second Cold Wars respectively) did the prob-lematic battles fought within them invalidate the larger struggle or the doctrine underlying it. The First Cold War suffered both Korea and Vietnam, and yet its containment doctrine remained intact for the duration of the conflict with communism. Indeed, not taking containment seriously, as Jimmy Carter did not, produced one of the least effective foreign policy presidencies. Between 1977 and 1980 the USSR invaded Afghanistan, the Cambodian genocide went unchecked, and Central America was victim to communist infiltra-tion. The war on terror is currently enduring Iraq. This 'catastrophe,' as Clemenceau would likely have labeled it, has not invalidated the

Bush Doctrine. As Lawrence Kaplan reminds us, 'when critics advertise the Iraq war as the decisive repudiation of a broader doctrine, they may be jettisoning the good with the bad.'[126] Iraq divides the American polity, and is the subject of our next chapter. The Second Cold War, like the First, embodies an enduring consensus. It does so on the basis of its utility, not its perfection.

5

Iraq: Vietnam in the sand?

As was often the case, Mr. Reagan did not seem to be paying close attention, according to one of those present. But when the briefing was over he had one question. He wanted to hear again the number of troops the planners were going to send in. He was told a figure and shook his head. 'Make it twice that,' he told a slightly puzzled general. Asked why, the President said calmly: 'If Jimmy Carter had sent 16 helicopters rather than eight to Desert One to rescue the US hostages in Iran in 1980, you'd be sitting here briefing him today, not me.'

Gerard Barker[1]

I cannot, alas, leave in such a cowardly fashion. As for you, and in particular for your great country, I never believed for a moment that you would have this sentiment of abandoning a people which has chosen liberty . . . I have only committed this mistake of believing in you.

Cambodian Prime Minister Sirik Matak, April 1975,
on the offer of asylum by the US ambassador after
US withdrawal from Indochina; Matak was killed
by the Khmer Rouge a month later[2]

Those who wallow in . . . Vietnam angst would have us be not only reticent to help the rest of the world but ashamed of our ability to do so and doubtful of the value of spreading democracy and of the superiority of freedom itself.

Melvin Laird, US Secretary of Defense, 1969–73[3]

The American liberation of Iraq was seriously mismanaged but not misconceived – an unsound execution of a sound doctrine. The invasion by the United States and its coalition allies in March 2003 was the most criticized act, among many, of the Bush administration. It was also one of the most controversial and momentous American military interventions in the Republic's history. While the initial war was won with ease by April 2003, confirming the supreme military might of the US in conventional battle, the subsequent occupation proved more difficult and deadly. Asymmetric warfare, as it had previously in Vietnam, Lebanon, and Somalia, posed fatal challenges to US forces in theater and public opinion at home. By the fall of 2007, nearly 4,000 Americans had been killed in Iraq, while many tens of thousands of Iraqis had also died, many through sectarian killings, others through deliberate targeting by al Qaeda in Iraq and its jihadist affiliates-in-terror. Iraq's rogue state neighbors – Syria and Iran in particular – proved actively complicit in financing and arming anti-coalition attacks and promoting sectarian strife. As a result, the prospects for the stability of Iraq and the wider Middle East are at best unclear, although no worse than in 1980 when a million Muslims stood poised to kill each other in the Iran–Iraq War.[4]

When combined with the political controversies that had surrounded the war's rationale(s), the illegality of preventive war under international law, allegations of manipulated and politicized intelligence, and above all the absence of WMD stocks in Iraq, the legitimacy of the war was discredited to many within and outside America. To its critics, the Bush Doctrine had been vitiated, not vindicated. The Iraq War divided and polarized America and pitted the presidency and Congress against each other in a serious constitutional confrontation after the 2006 midterm elections. Much as the 'Vietnam syndrome' shadowed successive presidents of both parties after 1975, rightly or wrongly shaping their judgments on the efficacy of using force, so an 'Iraq syndrome' now threatened similarly to constrain the freedom of action of future American presidents.

In this chapter we contest this interpretation and argue that Iraq was a 'necessary war.' We concur with the sentiments expressed by Senator John McCain (R-AZ) in his speech to the 2004 Republican Party national convention in New York City, in a succinct summation of the necessity to topple Saddam:

> Our choice wasn't between a benign status quo and the bloodshed of war. It was between war and a graver threat. Don't let anyone tell you otherwise . . . Whether or not Saddam possessed the terrible weapons of destruction he once had and used, freed from international pressure and the threat of military action, he would have acquired them again . . . We couldn't afford the risk posed by an unconstrained Saddam in these dangerous times.[5]

It was not the threat calculus behind the decision for war but the execution of the transition from long-term dictatorship to fledgling constitutional democracy that was mistaken. The implementation of the occupation revealed a woeful lack of careful planning, effective execution and judicious decision-making. Insufficient ground forces were deployed from the outset while certain key decisions concerning the disbanding of the Iraqi army, de-Baathification and drawing down the American presence over 2005–6 were demonstratively wrong. Mismanagement and conflict in Washington – nothing novel but especially serious in wartime – was as problematic and as poorly resolved as that in the Green Zone. But despite its terrible toll, the principles informing the decision to invade were the correct ones, and remain so. Moreover, the evolution of the Iraqi imbroglio is such that a premature US retreat would prove deeply injurious to American interests in the region and the prosecution of the Second Cold War. At minimum, such an exit could plausibly create the prospects for a full-scale civil war involving a genocidal level of sectarian violence, a humanitarian catastrophe with massive popular displacement, growing Iranian influence stoking a broader Sunni–Shiite conflict within Iraq and across the region, increased bloodshed throughout the Middle East and the degeneration of Iraq into a new 'failed state' perfectly placed to provide a haven for assorted jihadist organizations and homicidal terror operatives targeting the West. While some erstwhile realists now suggest, in a curious mix of complacency and cynicism, that the Middle East 'does not matter' and can safely be abandoned by Washington, such a course would be utterly counterproductive and irresponsible for the US.[6]

Our defense of the Iraq War rests, then, on both retrospective and prospective reasoning. We do not dispute the major criticisms of the occupation and its misconduct. The multiple failings in this regard, which have received extensive, cogent, and authoritative analysis by an array of thoughtful critics, were highly counterproductive and dealt a major setback to the US.[7] But they neither invalidate the logic and wisdom of the original decision to invade nor do they suggest that the US would be best served by a full or precipitate withdrawal.

The oft-employed Vietnam analogy is therefore, at best, imperfect. Analogies are ubiquitous in international relations, and not always constructive, but their utility derives from two functions. First, analogies offer the opportunity to reflect on the absence of uniqueness. That is, by casting our minds back over history we can usefully remind ourselves that, for all the breathless coverage of the mass media and 'in time' analyses of contemporary scholars, current predicaments – including international crises – are rarely without precedent. Secondly, analogies can help to craft a sense of where we are heading and where we should recalibrate strategy and tactics. In this regard, the appropriate First Cold War analogy for the Iraq case is more Korea than Vietnam. Like Iraq, Korea was seen as a war of choice by many of Harry Truman's critics. Like Iraq, an initial American military success was subsequently countered with major regional powers playing a crucial role in reversing the American gains. Like Iraq, by the time Truman left office, the war seemed mired in an intractable position and had eroded the president's standing in America and the world, with his domestic opponents seeking to capitalize on the war's setbacks for partisan and electoral gain. Like Iraq, it was left to a new president to try to resolve the apparent impasse. And, we believe, like Korea, Iraq will (and should) see the presence of sizeable numbers of American troops for many years to come as a prerequisite of regional peace and lasting national security for the US. Critics who see such a presence as doomed 'by their very existence (to) swell the ranks of *jihadists*' fail to explain how a Second Cold War against jihadist Islam can be won without a fight.[8]

In this chapter we make this case by first revisiting and evaluating the case for war as advanced by the Bush principals over 2002–3. We then assess the reasons for the relative failure of the occupation over 2003–8 and its consequences for Iraq and American power. Finally, we reiterate the crucial geo-political role that Iraq will play in years to come and its appropriate place in an American grand strategy that advances the war on terror.

Iraq: a necessary choice

Iraq has been a strategic albatross to the US since Saddam came to power in 1979. The dilemma was aptly summarized by Henry Kissinger, who, when asked whom the US should support when the Iran–Iraq War began in 1980, responded that it was a pity that both sides couldn't lose. Although the US tilted toward Baghdad, as a necessary counterweight to revolutionary Iran's expansive ambitions in the region, during Reagan's first term in office, that tilt was one typical of First Cold War geo-politics: unwelcome and contingent. With the Gulf War in 1990–91 to drive Iraq out of Kuwait after its August 1990 invasion, Saddam assumed a new status as the region's premier menace, a distinction that he would retain throughout the following decade (despite al Qaeda's increasing activity and Iran's equal status to Iraq as a pariah state subject to 'dual containment' by the US).

Indeed, the origins of the 2003 war need to be traced to the unsatisfactory conclusion of the 1991 campaign. As Robert Litwak argued, an 'underlying tension' persisted throughout the Desert Storm campaign and for years thereafter.[9] The UN Security Council resolutions authorizing the use of force by the US-led coalition in 1991 had been linked to a particular goal – liberating Kuwait – rather than overthrowing Saddam. The latter, however, was always an implicit American war objective. George H. W. Bush's refusal to pursue regime change after the coalition expelled the Iraqi army from Kuwait – despite encouraging Shiites and Kurds to revolt against the regime – meant that the tension between keeping Saddam 'in his box' in the near term and working for his ultimate overthrow remained throughout the 1990s. Presidents Bush and Clinton maintained a strong US military presence in the region, with forces in Saudi Arabia the principal – though far from single – cause of Bin Laden's animus toward America. They implemented 'no-fly zones' over large parts of Iraq, enforced a substantial (though, we now know, highly imperfect) set of sanctions on the regime, and authorized regular air sorties and occasional military engagements (most notably, four days of bombing in Operation Desert Fox, in 1998). Under pressure from congressional Republicans, Clinton made regime change official US policy in the 1998 Iraq Liberation Act. Iraq was widely seen as the single greatest state-centric threat in and to the region. It remained the most crucial focus of US policy. UN resolutions, congressional debates and foreign policy discussions about Iraq punctuated the entire decade. The Baathist state was a preoccupation of American policy-makers long before the George W. Bush administration.

According to a Pentagon official close to Colin Powell, then chairman of the Joint Chiefs, Clinton's 'comprehensive containment' approach meant treating Saddam 'like a toothache. There are periods when it doesn't hurt as much as other times, but it just doesn't go away and you never quite forget about it.'[10] The 'major liability of this strategy,' as Litwak noted, 'was that it relied on multilateral cooperation during a period when US allies, as well as Iraq's regional neighbors, were suffering from "sanctions fatigue"'.[11] While the toothache remained painful, by the time Clinton left office, the array of remedies was eroding. Bush officials who inherited this situation called for a 'smarter,' but not necessarily more belligerent, approach. While it is clear that Bush distrusted the Iraqi dictator he did not enter office calling for his forcible overthrow. Such a mode of redress, agitated for by neoconservatives at the Project for a New American Century (founded in 1997), was not contemplated by Bush. It followed that the prospects for decisive military action in Bush's first term were limited. It was the 9/11 attack that transformed the strategic calculus of the new president. It was this event, rather than anything new Saddam Hussein had done, that changed the American emphasis. The key figures in the foreign policy process – Rumsfeld, Cheney, Rice, and, most significantly, Bush himself – agreed that the vulnerability of the US, exposed on September 11, made action against Iraq imperative and likely unavoidable. 9/11, as we observed in chapter 4, altered 'the prism' through which Iraq and rogue regimes were now viewed in Washington. Saddam was now fast due a dentist's visit.

Any assessment of the wisdom of the Iraq war, regardless of the subsequent occupation, must therefore deal in an unsentimental fashion with the situation as it existed prior to and in the immediate aftermath of the attacks on New York and Washington. Indeed, this is the fulcrum of any analysis of the war as necessity rather than choice. In our view, the US-led wars of the 1990s (with the exception of Desert Storm in 1991) were wars of choice. The wars of the 2000s were wars of necessity. Strategically defensive, they employed offensive methods to take the war on terror into enemy territory. For neoconservatives, such an approach rightly adopted a 'distinctly American internationalism.' As Kaplan and Kristol observed, although liberals and realists typically approach the world from different directions, both ended up in the same place on Iraq, endorsing 'a minimalist approach to foreign policy – one because the very concept of self-interest provokes discomfort, and the other because it defines the national interest far too narrowly.'[12] The Bush administration rejected such minimalism on Iraq. But while, as we argue below, Iraq was not a 'neoconservative war,' it was one that neocons could and did support.

Critics of the intervention (both at the time and since), in stark contrast, viewed the intervention as, in Lawrence Freedman's words, 'a false move in a real conflict.'[13] Whether or not they approve of the war on terror more broadly, opponents of the Iraq campaign typically venture various combinations of five central arguments:

1. *Saddam was a rational actor.* As such, he would not have given WMD to terrorists, attacked the US directly, or threatened regional stability. The consequences of his doing so would bring about his rapid demise – so, the argument goes, he was effectively deterred.

2. *Saddam was being kept 'in his box.'* Through a combination of economic sanctions, diplomatic pressure and the US–UK military presence, Saddam was unlikely, and effectively unable, to make significant mischief.

3. *Saddam was in possession of insufficient WMD to pose a serious threat and was therefore not worth deposing.* Although his stockpiles had been substantially underestimated during the first Gulf War, many critics of the 2003 war were persuaded that UN weapons inspectors had forced Iraqi compliance; Saddam was far, far weaker than he had been prior to the 1991 war.

4. *If Saddam acquired, threatened, let alone used WMD, he would again face a considerable alliance of states against him.* The pattern of the first Gulf War would be repeated, but this time Saddam would be removed – so, he would not so act.

5. *Preventive war against Saddam would be illegal.* Many scholars of international relations and law argued this. Preventive war would violate international law. For the US to arrogate to itself, in the absence of an explicit *casus belli*, the power of judge, jury, and executioner over other sovereign states was unacceptable.

In short, while his regime was unarguably one of the most brutal and unpredictable on the planet, Saddam neither constituted nor was likely to constitute a threat sufficient to warrant another US military campaign in the Middle East.

Before addressing these criticisms, we should first comment on the debate over the war, which remains more a matter of heat than light. Contrary to the most common misperception, and despite the efforts of distinguished scholars to impress this point on students of international relations,[14] Iraq was *not* a 'neoconservative' war. It was not declared without debate. It was not imposed on an unsuspecting and innocent American nation by a secretive cabal of bellicose and naïve warmongers. The decision to go to war was made by a war cabinet comprising Bush, Cheney, Powell, Rice, and Rumsfeld – none of whom could be counted a neoconservative.[15] To be sure, some neoconservative arguments found their way into the justifications for war that they employed. For example, and especially after no WMD came to light after the war, the Bush team relied on the democratic peace hypothesis: America was safer in a world of democracies so why not create more when the chance presents itself. But these leading decision-makers were otherwise all traditional 'realists' or 'national interest conservatives.' Regime change in Iraq was justified in the American national interest. For most, the imperative to war stemmed not from a crusading desire to reshape the Middle East but from the need to staunch more permanently the threats to US interests and security emanating from that region. Warriors they may have been, but their swords were only intermittently unsheathed.

In addition, the war's main foreign supporter was the Labour Party prime minister, Tony Blair, a liberal interventionist whose concerns about WMD in general, and Iraq in particular, were strong from the time he entered office in May 1997.[16] In the Democratic Party, the leading Senate Democrats running for their party's 2008 presidential nomination – Hillary Clinton, John Edwards, Joe Biden, and Christopher Dodd – who were in office at the time, all voted for the

2002 use of force congressional resolution. Outside government the
case for war was advanced not only by the neoconservative *Weekly
Standard* but also the conservative *National Review*, the historically
liberal *New Republic*, and the center-right *Economist*. While most
neoconservatives supported the war (including Francis Fukuyama),
so too did writers across the spectrum: the leftist Christopher
Hitchens, the liberal Thomas Friedman, the centrist Fareed Zakaria,
the center-right Michael Kelly, the Tory Andrew Sullivan and the
quintessential realist, Henry Kissinger. The most persuasive, published case for war was penned not by a neocon but by Kenneth
Pollack, a leading Middle East authority in Clinton's National
Security Council.[17] To depict the war or the botched occupation as
discrediting the neoconservative tendency is shortsighted.[18]

Neoconservatives actually contended fiercely between themselves
over the war and the prospects for Arab democracy.[19] As Frederick
Kagan, usually identified as a neoconservative – though he decries
the label – has noted, neoconservatives differed on the military
approach to Iraq.[20] In 2002, he warned that the Wolfowitz 'Afghan'
model would be insufficiently light for a future Iraq war.[21] In 2006,
he observed that 'the "small footprint" approach in Afghanistan and
Iraq has led to disaster.'[22] In 2004, he derided the fantasies of neocons
like Richard Perle, that somehow regime change in Iraq would be
easy and staffed by returning Iraqi exiles: 'I think that was foolish at
the time, and it's turned out to be extremely foolish in hindsight.'[23]

While some of the most vociferous opponents of the war employed
highly dubious and tendentious assertions – that it was driven by
Israeli or Jewish influence in Washington; that it was a personal act of
revenge for Saddam's plot to assassinate George Bush Sr. in 1993; and
that finishing a job left incomplete in 1991 represented less a defeat
for a pariah regime than an Oedipal victory for Bush 43 over 41 – the
broad array of mainstream critics drew on carefully reasoned and discrete arguments. Some of these either had, or have since acquired,
undeniable force. Most notably, the post-war occupation did not

uncover substantial weaponized stocks of WMD, the central case for preventive war. Saddam's formal ties with al Qaeda have proven difficult to substantiate. He clearly played no role in 9/11. These unsettling attributes of the case for war combined with the failure to reconstitute effectively the Iraqi state and the revelations of prisoner abuse at Abu Ghraib to dent American credibility and claims of global leadership. These arguments from hindsight, however, do not invalidate the case for military action as it was put in 2002–3. In order to explain why, let us deal with each of the five main criticisms of the war.

1. Containment and deterrence: Saddam as a rational actor

While Saddam's rationality is difficult to prove, his irrationality is more easily documented. Some realists depict Saddam as ruthless but not reckless: he started 'only' two wars in a quarter-century in power (with Iran in 1980 and Kuwait in 1990), and both were rational responses to his geo-strategic situation. In terms of the latter, for example, Stephen Walt argues that in the context of an 'increasingly dire' economic situation and with little danger of outside military intervention to repel an Iraqi land and oil grab, 'Although the [Kuwait] invasion did not work out as Saddam expected, his decision to invade was neither reckless nor surprising.'[24] But such arguments are not especially persuasive, even in the febrile cauldron of the Middle East, where what passes for rationality has a quality all its own.[25] To commence an essentially futile eight-year war with Iran and then to invade another neighbor only two years after its cessation does not strike us as symptomatic of rational calculation. Similarly, to bank on an ambivalent American response to his invasion of Kuwait suggests a fundamental failure on the part of the Iraqi leader to understand how international relations work. His refusal to bow to US demands in March 2003 continued this pattern of unfortunate calculation – ultimately costing him his life.

However, even if one concedes that Saddam was in some sense a rational actor whose primary goal was self-preservation, he was undoubtedly a reckless gambler, a demonstrably poor calculator, and a confirmed megalomaniac. The official 9/11 Commission Report concluded that Iraq did have a relationship with al Qaeda.[26] Saddam's regime, even if had no formal operational links with al Qaeda, had a record of happily harboring terrorist organizations and jihadist operatives in Iraq while financing anti-Israeli suicide bombers and their families in the Palestinian territories. Evidence uncovered after the liberation revealed that the Saddam *Fedayeen* (a permanent state security force created in 1994) had, since 1998, trained Arab volunteers from across the region. In the year before his overthrow, Saddam's forces were planning terror attacks against Iraqi exiles and hostile groups in Europe (including the UK), Kurdistan, and Iran.[27] Saddam's loathing of the US was amply documented and long established. It is not inconceivable that a regime headed by Saddam or one of his sons would have facilitated and abetted direct or indirect attacks against the US. It was, after all, one of the few regimes – even in the Middle East – openly to celebrate 9/11 (which even the normally reliable 'Death to America' Iranian theocrats and Syrian rent-a-mobs did not).

As Saddam's calculations about America's willingness to use force in 1991 and 2003 revealed, his judgment was deeply and persistently flawed. Just as Soviet intelligence officials dared not tell Stalin that his ally Hitler was about to invade him,[28] so Saddam preferred a brutally enforced fantasy to reality:

> In the words of a senior Iraqi official, 'Directly disagreeing with Saddam Hussein's ideas was unforgivable. It would be suicide.' Indeed, Saddam decided to invade Iran in 1980 without consulting any of his advisors and made the decision to invade Kuwait in 1990 after talking only with his son-in-law. And he forbade his own intelligence apparatus from giving him analysis about America because he claimed a superior understanding of the Americans and their behavior. Saddam so intimidated his generals that they dared not tell him the truth about the rapid pace of the American offensive in March–April 2003, and even as US tanks entered Baghdad Saddam believed his forces were prevailing and was

still ordering the movement of Iraqi units that no longer existed. Even months after the fall of Baghdad, senior Iraqi officers who had been captured by the coalition forces continued to believe it possible that Iraq still possessed a hidden WMD capacity.[29]

Effective containment and deterrence rely heavily on the core premise that targeted opponents are value-maximizing, rational actors. There existed little reason for confidence that Saddam would ever fit such a description. As Stanley Renshon notes:

> The question of what to do about leaders like Saddam Hussein and Kim Jong-Il rests on deciphering their worldviews, calculations, and psychology. If they are sufficiently 'like us' to see their circumstances and ours the way we do, see their options and ours as we do, and act accordingly, the United States and the concepts of deterrence and containment are in good shape. If not, American national security policy had better consider other alternatives, perhaps something like the Bush Doctrine.[30]

2. Sanctions

As Litwak stressed in 2000, and as we now know beyond any reasonable doubt, the prospect for maintaining a credible international sanctions regime on Iraq was progressively crumbling with each successive month by the end of the 1990s.[31] Iraq was not in a state of stable equilibrium but was actively, and increasingly effectively, dismantling the sanctions regime. Not only had Saddam managed to evade – with Syrian and Turkish assistance – the international sanctions on Iraqi oil exports, but large-scale bribery and the massive corruption of the UN 'oil-for-food' program heavily compromised French, Russian, and Chinese positions in the UN Security Council. The continuing US and UK air sorties against Iraq regularly occasioned strong criticisms of Anglo-Saxon bellicosity, long before George W. Bush entered the White House. Indeed, it was Bill Clinton, who, on February 17, 1998, spoke of the imperatives confronting US policy in Iraq:

What if he fails to comply and we fail to act, or we take some ambiguous third route . . . [Saddam] will conclude the international community has lost its will. He will then conclude that he can go right on and do more to rebuild an arsenal of devastating destruction . . . And some day, I guarantee you, he'll use that arsenal.[32]

Both David Kay and Charles Duelfer, the successive heads of the CIA's Iraq Survey Group after the war ended, concluded that Saddam planned to resume production of WMD and delivery systems once the UN sanctions regime ended. But, far from being seen around the world as the pariah state that it was, Iraq was portrayed by influential voices in the media and academia as another benighted victim of western imperialism, a nation that had effectively served its sentence and no longer merited punitive international sanctions. Whether through a reformed but ineffective sanctions regime, illegal and corrupt measures by Baghdad or a collapse of the sanctions regime, that Saddam would resume full-scale oil exports and recover substantial oil revenues within a matter of one to two years seemed likely. As his prior behavior had always confirmed, those revenues would buy guns not butter. They would allow him again to threaten his neighbors, repress his own people, and rekindle his WMD ambitions.

3. WMD and intelligence

Every important national intelligence agency – the US, UK, French, Israeli, Australian, Russian and Chinese – was convinced that Iraq still possessed a WMD capacity in 2002-3. The exact make-up and extent of that capacity was not agreed, which is unsurprising. Intelligence is not synonymous with knowledge. The US has long experience of this unfortunate reality. Modern US history is punctuated by spectacular intelligence failure:

- Pearl Harbor in 1941;
- Soviet missiles in Cuba in 1962;
- failing to predict the 1979 Iranian revolution;
- the surprise of the Indian and Pakistani nuclear tests of 1998;

- 9/11;
- underestimating Saddam's pre-1991 capacities (when intelligence officials reported that Saddam had been within a few months of completing a nuclear weapon);
- failing to identify Libya's WMD stocks pre-2003.

Moreover, none of the major intelligence agencies possessed substantial human (as opposed to technical) intelligence on the ground in Iraq, the most valuable – albeit still not entirely reliable – type. As Richard Posner notes in assessing the March 2005 WMD Commission Report,[33] while a number of specific mistakes were committed by US intelligence officials,

> Almost all experts on national security were highly confident, even in the absence of concrete evidence, that Saddam Hussein had weapons of mass destruction. Everything in his history and character pointed that way and in particular it seemed inconceivable that he would risk his regime, liberty, and indeed life merely to create a mistaken impression of having retained them, if in fact he had discarded them.
>
> Because the logic of the situation created such a powerful expectation and because the 9/11 attacks were so dramatic a reminder of the cost of false negatives, the available evidence was quite naturally interpreted to support the inference that Saddam Hussein had taken advantage of the absence of United Nations inspectors (who had withdrawn from Iraq in 1998) to resume the production of weapons of mass destruction – especially since the evidence *did* support this expectation.[34]

The result was that the powerful *a priori* case for believing that Saddam possessed a WMD capability 'made it inevitable that the burden of proving the contrary would be placed on the doubters – of whom there were few.'[35]

Beyond these factors, Saddam's long history of non-compliance with, and evasion of, UN inspectors was a matter of record that remains beyond dispute. Saddam's pattern of behavior, from the imposition of UNSC Resolution 687 in 1991 – under Chapter VII – requiring Iraq to relinquish all WMD to Resolution 1441 on

November 8, 2002 (the seventeenth resolution since 1991), was one of 'cheat and retreat.' Even as late as January 2003, with coalition forces assembled in their tens of thousands on his borders and the Bush intent to achieve regime change crystal clear, Saddam refused to comply fully. It was on January 27, 2003 that Hans Blix affirmed that 'Iraq appears not to have come to a genuine acceptance, not even today, of the disarmament which was demanded of it,' with unaccounted-for materials including stocks of chemical bombs, bulk agents for chemical weapons, and munitions for their delivery.[36] Equally a matter of record, and at least as disturbing, is the remarkable ease with which amoral WMD proliferators have been able (prior to 9/11 and in some cases, such as A. Q. Khan, since, in the passive knowledge or active complicity of national governments) to flog their lethal wares to sufficiently high bidders. As long as these two conditions obtained, the risk that Saddam would use existing capacity or acquire an enlarged WMD arsenal was entirely genuine and urgent. For an American president after 9/11 to discount such an occurrence would have been strategically unthinkable and politically irresponsible. As former Secretary of Defense Melvin Laird put it, 'it was better to find that Saddam had not progressed as far as we thought in his WMD development than to discover belatedly that he had.'[37]

None of this is to deny that the intelligence services committed important errors here. Nor do we contest that any case for war that relies in large part on intelligence about capacities, not as a just response to malign intentions as revealed through actual attack, is a very risky undertaking. But the importance of the errors on Iraq's WMD was less in their inherent inaccuracy than in their consequences for the domestic and international credibility of the Bush administration. That is, serious as the error was on WMD, it was not easily avoidable. In part, this stems from the inherent difficulties in intelligence collection, where dangers of 'confirmation bias' and 'mirror imaging' are ever present (whether imagining falsely that an enemy has the same mindset as one's own [as in Saddam's 'rationality'] or failing to credit an enemy with such a mindset [as occurred in American underestimation of Japanese technical prowess at the outset of the Second World War]). A mass of weak evidence all supporting a proposition can, cumulatively, amount to strong evidence for it. In the Iraq case, even today, no one disputes that the decisions to coerce Saddam into readmitting inspectors or equipping coalition troops with chemical protection suits on the eve of war were wrong. The most central problem over intelligence was that the degree of certainty necessary for a totally undeniable or compelling case for war was not providable by intelligence alone. The policy-makers' convictions were stronger than the intelligence agencies in this instance, an understandable but highly significant difference post-9/11. That key Bush principals – along with Blair – wanted the evidence to support the case for war, and that intelligence officials have a natural desire generally to please their political masters is clear enough. Without question, more weight was placed on the intelligence evidence than it could, in retrospect, have reasonably borne. But the WMD Commission found no evidence of pressure from administration principals to distort intelligence. 'In short,' as Posner argues:

> it is only with the blinding clarity of hindsight, and an unrealistic optimism about what can be expected of intelligence, that the CIA and the other services (the WMD Commission criticized the Defense Intelligence Agency even more harshly) can be confidently declared to have blundered inexcusably in the matter of the Iraqi WMD, rather than to have done the best they could with the usual inadequate evidence on which intelligence services have to rely and the usual quota of blunders ... that all human activities involve, confronting – against a background of budgetary stringency throughout the 1990s – an unprecedented range of intelligence challenges.[38]

When dealing with rogue states, the partial reliance on intelligence – in the absence of effective enforcement of UN resolutions on transparency, access, and compliance – is likely to remain an unavoidable feature of risk assessment in the coming decades.

4. Desert Storm Mark II

Critics who claim that, even in the event of a threatened or actual Iraqi military attack with WMD, the West could simply repeat the 1991 campaign in response, are unpersuasive. Saddam's dogged pursuit of WMD since he came to power was one of the few constants of his dictatorship. Indeed, it was during Desert Storm that then Secretary of Defense Dick Cheney thanked the Israelis for their 1981 preemptive strike on the Osirak nuclear reactor, for which they had at the time been condemned by a unanimous UN Security Council (an attack the Iranians had also mounted earlier that year but failed to execute successfully, though tellingly to no subsequent UN condemnation). Without nuclear weapons, Saddam invaded Iran, murdered over 180,000 Kurds in Al Anfal in 1988, invaded Kuwait, launched missiles at Israel, Saudi Arabia, and Bahrain, and killed some 400,000 Iraqis. There is little doubt that for Saddam nuclear weapons would have been a 'menace multiplier' of incalculable dimensions. Had he possessed them in 1991, it is difficult to see whether or how the US would have deployed conventional force to eject him from Kuwait. The incentive to attack his neighbors and achieve regional hegemony, not least over energy supplies, would have been too tempting for Saddam to refuse. To all intents and purposes, the Iranian threat today echoes that of Saddam. Indeed, it was more the successful UN-sanctioned coalition attack in 1991, not bellicose threats of regime change after 2001, that reinforced the strong conviction of both Saddam and Tehran that acquiring nuclear bombs was a precondition of regime survival in the face of another US military response to their expansionist regional ambitions. The destabilization of the region, with all the consequences for oil supplies and global economic growth that would ensue, would have been as urgent (and perhaps more so) with Saddam still in power then as with the Iranian theocrats now. Not permanently divesting Saddam of WMD would have been an abdication of international responsibility of the highest order.

5. Preventive War

Iraq was a preventive, not a preemptive, war. As such, it was illegal under international law and the UN Charter, which allows for preemptive action against imminent attacks – such as Israel's preemption of Egypt, Syria, and Jordan in the 1967 Six-Day War – but not against emergent threats. But while illegal, in 9/11's aftermath the Iraq War was not illegitimate, any more so than the Kosovo War of 1999. Far from hiding his intentions, President Bush had explicitly acknowledged that the notion of waiting for an imminent threat to appear was one he rejected. As Bush declared in the 2003 State of the Union, 'Some have said we must not act until the threat is imminent.' But Bush expressly rejected such a pre-9/11 calculus. As then CIA Director George Tenet conceded, 'It was never a question of a known, imminent threat; it was about an unwillingness to risk surprise.'[39] Indeed, as even the UN implicitly recognized subsequently in developing the concept of the 'responsibility to protect,' it was more international law that was the problem than the appropriateness of the war.

It is indubitably the case that a more stable world would comprise a system whereby states recognized mutually agreed norms and adhered as closely as possible to these, both in terms of their external relations and their internal configuration. As Renshon notes, for all their sophistication, the closest that international relations theories have come to a near-scientific law is that mature democracies do not go to war with each other.[40] But as we know all too well, that universal concert of democracies is far from being realized. At the same time, moreover, it is necessary to accept the fact that not all states occupy the same position of power and responsibility for international order. Unless international law accommodates the realities of changing

power flows and imbalances, it invites irrelevance. In the post-9/11 era, it makes no sense to adhere without exception to norms that are eroding in the face of non-state transnational terror threats. It is not the notion that attacks should be preempted before they occur that is problematic, a notion that to most observers is less a radical innovation than long-acknowledged common sense.[41] Rather, the difficulty resides in gauging correctly what threats exist, where, and how best to engage in effective anticipatory defense against them.

In sum, we were unconvinced in 2002–3 of the more sanguine case against war. Saddam was certainly no Hitler, in 1991 or 2003, either in terms of his ideological convictions or the magnitude of the direct and immediate threat that he posed to the West. Nor was he a committed jihadist or Islamist in the mold of Khomeini or Bin Laden (although his instrumental willingness to invoke Islam when it suited his political purposes was as great as other Arab leaders, such as the Assads, as was his tactical pragmatism in the service of militarism). But he had a similarly megalomaniacal and inhumane personality. He was insulated from constructive or effective internal criticism. He was casual in his indiscriminate barbarity. Whether one regards him as inherently irrational or merely a recklessly poor gambler is less important than his abiding ambitions for military power, consistent record of territorial expansionism, and utter disregard of civilized norms of (internal and external) state conduct. For all the febrile focus of the international media and commentariat on Washington's machinations during 2002–3, it was the calculations in Baghdad that proved crucial and, ultimately, determinative of war.

Was it credible that an individual with Saddam's record would have voluntarily given up all his WMD? Had Saddam genuinely known that he lacked WMD, why did he not afford the UN inspectors complete and unfettered access? After all, this was all that was necessary to prevent an invasion. Instead, with coalition forces about to invade, with his presumed awareness of America's logistical and technical superiority gleaned from 1991, and with the obvious private enthusiasm of Iraq's neighbors for his removal all to hand, Saddam deliberately chose a course of steadfast defiance. Such a wanton disregard for his own regime's prospects, never mind the Iraqi people, plainly illustrated the danger that Saddam consistently constituted. Had the US not gone to war in 2003, then it would surely have had to do so later in the decade, albeit at a much greater risk of failure at a far higher cost in American fatalities. The dangers posed by Saddam may not have met the test of being 'clear and present' but, as Robert Lieber concluded:

> The prospects for containment and deterrence thus were not encouraging. The weight of the evidence suggested that Saddam constituted a dangerous and long-term strategic threat and that it was preferable to act before that threat materialized.[42]

On grounds of national and collective security, then, the case for a necessary war was compelling. As has been noted by critics of Bush, the WMD rationale was reached because it was the one imperative that the senior foreign policy principals were able to agree upon. Other elements of the case for war – the humanitarian case against dictatorship, the possibility of enhancing democratization and liberalization in the region through a successful 'demonstration effect,' the authority of the UN to enforce its own resolutions or risk a collapse of its political credibility – were also articulated by the administration in its effort to rally public support. That effort succeeded within America, despite vocal criticism. Washington failed, however, to win over international opinion. But this was less a matter of effective presentation and public relations than the more fundamental differences in threat perceptions that had arisen since the First Cold War's end. At its most elemental, as we stressed in chapter 3, Americans perceived the world still to be a very dangerous place, with threats requiring confrontation. Many others, especially in continental Europe, viewed the world through the peculiar prism of the EU, as a peaceful and benign order where negotiation and compromise could solve any and all misunderstandings. It is this more entrenched 'syndrome' – strategy versus sociology – as much as any Iraq one that will likely shape international relations for years to come.

Occupying Iraq: the lessons of Mesopotamia

Whatever the original reasons for supporting or opposing the war, once Saddam had been toppled in April 2003, the remarkable possibility of building a democratic and prosperous Iraq was at hand. But although Iraqis eventually tasted self-rule and twice, in their tens of thousands, braved murder to go to the polls to establish a new constitution and accountable governing authorities, the subsequent years of occupation proved desperately difficult and disappointing to all who hoped for a new, peaceful settlement.

Contrary to those many accounts that portray the occupation's problems as inevitable, apportioning blame in this regard is far from easy. Mismanagement and poor decision-making in Washington played a key role, as did the pressures for rapid results and a decisive draw down that the American political timetable invariably imposes on America's leaders. But so, too, did the failure of Iraqi leaders to grasp the opportunities that liberation had presented. While the term 'reconciliation' has no equivalent in Arabic, the mutual interests of Shiites, Sunnis, and Kurds in a viable and self-governing Iraq too often assumed second place to narrowly self-interested actions that inhibited effective state-building. The active obstructionism of Iraq's external neighbors – who shared an abiding interest in the failure of the US and of democracy-building in the Middle East – powerfully exacerbated its internal fissures.

Was the 'foreigner's gift' of liberation and democratic transformation doomed to fail?[43] In our view, no. Counterfactual reasoning is rarely scientific but four developments proved especially inimical to

presence would have prevented or effectively dealt with such a challenge to the fledgling Iraqi state but, as we note below in relation to the 2007–8 escalation of US forces, a larger military footprint together with a more judicious political strategy might well have facilitated the conditions (not only in Iraq but also in America) successfully to forge the new settlement in Mesopotamia.

2. Political failure

The second failure was that neither Jay Garner nor Paul Bremer achieved an effective system for managing the transition from Baathist tyranny to constitutional democracy. As Dodge observed, thirty-five years of Baathist rule meant that 'There was no civil society in Iraq before the US military reached Baghdad; Iraqi politics began from scratch in April 2003.'[46] The national elections of January 30, 2005 (that saw eight and a half million Iraqis vote, 58 percent of those eligible) and December 15, 2005 (with voter turnout increasing to 76 percent) represented triumphs of popular participation. All too peremptorily downplayed amid the growing chorus of criticism of the war effort, the elections testified to the Iraqi peoples' desire to participate in self-rule. In this respect, the hope of the war's supporters that a rare Arab democracy could be established in the aftermath of decades of tyranny was vindicated. In effect, though, the elections also represented and heralded a 'Lebanonized' acceptance of sectarianism in politics, with all the lack of coherence at the center of power that that implied. The electoral system based on large multi-party coalitions, combined with the relative powers accorded the president and prime minister, undermined the coherence of the new central government. By vesting real political power with political parties contesting elections, the cabinet was effectively rendered a mechanism for dividing up the spoils of office rather than a vehicle for national unity and state-building; post-war Iraq echoed the instability, parochialism, and corruption of post-Second World War Italy. A recipe for stability and national cohesion this was not.

3. State-building

The third negative development was the woeful absence of international support for reconstruction and state-building. As with the issue of the size of the occupation force, it is impossible to know with hindsight whether and how much a more concerted and broad-based international effort would have helped the occupation to succeed. But, as Cohen has stressed, even, indeed, especially, progressives could and should have embraced the effort to build a secular, self-governing, and economically viable Iraq once Saddam had been toppled. Just as opinion surveys reported that one-quarter of the French had wanted Saddam's Iraq to defeat the invading coalition forces in 2003, so for non-Americans to regard the 'insurgents' as anti-imperialist forces and therefore 'objective' allies of progressives was historically ill-informed and tragicomically wrong. It was an unfortunate measure of the degree to which the war had been so polarizing and divisive, however, that nations that 'objectively' had a stake in the success of the Iraq project, both in the region and further afield, lent neither finances nor personnel to assisting the transition to a stable and secure nation state:

> The anti-war movement disgraced itself not because it was against the war in Iraq, but because it could not oppose the counter-revolution once the war was over. A principled left that still had life in it and a liberalism that meant what it said might have remained ferociously critical of the American and British governments while offering support to Iraqis who wanted the freedoms they enjoyed . . .
>
> But again, no one who looked at the liberal-left from the outside could pretend that such principled stands were commonplace. The British Liberal Democrats, the continental social democratic parties, the African National Congress and virtually every leftish newspaper and journal on the planet were unable to accept that the struggle of Arabs and Kurds had anything to do with them. Mainstream Muslim organizations were as indifferent to the murder of Muslims by other Muslims in Iraq as in Darfur. For the majority of world opinion, Tony

Blair's hopes of 'giving people oppressed, almost enslaved, the prospect of democracy and liberty' counted for nothing. The worst of the lot were the organizers of the British anti-war demonstrations who turned out to be not so much against the war but on the wrong side.[47]

Disgracefully for many erstwhile progressives, 'punishing' Bush and America assumed a greater priority in their approach to Iraq than assisting state-building and opposing the forces of jihadism and tyranny in a newly liberated nation.

4. Maintaining public opinion at home and abroad

The fourth main error in the occupation was that the failure to deal effectively with sectarianism and terrorism strongly hampered coalition efforts to win enduring popular support, both in Iraq and the US. In essence, the occupation was being waged on two unsynchronized time-lines: those of Iraq and America (or, more precisely, Washington). As Niall Ferguson has compellingly argued, modern America suffers from three deficits: of manpower, of budgetary resources, and of attention.[48] Any one of these would pose serious problems in wartime. In Iraq, all three were painfully apparent and linked. Discharging the heavy responsibility of a successful occupation required not only patience but also a willingness to shed the blood and pay the heavy financial price that many Americans, particularly Democrats, were unwilling to accept. In some respects, this is eminently understandable. Non-existent WMD, abuse scandals and the daily media coverage of enduring violence together provided a graphically grim picture of the war's aftermath. In stark contrast to Germany and Japan after the Second World War, two nations thoroughly defeated, disgraced, and exhausted by war, Iraq appeared at best indifferent, at worst deeply hostile, to the forces that had achieved the end of Saddam's tyranny. Losing American lives every week and month in such an inimical setting required, on the part of many Americans, a willing suspension of disbelief they were unminded or unable to give. Increasingly, Iraq appeared to resemble a 'Vietnam in the sand.'[49]

But unlike Vietnam, the need for a lengthy US military presence was all the more pressing in Iraq precisely because of the historical divisions that any failure of state-building would exacerbate to lethal effect. As Robert Brigham observes, 'Iraq may have had all the essential elements of a state in the twentieth century, but there is little evidence of nationhood.'[50] The effort to rebuild the state and forge a new national settlement demanded patience from Americans as well as Iraqis. Compelling research shows that when the American public broadly agrees with the goals of a US military deployment and believes that it has a good prospect for success, Americans will tolerate significant military losses. In the Iraqi case, however, John Mueller contended that the lower tolerance for casualties and the precipitous decline in public support for the war were faster than most experts predicted because the American public 'places far less value on the stakes in Iraq' than it did previously on those in Korea and Vietnam.[51] Whatever the underlying reasons for that value judgment, Iraq reconfirmed a constant in American history that 'Americans do not have much patience for inconclusive conflicts.'[52]

Despite its geo-strategic imperatives, these four failures were calamitous for the success of the Iraq War. When and how America achieves an honorable exit from Iraq is as unclear as the prescriptive lessons that Iraq offers for future American strategy. But, as Steven Miller argues:

> Whatever the outcome in Iraq – however good or bad – no one is going to come away from this experience believing, as the Bush administration did at the outset of its Iraq experiment, that the political renovation of distant and alien lands is cheap and easy. On the contrary, Bush's experiment in social engineering in Iraq leads to the conclusion that externally imposed reform – gunpoint democratization – is very difficult and costly, as well as risky, hard to control, and unpredictable in result. It is unimaginable that this lesson will not color the perceptions of future decision-makers as they contemplate using force for the purpose of regime change.[53]

In the short to medium term, Iraq's legacies point to important – but not decisive – constraints on American primacy, unilateral action, and military might. Intelligence is as questioned as it is vital. Ironically, twice shy after its overestimation of Iraqi WMD, US intelligence agencies may now be seriously underestimating Iran's nuclear capacities. High-tech warfare alone cannot guarantee success against low-tech opponents engaged in the type of asymmetrical warfare – a concept embracing not just terrorism but propaganda, agitation, subversion, economic warfare, hit-and-run attacks, and cyber-warfare – that is now the warfare of choice of any opponent contemplating a fight against US power.[54] Approximately half a million troops is insufficient for an effective US military in the first decade of the war on Islamic terror. In the short term, other regional actors have gained in their ability to act as gadflies. Similarly, the US preoccupation with Iraq has hampered its ability to deal as effectively as it might in other pressing areas. Few analysts dispute that the war in Iraq has increased the number of terrorists operating in the region. The Bush administration's own NIE estimates agreed with this analysis. Against this, however, need to be placed three key points.

First, we simply have no way of knowing how many jihadists the war brought into existence who were not already becoming active, nor whether – in the absence of Iraq – these terrorists would instead have been peaceful and constructive citizens in their respective states and communities. A common criticism of the decision to wage war on Saddam was that it deflected attention from Afghanistan. This is valid inasmuch as it clearly did require significant redeployments from one theater to another. But the dispatch of some 160,000 forces to Afghanistan was never on the Bush administration's agenda, nor would it have been. In the absence of Iraq, al Qaeda's efforts to recruit jihadists would have continued apace. They would likely have been deployed in Afghanistan, Kashmir, Chechnya, Sudan, Somalia, Indonesia, Western Europe and elsewhere. Indeed, the greater the US and western presence – wherever in Muslim lands they are located – the more such forces become a priority for jihadist designs. The logical inference of the criticism is that Washington should simply never deploy forces to fight in Muslim nations for fear of generating new terrorists, a conclusion that may accord with some analysts' prescriptions but serves al Qaeda and jihadists most of all. 9/11 pre-dated Iraq and was, at root, the result of an excessive passivity on America's part in the 1990s. A return to passivity post-Iraq will not augur well for American security.

Second, the war brought many jihadists to Iraq but thereby killed many in the process. Indeed, the targeting of their fellow Muslims exposed jihadi piety and respect for Islam as a bogus fiction. The central fact of the 9/11 world, so graphically revealed on that clear September morning in 2001, is that the US and the West are engaged in an on-going generational conflict against jihadist Islam wherever it manifests itself. The implicit prescription of critics of the Iraq War – that, had it not been waged, the US would be safer – cannot be sustained without reverting to a pre-9/11 mindset. It is one which insists that a Middle East in which America is absent is a Middle East indifferent to America's fate.

Third, as we examined in the previous chapter, the linkage between increases in terrorist numbers and attacks in and on the West is simply unknowable. There can be no doubt that the war antagonized Muslims around the world, including those in America and Europe. But, as a number of first-hand accounts of radicalization attest, many so-called 'home-grown' and 'clean-skin' terrorists were motivated by conflicts far from Iraq, many of which had no direct connection to the 'West' such as Chechnya and Kashmir.[55] It is ironic that opponents of the war who castigated those linking Saddam and terrorists now attempt to link the war and terrorism in such all-embracing fashion. Had there been no invasion, the excoriation of Washington, for its sanctions and no-fly zones in Iraq, would have continued. Local conflagrations of Muslim-on-Muslim and Muslim-on-non-Muslim violence would have precipitated Islamists to castigate the West either for its omissions or its commissions. Alienated young Muslims across the globe would have located a convenient scapegoat for their predicaments in mendacious American/neoconservative/Jewish/British plots.

It is curious, then, that critics who deny that the war on terror has any affinities with the struggle against communism so readily employ the Iraq/Vietnam analogy. As Brigham notes, 'To reason by historical analogy requires making distinctions.'[56] Comparisons of Iraq with Vietnam should be ventured with care. Indeed, when George Bush used the analogy himself, to highlight the costs of US withdrawal from Iraq, he was berated by those who treated the analogy as their exclusive preserve.[57]

As even war critics such as Freedman have noted, we still do not know the ultimate outcome in Iraq. Even if a substantial US draw down occurs:

> The presumption of an orderly transition may involve a suspension of disbelief, in terms of the assumptions made about governmental authority, national unity and embryonic democracy. Yet the result is also unlikely to involve a clear victory for an organized enemy. The problem left behind after Vietnam was a unified country under a communist regime; the problem left behind after Iraq is more likely to be fragmentation and anarchy.[58]

Proponents of American withdrawal, who simply assume that Iraqis will then roll up their sleeves and get down to the task of rebuilding their nation that they shirked while free-riding on American goodwill, are unlikely to be vindicated.

If the problem for the invaded nation is dissimilar, so too is the home context of the war. While the US military emerged after Vietnam with an aversion to counter-insurgency operations and a commitment to greater care in choosing its battles and using force, its reception back home was wholly dissimilar during the Iraq War. In Vietnam, there was no welcome for many veterans. Many were

shamefully pilloried and abused by their countrymen, an experience
that soured American politics during the 1970s and contributed to
the shift of veterans and the military into the ranks of the Republican
Party. In Iraq, by contrast, there was powerful recognition and thanks
for their sacrifice among the American public even as that public
turned decisively against the war. 'Support Our Troops' yellow ribbon
bumper stickers are commonplace in America today. If Americans
increasingly came to view Iraq as the 'wrong war' to fight, it did not
taint the rightness of the broader war on terror.

Iraq's implications for military doctrine are also rather different to
those of Vietnam. It was clearly the case that Vietnam inhibited the
use of force by successive administrations. From the beginning of
the Korean War in 1950 to Vietnam's conclusion in 1975, 100,000
American troops died in combat. From 1975 until 2000, a similar
twenty-five-year period, fewer than 5,000 troops lost their lives in
combat.[59] The Weinberger and Powell Doctrines on the use of force,
while widely accepted in the military, caused notable concern among
diplomats from George Shultz in the 1980s to Madeleine Albright in
the 1990s, who knew that diplomacy without the threat of force was
usually doomed. But America's military superiority is now so great,
and the number of circumstances requiring large-scale deployments
of ground forces so modest, that any inhibition on the use of force is
likely to be limited post-Iraq. Even had Iraq been a rapid and decisive success, the notion of American ground forces then merrily
moving on to invade Syria, Iran, and Saudi Arabia was fantasy.

Finally, while Vietnam complicated but essentially reinforced an
existing doctrine of containment of communism, Iraq is unlikely to
undermine the 'meta-narrative' of the war on terror. Certainly, as
with Vietnam, the lessons that politicians draw – whether welcoming
restraint as wise prudence or regretting an aversion to force as an
unfortunate pathology in a dangerous world – are unlikely to be
uniform. Moreover, it is improbable that future administrations and
congresses would wish to repeat the Bush experience in Iraq. But while

some Americans embraced notions of détente with the Soviet Union and China and others human rights and limits after Vietnam, the geo-political realities post-Iraq remain largely the same. Détente with jihadists or Iran is a notion that few Americans entertain seriously. As the 2006 NSS warned on the dangers of inaction in a post-9/11 world:

> The greater the threat, the greater is the risk of inaction – and the more compelling the case for taking anticipatory action to defend ourselves, even if uncertainty remains as to the time and place of the enemy's attack.[60]

For those who are already penning their rejoinders to future assertions of US power under the title 'Another Iraq?,' it is worth recalling Mel Laird's retort to those who used the Vietnam war 'as their bully pulpit to mold an isolationist American foreign policy':

> They join their voices with those who claim that the current war is 'all about oil,' as though the loss of that oil were not enough of a global security threat to merit any US military intervention and especially not "another Vietnam".[61]

Brigham does see a parallel 'Iraq syndrome' now echoing that of Vietnam. But he also observes that, if one lesson of both conflicts is that America must use its power wisely, 'Another is that trouble will find a nation of America's power and responsibility without the United States looking for it.'[62] Post-9/11, that is especially resonant. As we emphasize in chapters 7 and 8, the international system's contours remain familiar, and the fundamental strategic logic underlying the decision to go to war in Iraq has not been abandoned and remains influential, and deeply rooted, in both American political parties. It is therefore not a question of whether America will go to war again in coming years, but when and how. In that regard, neither the specific option of preventive war nor the broader Bush Doctrine has been exhausted by the mismanagement in Iraq.

Iraq and the future of American power

Three features of the Iraq War's conduct stand out for future administrations and the fate of American power.

First, while the American public is unlikely to exhibit unanimity
over war, the case for war needs to be made clearly and fully so as to
guarantee maximum public support. It needs, as Dean Acheson once
said of the case for containing communism, to be 'clearer than the
truth.' As we noted in chapter 2, Americans are 'pretty prudent' and
rational when it comes to questions of war. Americans are neither
warmongers nor pacifists. But the contours of the post-9/11 world are
more complex and opaque than those of the First Cold War. The
combination of technological superiority, skill, and sophistication of
the US military helped wage increasingly 'bloodless' interventions
during the 1990s, a development that contributed to public disillu-
sion with American losses in Iraq after 2003. Wars involving large-
scale ground forces and occupations are, and always were after the
First Cold War's end, likely to be few and far between. But selective
and small-scale ground deployments, military strikes, naval block-
ades, special operations, and 'black-ops' are all going to continue to
be a necessary part of the Second Cold War. Whether it proves a
success, a calamity or something in between, the broader security
conflict should not be obscured by the specific case of Iraq. As such,
the political class needs to articulate the stakes, rationale, and costs
of America's global commitments. However apparently peaceful and
prosperous it may be, America cannot afford another 1990s-style
'holiday from history.'

Second, political and military leaders need to prepare adequately
for the aftermath of war as well as its execution. There remains no
other military that can overcome the US in a direct war. But much
of the function that the US will need to perform will involve state-
building activities. There is no reason why a revival of the Powell
Doctrine of overwhelming force cannot also be married to a diversity

of post-conflict and stabilization activities. To some extent, as it invariably does, the military has already analyzed its recent experiences and recalibrated its posture.[63] Counter-insurgency now looms larger in its strategy and preparations. Doctrine has been modified. Calls for a substantial increase in permanent-level army and Marine personnel now receive sympathetic hearings on Capitol Hill. But there remains much more to be done to preserve and refine the capacity of the world's finest fighting forces to meet the challenges of this century fully and effectively. Politics, domestic and international, and contingency will shape decisions as to how and when to deploy, but an adequate pool of personnel, resources, and platforms is a prerequisite of defense policy.[64]

Third, coordination within Washington, as well as between Washington and other capitals, is paramount in time of war. There are no academic models that can guarantee that this occurs. If it is a hallmark of academic life, it is also ironic that so many critics with relatively modest records are so generous in their public advice on strategy, tactics, and planning. Indeed, it is something of a paradox that so many Democrats criticized the 2003 invasion partly by comparing it unfavorably with the 1991 war, a campaign that most congressional Democrats at the time voted against. At minimum, however, the president needs to be actively involved in the process at all stages. The balance here is a delicate one. Military planning should not be micromanaged by civilians with minimal experience of conflict situations, whether in the Oval Office or Congress. As we observed in chapter 1, it is a peculiar but recurrent pattern now that most modern presidents, and most aspirant presidential candidates, have little if any prior experience of combat or of diplomacy before entering the White House (Eisenhower, Kennedy and George H. W. Bush were exceptions). As the Democrats' difficulties in imposing political conditions on the presence in Iraq over 2007–8 attested, the military has a level of respect among Americans matched by few other institutions.[65] At the same time, though, the principle of civilian control of the military remains sacrosanct under the Constitution.[66] Ultimately, it falls to the president to make the decisions that matter on such questions – all the more reason why national security should and will be a key consideration in presidential elections. The time when grand strategy did not figure in such elections is, thankfully, long past.

Ultimately, in strategy, as in medicine, diagnosis dictates remedy. Whether or not the 'surge' strategy adopted by the Bush administration in early 2007 ultimately succeeds or is ended by congressional efforts to pull out remains to be seen. Powerful arguments were ventured for its success, and for sufficient patience and resolve in Washington to allow this to occur.[67] In 2007, there were witness indications of an effective new strategy under General David Petraeus. Rather than pursuing General George Casey's strategy of 'clear, hold and build,' which had the inadvertent effect of leaving Iraqis vulnerable to sectarians once the US forces left an area, the counter-insurgency approach looked to protect those parts of Iraq's population in trouble. Rather than hand over responsibility to Iraq's government, which often saw serious weaknesses in central government ministries and non-existent links between the center and provincial and local governments, the new approach focused on the government's capacity to function effectively. Finally, rather than tolerate sectarianism and corruption within the government and armed forces, the new approach sought actively to empower Iraqi nationalists while purging militant sectarians and corrupt officials. As even two critics of Bush noted, the surge had created the possibility that Iraq could still be 'a war we just might win.'[68]

But many of the changed realities on the ground did not register in Washington, where the impetus to withdraw had made critics of the administration impervious to the possibility of success. Much popular commentary on the war depicted a wholesale American exit from Iraq as politically imperative and easily achievable. But more judicious commentators appreciated that no precipitous withdrawal was possible, for strategic and political reasons. Logistically and tactically, some twelve to eighteen months was a minimum for a consequential withdrawal. Moreover, in order to draw down deliberately while preserving maximum credibility in a painfully compromising situation, the 'narrative' would need to be shaped simultaneously to deter insurgent attacks and maintain the confidence of allies while not emboldening adversaries. This narrative, as Steve Simon described it, 'comes down to ensuring that no American leaves under fire from the embassy roof in a helicopter':

> Disengagement and the diplomacy that must accompany it should be initiated immediately, before the costs of the war begin to widen: a looming threat to Jordan's stability; the empowerment of a radicalized Iran; rise of ominous anxieties in Turkey and the Persian Gulf states; strained alliance relations; Washington's prolonged distraction from seething problems in Afghanistan, Pakistan and Palestine; the weakening of Arab moderate voices; fuming animosity toward the United States throughout the Muslim world; reinvigorated jihadi sentiment; and of course the direct cost measured in the loss of American blood and treasure.[69]

But, as Simon acknowledged, the prospects for acting 'decisively and creatively' across the Middle East to 'offset perceptions of American weakness' were hindered by the on-going weakness and unwillingness of other interlocutors, respectively, the Palestinians and the Iranians. Those well-intentioned and distinguished American critics calling for a withdrawal believed that this was the least painful and most promising option for America and Iraq. On both scores, their confidence was perhaps less than well founded.

Contrary to some commentary on a possible exit from Iraq, a withdrawal would likely require US logistical, command-and-control, and airpower support for years to come. A withdrawal from Baghdad and Anbar province would require not just troops but civilian reconstruction teams and contractors, along with embassy personnel and thousands of ordinary Iraqis who assisted US forces, to be protected.

American training and mentoring units would be extremely vulnerable. At minimum, a substantial rapid reaction, and possible evacuation, force would be required to be located nearby to extract those in threat. Some residual capacity to strike al Qaeda and associated terrorists and to deny them an uncontested sanctuary would also be necessary, requiring intelligence units and Special Operations who in turn would need back-up from rapid reaction and logistical support.[70]

Any proposal to pull most American forces out of Iraq by the end of 2008 would run up against what Kitfield and Friel termed the 'ineluctable logic of the military's strength curve': 'The more forces you withdraw and the farther away they are from the point of any required action, the more risk you assume in terms of their effectiveness and vulnerability.'[71] They cited a January 2007 report by Kenneth Pollack and Daniel Byman that examined eleven civil wars from Lebanon to Somalia and found that in nearly every instance civil wars and collapsed states attracted the military intervention of neighbors who saw their interests threatened.[72] Were such a civil war to follow a US withdrawal, a similar scenario would arise:

> If US forces withdraw, there's a good chance the Iraqi conflict is going to escalate, and that will almost certainly draw in neighbors who feel compelled, for opportunistic or defensive reasons, to get involved.[73]

A redeployment that seeks to contain any such spillover effect would at minimum see US forces remaining on Iraq's borders, most plausibly in Kuwait and possibly Jordan, and even in Iraq's relatively peaceful Kurdish north to stave off a move towards independence that might incite conflict with Turkey. A US force posture relocated north and south of Baghdad with eventual redeployment to these areas could perhaps offer a possibility to deal effectively with the range of likely eventualities – from terrorism to refugee flows – that would likely ensue. How stable such a posture could be over the longer term, however, remains uncertain. In short, no complete withdrawal is feasible without precipitating painful consequences.

Even were an orderly and effective exit to be feasible, its benefits would likely be short-lived at best. Leaving a broken Iraq in the Middle East would offer international terrorists a reliable and strategically promising safe haven and ensure a legacy of chaos for future generations. In the face of a collapsed state dominated by a full-scale civil war, the immense sacrifices of the Iraqi men and women who stood up to the terrorists and sectarians would amount to naught, while extinguishing the last shreds of Arab and Kurdish confidence in American good intentions and credibility. However carefully presented the justification, the retreat from Iraq will be interpreted in the Middle East as a defeat as momentous and consequential as that of the USSR in Afghanistan. As such, it will be seen as vindication of the notion – long held by Bin Laden, Saddam, Khomeini, Assad, and other anti-American despots – that the US is a paper tiger, unwilling to expend the blood and treasure necessary to maintain global order. Moreover, Washington's ability to force upon the region, and the distinct terrorist strands within, what we describe in chapter 7 as the necessary choice between violence and politics, will be severely compromised at a moment when the need to counter sectarian forces of bigotry and violence is greater than ever. As David Rothkopf observes:

> Whether stability is brought about by the spread of democracy or by other, interim means, we must recognize that it is the decay of Middle Eastern civilization that is the threat to us; the terrorists bred by that decay are only a symptom of the bigger problem. They must be crushed, but we must also eliminate the forces that create new armies of terrorists each year.[74]

A precipitous departure from Mesopotamia is likely to retard, not advance, America's Second Cold War against jihadist terror.

Conclusion

As Tocqueville observed, 'There are two things that a democratic people will always have much trouble in doing: beginning a war and ending it.'[75] Iraq, for Americans, is a clear example of his maxim. Historians, political scientists, and international relations scholars even today are divided over the merits of the Vietnam War, its strategies, tactics, and consequences. Some, who strongly opposed the Iraq War, had previously adopted revisionist interpretations of Vietnam that judged it, in hindsight, a 'necessary war.'[76] We doubt, in terms of popular and academic controversy, that Iraq will prove much different. The Bush administration's mistakes in not planning for the post-war occupation, 'unconscionable' as they were,[77] should not detract from the fundamental correctness of the original deci-sion to invade, and the grand strategy and national security calculus underlying that decision. Robert G. Kaufman summarizes the case well:

> Victory in Iraq is a vital national interest for the United States in waging the war on terror. It will make America safer and stronger by removing a dangerous tyranny, keep terrorists on the run by depriving them of the sanctuary of a rogue regime, and embolden the forces of democratic reform in a region that sorely needs freedom to address the real root cause of terror. Conversely, failure in Iraq would undermine the credibility of American power in the eyes of our friends and enemies, destabilize the entire Middle East, vindicate the brutal tactics of our adversaries, and hence invite more dangerous attacks on the United States and its allies.[78]

The potentially catastrophic risks of inaction on Iraq in a post-9/11 era – for the nation, region and world – had to be set against the potential risks of action. Reasonable people did, and still do, disagree on that balance, as they do over the vexing problem of Iran's nuclear ambitions. In the context of the unfolding situation on the ground, however, history's verdict is unlikely to be clear or conclusive for many years to come.

The decisions of the next administration and Congress will exert a powerful influence on the outcome of the occupation. If an 'Iraq syndrome' does condition American foreign policy, few within or outside America should welcome the prospect. The years following America's exit from Vietnam were undistinguished ones for the US and the democratic world. Nor, ultimately, did the most vocal opponents of Vietnam benefit from America's defeat. Indeed, just as congressional Democrats were in the vanguard of the push to quit Vietnam, only subsequently and for decades to be branded as 'weak on defense,' so a perilous and messy exit from Iraq may 'blowback' on today's generation of Democrats (a fact readily appreciated by more pragmatic progressives who recognize the imperative of strong national security credentials).[79] To the extent that the 'Democratic party is beginning to sound like an echo chamber for Zbigniew Brzezinski, the national security adviser for the most inept and calamitous Democratic administration of modern times,' its fate is bound to the outcome in Iraq as much as that of the Bush administration itself.[80]

Iraq was mismanaged but not misconceived, an unsound application of a sound doctrine. That distinction remains crucial to current and future American commitments of blood and treasure. As Steven Miller has written:

> the disappointing experience in Iraq undermines the appeal of Bush's strategy but does not overturn the logic of preventive war and regime change as the Bush administration has articulated it. Iraq suggests that the costs of this strategy are significantly higher than proponents of the war had hoped, but Bush and Cheney have made it abundantly clear that to prevent a future 11 September – in particular a nuclear 11 September – they are prepared to pay whatever price is necessary. If it is costly to undertake steps essential, as they see it, to protect the United States from terrible attacks, so be it. Despite Iraq, for many in the American debate and for those at the highest levels of the Bush administration, the rationale that weaves together a preference for the offensive, regime change and preventive war is still operative. Viewed through this lens, the painful experience in Iraq, however unpleasant and undesirable it may be, does not undercut the premises that led to the adoption of the Bush strategy in the first place.[81]

In crafting US grand strategy, those premises – disturbed but not displaced by Iraq – are ones that Bush's successors should, and in all likelihood will, attend to at least as closely. We hold that they should also inform strategy toward the broader Middle East, to which we turn next.

6

The Middle East: reformation or Armageddon

Nuclear arms in the Middle East
Israel's attacking the Iraqis
The Syrians are mad at the Lebanese
And Baghdad does whatever she please
Looks like another threat to world peace
For the envoy
Warren Zevon, The Envoy (1981)[1]

The main concern of fundamentalist Islam is with moderate Islam, and especially those Islamic states which, if they have not precisely embraced democracy, have nevertheless tried to banish theocracy from the business of government. That fundamentalism loathes the Western democracies goes without saying: or rather, it goes with a lot of saying, at the top of the voice. But the real horror, for the diehard theocrats, is the country with a large number of Muslims that has been infiltrated by the liberal ideas of the West. As a rule of thumb, you can say that the terrorists would like to wreak edifying vengeance on any predominantly Islamic country where you can see even a small part of a woman's face.
Clive James, 'A Nightclub in Bali'[2]

When you say 'Islamic terrorists,' the only people you're insulting are . . . Islamic terrorists. And really, we don't care if we insult them.
Rudy Giuliani[3]

Why is foreign aid not contingent upon warning recipient states that
they will forfeit it if clerics they subsidize preach hatred of the West?
Why aren't we helping Afghanistan or Pakistan to build secular alternatives to the Saudi-financed madrassas where children are brain-
washed with cartoon Jew killers? If this is a neo-Cold War, why are we
failing to help the four fifths of Muslims who are not from the Middle
East to assert themselves against that demented region?

Michael Burleigh[4]

In this chapter, we advance the argument that the key to winning the
Second Cold War on Islamist terror rests on successfully reforming the
Middle East and assisting its peoples to reach a genuine and lasting
reconciliation between the 'non-negotiable demands of human dignity' and the faith of Islam. However skilled or fortuitous, no single
American administration will be able to accomplish this formidable
task, which is the work of decades ahead and will witness many rever-
sals before any eventual success is in prospect. Indeed, ultimately,
Washington can only cajole and nudge a steady reformation of the
region's political, economic and religious transformation. The central
force in establishing regimes that are accountable, self-governing,
based on the consent of the people and respectful of human dignity
must be the people of the Arab and Muslim states themselves.

Nonetheless, this task is as urgent as any in international affairs,
and the US can and must assist this modernization process as fully as
possible. A continuation of the present dysfunctional regimes will
not only deepen the parlous state of the region and the deprivation
of millions within but will hasten a regional conflagration with devastating consequences for the people of the Middle East and for
American, European, and other interests worldwide. 9/11's central
lesson – that no nations, however powerful and distant, can isolate
themselves from the deep maladies and profound antagonisms of
other parts of the globe – needs still to be forcefully understood.

We proceed by first considering the nature of America's involvement in the Middle East and the powerful continuities underpinning

this. We then examine the merits and demerits of Bush foreign policy toward the region. Finally, we discuss possible alternative courses and make several recommendations. In analyzing the region's maladies and the dim prospects for their amelioration, we are mindful of the fluidity of politics, the profound challenge that the region poses policy-makers and the limits on American influence. The region is, in the apt characterization of Richard Haass, 'an unstable and often violent cauldron of competing local states, terrorist groups, failed and failing countries, and sectarian violence with outside powers possessing only limited capacity to order regional developments.'[5]

Dennis Ross, a former US envoy, outlined three abiding features of the dismal regional landscape: 'first, every vacuum in that region is filled by violence; second, every diplomatic opening tends to close quickly; and third, the war on terrorism is actually a war against radical Islam.'[6] While Washington and its allies need to craft their priorities and policies to attend to the particular vagaries, distinct interests, and divergent peoples of each nation in the region, the overarching vision uniting these policies needs to be premised on the twin imperatives of advancing reform and ending the 'terror dividend' that erstwhile allies currently reap. Brzezinski, Nye, and other international relations scholars are right to employ the metaphor of a 'grand chessboard' to characterize international affairs, in which the moves of individual players are intimately and inextricably connected.[7] But they need also to pay greater attention to the central fact about the 'game' of chess, one ironically missing from their accounts: the game consists of two sides only, each intent upon a clear and decisive victory. This is as true of the Second as it was of the First Cold War.

Power, faith, and fantasies

The 9/11 attacks, followed by the US military campaigns in Afghanistan and Iraq, made Middle East policy the defining and most controversial feature of George W. Bush's presidency. Whilst prior presidents had pronounced 'doctrines' that conceded the importance of the Middle East to US interests (the Truman Doctrine indirectly, and the Eisenhower and Carter Doctrines directly), the change under Bush was as courageous to his supporters as it was reckless to his critics. For the first time, the Middle East assumed center stage in American foreign policy. Beyond the shift in priority, the substance of policy also appeared to assume a new direction. Bush's public commitment to a 'forward strategy' of freedom, his commitment ultimately to 'end tyranny' around the world, and his Doctrine's embrace of preventive war, regime change and democratization rejected and reversed the stability-oriented principles and caution of his White House predecessors. In grasping the 'third rail' of international politics, the president took an immense gamble on his place in history, on the fate of millions within and outside the Middle East, and on the shape of international security for years to come.

Yet, as Michael Oren has argued, strong elements of continuity exist in relations between the US and the Middle East. America's entanglement in the region, from North Africa to Afghanistan, has been reliably shaped for 200 years by a combination of 'power, faith and fantasy.'[8] From the wars against the Barbary pirates – America's first encounter with Islamic terrorists (when 'Mussulman' pirates terrorized shipping and threatened trade along the North African shore of the Mediterranean), America's relations with the region were shaped by a mixture of war, trade, and evangelism.[9] Washington's rise to globalism during the twentieth century increasingly placed an American geo-political imprint upon the Middle East. American idealism not only caused missionaries to evangelize and establish liberal schools and colleges there (such as the American University of Beirut, established in 1866) but also to support efforts to resist European colonialism and restore the Jews to the Promised Land. American fantasies, too, played an influential role in romanticizing the mysterious East among American elites. The relative weight of these three forces inevitably shifted over time, not least in the post-1945 period as the demands of geo-political leadership caused Washington mostly to allow its interests to trump its idealism, as the containment of communism and the imperative of assuring access to reliable and affordable oil supplies led successive administrations to align alongside repressive regimes in Iran, Saudi Arabia, the Gulf states, and Egypt. Such an alignment, along with the strong support accorded Israel, together yielded a lethal form of 'blowback' in rising Islamist terrorism against American interests, personnel and the homeland itself in the latter decades of the twentieth century and the first decade of the twenty-first. As Oren notes, though, the same confluences and divergences between power, on the one hand, and faith and fantasy, on the other, animated America's relations with the region throughout its history.

It was not only the American side that displayed such tensions. For much of the last century, America was viewed positively across the region. To the extent that Arab encounters with America occurred, unsullied by European colonialism, they were relatively modest and positive. Even during the post-Second World War years, few Middle East states displayed a consistent, principled anti-Americanism. As Rachel Bronson details, for example, Saudi Arabia shared America's detestation of godless communism and benefited immeasurably from American know-how to exploit its oil resources.[10] Egypt equivocated between hopes of enlisting the American giant on its side and resisting its encroachments. During their on-going conflict, Iraq and Iran, despite (or rather, in part, because of) their deep animosities, hoped to find a decisive partner in Washington. For many states, trapped in a Byzantine maze of shifting antipathies and pathologies, pragmatism frequently triumphed over principle. Power, faith, and fantasy (the latter extending to conspiracy theories about American, British, and Jewish designs and influence) applied to the region's take on America as much as Washington's on the region. If too many American leaders evinced a crude orientalism, that crudeness was mirrored by the 'occidentalist' view taken of the West, and America in particular, by many Arabs and Muslims.[11]

A recognition of the competing impulses to US policy, and the tensions inherent therein, is therefore a prerequisite to understanding past, present, and future strategies. As we argue elsewhere in this book, too great a focus on the particular personalities of the day can obscure the forces of continuity that typically underpin international relations. This is doubly so in that any international relationship displays structural features that condition the reciprocal interaction of both parties. In the US case, these encompass American exceptionalism, Washington's preeminent position in the international system, and the domestic political setting (from the constitutional design to the two-party system). In the Middle East, these include thousands of years of development, antagonisms within the region and toward outside powers, and a range of successes and failures, fissures, and coalitions that have shaped its rise and fall.

Echoes of recently damning assessments of Bush's policies can easily be found in relation to his predecessors. For example, in reviewing the legacy of one much misunderstood and 'misunderestimated' Republican president's Middle East policy, John Lewis Gaddis wrote that:

> Unilateral security guarantees could be taken as excuses for American intervention, as the hostile Arab reaction to the 1957 Eisenhower Doctrine showed: that single proclamation, pledging the United States to defend 'the Middle East' against 'overt armed aggression from any nation controlled by International Communism,' dissipated overnight the goodwill Washington had won in the Arab world by opposing the British-French-Israeli invasion of Egypt the year before. And, of course, none of this ensured that nations being protected by the United States shared the administration's perception of interests and threats, or that they would turn their nationalism against communism in the way Washington wanted them to.[12]

Such a perception gap has been a relative constant throughout the First Cold War period down to today, partly because of a failure to accept the fact that the US has pursued multiple goals that have been in tension, if not outright conflict. Four lodestars shaped American interests, ideals, and interventions from 1945 to 2001. First, Washington's key First Cold War priority was vigorous containment of communist expansion, a policy that necessarily entailed according support to authoritarian opponents of godless Moscow – Saudi Arabia, the Shah's Iran, and Pakistan – and assistance to Islamist forces resisting the Soviet occupation of Afghanistan after 1979. Second, a commitment to the establishment, and subsequently the preservation, of the state of Israel made Washington's dealings with Arabs and Muslims immensely more difficult. This was especially the case after the US provided decisive military assistance to Israel during the Yom Kippur War of 1973, prior to which its support had been clear but relatively modest. Third, reliable access to energy supplies represented a necessary, if insufficient, condition of American and global economic well-being, requiring cordial relations with oil-producing states in the Persian Gulf. At times, as during 1987–8, this entailed the dispatch of naval forces, which heightened the possibility of war. Fourth, extending support to 'friendly' authoritarian regimes was typically viewed by Republican and Democratic administrations as the optimal means to contain regional security threats and guarantee energy access while providing a modicum of stability to a region plagued by internecine conflicts of religion, tribe, ideology, and nationalism. Presidents from Truman to Clinton rarely challenged the premise that American interests required that Washington play down its ideals and ignore the reality of repressive Arab governance. Indeed, with few (though significant) exceptions, Washington's attentions to the region were invariably spasmodic and reactive rather than anticipatory and proactive in advancing internal change. Moreover, until 9/11, the Middle East was secondary to Europe and Asia in American grand strategy.

Striking the 'Great Satan': sympathy for the devil

After 9/11, the Middle East became the central focus of American foreign policy. Al Qaeda's attack prompted an alteration in Washington's preferences as well as priorities. First Afghanistan, then Iraq and the broader region, became the focal point for applying the Bush Doctrine. Initially, until 9/11, Bush had evinced minimal interest in Middle Eastern problems or politics, with the exceptions of Israel and Iraq. In one of his relatively few international forays prior to 2000, Bush's visit to Israel before becoming president confirmed the pro-Israeli political dynamics of the Republican electoral coalition – this despite the fact that historically American Jews vote Democratic. Clinton's failure to secure a peace deal in 2000, the second *intifada* and concomitant Israeli security response, and the highly personalized politics favored by Bush in his diplomacy (that cast Yasir Arafat as a mendaciously unreliable supporter of terror) augured strongly against a direct and intimate involvement in the search for peace in the Holy Land. Iraq, on some accounts, was one example of presidential curiosity as to available policy options, including military action, for change. However, prospects for an invasion were slim in 2001.[13] It was 9/11 that transformed the direction, priorities, and instruments of Bush's Middle Eastern agenda.

Three aspects of the region informed Bush's response. First, the supply of 'superterrorists,' although not exclusively located there, drew most directly and to most destructive force from the Middle East's conflicts. Second, the three Ts nexus – of terrorism, technology, and tyranny – threatened more costly 9/11s. Third, to the extent that the domestic structures of undemocratic regimes could be linked to their destabilizing behavior in foreign policy, the issues of liberalization and democratization and the most effective instruments and tactics to promote these became urgent matters for America. As we outlined earlier, Bush's response was to reject the 'narrow realism' of his father's administration and the 'wishful liberalism' of Clinton in

favor of a 'distinctly American internationalism.' This married
Wilsonian ideals to realist means, focusing on regime change in addition to containment, prevention as well as deterrence, and preserving American primacy. It also appeared to reject the stability-based
precepts of prior administrations. As Bush put it during a speech in
London in November 2003:

> We must shake off decades of failed policy in the Middle East. Your
> nation and mine, in the past, have been willing to make a bargain, to
> tolerate oppression for the sake of stability. Long-standing ties often
> led us to overlook the faults of local elites.[14]

But the faltering Iraqi occupation, continued violence in Palestine,
growing instability in Lebanon, the resurgence of the Taliban in
Afghanistan, and the rise of Iranian influence together suggested to
critics that a forward strategy of freedom was causing America's
regional influence to regress. The transformation that Bush had
promised was working against American interests, not for them:

> With the air already poisoned by Iraq and continued violence in Israel
> and Palestine, this *mea culpa* generated very little (if any) goodwill.
> Simply put, US action abroad sets the context for dialogue, and even
> significant shifts in rhetoric *vis-à-vis* the Middle East will remain a
> distant second to recorded votes (in the UN), the distribution of aid and
> observable intentions. This is particularly true when those interven-
> tions are as momentous as regime change in Iraq and tend to reinforce
> the prevailing views of what really drives American foreign policy.[15]

There certainly can be little doubt that anti-Americanism has
grown from an already fertile base, not least among those allies and
aid recipients most favored by America (Egypt, Saudi Arabia, and
Jordan). The depth and breadth of anti-Americanism meant that, as
Jonathan Stevenson argued:

> Negative Muslim perceptions of the United States make controversial
> but largely non-optional US policies in the Middle East, the Gulf and

the wider Muslim world all the more difficult to execute. Immediately after 11 September, the Qatar-based satellite television station al-Jazeera resolutely portrayed Muslims as victims of a 'crusade' in Afghanistan – a term initially and unfortunately used by the Bush administration itself in characterizing the intervention – rather than culprits in the attacks that necessitated a self-defensive intervention against the Taliban and al-Qaeda. The network also manifested a kind of cognitive dissonance, championing Bin Laden as a righteous defender of Islam . . . while denying his involvement in the attacks that bestowed that status.[16]

Such perceptions reflect and reinforce a widespread view of America that is untroubled by dispassion and balance. Any objective analysis of American military interventions can hardly cast Washington as a regional villain or Islamophobic power. During the last half-century, in eleven of twelve major conflicts between Muslims and non-Muslims, the US sided with the Muslim/Arab groups. American backing for Israel has been the sole significant exception, with the US helping Israel to survive efforts from Arab states and terrorists to remove it from the map. As Barry Rubin notes:

It has been the United States' perceived softness in recent years, rather than its bullying behavior, that has encouraged anti-Americans to act on their beliefs. After the United States failed to respond aggressively to many terrorist attacks against its citizens, stood by while Americans were seized as hostages in Iran and Lebanon, let Saddam Hussein remain in power while letting the shah fall, pressured its friends and courted its enemies, and allowed its prized Arab–Israeli peace process to be destroyed, why should anyone have respected its interests or fear its wrath? . . . further concessions will only encourage even more contempt for the United States and make the anti-American campaign more attractive . . . If Arab anti-Americanism turns out to be grounded in domestic maneuvering rather than American misdeeds, neither launching a public relations campaign nor changing Washington's policies will affect it . . . Only when the systems that manufacture and encourage anti-Americanism fail will popular opinion also change.[17]

The tenacity with which febrile notions of American designs and influence win currency in the Islamic world is remarkable. Indeed, this should be factored into discussions of American 'soft' power winning 'hearts and minds.' As Bernard Lewis noted, when Khomeini and other fanatics labeled America the 'Great Satan' they chose their term carefully. Satan is a seducer more than he is a warrior. It is the power to tempt 'good Muslims' into a degenerate, infidel mindset and lifestyle that is the devil's greatest threat. It is not what America does that accounts for Muslim rage. To parrot this notion as a rational explanation, demanding a change in policy that will then lead to cordial relations, is to ignore the reality that, for Islamists, what America is generates resentment, anger, and envy. It is this paradox ('Yankee go home! And take me with you!') that, among other problems, precludes the success of a 'hearts and minds'-based strategy. As Lewis observed:

> from the writings of Khomeini and other ideologists of Islamic funda-mentalism, it is clear that it is the seductive appeal of American culture, far more than any possible hostile acts by American govern-ments, that they see as offering the greatest menace to the true faith and the right path as they define them. By denouncing America as the Great Satan, the late Ayatollah Khomeini was paying an unconscious tribute to that seductive appeal.[18]

Given this, and the societal, economic, and political deficiencies that generate anti-Americanisms in the region, what can feasibly be done?

Toward a new Middle East?

What kind of vision should we advance for the Middle East and what grand strategy best advances it? In much commentary on the region, at least by western analysts, there exists little sense of an end point. The First Cold War saw a self-confident West contain Soviet

communism with, at its end, reasonable (if never certain) expectations
that the former states of the USSR along with its Eastern European
satellites would embrace market democracies. Yet in relation to the
Middle East no comparable western confidence exists. For decades,
mainstream discussion has veered between reluctantly conceding that
the US, as a major power, has to assume a role in the region, despite
occasional costs entailed in blood and treasure, and a neo-isolationism
that recommends exit. Both approaches more or less concede that the
region is beyond redemption or even comprehensive understanding,
that its problems and conflicts are too intractable to be enable to
effective crisis management or resolution, and that the quasi-imperial
role America has inherited runs against its interests and values. After
the seizure of the US hostages in Tehran in 1979, the murder of 241
Marines in Lebanon in 1983, the sending of half a million military personnel to the Gulf in 1990–1, the al Qaeda attacks of the 1990s and
9/11, and the loss of over 3,000 Americans in Iraq since 2003, such
sentiments are understandable. They are, however, poor guides to a
sound policy. Whatever short-term palliative they offer, American
interests and ideals can only be served by a more ambitious strategy.

There does exist a desirable and attainable end point. It is one that
many, and perhaps most, observers from across the political spectrum
can agree on with relative ease, at least in the abstract. It envisages
a Middle East:

- which includes two independent states, Israel and Palestine,
  existing in peace alongside each other;
- where Israel and Palestine are both recognized by all other states
  in the region and wider world;
- in which there is no WMD (with the necessary exception of
  Israel);
- with a set of growing market-based economies;
- where wealth is distributed widely among the people;
- where a radical advance in education, employment, and women's
  equality obtains;

- where governments are elected by and accountable to their electors – men and women;
- where a reformation of the relation between mosque and state means religion does not suffocate public life;
- where all states and peoples renounce the use of violence against civilians;
- where governments are empowered to deal with terrorist networks in order to disrupt and eliminate them;
- where the protection of property rights, the abandonment of command economies, and the encouragement of private entrepreneurship and outside investment are facilitated;
- where broad guarantees of freedoms to speech, assembly, and religion are established;
- where the promotion and proselytization of extremist religious doctrines are met with disdain rather than relativistic appeasement; and
- where the steady reincorporation of the region's states into the community of nations is advanced, with a combination of bilateral and multilateral free trade pacts concluded and vigilant international monitoring to ensure that the rights of the UN Charter to which the nations are signatories are respected.

To be sure, such a vision represents a monumental undertaking, one that we have little optimism will be achieved soon. But for critics who reject such a blueprint as naïvely ambitious, we offer two rejoinders. The first is that, at the Second World War's end, an ambitious and judicious American administration developed the vision (albeit in fits and starts) of a Europe whole, prosperous, and free and managed to convince domestic American opinion of its desirability and feasibility. Europeans who now treat American ambition with scorn would do well to remember how distant such a European peace looked even in 1985, much less 1945.

The second, rather less optimistically, concerns the consequences of failing to achieve this vision. Middle East-based threats to the

security of America and Europe are serious and multiple. Political,
economic, and structural changes partially explain the appeal of 'Bin
Ladenism' to sections of Middle East opinion. Recent decades have
seen the end of the Arab nationalism/radicalism that began in 1954
with Nasser's ascendancy in republican Egypt and the erosion of the
appeals that Arab despots such as Saddam, Gaddafi, Arafat, and
Assad enlisted over time to shore up their domestic bases (anti-
monarchism, anti-colonialism, anti-Zionism, socialisms, secular-
ism, pan-Arabism). Conservative rather than radical command
economies, plagued by corruption and nepotism, have produced disastrous effects despite the resource-rich base of many Arab states, the
seemingly perpetual backwardness of which contrasts sharply with
the rapid advance of Israel's economy. The 2002 UN Arab Human
Development Report, authored by Arabs, noted that the entire Arab
world had the same GDP as Spain and lower per capita economic growth than any other region except sub-Saharan Africa.[19]
Authoritarianism and nepotism together made changes of Middle
East governments rare and political repression widespread. Partly as
a direct result, the growth of 'political Islam' as the only viable
expression for new radicals provided a key supply source for the
region's most deadly cohorts of terrorists. Finally, economic and
political stagnation, technological backwardness (total Arab internet usage was 2 percent in 2002), and a burgeoning demographic
crisis (the twenty-two Arab states plus Iran are estimated to grow
from 304 to 400 million people between 2001 and 2015, with several
states' populations having majorities under thirty years of age)
together pose profound dangers. The 2003 UNDP report was clear:

> AHDR 2002 challenged the Arab world to overcome three cardinal
> obstacles to human development posed by widening gaps in freedom,
> women's empowerment and knowledge across the region. AHDR
> 2003 makes it clear that, in the Arab civilization, the pursuit of knowl-
> edge is prompted by religion, culture, history and the human will to
> achieve success. Obstructions to this quest are the defective structures

created by human beings – social, economic and above all political. Arabs must remove or reform these structures in order to take the place they deserve in the world of knowledge at the beginning of the knowledge millennium.[20]

Whatever the flaws in his argument, Samuel Huntington was right to note that a central part of the region's problems resides in the disjuncture between Muslim conviction in their superior culture and Islamist obsession with the inferiority of their power.[21] With the Middle East's population estimated to grow by 132 percent by 2035, the urgency of achieving some kind of regional normalcy is starker than ever. The history of Arab civilization, a once influential force, stands as a constant reminder to the peoples of the region of their current dystopia.

If such backwardness continues, socio-economic and political stagnation will offer ever more plentiful supplies of disaffected young men to whom jihadist appeals are even more seductive than the temptations offered by the 'Great Satan' – with potentially apocalyptic effects. A nuclear Iran, for example, would precipitate a regional arms race that would cause all hopes of non-proliferation in the region to evaporate. Even the French president, Nicolas Sarkozy, declared a nuclear Iran 'unacceptable.'[22] Prospects for peace would recede rapidly while the potential costs of regional war would be ratcheted up. The effect of conflict on the price and supply of energy would likely devastate the global economy, a downturn in which would wreak havoc on Asia, Africa, and Latin America. The prospect of trans-national terrorists gaining usable forms of WMD, or even a WMD-equipped state, would be immeasurably greater with a proliferation of such weapons across the region and the possibilities of several lucrative A. Q. Khan-style networks becoming operative. Nuclear, biological, and chemical weapons cannot be uninvented, and there exist few reasons to suppose we can prevent their spread, in small numbers, any more than we have illegal drugs. For once, the claim that 'the stakes could not be higher' rings true.

It is therefore curious that so few of Bush's critics have offered coherent or compelling alternatives. Indeed, the vituperative opposition to Bush has ushered into being an odd *de facto* alliance, in which he and 'neoconservatives' are castigated by the left and the right for excessive idealism. But progressives should be wary of seeing in Islamists, 'insurgents,' and Mullahs forces of anti-imperial resistance. To the extent that this has already occurred, a left that once believed in universal ideals has apparently abandoned them (at least if it is Washington that seeks to advance them). The realist right, meanwhile, appears to disregard the notion that America's steadfast support for the shah, Riyadh's royalty, and Hosni Mubarak might partly explain why al Qaeda profitably targeted its 'far' rather than its 'near' enemy in 2001. The realist prescription is that the existing regimes, however toxic and linked to the spread of noxious anti-American, anti-Semitic and anti-Christian notions among Muslims, are preferable to what might result from free and fair elections.

In the short term, realists are correct. Elections, of themselves, do not constitute a working constitutional democracy. The prospect of illiberal Middle Eastern regimes arising is real. As the experience of Hamas in the Palestinian Authority and Hezbollah in the Lebanese government has shown, not to mention the warped democracy in Iran, elections can yield governments that are decidedly anti-American. But a strategy premised on promoting forms of self-government (not, as the caricature has it, at the point of a gun) is the only one that promises, over time, getting closer to the end point that we sketched above. There are four reasons why.

The first is that, as we have emphasized elsewhere in our discussion of continuity, 9/11 did not alter the structure of the international system. It did prompt a new sense of vulnerability. Non-state actors such as al Qaeda and Hezbollah nonetheless operate within states. As Litwak notes, 'the prerequisite for addressing the non-state threat is the design and implementation of effective strategies on the state level.'[23] In that regard, and as successful non-proliferation efforts in

South Africa, Ukraine, Brazil and Argentina attest, a model exists for the post-9/11 era: 'nonproliferation through democratization, security assurances, and integration into the globalized economy of the liberal international order.'[24] Or, as Michael Mandelbaum observes:

> The world of the twenty-first century is marked by a broad and unprecedented consensus in favor of three great ideas: peace as the optimal condition of international relations and the proper aim of foreign policy; democracy as the best form of government; and the free market as the only satisfactory way of organizing economic affairs.[25]

Second are the lessons of Afghanistan and Iraq. When given the opportunity, millions of Afghans and Iraqis seized the chance to exercise a right long denied them, in many cases braving death to cast their ballots. In Lebanon, the 'Cedar revolution' saw millions of Lebanese seek to regain sovereignty over their nation from Syria. Even in Egypt and Saudi Arabia, small steps were taken toward political liberalization – ludicrous to western eyes but in the nations and region they represent momentous beginnings. To dismiss the masses of the Muslim world as unable to grasp the forms of self-government that other peoples have taken on board is not only a form of bigotry but also runs against the reality of human experience. Fragile the democratic regimes in Turkey, Indonesia, Afghanistan, and Iraq most certainly may be but the faltering steps toward a new settlement across the Middle East are ones to be offered support rather than derision. It may be that liberalization and modernization need to precede democratization in several cases. But that elections are insufficient does not negate the notion that they are necessary parts of a successful reform agenda.

Thirdly, it is unclear that, as realists claim, the outcomes of democratic choice would be significantly worse than current regimes. The alacrity with which corrupt regimes from Islamabad to Cairo cling to this thesis ought to induce pause among US policy-makers. Groups such as the Muslim Brotherhood would certainly gain seats in assemblies and possibly even governments in states such as Egypt, Syria, and Jordan. But the extent of their support is far from obvious. Moreover, as Leiken and Brooke argue, while western commentators condemn the Brotherhood for its Islamism, radicals in the region condemn it for rejecting jihad and embracing democracy. This suggests that, providing policy-makers recognize the substantial variation in the group's branches, agendas and tendencies, relative moderation can be engaged.[26] Certainly, the notion that the most odious Islamist fanatics such as al Qaeda would win broad support is not credible. As Lieven and Hulsman note, contemporary surveys of popular Muslim opinion reject the imposition of Taliban-style fundamentalism and a universal caliphate (even in Saudi Arabia) and reveal alienation from Islamist terror and a combination (rather ironically) of hostility to US policies with support for democracy.[27] In Iran, having established an Islamic theocracy, few Iranians harbor illusions that their economic and social problems are the result of insufficient conformity to Shia Islam. With, for all its faults, the rise of independent media outlets such as al-Jazeera allowing Arabs and Muslims access to critical, non-governmental voices, the possibility for popular forms of self-government to be achievable and sustainable is arguably genuine. While this would not be a copy of Washington or Westminster – and while an Islamist regime with nuclear weapons is an unacceptable 'redline' (whether in Pakistan, Iran, or Saudi Arabia) – hardly disqualifies the prospect for an indigenous form of constitutionalism that combines self-government with Islam.

The fourth and final reason why a pro-democracy agenda is essential, however, is at once a typically American combination of pragmatism and idealism. On the pragmatic side, let us assume that a group such as the Brotherhood did come to power in a regional state. In general, an accountable regime is tempered in its radicalism. The responsibility of delivering tangible material benefits to a mass citizenry typically concentrates minds in power. Over the medium term, the appeal of radical solutions and the groups who espouse them diminishes when those groups prove unable to deliver the goods. In Europe, for example, there exists no mass support for Marxist movements or socialist parties precisely because Europeans have had to endure the experience of what such governments are like in the concrete, not merely in the abstract designs of academics.

Yet, beyond this point, realists need to confront a failure in their own logic. If states are the key actors in the international system, are generally rational actors, and are more easy to contain, confront, and influence than non-state actors, is it clearly so preferable to leave nationalist Islamists – as distinct from international jihadists – at large rather than burdened by office? Even were several such states to band together in a form of quasi-caliphate (an impossible undertaking given the profound and enduring fissures among them) such an entity would provide a more familiar strategic rival than the stateless, virtual networks that currently threaten to bring about an apolar region characterized by vacuums of power.

The idealism underpinning democratization draws on the notion that there exist certain universal truths that can be promoted. Part of the problem in advancing this case, however, stems from the transatlantic division in lenses in which it is typically framed. For most Americans, religiosity is a positive force, and hence there is nothing inherently dysfunctional about Islam as such. For secular Europeans, however, religion is frequently seen in negative terms, as a rejection of Enlightenment values. The multiculturalism, cultural relativism, and anti-racism that animate many Europeans, though, caution against suggesting that other cultures are underdeveloped. Thus we reach a curious impasse. The left is divided internally, between those who see no clash of civilizations and reject the notion mostly on ethnic and racial grounds, and those who see religion (whether Islam or religion generally) as being the problem. As Sam Harris puts it, in a way that few conservative commentators dare:

We are at war with Islam. It may not serve our immediate foreign policy objectives for our political leaders to openly acknowledge this fact, but it is unambiguously so. It is not merely that we are at war with an otherwise peaceful religion that has been 'hijacked' by extremists. We are at war with precisely the vision of life that is prescribed to all Muslims in the Koran, and further elaborated in the literature of the hadith, which recounts the sayings and actions of the Prophet. A future in which Islam and the West do not stand on the brink of mutual annihilation is a future in which most Muslims have learned to ignore most of their canon, just as most Christians have learned to do. Such a transformation is by no means guaranteed to occur, however, given the tenets of Islam.[28]

Candor on this topic is as necessary as courage in Enlightenment convictions. From the end of the First Cold War to 2006, the UN, on average, intervened in the territory of one of its member states every six months. Of the last nine interventions, six were in Muslim nations (Somalia, Kosovo, Iraq, Afghanistan, Lebanon, and Bosnia). In this respect, while the framing of the war on terror was entirely understandable from a motivational viewpoint, the Second Cold War's real focus is radical Islam and the battle that rages between those Muslims who want Islam to dominate public life and those who see it as an important but essentially private force. If Harris is correct that the religion is the problem, not the fundamentalism, then we are indeed in a global war that promises no respite for decades. If, however, sufficient numbers of Muslims wish to 'ring fence' the public sphere, to achieve a reformation that places limits on the extent to which Islam trumps a secular state, then some genuine progress can be achieved. It is perhaps most centrally here that the limits of US power are starkest. For the US and the West to achieve lasting security, it is not so much winning as changing hearts and minds that must occur.

A tailored approach toward both states and sub-state actors is a necessity. Assessing the 'strategic personalities' ('the long-term historical and cultural forces that uniquely shape each state's world view and decision-making calculus')[29] is vital, albeit that this is more art than science. Nevertheless, Washington cannot achieve all its regional goals at once. Recognizing the distinctions between 'nationalist Islamists' and 'international jihadists,' on the one hand, and within nationalist Islamist groupings, on the other, is a prerequisite of an effective policy. There is good reason to fear that the embrace of democracy by groups like the Muslim Brotherhood is tactical – 'one man, one vote, once' – rather than sincere. But there is also some modest reason, selectively, to be hopeful that the lessons of decades of dictatorship, nepotism, and corruption have left a deep suspicion of authoritarianism among most Arabs and Muslims. If the risk of such engagement is certainly real, the costs of ostracism are arguably greater. The possibility that selective engagement and clear conditionality can yield regimes committed to regional peace, human rights, and modernity is not fantastical.

As Harris notes, however, the prospects are not good. Most obviously, the US will remain compelled to be a player in the region, whatever the outcome in Iraq. Bush warned in his 2006 State of the Union address that 'America is addicted to oil, which is often imported from unstable parts of the world.' In fact, it is largely stable regimes that provide the bulk of those energy exports. Haass is correct that the 'solution lies in some mixture of near and mid-term policies designed to hasten the emergence of alternatives to oil and gas and in reducing the amount of oil and gas consumed.'[30] But however desirable and feasible such policies, their effects on the region's other major export – terrorism – are less far-reaching than typically claimed. Even were American energy security to become less dependent on the region – a development that will occur, but not for some years – other players will replace the diminishing US dollars in the coffers of Riyadh, Tehran, and the Gulf states. The finances that bankroll terror, arms, and WMD will therefore remain buoyant even in the face of a new American energy compact. Equally, as long as corrupt and repressive regimes deny political outlets to the mass of

alienated citizens and fail to deliver decent levels of secular education, economic growth, and prosperity, their stability will remain
predicated on projecting animus toward foreigners. In its public
diplomacy, then, Washington should remain clear and steadfast in its
commitment to peaceable, democratic change and liberalization.
That message, like the message of anti-communism that American
presidents sent to the peoples of communist regimes, should be loud
and clear. As Natan Sharansky argued:

> it is hard to imagine many who would contend that if the region's
> tyrannies were transformed into genuinely free societies, the world
> would not be more secure. Surely, few would argue that the successful
> transformation of the Middle East into governments that respect the
> rule of law, protect individual rights, cherish human life and dedicate
> themselves to improving the well being of their citizens would not be
> better for everyone.[31]

Americans should have the self-confidence to propagate such a
vision in an unabashed fashion. They should ignore – or confront
directly – the hypocritical charges of imperialism and cultural relativism from those in the West who enjoy the benefits and protections
of American-made constitutional liberalism and free markets. They
should challenge Arab governments that refuse to their own people
the blessings of such liberties.

Recommendations: recalibrating Mid-East policy

Beyond the broader vision that American grand strategy needs to articulate, concrete and particular steps need to be taken to advance it.
Although the problems are distinct, and the process for resolving each
is protracted and difficult, seven key measures present themselves.

1. Terrorism

As long as the resort to terror is subsidized and sanctioned as divinely
ordained and rewarded, lasting Middle East peace will remain a

chimera. Moreover, as long as terrorism is legitimated while regional powers pursue WMD, the region's status as the preeminent security threat to the West will remain intact. Both the peoples of the Middle East and the West therefore have a shared interest in seeing all available measures employed to prevent, preempt, and ultimately delegitimate terrorism. Both need to emphasize that the main victims of terror by Muslims, currently, are other Muslims. Similarly, while it remains important to recognize the distinctions between ethnic, nationalist, and globalist terror groups, the practical value of these analytical distinctions to policy-makers needs to be carefully calibrated on a continual basis.[32] In practice, nationalist groups and states such as Syria have increasingly employed Islamist language and jihad to justify and expand their murderous ranks. Until and unless the West, governments in the region, and figures in the religious, media, and educational worlds take decisive action to address what regional grievances are tractable and to delegitimate the political use of violence – the two cannot be separated – the Middle East will grow in its threat to world peace.

In this regard, the US should pursue two tracks. First, it should make it clear to state and non-state actors that mass terrorism as practiced by al Qaeda will provoke a full American retaliatory response. Groups such as Hamas and Hezbollah that fantasize about an Islamist bomb should be made fully aware of the consequence of its attainment, let alone of its use. Second, America should prioritize its threat perceptions. Currently, al Qaeda, Iran, Syria, and their terror clients are the main forces working against US regional interests, and an effective strategy needs to contain all of them, even at the cost of accepting the temporary utility of Faustian bargains with repressive 'allies' in Cairo and Riyadh.

But the US should make clear that those who seek a non-violent road to state power do not, *a priori*, pose a threat to America and can be *bona fide* members of the international community. The renunciation of violence should be rewarded by concrete steps, from

meaningful negotiations to tangible benefits in the form of diplomatic recognition, economic assistance, trade, and exchanges.
However, as Bruno Tertrais notes, 'to argue that military action is not
the appropriate way to deal with terrorism, as some did after the
Madrid bombings, is to misconstrue the nature of the adversary.'[33]

2. *Israel and Palestine*

The Arab–Israeli conflict is not the bloodiest, most dangerous, or
most complicated of the Middle East's problems. Contrary to mainstream European opinion, a lasting solution to this particular conflict
will not bring an end to the region's pathologies and psychoses. As
Josef Joffe has argued, even a 'world without Israel' would not address
the region's multiple dysfunctionalities.[34] Moreover, the notion that
Washington can simply force a solution on recalcitrant parties if only
it devoted sufficient time and energy to the process is misleading and
flies in the face of the efforts of several administrations. Bush, for
example, was right to declare for the first time, and to remarkably
modest international enthusiasm, that Palestinian statehood was
official US policy. But he was also correct to note that the US could
do little until conditions on the ground so permitted. As the Syrian-
and Iranian-supported Hezbollah attacks and the fraught relations
between Fatah and Hamas both demonstrated over 2006–7, there
can be no peace until an Israel that continues to face an existential
threat of annihilation receives genuine and concrete assurances that
a Palestinian state, and its Arab neighbors, will recognize it, abide by
agreed peace accords, and renounce violence. As long as Palestinians
and their state and sub-state allies seek to push Israel back to its pre-
1948 borders, no negotiations can yield a settlement, and aggressive
action against terrorists is entirely justified. Israel's stance on matters
such as construction of the security barrier should, as Campbell and
O'Hanlon suggest, be understood as 'an unfortunate but reasonable
exercise of sovereignty by a state repeatedly attacked by its neighbors.'[35] Should the Palestinian Authority recognize and abide by

established accords and take concrete measures to renounce violence, however, the US and other members of the Quartet should take what steps they feasibly could to facilitate the parties reaching final status agreements. The broad outlines of these would include at least six key elements:

- two states for two peoples, both democratic and living in peace alongside agreed borders;
- a Palestinian state established on parts of the West Bank and Gaza Strip;
- Palestinian refugees to have the right of return to Palestine, but not to Israel, with commensurate compensation and resettlement options in other third countries in the region;
- Jerusalem as the one capital for the two states, with Arab east Jerusalem under Palestinian sovereignty and the Jewish part of the city under Israeli sovereignty;
- recognition of Israel by all Arab states in the region;
- multilateral trade and investment initiatives to provide employment, education, and infra-structural development.

Security guarantees are also vital to confidence building, especially on the Israeli side. Disengagement from Lebanon in 2000 and Gaza in 2006 did not bring about improved security for Israel, and similar retreat from the West Bank – without guaranteed security measures – is unlikely to do so either. Such measures should include the demilitarization of the Palestinian state and a mutual security accord between Israel and Palestine. If necessary, NATO should provide a substantial peacekeeping force with permissive rules of engagement to maintain an interim consolidation of Israeli borders. Washington should coordinate a substantial program of inward investment and trade accords while being mindful that aid without conditionality (whether the EU's Barcelona Process or US assistance to Egypt and Jordan) cannot guarantee lasting improvements in security. Security guarantees to Israel could also be rendered more credible, not least to those in the region seeking its destruction, if

Israel's informal security partnership with the United States was made official by bilateral treaty.

Resolution of this conflict would achieve three advances in the region. First, it would settle a longstanding conflict that would help both parties toward a more stable and prosperous future. Second, it would remove one of the few grievances uniting Arabs, Persians, and Muslims within and without the region, thereby making explicit the many intra-Muslim fissures in need of resolution. Third, and related, it would deprive several corrupt regimes of one of the few powerful themes that are wheeled out to pacify otherwise alienated citizenries, making pressure for internal reform more intense. We remain cautiously optimistic that a genuine and enduring peace can be reached. But that requires not so much American will as a reciprocal effort by the key regional interlocutors. As Martin Indyk cautioned:

> There were many reasons for the Clinton administration's failure to achieve comprehensive peace and for the Bush administration's inability to stop the violence in its first term. But one challenge beset progress at every stage: terrorism. Western powers should be under no illusion. Arab–Israeli peace is one of the most threatening challenges to Islamic extremists. Backed by Iran, they can be expected to do everything possible to thwart US efforts.[36]

That reality must again be central to the next administration's counterterrorism strategies. As with Iraq, achieving lasting security for Israel – a democracy surrounded by hostile undemocratic regimes where ceding territory now encourages not simply Arab land grabs but jihadist ambitions for its destruction more broadly – must be the primary starting point for a meaningful peace process.

3. Iran

In assessing Iran's 'strategic personality,' Geoffrey Kemp questions whether Iran is 'an aspiring regional hegemonic power, intent on eventually dominating its neighbors once the Americans have left, or is it a chronically insecure state, determined to protect itself against Western imperial aspirations that include regime change?'[37] It is both, simultaneously. As Kissinger noted, Iran has yet to decide whether it is 'a nation or a cause.'[38] The resulting dilemma for the US is that the short-term 'timeline for Iran's potential acquisition of nuclear weapons is not in sync with the indeterminate timeline for societal change. That hard reality presents US policy-makers with two policy options for addressing Iran's nuclear program: military preemption or negotiation.'[39]

When Khomeini took power in 1979, he made anti-Americanism a core of Iranian foreign policy and, lacking diplomatic relations ever since, the US and Iran have periodically confronted each other.[40] Mark Bowden argues that the hostage crisis was America's first battle in its war with radical Islam, its 'first encounter with Islamo-fascism and, as such, can be seen as the first battle in that ongoing world conflict':

> Iran's hatred of the United States was in part a consequence of heavy-handed, arrogant, and sometimes criminal twentieth-century American foreign policy, but it was also rooted in something that has nothing to do with that. It grew out of anger over the erosion of tradition. The modern Western world does not recognize revelation and divine right as the root of government authority. The trend of history has long been away from strict tribal authority grounded in one holy book or the other, whether the Koran, the Torah, the Bible, or any other ancient text, and toward those strictly human values distilled so well in the Declaration of Independence as 'life, liberty, and the pursuit of happiness.' The murderous terrorism that has become a fact of modern life is part of the death throes of an ancient way of life. The glorious Islamist revolution in Iran, which a quarter century later has produced a despised, corrupt, and ineffectual religious dictatorship, will wind up little more than a footnote in the long and colorful history of that nation, and probably an embarrassing one, judging by the disgruntlement of many Iranians, including at least some of the old hostage takers.[41]

As Daniel Byman notes:

In the decade before 9/11, Iran structured its military forces to fight
America, even when the US military presence in the Persian Gulf
region was confined to the conservative oil states of the Arab peninsula . . . Tehran does not want the secular and pro-Western Iraq that
America dreams of, and it wants to ensure that the US doctrine of preventive regime change is dead.[42]

Admittedly, despite its political and religious elites' Islamic fervor,
anti-Americanism, and anti-Semitism, the regime has been highly
pragmatic – reaching out to Sunni groups, Syria, Palestinian Islamic
Jihad, and Hamas (whose ideologies are closer to Bin Laden's than
Khomeini's), working with Israel and the US during the Iran–Iraq
War and building Hezbollah from disparate Shiite movements. Iran
has also trained terrorist groups in Bosnia, Lebanon, and Palestine.
But its moves are above all calculated to divide its regional neighbors
and the West and to cause maximum trouble for the US in Iraq.

Moreover, as Therese Delpech argues, 'Despite all of Tehran's talk
of the peaceful purposes of its nuclear program . . . Iran wants the
bomb.'[43] Western sanguinity in the face of an Iranian nuclear WMD
capacity would be deeply troubling. As Haass describes it:

> Although it is right to oppose the emergence of new nuclear weapon
> states in all circumstances, it is also right to oppose it more in some
> than in others. The character and behavior of the regime – its record
> of aggression, its history of supporting terrorism, its stability, its record
> on preventing exports of sensitive technologies, whether it is a democ-
> racy, its involvement in a dispute with a neighbor that could lead to a
> conflict that in turn could involve nuclear weapons – all can and
> should influence the intensity of US and world opposition to prolifer-
> ation and what the United States and other countries should be pre-
> pared to do to prevent or counter it. While the emergence of a nuclear
> Iran and a nuclear Switzerland would both be of concern, they would
> not be of equal concern.[44]

How the world deals with Iran goes to the heart of the collective
security system. As Delpech, director of strategic studies at the

French Atomic Energy Commission and an UNMOVIC commissioner, notes, 'there is a danger for the United Nations of a gradual return to the impotence of the Society of Nations if the violation of agreements as important as the NPT does not lead to any kind of sanctions.'[45] As such, a nuclear Iran should be a clear and abiding 'red line' for any American administration and its allies.

The White House should and likely will engage in more concerted and clear public diplomacy to make apparent why this is the case. That is, the argument should be predicated not simply on the Shia tradition of martyrdom, the sanity or otherwise of the Iranian leadership, or a direct conflict between Tehran and Tel Aviv or Washington. Rather, the case should be made that the consequences of regional proliferation are such as to render a nuclear Iran a step too far. In spring 2007, six Arab states made clear to the IAEA that if Iran gained nuclear capabilities they would also seek them. The exposure of the A. Q. Khan network has made apparent how easy it is to advance proliferation. Given the region's history and its centrality to the global economy, the notion that a 'crescent of crisis' could become cradle to a burgeoning supply of WMD – where the only three modern uses of chemical weapons have occurred (by Egypt in Yemen in the late 1950s, by Libya in Chad in 1987, and by Iraq in the Iran–Iraq War of 1980–8 and in Halabja in 1987) – is too terrible to contemplate. As Kissinger put it, 'Iran will get us probably beyond the point where non-proliferation can be a meaningful policy, and then we live in a world of multiple nuclear centers. And then we'd have to ask ourselves what the world would look like if the bombs in London had been nuclear and 100,000 people had been killed.'[46]

Several Iranian experts urge caution and reject a military option.[47] But the regime's hardliners are likely to be strongly resistant to a grand bargain curbing the Islamic Republic's external mission (supporting terror), since this provides one of the few domestic legitimating devices they possess. Moreover, in terms of action, as Bruce Jentleson has argued, 'Force rarely if ever should be a first resort, but it needs to be more of an early resort . . . [Without the credible threat of force, a] preventive diplomacy strategy will lack the coercive component essential to success in most cases.'[48] No measures should be ruled out if Iran continues to refuse to comply with its obligations. Serious sanctions must affect the oil and gas industries. An embargo on refined oil products and investments in oil and gas could have an effect on Iran. The nation cannot meet domestic demand for oil and imports around 40 percent of its refined oil from abroad. But if diplomatic pressure is insufficient to achieve the result, as seems inevitable given the obduracy of Russia and China, then military strikes on Iran must be contemplated. While these risk only retarding the program, that is a necessary part of moving toward a full solution. If the Iranian nation, rich in oil and natural gas reserves, genuinely needs peaceful nuclear power as well, it should either accept the previous offer of Russia to supply this, or admit to full, unannounced, and frequent IAEA inspections to trust and verify its activities in full.

Beyond this, the stark centrality of the region to global economic well-being needs to be made clear. An expansionist Iran – especially one protected by a nuclear arsenal – would pose grave threats to Israel and to the safe passage of oil supplies through the Strait of Hormuz. It is incumbent upon critics of the US to explain how a strategy of carrots without accompanying sticks will dissuade Tehran from precipitate action or would, in the event of that action, reverse it. A nuclear Iran would be disastrous for the international non-proliferation regime, the parlous credibility of the UN, and the entire strategic situation of the Middle East. Some hold that, if the problem is not resolved before Iran acquires the bomb, an Iranian crisis similar to that of the Cuban Missile Crisis of 1962 will become inevitable.[49] As Robert McNamara has recounted, the premise of universal rationality needs to be set against Fidel Castro's later revelation to him that he was prepared to sacrifice Cuba for the advance of international communism. The risk of an uncontrollable and devastating situation developing requires concerted action by the West because 'the future must not be sacrificed to the present.'[50] Failing that, America should act alone. As Mandelbaum noted, the lesson that responsible officials drew from 9/11 was that 'in dealing with aggressive terrorist groups or rogue states, the better part of valor is not discretion but boldness.'[51] It is a lesson that applies especially to Iran, a nation purporting to be a firefighter while acting as a regional arsonist.

4. Saudi Arabia

The US can no longer tolerate Riyadh's financing of Wahhabism in the Muslim world and beyond. In the short term, US interests are such that it continues to need a relatively supportive Saudi relationship to continue. Riyadh's considerable influence on the Israeli–Palestinian issue, Sunnis in Iraq, counterterrorism and the international oil market together make a severing of the relationship, currently, an impossibility. Action against Iran, for example, whether via sanctions or military strikes, requires Saudi Arabia to play a proactive role in maintaining the flow of oil and minimizing price fluctuations. An effective effort to secure a meaningful Israel–Palestine peace also demands active diplomacy and serious financial largesse from the Kingdom. Nonetheless, a recalibration of the terms of the US–Saudi relationship needs to begin in earnest with a view to, at a later stage, a drastic and abiding alteration. As noted above, the false panacea of energy security and independence is not one that will substantially reduce the monies going to subsidize the most extremist and pernicious form of anti-western Islamist dogma around the world – those propagated from Riyadh, Tehran, and Damascus. Yet to ignore that this is occurring is politically irresponsible and counterproductive in the long run. The Saudis should be made clear that, should their nefarious activities continue, a decisive reckoning with Washington will occur.

5. Syria

Bashar Assad's regime is an aggressive and opportunistic irritant. It is not a potential solution to the region's problems; it is part of the problem. Damascus felt substantial pressure over 2004–6. The joint US–French-sponsored UNSC Res. 1559 mandated that Syria evacuate its forces from Lebanon, a measure supported by Saudi Arabia. That incomplete withdrawal (Syrian intelligence operatives remain) encouraged Syrian opposition groups, reformists, and civil society activists to become more vocal in their demands for a liberalization of Baathist control. Progress has been very slow. Damascus was widely held to have masterminded the assassination of former Lebanese prime minister Rafiq Al-Hariri, along with other anti-Syrian political figures in Lebanon. Syria's alliance with Iran against Gulf and other Arab states, its support for Hezbollah's attempts to topple Lebanon's Al-Siniora government, along with its facilitating passage of jihadists into Iraq through its territory, further isolated the regime. Assad's description of other Arab leaders as 'half-men' in August 2006, as the Israel–Hezbollah summer war was ending, fueled Arab ire. The regime's political isolation, combined with a long-lasting recession and US sanctions, nonetheless did not result in meaningful changes. The dictatorship relies on fomenting terrorism, instability, and anti-western appeals to maintain its grip on power.[52]

As such, Washington would be well advised to proceed with a profound skepticism toward Damascus. In some respects, Syria has more potential for successful transition to an open society than other Arab states. The state retains a monopoly on the legitimate use of coercion, state institutions have widely penetrated society, the population is largely well educated with a growing middle class and opposition groups mostly reject terrorism as an instrument of change. But if Assad has proven to be a tyrant marginally less brutal, but also less politically adept, than his father previously, his leadership is at best only symbolically committed to a gradualist program of technical and economic modernization. Substantive moves to a market economy, the rule of law, and constitutionalizing rights and liberties are yet to be seen. There exist few reasons for optimism. As with Iran, a modification in the regime's behavior is more tenable than a change in that regime in the short term, since at best the US could only seek 'regime change on the cheap' given its on-going commitments in Iraq. But, as Goes and Leenders note, 'If one lesson can be drawn from recent developments in Lebanon and Syria, it is that external pressures for political change can be effective in creating a momentum for change if they result from a concerted campaign.'[53]

While the Syrian regime will not relinquish power of its own accord, it is possible to envisage an American effort that provides a robust mix of incentives and sanctions to pressure Assad, as occurred over 2001–3. This cannot be separated from the Israel–Palestine issue. Nonetheless, while the US can seek a separate Israeli–Syrian dialogue along parallel tracks to an Israeli–Palestinian one, its prospects for success are minimal. The kind of 'dialogue' favored by the Baker–Hamilton group holds Syrian consent as a precondition of regional peace and Arab 'normalization' with Tel Aviv. A form of 'conditional engagement' is perhaps possible. As Volker Perthes suggests, 'this would involve a clear message that there is room for increased cooperation, including trade, an enhanced political dialogue – as foreseen, on Europe's part, under the EU–Syria Association Agreement – the modernisation of economic and administrative structures, technology and education and cultural and civil-society exchange.'[54] A staggered set of conditional and reciprocal measures that build multi-party reassurance can be envisaged. This would entail clear steps toward full compliance with Res. 1559 by Damascus and a cessation of its active military support for Hezbollah, Islamic Jihad, and Hamas (and political violence in Israel, Lebanon, Palestine, and Iraq). In return, Syria could expect a reduction in US sanctions so long as it submitted to a coordinated effort – involving NGOs as well as governments – to promote trade exchanges and other political and economic reforms.

But such reforms require an end to a pattern of behavior on the part of the Baathist regime – a Damascene conversion if you will – that seems highly improbable. The regime has, contrary to proponents of diplomacy, dialogue, and engagement, no interest in regional peace, an end to terror, or in ceasing to target Israel for extinction. These are precisely what ensure its continuation in power. Moreover, its demand for the return of the Golan Heights is not a realistic proposition, given Israel's strategic vulnerability and Syria's active sponsorship of terror against it. Again, while an end state can be envisaged, the prospects for its realization are unimpressive.

6. Education, economic development, and reform

Although the simple equation of poverty with terrorism is false, endemic poverty and competition over scarce resources is undeniably a major source of instability and extremism in the region.[55] But despite the popularity of post-colonialist narratives and projections onto America and Israel of malfeasance, the fundamental source of inequality in a region with abundant natural resources and a highly cultured set of peoples is human: the choice of command economies wracked by inefficiency, corruption, nepotism, and a lack of accountability of those in power. Liberalization, modernization, and democratization are perforce linked. The US should coordinate the agreement of a regional free trade pact. The four accredited universities operating in the Middle East (teaching some 20,000 students and more than 100,000 alumni) offer encouraging evidence that a mission to spread liberal and democratic values in the region is 'not quixotic.' As Jackson Diehl observes:

> To a large and growing extent, US-chartered or accredited universities are training the elite of countries such as Egypt, Lebanon, Jordan, the Persian Gulf states and, soon, Iraq. They are teaching women equally with men; opening programs in Western-style journalism; offering cutting-edge courses in capitalism, science and politics; and providing a refuge for free intellectual and political debate.[56]

We hope for the continuance of such developments and a diplomacy that makes this more likely.

7. Afghanistan and Pakistan

The US should further tilt toward New Delhi in a fashion that deliberately stokes sufficient alarm in Islamabad as to cause decisive action against the training, funding, and equipping of both al Qaeda and the Taliban. Whatever the tactical errors of the Bush administration in terms of its military deployments in Afghanistan, the central fact of that tragic nation is that the Taliban were – and remain – primarily a Pakistani product. While Washington may – out of ignorance, diplomatic calculation, or partial concurrence – have accepted Islamabad's assertions of the difficulties of the border terrain, the evidence is compelling that elements of both the government and the Pakistan ISI recruited, trained, financed, and armed Taliban renegades, at times with American dollars. As with the Saudis, the fiction of the alliance should now be threatened with exposure and decisive change. Islamabad should be denied a terror dividend and instead be provided with a structured set of choices, contingent on which Washington will either reinforce or reduce – even abandon – its reciprocity. As Seth Jones argues, the US can offer a judicious combination of carrots and sticks.[57] Removing the restrictions on imports of Pakistani textiles would be a major boost to the economy, for example, while mediation to settle the on-going Afghan–Pakistani border dispute could also be beneficial. Beyond this, Washington can and should tie assistance in areas such as health, economic development, trade, and law enforcement, as well as support in multilateral bodies such the IMF and World Bank, to progress in defeating Afghan insurgents and their support networks. Failure to meet certain clear metrics of progress – from the firm interdiction of Taliban insurgents to the arrest of al Qaeda operatives – should result in the imposition of such sticks, along with a concerted effort to implement reforms to make the political process more open, inclusive, and legitimate. As Jones argues, successive US administrations during the First Cold War understood the changing nature of international politics:

> When US and Egyptian interests began to diverge in the 1950s as Gamal Abdel Nasser gravitated toward the Soviet Union, President Dwight D. Eisenhower cut ties and moved on. NATO is at an important crossroads with Pakistan today. The rising level of violence in Afghanistan has fundamentally altered NATO's cost-benefit calculus. Afghanistan has made notable strides since 2001. It would be a tragedy and a disaster to see this progress unravel at least partly because of the failure of Pakistan to act, and of the United States and Europe to do anything about it.[58]

Conclusion

To that most frequent contemporary question, 'are we in a clash of civilizations?', it is tempting to evade a clear answer even now. The reply that we have given for some years has been that those who answer unequivocally 'yes' or 'no' are missing the point. The accurate answer is 'not yet.' However, there are now strikingly few sands left in the hourglass. It is incumbent on all of us to recognize that, to the extent that civilizations exist, they are not all at the same stage of moral, political, and economic development. What Bowden characterized as the 'sorry course' of the Iranian revolution suggests a retrograde Islamist movement currently 'terrorizing the world':

> Driven by a vague goal of establishing a Koranic utopia, a fanatical fringe allies itself with mainstream political disaffection, but instead of opening the doors to liberty and prosperity it succeeds only in creating a closed and stunted society under the thumb of so-called spiritual leaders who prove, in the end, to be merely human, subject to the same temptations of power and wealth as rulers everywhere and always. The only political system that serves the majority is one that respects true human spirituality, something deeply personal and almost infinitely various.[59]

As such, and as Harris argues from the standpoint of western societies, 'We are now living in a world that can no longer tolerate well-armed, malevolent regimes':

> Unless Muslims can reshape their religion into an ideology that is basically benign – or outgrow it altogether – it is difficult to see how Islam and the West can avoid falling into a continual state of war, and on innumerable fronts.[60]

As the leading western power and provider of global public goods, the US must either lead the fight to ultimate victory or beat a retreat to defeat. That does not mean that the struggle necessarily has to assume a military form, since economic development, education, diplomacy, and other instruments can be of substantial utility in transforming Islam within and without the Middle East. But neither weakness (a European Teddy Roosevelt: 'speak softly and carry a big carrot') nor stasis will suffice.

If this is the case, an American withdrawal from Iraq, much less the region, would provide no palliative to the United States, much less a panacea for the wider West. To the reflexive response of those who either see the US as the cause of the region's problems or who prefer to avoid marrying ideals to interests, such a retreat would not be advantageous to its prospects for a better future. Such a retreat would hasten the prospects for a precipitate, wide-ranging, and potentially devastating regional conflagration the consequences of which for the region and the wider world could be grave. As long as the US remains the world's leading power, moreover, the demands for it to intervene in the region will remain vocal. The ultimate solutions to the multiple problems from Algeria to Afghanistan depend not on Washington but on the regimes and peoples of the region. As Indyk observes, 'the Middle East is notorious for confounding expectations and generating unexpected developments,' for worse and on rare occasion better.[61] The Middle East cannot afford to wait for democracy before it achieves peace. But the US can and should assist the promotion of good governance, the rule of law and human rights on the basis that an accommodation can eventually be reached between the development of such constitutional government and Islam. Far from being about 'imposing' Western values on a recalcitrant people, it should be clear that in encouraging the growth of market democracies the West is seeking to enable Arabs and Muslims to find their own path to remedy the deficiencies so comprehensively detailed by Arabs themselves in successive UN reports. For those who oppose such a course, it is incumbent on them to explain why the mechanisms that have assured economic prosperity, civil liberties, and political rights elsewhere are inappropriate for, or unachievable in, this particular part of the world.

7

Friends and foes after Bush

The nation which indulges towards another a habitual hatred or a habitual fondness is in some degree a slave. It is a slave to its animosity or to its affection, either of which is sufficient to lead it astray from its duty and its interest.

George Washington[1]

We act in alliance or partnership when other states share our interests, but will act unilaterally when compelling national interests demand.

Bill Clinton[2]

Judge me by the enemies I have made.

Franklin D. Roosevelt

Just as we do not today differentiate between the Roman Republic and the imperial period of the Julio-Claudians when we think of the Roman Empire, so in the future no-one will bother to make a distinction between the British Empire-led and the American Republic-led periods of English-speaking dominance between the late-eighteenth and the twenty-first centuries.

Andrew Roberts[3]

In this chapter we extend our case for continuity by assessing the condition and likely future course of America's foreign relationships with key friends and foes, states, and international organizations. We argue that President Bush altered the substance of several relationships and that his successors' diplomacy and statecraft will continue to reflect this. Rather than being responsible for an enforced American solitude, Bush shifted his alliance-making and use of international institutions to reflect the demands of the war on terror. He also adapted to the many continuities of international relations. Ensuing US administrations will depart very little from this approach. Those expecting a return to 'normalcy' in American diplomacy after Bush should prepare for disappointment; Bush was a very normal president.

This normality resides in the following key features of his bilateral diplomacy, as examined in this chapter. He maintained the primacy of international cooperation – *not* international law – as basic to the prosecution of the Second Cold War. He was willing to embrace the old maxim – 'the enemy of my enemy is my friend' – that conditioned the alliances of his successful predecessors in previous global wars against existential enemies. He continued the long tradition of US military interventions on behalf of American interests and values; he was not the first, and will not be the last, American president to work on the assumption that democracy is the only legitimate form of government. Most fundamentally, he rediscovered the strategic and political efficacy of the English-speaking alliance in the face of obfuscation from a briefly nascent Franco–Russo–Sino–German axis.

International organizations

We begin our analysis with international organizations (IOs) since it was Bush's relationship to them that colored so much of the criticism of his foreign policy. Like his predecessors, Bush chose to use IOs not on the basis of their conformity with notions of global justice but for their practical utility. If they contributed to the war on terror they were to be included; if they retarded that war effort they were to be

marginalized or skirted. We can see no president in the future alter-
ing this substantive and sensible calculation very much. Bush, after
all, was like all CEOs in not being keen on arbitration that might
reduce his room for maneuver. In the summer of 2001, to much international hand-wringing, he rejected the Kyoto treaty on climate
control (a treaty that had been rejected by the Senate in 1997 by a
95–0 vote, let us recall). September 11 increased this distrust of
internationalized solutions to global problems. The UN's failure to
enforce its resolutions against Iraq convinced Bush of the body's
redundancy. The war on terror was a truly global fight, Bush declared,
but one which only America could and would lead – even if many
chose not to follow.

NATO

Just as NATO seemed to be expanding and thus fading in its central
role in US foreign policy, 9/11 happened.[4] After that day, according
to the then Russia defense minister Sergei Ivanov, NATO was better
understood as 'Nations Against Terrorist Organizations.' The immediate invocation of Article V, the mutual defense clause – which had
the effect of making the al Qaeda attack a generalized one on all the
then nineteen NATO members – offered the organization a renewed
relevance that was long overdue. It has certainly been responsible for
a clear front in that war – in Afghanistan – and offers the clearest
example of the 'strategy of partnerships' Bush has pursued since late
2001.[5] Indeed, it is via NATO that America's partners have the
strongest formal influence on US foreign policy. No such influence
accrues from EU membership. In the 1990s, the primary ambition of
the Czech Republic, Hungary, and Poland was to join NATO
(secured in 1998), not the EU (achieved six years later). The first
club the newly liberated nations of Eastern Europe – comprising
some 40 percent of the new NATO[6] – wanted to join was US-led,
not Franco-German. Despite realist predictions and liberal hopes,
NATO has not gone away in the war on terror.[7] Indeed, the newest

members of the alliance have been those states most supportive of American foreign policy since 9/11 – 'new Europe'.[8] On March 29, 2004, Bulgaria, Estonia, Latvia, Lithuania, Romania, Slovakia, and Slovenia formally became members of NATO. All except Slovenia have fought alongside US forces in Iraq.[9]

NATO is likely to remain relevant but not a decisive tool for the next several American administrations for a number of reasons. As Patrick Keller argues, the values that underpinned NATO at its inception endure. The 'Atlantic Spirit,' he says, remains NATO's 'animating force.'[10] A commonality of regime type makes the organization cohesive in a manner denied to more diverse and consequently ineffective IOs like the UN and G8. It is an alliance whose origins were forged in successful war against the Axis in the Second World War and tested over the long term against Soviet communism. With France – recurrently uncomfortable with the Anglo-American pre-eminence NATO facilitates – excepted, its members are keen to remain, and prospective members are eager to join.[11] NATO, despite predictions of its demise, has demonstrated a considerable 'institutional flexibility,' both in terms of members and structure. It has not ossified with the demise of the Warsaw Pact.[12]

The problem of 'interoperability,' the downside of America's 'revolution in military affairs,' is partially resolved through NATO.[13] The increasing sophistication of American weaponry, coupled with the flat-lining of European defense research and development, makes partnership in foreign adventures technologically difficult, even before political considerations are factored in. Systems do not integrate as well as they used to. This situation became especially apparent in NATO's Kosovo campaign in 1999 and has grown through the Second Cold War.[14] Allies that might want to be far more involved in supporting American operations are, in the absence of an unlikely comprehensive sharing of US expertise, rendered technologically incapable of doing so. The new Eastern European member-states seem especially keen to force the pace of this sharing. The Czech

Republic and Poland, for example, want to have a US missile defense
shield built on their soil, judging the technological and economic
spin-offs to be worth Russian anger; Poland, especially, hardly owes
its former colonizer.[15] If the US is to bestow the benefits of its military revolution abroad – a situation the war on terror has made
imperative – the most secure means of doing so is under the auspices
of NATO, where US influence is fundamental and its partner
regimes democratic.

However, certain features of the Second Cold War on Islamist terrorism have reduced its operational capacity.[16] The covert nature of
counterterrorism lends itself not to the coordinated military command
and attendant bureaucracy of the alliance but to foreign intelligence
sharing and routine policing – often with nations that will never join
NATO. The Second Cold War, despite Afghanistan and Iraq, is only
partially a military endeavor, and thus only partially draws on NATO's
expertise. NATO is a formal alliance – a considerable strength – but
Bush has been explicit in utilizing temporary, ad hoc coalitions of the
willing in order to realize objectives and circumvent the obstructionism of formal allies.[17] This is hardly a new development. America has
been prepared to act without NATO – in Vietnam, for example, and
in numerous interventions since, such as Grenada (1983), Panama
(1989), and Somalia (1992–3). Meeting NATO objectives is secondary to meeting US security interests.

United Nations

The absurdities of the UN contrast sharply with the efficiency of
NATO. The principles on which it operates are far more attractive
than the vague egalitarianism of the UN. Its members are democracies – it is a *de facto* admission requirement – 'determined to safeguard
the freedom, common heritage and civilization of their peoples,
founded on the principles of democracy, individual liberty and the
rule of law.'[18] The UN will take anybody and is dedicated to a contradiction. It operates an international egalitarianism – Zimbabwe

chairs the Commission on Sustainable Development, Saudi Arabia adjudicates on human rights[19] – regardless of regime type, and yet its permanent Security Council cements historical power inequalities; France, Russia, the US, and the UK sit on the UNSC because they were victorious in the Second World War. For any US president, the exclusivity of NATO, even in its enlarged form, has much to recommend it. Symbolically, his use of it evokes NATO's Second World War genesis and First Cold War success. It is observable that when NATO has not functioned US foreign policy has been less effectual. NATO was not involved in Vietnam, for example. The UN, in contrast, has operated as a talking-shop for developing-world dictatorships, a forum for anti-Americanism, and a mechanism to elicit western aid by stoking western guilt and division.[20] Harry Truman fought under its banner in Korea (1950–3). The experience was not precedent forming. Bill Clinton's most successful war, against Serbia in 1999, was waged without UN approval and by NATO. George W. Bush came to the same conclusion: a just war does not necessarily have to be a UN-sanctioned one.

Liberal illusions that the United Nations is, or can be made into, what Jacques Chirac called the 'guardian of the peace and democracy in the world' did not substantially inform the diplomacy of Bill Clinton or George Bush.[21] They will not inform that of their successors either. The UN will not solve Iraq for the next American president, despite demands that the organization re-establish itself in Baghdad.[22] This descent into an ineffectual internationalism might please the academic left but would condemn Iraq to a fate likely worse than we see unfolding presently. The UN was there before, was attacked (despite the comforting equation of insurgent rage with American occupation), withdrew and has not returned; UN staff have persistently refused to serve there since the murder of UN envoy Sergio Vieira de Mello and twenty-one others in August 2003.

The UN has shown a marked reluctance to prevent war and genocide. The Serbian massacre of some 7,000 Muslim men and boys in

Srebrenica, Bosnia, a UN 'safe area,' in July 1995 – observed by UN soldiers – remains symbolic of a blue-helmeted aversion to fighting.[23] The more reliable agency to call upon in emergencies is the US Pentagon. Indeed, the failure of the American military (and its political leadership) to establish a sufficient level of order after Saddam's fall accounts, sadly, for the UN's reluctance to re-engage. The problem remains primarily an American one.

The stature of the UN cannot grow by negatives. Its worth comes from what it does (or does not do) in the world, not for what it symbolizes for liberals. The fact that it offers, to some, the antithesis of Bush statecraft does not make it a positive force for freedom and peace. If anything, the Iraq War, like Kosovo before it, highlighted the persistent inability of the UN to enforce its own charter and resolutions. It is difficult to see how the most UN-friendly of American presidents – and there are none on the horizon – could imbue it with an authority, utility, and effectiveness that the UN itself is incapable of realizing. The increasing irrelevance of the UN was, even for Anne Marie Slaughter, a Democrat and possible future secretary of state, indicative of a wider failure of IOs to assert themselves in the post-cold war system. 'The system of international institutions that the United States and its allies built after World War II and steadily expanded over the course of the Cold War,' she wrote, 'is broken.'[24] 'Hard power' Democrats Campbell and O'Hanlon concur: no Democratic president, who must have won office by proclaiming his or her 'hard power' credentials – being 'timid and right,' they argue convincingly, is a doomed electoral combination – will cede American security to an international body. No president ever has, none ever will. The authors insist that Democrats face reality:

> Although reviving America's international economic competitiveness, reaffirming the US commitment to global partnerships and multilateral diplomacy, and improving living standards in the developing world are each and all manifestly important objectives, Democrats and like-minded moderates and internationalists will need to go beyond

stating these soft-power objectives and offer hard solutions – including some that could involve the unashamed application of military power – to the most immediate threats facing the United States.[25]

The international institutions that count are those that unite nations with broadly shared values. NATO has endured for this reason. The UN remains mired in a peripheral role because it does not and cannot represent a common character or set of shared values. Anne Marie Slaughter and, separately, Robert Kagan have both urged American leaders to recognize that the only IOs likely to advance the interests of the democratic world are those run by democratic countries.[26] Expecting an increasingly autocratic Russia and China to use the Security Council as anything other than a vehicle to stymie western democratic interests is a fantasy. A more realistic reliance on what Slaughter calls 'a concert of democracies' commends itself.

Old Europe vs. new Europe

Such a concert of democracies led by the United States is all very well, critics might respond, were it not for the fact that Bush ruined the US–Europe relationship, rendering such a concert unlikely. Moreover, it seems that American and European publics have increasingly divergent world views. Unlike Americans, where polling suggests support for the war on terror remains high (at about 70 percent), 'old' Europeans, to perpetuate Donald Rumsfeld's not unhelpful bifurcation, refuse to accept the legitimacy or necessity of the struggle. According to a 2007 Pew poll, the following majorities 'oppose[d] the US-led efforts to fight terrorism':

France	57 percent
Germany	51
Spain	67
Sweden	52

Support for the war in China (26 percent) was higher than in Spain (21).[27] Eighty-two percent of Americans think that war is sometimes necessary to obtain justice. Only 41 percent of Europeans feel the same.[28]

However, transatlantic differences can be exaggerated. Bush's diplomacy earned a media reputation that was often at variance with underlying realities. It was 'old Europe,' far more than new, that provided the US with significant hard power in the Afghan and Iraqi theaters – which is why a gradual cooling on the NATO mission in Afghanistan by Belgium, France, and Germany has rankled in Washington.[29] We tend to remember the diplomatic fallout over Iraq more than we do the 13,400 British, Italian, and Spanish troops who fought alongside the US in 2003. 'New' Europe's military contribution has been longer (as against Spain's certainly) but much smaller. Moreover, whatever the political symbolism, there is a marked hierarchy as to which nations matter to Washington in dangerous missions. A UK or France that did not support the US would be a greater blow militarily than an Italy or Denmark that opposed American actions.

There has also been a tendency in Europe to recall Bill Clinton with a misplaced nostalgia. In the 1990s, arguments over the appropriateness of military force were as fierce as those after 9/11. There was at least as much contestation over the Balkans, for example, as there was over Iraq.[30] The US and Europe usually shared the same objectives but differed over the means to realize them. In Kosovo, for example, France wanted a ground invasion; America did not. In Iraq, America wanted a ground invasion; France did not.[31] France has been prepared – with, of course, a UN mandate – to deploy its troops in the Ivory Coast, suggesting that claims of French pacifism (if not of effectiveness) in world affairs are an exaggeration.[32]

France and Germany

A complicating factor in estimating the future course of transatlantic relations is the rather opaque ambitions of the EU's largest nations.

France and Germany, according to Walter Russell Mead, constitute
the 'odd couple' of Europe:

> Germany wants the old games of power politics and national rivalries
> to end; it has been burned too badly, and both inflicted and suffered
> too much pain to want to venture down that ominous path again. The
> French elite, however, like an old and fading roué, just wants to get
> back in the game. It is addicted to the thrill of the game and it has lost
> sight of something that both Germans and Americans know: old fash-
> ioned power politics in an era of weapons of mass destruction is a sure
> road to ruin.[33]

After the liberation of France in 1944, Charles de Gaulle warned
Dwight Eisenhower, 'You will be overwhelmed by our ingratitude.'
As president, Ike came to the conclusion that the French were 'a
hopeless, helpless mass of protoplasm.'[34] American perplexity at this
state of affairs has endured. Consider the poem by a retired US major,
written after the fall of Saddam Hussein:

> Eleven thousand soldiers
> Lay beneath the dirt and stone,
> All buried on a distant land
> So far away from home . . .
> And now the shores of Normandy
> Are lined with blocks of white:
> Americans who didn't turn
> From someone else's plight.
> Eleven thousand reasons
> For the French to take our side,
> But in the moment of our need,
> They chose to run and hide.[35]

Any number of cultural and historical interpretations might
explain why the French government has sought to weaken the Pax
Americana pursued by every president since FDR. We will resist the
temptation to trace French antipathy to the divergent legacies of
1783 and 1789 – the American revolution worked, the French did

not; the French revolutionaries misread the American Revolution and made individual freedom contingent upon the power of the state; we speak today of an American rather than a French empire; the world's lingua franca is English, not French – and instead explain the affinity of new Europe and the antipathy of old Europe to both internal and external factors. New Europe, having been, for half a century, vassal states in a communist experiment, was predisposed to recognize serious threats to free systems from closed ones. Dictatorship, these post-Soviet governments concluded, is not relative or equivalent to democracy and should be countered rather than 'engaged' or appeased. Václav Havel and Lech Wałęsa, the first leaders of a liberated Czech Republic and Poland, respectively, are examples of a remarkable resistance to state oppression.[36] Fifty years of communist misrule tends to make people rather resistant to excuses for, or arguments on behalf of, the perpetuity of oppression in other lands.

President Chirac's absolute refusal to pass a second UN resolution authorizing regime change in Iraq – that is, he made plain that he would deploy the French veto in the Security Council irrespective of the success of Anglo-American diplomacy – symbolized the counter case. Where new Europe recognized the logic of freedom inherent in the war on Saddam and the war on terror more broadly, old Europe (ostensibly France joined by Germany) favored stability and the status quo. Democracy, argued Chirac in effect, is a delicate seed, and the Middle East infertile soil.

This is hardly the first time the French have not shared an American analysis. The First Cold War was punctuated by an entente that was often less than cordial. As we have seen, France's withdrawal from Indochina took place despite American objections and fears. Eisenhower doomed an Anglo–French bid for regime change in Egypt in 1956 by withholding his support over Suez. De Gaulle walked out of NATO. French defeat in the Algerian War convinced Paris that supporting America's war in Vietnam, which soon followed, was futile. The EU project has been as propelled as much by a French desire to balance US power as it has been to realize a still opaque vision of European civilization.[37] The greater the disparity between American and European military capacities, the more Europe – and here France has taken the lead – will rely on international law (a commodity the EU has in abundance) to check American strength. For example, it is evident that France would like to see the US bound by the Kyoto Protocol and International Criminal Court not to advance a better world but, rather, to constrain US economic and military power. France and America have maintained a long history of fluctuating dependency, antagonism, revulsion, and amity. This has been compounded by an increasing power disparity in the modern era. It is unlikely that a diplomatic policy shift on the behalf of Washington or Paris can change this underlying dynamic. President Sarkozy's rapprochement with the US – he chose to holiday in New Hampshire in July 2007 – is more notable for the domestic French opposition it has engendered rather than the diplomatic rift it has healed.[38]

The ex-Soviet satellite states of East Europe certainly related to Bush's war on terror differently from Germany and France. Those that suffered most under Soviet domination have proved warmer to the United States than the states that did best under the US security umbrella during the First Cold War. Gratitude is rarely a sound basis for any government's foreign policy, but the truism that people never forgive a big favor granted them explained much of the antipathy of old Europe toward the Bush administration, the French government's especially so. New Europeans were keen on joining the US economic and security imperium at the end of the First Cold War and the advent of the war on terror has provided unique opportunities to do so. France and Germany, on the other hand, saw the end of the USSR and the rise of global Islamist terrorism as an opportunity to tread a more independent path from Washington. The passing of the Bush administration is unlikely to alter Franco-German calculations. As we observed in chapter 3, the distaste shown toward the Bush administration in Paris and Bonn did not make their foreign policies any more cohesive or effective. 'When I want to speak to Europe,' asked Henry Kissinger some three decades ago, 'whom do I call?' The EU is no nearer to providing a telephone number.

Russia

In some ways, America's former First Cold War adversary, the regime Kissinger felt could be accommodated into peaceful coexistence, will continue to matter significantly. In others, it will remain decidedly second tier. Let us consider first the argument that Russia still matters. Since 9/11, Russia has occupied a somewhat ambiguous position vis-à-vis the United States. On Bush's plans for missile defense, for example, Russia emitted some mixed signals. At the June 2007 G8 summit, President Putin warned that, if the US went ahead with a missile shield in Poland and the Czech Republic, he would be forced to train Russian missiles on European cities. He then offered to house the shield system in Azerbaijan.[39] The first posture was dictated by Putin's need to impress his domestic audience – of Russian toughness and great power status. The second reflected the realities of state security in an age of increasing WMD proliferation. Indeed, Putin's offer confirmed the underlying utility of the Bush Doctrine to nations facing comparable threats from terrorists and their sponsors. Islamism has killed far more Russians than it has Americans. Some 15,000 Soviet soldiers died fighting the Mujahadeen in the Afghanistan War (1979–89). Islamist separatists killed 344 Russian civilians (186 of them school children) in Beslan (September 2004). In its war against them in Chechnya since 1994, Russia has lost an estimated 25,000 soldiers.[40] The Russian war against Islamism has a longer and fiercer history than America's. It is likely to remain at least as protracted.

Bush was keen to play on this commonality of threat.[41] It is probable his successors will do likewise. A 'second' US–Russia cold war is in the interests of neither Washington nor Moscow. Joint efforts in a Second Cold War against Islamist terror offer a better prospect. Since the demise of communism as the organizing principle of Russian society – an event which occurred some time before the formal dissolution of the USSR[42] – the grounds for cooperation have increased. The war on terror has amplified them further. On the evening of September 11, Bush 'noted that the attacks provided a great opportunity to engage Russia and China.'[43] To a significant extent, Bush's prediction was correct. The use of former Soviet central Asian republics by American forces in Operation Enduring Freedom (in Afghanistan) was largely dependent on Putin's consent.[44] 'Sixteen years after the end of the Cold War,' Condoleezza Rice declared in 2007:

> the transatlantic community and Russia are not adversaries. Indeed, on a number of issues, we are partners. We both face a number of common challenges, among the most threatening is the possibility that a dangerous state will use ballistic missiles, tipped with nuclear or other weapons of mass destruction, to hold our societies hostage – or worse.[45]

Russian helpfulness – a consistently rationed commodity – conceals, however, several fundamental weaknesses in Russia's position, making it progressively less vital to American interests. Presidents after Bush will be faced with the enduring strategic and economic decline of the Russian Federation. The nation's enormous landmass and imperial past mask one of the lowest fertility rates in the world (1.4 children per woman) which presages a demographic disaster worse even than Europe's (1.5).[46] Russia's population, the nation's 'most acute problem today,' according to Putin, is decreasing by 700,000 each year.[47] Economically, Russia remains dependent on its energy exports and foreign investors. Increasingly, the Kremlin's international leverage extends not much beyond the turning of a gas tap. 'Fluctuating energy prices, not nuclear warheads, are what really matter to Moscow.'[48] As Robert Kagan explains,

Russia has been using its vast reserves of oil and natural gas as a lever to compensate for the lack of military power, but it either cannot or does not want to increase its military capability sufficiently to begin counterbalancing the United States. Overall, Russian military power remains in decline.[49]

Moreover, whilst the EU might feel the effects of an interrupted gas supply, US consumers are relatively immune to such Russian tinkering. Only 3 percent of US domestic electricity is generated by imported gas. This also provides an important reason why no American president – even Al Gore – will sign up to global carbon emission targets, irrespective of whether he or she has faith in the climate change theory. Over half of America's domestic electricity comes from coal-fired power stations, one of the dirtiest forms of power generation. Closing them, as environmentalists demand, would shift the burden to natural gas, a resource in which the US is not rich, and thus render it more dependent on foreign supply. Russia and the Middle East produce more natural gas than any other region. No US president would choose to be dependent on Scandinavia let alone on Arabs, Iran, and former Soviets, especially after 9/11.[50] The United States, having seen off the Soviet ideological threat, is hardly likely to imbue the children of that failed experiment with control over its domestic energy supply.

Like its French counterpart, Russian awkwardness is hardly a new phenomenon in world politics. Presently and in the future, that awkwardness is unlikely to make Russia a primary concern of American foreign policy. Russia has eminently strong grounds for fearing a terrorist nuclear strike – given its treatment of jihadists – as much as America but is also positioned to counter it, given its stockpile of nuclear weapons, and to pressure its former colonies into doing the same. Whilst Russia has given covert support to North Korean nuclear ambitions – its Scuds have been the model for Pyongyang's Nodong missile, according to US intelligence – this has hardly increased Russian security from American, Chinese, and Japanese reprisal should North Korea ever use them. Russia may well be a military 'Toys Я Us' for China and North Korea, but a toy store is hardly a world power.[51] 'Russia Inc.' now proliferates for profit rather than for strategic advantage or from ideological compulsion.[52] Proliferation on such a basis is much more open to suasion than when an ideologically inspired Russia was deploying missiles to Cuba in 1962.

The ongoing deployment of an American defensive shield into Russia's front yard demonstrates with rare clarity the impotence of Russian power in the current international system. Putin and his successors will no doubt continue to bluster over this US deployment. They are, however, incapable of doing anything to prevent its happening. Indeed, as Putin's 2007 offer to facilitate the American system highlights, Russia sees that it stands to gain from American projection into its former satellites and the defense blanket such projection affords Russia itself. This does not quite make Russia a victim of anything a US president chooses to do but it does indicate the room for maneuver Washington has in its diplomacy with Moscow in the Second Cold War – a latitude that could only be dreamed of in the First.

China

Is China a threat to the United States? Those who fear China argue that its economic power is translating into military ambition. This fear is compounded by an ideology that prizes state power and treats human rights as a western construct wielded to demonize China. 'In its entire 3000-year history,' argue Richard Bernstein and Ross Munro, 'China has developed no concept of limited government, no protection of individual rights, no independence for the judiciary and the media.' The country, they conclude, is likely to become a 'kind of corporatist, militarized, nationalist state, one with some similarity to the fascist states of Mussolini or Franco.'[53] Michael

O'Hanlon and Richard Bush do not rely on this analogy. They do, however, argue persuasively that US–PRC conflict is inevitable.[54]

Arguments against this interpretation observe the regionally circumscribed ambitions of the Chinese leadership; Beijing has no plan for world domination. It does seek regional hegemony because this, it calculates, will buy it a security elusive in Chinese history. The PRC is surrounded. Until the dissolution of the USSR, it had more land borders than any other nation on earth – today only Russia has more. It has been prey to recurrent invasion and foreign interference, from the humiliating asymmetry of relations with the West, especially Britain, in the nineteenth century, to the genocidal occupation of the Japanese in the 1930s. We argued in chapter 1 that the world view of Americans was shaped, in significant measure, by their geography. It has, indeed, become a truism that geography is destiny. In China, the impact of location is especially clear. According to this interpretation, it is fear that motivates Chinese behavior rather than hubristic ambition.[55]

Which side of the debate was reflected in Bush's China policy? The diplomacy of George W. Bush toward China was in some ways more temperate than that of his predecessor. The furor over the accidental bombing of the Chinese embassy in Belgrade, which killed three Chinese journalists, during the Kosovo War in May 1999 stands in contrast to the careful negotiations that resolved the US–PRC standoff over a downed American spy plane in April 2001.[56] Indeed, in several respects, his China policy looked more liberal than Clinton's. Bush recurrently engaged China in order to temper the North Korean threat. Unlike Clinton, who nearly became embroiled in a war on the Korean Peninsula in 1994, Bush used multilateral diplomacy to forestall Pyongyang's nuclear program.[57] Howard Dean and Senator Russ Feingold (D-WI), among several other prominent Democrats, actually chided Bush for having 'outsourced' – i.e., multilateralized – America's North Korean policy. 'The stakes are too high,' said Feingold, 'to rely on others to address the North Korean crisis.'[58]

Bush, with some success, was able to use China in stabilizing East Asia. China bought into this because stabilization is in its interests. It is notable that the United States has become as reliant on Beijing limiting North Korean excesses as Beijing has become on America's negation of Japanese regional ambitions. China fears Japan more than it craves Taiwan. If realists are correct, Beijing would not risk conflict over the island at the price of a Japan unchecked by American power. The US would almost certainly urge Japanese militarization, even nuclearization, in response to Chinese aggression against Taiwan.[59] Bush accepted the logic of this situation, as did the Chinese leadership. Realists have referred to this as a case of 'mutual deterrence.'[60] Others, such as Robert Lieber, prefer to think of America as 'Asia's pacifier.'[61] In both analyses, however, China has, at least to date, accepted the utility of US power in its backyard.

What Bush sacrificed in his China policy, to the chagrin of several neoconservative and liberal commentators, was the pretense of a values-driven approach.[62] Human rights in China are no better today than they were in 2001 and in several respects much worse.[63] The Bush administration also appeared relatively sanguine about the remarkable penetration of Africa by China. Trade between them increased from $5.6 billion in 1999 to $32.2 billion in 2005.[64] It has been argued that what African regimes prize is the absence of a moral agenda and any colonial baggage attaching to their Chinese backers. The conditionality of much western aid – tying it to political reforms and human rights promotion – is entirely lacking in Chinese subventions of African industry. The fundamental amorality of Beijing's approach was captured in its recent designation of Zimbabwe's Robert Mugabe as a 'brilliant diplomat.'[65]

Bush's tolerance of Chinese soft power in Africa extended to Chinese intrigue in the Middle East. Despite emerging evidence that Beijing has been selling arms to America's enemies in the region – to Iraqi insurgents via Tehran, for example – Bush applied 'the China exception.'[66] Rather than risk losing China's cooperation over North

Korea, Bush followed the State Department line and denied that arms shipments were officially sanctioned. China was, after all, not seeking to spread the Shiite revolution but to gain access to Iranian oil. This objective, as Arthur Herman has argued, could well eventually entail 'an aggressive military strategy' but presently is better advanced by a rather nefarious trade arrangement.[67] China's Middle East policy seemed to Bush, as it did to Clinton, entirely economically self-interested.

This all illustrates an American China policy that was remarkably non-doctrinaire under Bush. In this regard, at least, he was most unlike Harry S. Truman. Bush consistently refused to take sides on the China threat debate. He rarely made a speech about it, continuing his father's ambivalence toward his one-time ambassadorial home.[68] Rather than pursue an aggressive strategy, Bush has trusted that the economic transformation of China, with its dependence on western, and especially US, markets, will result in a political liberalization. His position was essentially that of Bill Clinton in trusting that trade, eventually, would bring democracy, as if the progression from one to the other was a social scientific certainty. That faith in trade, as we examined in chapter 1, has been a consistent theme of American foreign policy since 1787.

Whilst cultural differences are marked, especially when it comes to human rights, the rule of law, and the power of the state, ideologically China is ambiguous.[69] It poses no obvious ideological threat despite being ideologically suspect. The pro- and anti-China lobbies in the US do not fit into neat partisan or ideological pigeonholes. In several important respects, its murky relationship with Iran and Pakistan excepted, China shares the broad goals of the Bush Doctrine – the defeat of Islamism – even if it balks at America's chosen means: democratization. A similar situation obtained in the First Cold War. Both the US and China shared an interest in containing Soviet power. This made relations between them, after a frosty 1950s and 60s, amicable, if never warm. America used China then, as now, as 'the regional power of choice.'[70] This does not mean that they will ever come to share a common world view. Hopes that they might remain the preserve of idealists. As Aaron L. Friedberg warns, 'The American people are never going to fully trust a government that restricts freedom of religion, speech, and political competition.'[71]

An English-speaking alliance?

The antipathy of the United States toward China, despite some common interests, is grounded in a more fundamental difference between the democracies that speak English and the rest of the world, democratic or not, that does not. The great US foreign policy presidencies of the last century were built on the moral unity and military interoperability of North America, Britain, and Australasia. In union, this alliance enjoyed a remarkable war record. When it has fractured, wars have gone less well. Suez was a debacle for London because Washington withdrew support. The US war for Vietnam enjoyed no Canadian or British support (though Australia did commit troops in the South Vietnamese cause) and was ultimately abandoned. This is not to argue that America cannot fight without the explicit sanction of its 'cousins.' But it does suggest that failure to unite them damages the moral claims of American action.

According to Andrew Roberts' definition, 'the first great assault on the English-speaking peoples' was 'Prussian Militarism' (c. 1900–1918), the second 'Axis Fascism' (1939–45), the third 'Soviet Communism' (1945–1991), and the fourth 'Islamicist Terrorism' (ongoing).[72] His argument is not built on the military prowess of those united by this particular language but rather on the values and legacy of British rule that have tied the English-speaking peoples together. That we do not speak about the cohesion or history of the French- or Spanish-speaking peoples highlights a special narrative afforded to the English-speaking alliance in modern history. This is not to deny the American Revolution drew its moral justification from the French *philosophes* of the eighteenth century. However, the notion of human rights and the principle of political freedom that grew from the European enlightenment have been advanced more by an English-speaking alliance in the modern era.

Our argument here is that Bush's foreign policy was built on that alliance. His war on terror was symbolically if not logistically dependent on winning the Australian, British, and to a lesser extent, Indian governments to the American cause. Symbolism matters. Here we agree with the 'ethical realists' Lieven and Hulsman who note that 'the influence of the American system on the world is something that should be seen as greater and more important than raw power.'[73] An American global war fought without English-speaking allies would be unsustainable. By the same token, the leaders of these nations, whilst their levels of physical commitment have varied, accepted the moral necessity of backing the US in the Second Cold War, as they did, with remarkable success, in the First. Each has been subject to jihadist attack. Each believed they were attacked for what they represented to the enemy, not for what they had done to him. Each responded by moving toward rather than away from Washington. No future US administration is likely to forgo the legitimacy such cooperation affords its foreign policy. Likewise, no English-speaking leader can resist American overtures without compromising his international leverage.

United Kingdom

Books that examine the Anglo-American relationship since 9/11 will increasingly have to account for the crucial supporting role the former British prime minister played in lending both political legitimacy and military efficacy to the Bush Doctrine. Without the support – moral and logistical – of this English-speaking alliance, America would have faced a uniquely hostile international environment after its ousting of the Taliban in 2001. How do we account for the strategic intimacy of the Bush–Blair relationship?

The popular answer is that Blair was drawn to power like a bee to honey. In this formulation, the prime minister sought to use his kinship with Bush as a lever for his European aspirations; being powerful in Washington made him powerful in the EU. Of what worth is British power in Europe, calculated Blair, if it does not act as a bridge to the US? There is some logic to this interpretation. What it downplays is the ideological amity of the Blair years, after a period of post-First Cold War estrangement during the John Major government (1990–7).[74] Blair connected American primacy with his aspirations for a moral world order, in which tyranny would be confronted rather than, pace the EU, appeased. He called it his 'doctrine of the international community,' and there is strikingly little in its accompanying rhetoric that Clinton or Bush did not sign up to.[75] In this regard Blair was not aberrantly pro-American, and certainly no poodle. Rather, as a commentator scathing of Blair's foreign policy put it, the PM used 'his heroine' Margaret Thatcher as his model:

> He soon turned his back – seeking 'the heart of Europe' – as she and Major had both done on taking office – in favour of the American bond. While half-hearted attempts were made by Robin Cook [British foreign secretary, 1997–2001] to clothe Blair's adventurism in 'ethical' garb, it was essentially if vaguely neo-imperial. It pronounced a 'Western values agenda' to be imposed on sovereign states at will. The politics of fear and a wildly inflated war on terror became the leitmotif of speech after speech. Told by Thatcher to 'hug Washington close,' Blair did so to a fault, from the mountains of Tora Bora to the streets of Fallujah and the cells of Guantanamo Bay.[76]

Just as Blair's Bush bias was not unusual – the most successful prime ministers since the Second World War have been solidly westward looking – neither was Bush's treatment of Blair and the British alliance. Bush was hardly revolutionary when it came to using the special relationship. Like FDR and Reagan before him, his foreign policy ideology synchronized with his British counterpart.[77] Presidents and prime ministers have invariably found themselves isolated, and their foreign policy compromised as a result, when they have failed to convince each other of their moral purpose. Suez (1956) was proof positive of this for the British, Vietnam for the Americans – both campaigns waged without the military support of the other.[78]

It is difficult to imagine, therefore, the special relationship after Bush and Blair as being anything other than one based on strategic alliance and managed intimacy. British power in world affairs is proportionate to British influence in Washington, not in Brussels. Blair grasped this with pristine clarity, especially after 9/11. Gordon Brown has done the same if in a more understated manner. Indeed, his abiding coolness toward the EU – *pace* Thatcher – is likely to enhance the US–UK relationship rather than degrade it as any number of anti-Bush commentators have hoped. For most Brits, the Channel remains wider than the Atlantic.

Australia

John Howard, the Australian prime minister from 1996 to 2007, Tony Blair, and George Bush each won post-9/11 national elections. Whilst we cannot prove that their unity or steadfastness in the war on terror caused their re-election, their continuance in office gives the lie to claims that counterterrorism has been uniquely unpopular among western, particularly English-speaking, publics. John *Winston* Howard actually won two general elections after November 2001 (a record arguably greater than the PM he is named after; Churchill lost the British general election two months after VE day, 1945).

As one scholar observes, the American–Australian alliance is deep and longstanding. 'In conflicts in the South West Pacific during World War II and later in the Korean peninsula, and then from Vietnam to Afghanistan and on to Iraq, Australia's and America's armed forces have repeatedly found themselves engaging common enemies.'[79] Australia has committed some 1,400 troops to the Afghan and Iraq Wars, losing three men by summer 2007.[80] US–Australian relations were especially strong in the Bush era. Indeed, according to one regional expert, the Australian government 'has offered almost unreserved support for the US . . . and seems remarkably comfortable with Bush's National Security Strategy.'[81] In contrast to Canada and New Zealand, Australia – in the shape of John Howard – has recognized the legitimacy of US objectives in the war on terror. He has done so despite the near 75 percent of Australians who believe the Iraq War has increased the likelihood of terrorism.[82] Howard has refused to allow this domestic pressure to alter his alliance with the United States. Indeed, as Mark Steyn has argued, Howard has succeeded in maintaining a domestic consensus on strategy despite public reservations over tactics:

> The Iraq war is unpopular in Australia, as it is in America and in Britain. But the Aussie government is happy for the opposition to bring up the subject as often as they want because [Alexander] Downer [Australian foreign minister] and his prime minister understand very clearly that wanting to 'cut and run' is even more unpopular. So in the broader narrative it's a political plus for them: Unlike Bush and Blair, they've succeeded in making the issue not whether the nation should have gone to war but whether the nation should lose the war.[83]

Australia's political character and geographic location are likely to make it more important in US foreign policy as the war on terror continues. Australia offers a balancing force against China and, to a lesser degree, Japan in Asia generally. It has also been important in counterterrorism efforts in Southeast Asia specifically. In the aftermath of the Japanese attack on Pearl Harbor, Australian prime minister John Curtin called America 'the keystone of Australian defence.'[84] It is an analysis John Howard has reapplied since 9/11. Rather than cause it to flee, the Australian government calculated that its own security was better met by joining the American-led war. The Bali bombing merely served to convince Howard that Australians would be targeted for their values irrespective of his intimacy with the Bush White House.

It is difficult to prove a commonality of response grounded in a shared value-system and certainly not in a common language.[85] But if one were to compare how Australia reacted to the 2002 Bali bombing, which killed 88 Australians, with how Spain reacted to al Qaeda's 2004 attack on Madrid, which killed 191, mostly Spaniards, one would see two different sets of values determining the respective behavior of these states. For the Australian government, Bali meant a renewed commitment to the American war on terror and a deeper engagement against jihadism in Southeast Asia. For the Spanish government elected in its wake, the Madrid attack symbolized the problem of alliance with the United States, one it swiftly downgraded (by withdrawing its troops from Iraq). Again, we make this observation not to prove the superiority of English-speaking values over Spanish but to highlight the broad, but certainly not perfect, cohesion of the English-speaking response to Islamist terrorism – at least at the elite level. Speaking English does not make a people brave but it is indicative of cultural patterns that tend to recur in the face of similar phenomena, like foreign attack.

India

Arguably the greatest bilateral success story of the Bush years was the transformation of America's ties with India. Despite an often discordant relationship between America and India since independence in 1947, after which New Delhi tilted toward Moscow, 'it is safe to say,' according to a former US ambassador, 'that the alignment between India and the United States is now an enduring part of the international landscape of the 21st century.'[86] Clinton deserves some credit for beginning a steady embrace, but Bush advanced the breadth and depth of the links in remarkably bold fashion. Three points of convergence will likely compel even greater US–India cooperation: Iran, Pakistan, and the threat of Islamism pose both to the English-speaking alliance and to India in particular.

The achievement of an offensive nuclear capacity by Tehran is feared by both Washington and New Delhi. The gloomy scenario with which we opened this book – an Iranian-backed nuclear deto-nation in several US cities provoking an American response in kind – might equally apply to India. It has endured more Islamist assaults than any other nation in the English-speaking world. Theologically, Hinduism is beyond the pale for Islamists. India possesses the second-largest Muslim population, after Indonesia. Historically, India has been subject to especially intense sectarian violence that resulted in the creation of the Islamic Republic of Pakistan and the transference, thereby, of a domestic tension into an intractable international dispute – symbolized but not limited to the conflict over Kashmir. Thus, the disposition of New Delhi, even before the war on terror, favored a diplomacy that sought to contain and reduce Islamism in the Indian sub-continent. It followed that Indian suspicions about Chinese support of Pakistan and Iran, given traditional Sino–Indian tensions, would naturally result in a warming of US–India relations.

Yet this assessment of Indian motivations ignores the cultural com-monalities that propel India toward America and the *de facto* alliance it leads. India opposes Islamism not because of Pakistan or Kashmir but because it represents a threat to values that India and its English-speaking allies deem worth protecting: the rule of law, economic opportunity, free trade, individual rights, religious freedoms, liberal democracy, and limits on the power of the state. It is these values which, more than geo-strategic interest and balance, will increasingly bind India to America, as they bind Britain and Australia as well. This was confirmed by Prime Minister Manmohan Singh:

> Our notions of the rule of law, of a Constitutional government, of a free press, of a professional civil service, of modern universities and research laboratories have all been fashioned in the crucible where an age old civilisation met the dominant Empire of the day. These are all elements that we still value and cherish. Our judiciary, our legal system, our bureaucracy and our police are all great institutions,

derived from the British-Indian administration, and they have served this country well.[87]

In the First Cold War, India survived a disastrous attempt to emulate the Soviet economic model. This futile effort to manufacture a value-system antithetical to its former British colonizer only suggests the permanence of values in the shaping of foreign relationships. It is impossible to expect any nation to operate on the basis of that which it is not. This argues for a strengthening of the US–India relationship in coming years. As Robert Blackwill observes, there was strong agreement from congressional Democrats on the course the Indian relationship took under Bush, especially the civil nuclear deal that he struck with New Delhi.[88] This American consensus suggests that 'the fundamentals of the new strategic direction will not change.'[89] Unlike US China policy, US–India relations have not inspired vociferous lobbies for and against India. This should not surprise us. India is, after all, the world's largest democracy, America the oldest. Again, this highlights the recognition of an English-speaking order, of ideals as well as of interests, embedded at the heart of US foreign policy.

As Bill Emmott notes, just as Nixon is remembered more for his opening to China than failure in Vietnam, Bush may well gain credit from future historians for recognizing the importance of India. His sealing of the new relationship – in the form of the US–India nuclear pact – will endure for a considerable time to come.[90] In assisting India to become stronger, to extend its political and economic clout into the rest of Asia and thereby to prevent China from dominating, Washington has played a key role in helping India balance Beijing, and in extending the English-speaking alliance.

Conclusion

According to al Qaeda, 'the Zionist–Anglo-Saxon–Protestant coalition' was the specific target on 9/11.[91] The consolidation of that powerful coalition was certainly the response to that attack. It is a coalition with considerable historical success on its side. Unfortunate, also, for al Qaeda, is that its success was against ideological and existential threats. In the First Cold War, the United States relied on a series of alliances that shared a common distrust of communism and, where possible, united in liberal democratic values. Not every bilateral relationship was grounded in a formal treaty. Those that were operated, via NATO for example, on the basis of their utility – did NATO help America realize its interests? – rather than because the alliance embodied an institutional significance so great that the US could not countenance operating outside of it. America surely did and surely will again.

The English-speaking alliance that has reassembled in the Second Cold War exemplified the thrust of Bush statecraft, that is, toward friendships that advanced common values even as they remained non-institutionalized and informal. It is difficult to imagine how a deeper ingratiation on America's part into the formal international institutions that liberals hold dear could have prevented the jihadist attacks that shaped foreign policy in the Bush era. Working more closely with the UN guarantees no more security for the United States than ignoring it. As in its previous global wars, America has been forced to rely on what works in practice, not on what should work in theory.

The Bush administration, faced with 9/11, relied on flexible coalition-building to answer the new threat, just as his predecessors had done against the enemies of their day. As we have observed in this chapter, especially in regard to China and India, Bush did not run a doctrinaire foreign policy so much as he did a strategy that relied on expediency to advance democratic values. There is a common misconception that Bush was a democratic zealot. His diplomacy reveals no such thing. His ambivalence toward China, for example, sprang from a healthy sense of the limits of American power. Like every president since Nixon, he trusted that trade and engagement would moderate Beijing. His ambivalence toward Islamabad and Riyadh testified to a recognition that no nation – not even America – can accomplish every goal at once. This was 'democratic realism,' not 'democratic globalism,' in action. In prioritizing, the charge of American 'double standards' over democracy promotion was no greater or lesser than it had been to his predecessors nor, in all likelihood, to those who will follow him in the White House.

Our contention throughout this book has been that values explain much of the international conduct of the United States. Not values in place of interests – no state so dedicated could long endure – but, rather, the pursuit of interests that tend to the survival, maintenance, and expansion of American values. This approach was manifested in the bilateral diplomacy of the Bush White House. There exists an ease to relations between Washington and London, Tel Aviv, Tokyo, Canberra, and, now, New Delhi, that is denied that with Cairo or Moscow. Bush was not unique among presidents in pursuing a values-based response to America's friends and foes alike.

An appropriate question in conclusion is 'how will his successors change Bush statecraft?' Our answer is 'not much.' A change in White House personnel, despite the delusions of some European elites, will not alter fundamentally the direction of US–EU relations – evident as much under Clinton as Bush – nor the way old Europe deals (inadequately) with the global Islamist challenge. On China, it seems likely that the next few US administrations will do as Bush has done and avoid tipping their diplomacy too far in either a pro- or anti-China direction. Like him, Bush's successors will likely feel at home within a *de facto* English-speaking alliance, one symbolic of a remarkable history and still capable of future victories.

8

The emerging consensus at home and abroad

Truth . . . has to be made by the rough process of a struggle between combatants fighting under hostile banners.

John Stuart Mill, *On Liberty*

. . . is it so preposterous to suggest that a global ideology that justifies the use of limitless violence against civilians, and whose adherents are immensely inventive (if not always competent) in discerning methods of delivering that violence, could present an 'existential' threat?

David Aaronovitch[1]

When Obama, in a speech on terrorism at the Wilson Center in Washington, said 'If we have actionable intelligence about high-value terrorist targets (in Pakistan) and President Musharraf won't act, we will,' he came under attack not only from Hillary Clinton but also from Senators Joseph Biden and Christopher Dodd. It turned out, though, that their objection was not to what he said – which they agreed with – but to the undiplomatic indiscretion of saying it out loud.

Hendrik Hertzberg[2]

There's a warning sign on the road ahead
There's a lot of people saying we'd be better off dead
Don't feel like Satan but I am to them
So I try to forget it any way I can

Neil Young, 'Rockin' in the Free World' (1989)

In this chapter we consider the future of American foreign policy and explain why its strategic shape is more likely to resemble rather than reject that established under Bush, regardless of who is president into the 2010s and beyond. We argue that both at home and abroad the Bush approach has generated a consensus likely to endure.

The White House is not a black box, and who occupies it after 2008 matters. Unlike some international relations theorists, we take seriously the differences that political leadership, especially in a state as powerful as America, can make. As Ian Kershaw has shown, in democracies as well as dictatorships leaders can make fateful decisions that shape the futures of entire nations.[3] We cannot therefore discount the possibility, in the abstract, that the next American president will declare the war on terror over or lost, retreat from Iraq and the Middle East, refuse to deploy force without a prior UN authorization, and strike a new concordat with Tehran and Damascus. But we rather doubt it. In this chapter we contend that the case for an essential continuity in the architecture of US foreign policy after Bush rests on five strong foundations:

- the severity of the clear and present security threat from internationalist Islamism;
- the continuance of American primacy and a unipolar world;
- the appeal of a distinctly American internationalism as the best strategy to preserve this primacy, alongside the unappealing nature of alternative prescriptions;
- the continued and reinvigorated bipartisan support for the Second Cold War 'beyond the desert's edge'; and
- the resilience and vitality of American exceptionalism.

We will deal in turn with each.

Clear, present and growing dangers

Although other concerns loom large, the most pressing task of Bush's successors in the White House is prevailing in the global struggle against jihadist Islamism. To do so, it is imperative that the nature of that struggle be properly appreciated and articulated. The president in particular – and the American political class more broadly – must make clear to the American people that this effort needs to be accorded the national seriousness, priority, and resources necessary for ultimate success. In particular, the competing terms employed to describe this struggle – war on terror, the 'long war' – would be better served by a simple yet clear recognition that a Second Cold War is now well underway. In its mix of tactical weapons, multiple fronts, and barbaric enemy the Second Cold War strongly resembles and echoes the First. Moreover, the success of western market democracies in prevailing in this struggle demands re-creating the types of creative and long-term thinking that characterized the First Cold War. If Muhammad remains less attractive today than Marx did previously in the West, this should be no cause for complacency. The ideological, political, economic, diplomatic, covert, intelligence, and cultural fronts will assume at least as much importance as the military one in this generational conflict. Shying away from recognizing the scale and nature of the struggle has its attractions. But ultimately this serves the American interest, and a more stable and just world order, poorly.

In confronting jihadist Islam explicitly, Bush's America joined a war already underway ('the terrorists' war on us,' in Rudy Giuliani's formulation). On some accounts, this war was first declared by al Qaeda in 1996. On others, the war has been fought since 1979. On still others, the war has been waged since at least 1945.[4] For some, including Islamists themselves, it has been on-going for several centuries. Whatever the preferred chronology, the Bush administration's response to 9/11 was commensurate with the security challenge America confronted. Contrary to the increasingly fashionable notion among some academics that 'mature' democracies should treat Islamist terror as a nuisance, the modest cost of a free and open society to be endured but pursued through police and intelligence work,[5] the administration correctly faced up to jihadist Islam as an existential threat of generational character. To be sure, the threat thus far remains on a lesser scale than Nazism and communism, inasmuch as entire nations (whether the US, UK, or Australia, but not Israel) do not face the imminent prospect of total annihilation. But the potential for entire cities to be vaporized and tens of thousands of lives lost is more real than ever.

Moreover, the intent to wreak catastrophic havoc in the West is at least as great as that of Nazi Germany. Al Qaeda's avowed preference is for terrorist 'spectaculars' – the simultaneous assault of multiple targets, causing maximum fatalities. Non-proliferation experts anticipate that – given the availability of technology, the black markets in weaponry, and the fanatical nihilism of jihadist networks – the likelihood of attacks during the coming decade with some form of WMD is around 70 percent.[6] The nexus of terrorists and WMD, and the shared anti-Americanism uniting otherwise disparate and antagonistic entities around the world, demand constant surveillance, covert action, and preventive interdiction. But mass publics in America, Europe, and elsewhere remain reluctant to comprehend the scale, variety, and lethality of the challenges that Islamist terror poses and the multiple mechanisms by which it seeks to attack national homelands. Bush rightly vowed that America would not seek a 'permission slip' from others to ensure its security, a position echoed (albeit more weakly) by Senator John Kerry (D-MA) in the 2004 presidential election. No successor, Democrat or Republican, will repudiate that vow since no president will accord a veto on national security to the UN or another state.

But with the 9/11 attacks receding in time, forgetfulness and complacency are gaining ground. The absence of a second 9/11 increases the propensity to believe that the threat has receded or disappeared, thereby unburdening Americans of the need for an assertive foreign policy and global presence. The failed occupation of Iraq dovetails for some by illustrating the high, even prohibitive, price of such assertiveness. The combined result is one where many Americans do not know if they truly *are* safer at the end of Bush's two terms or whether they merely *feel* safer. Notwithstanding the tendency of some analysts to use statistical 'truths' to discount terrorist attacks as less likely to occur than car accidents as a basis for crafting national security policies, we still have no idea – as we conceded in chapter 4 – whether the probability of another 9/11, or worse, is one in ten or one in ten million.

Moreover, because the war on terrorism is not a war with a conventional state, it is self-evidently not a conventional war. But it possesses the essential features of such a war – indeed, a total war. As Barack Obama noted, 'Because this enemy operates globally, it must be confronted globally.'[7] While it is a multi-dimensional conflict in which intelligence, ideas, and diplomacy all loom large, in its military dimensions it is a violent conflict against a resilient enemy whose publicly declared goals are to wound the West as grievously as possible, to overturn governments across the Middle East, Africa, and Central and Southeast Asia, to destroy Israel, and to cause an exhausted and demoralized America to withdraw from the Middle East. Posner argues that America's enemies are:

> numerous, fanatical, implacable, elusive, resourceful, resilient, utterly ruthless, seemingly fearless, apocalyptic in their aims, and eager to get their hands on weapons of mass destruction and use them against us. They did us terrible harm on September 11, 2001, and may do us worse harm in the future. We know little about their current number, leaders, locations, resources, supporters, motivations, and plans; and in part because of our ignorance, we have no strategy for defeating them, only for fighting them.[8]

Continue to fight them we must, but the strategy to defeat them and emerge victorious is one that requires careful calibration.

As we argued in chapters 3 and 4, the Second Cold War has made strong headway against al Qaeda and its affiliates. Were this not so, we would currently be entertaining measures far more draconian at home and abroad than those that have thus far come to pass. Terrorist attacks have taken innocent Muslim and non-Muslim lives with seemingly remorseless, year-on-year repetition. But in terms of the metrics of this war, much has been achieved. To reiterate, there has been no repetition of a 'spectacular' such as 9/11, much less a 9/11 with some form of nuclear, biological, chemical, or radiological weaponry. The Islamist attacks that have occurred, though many, have largely been confined to public transportation or public arenas such as bars and hotels, none approximating the scale of 9/11. Each assault has been another signal of the murderous intent of jihadists – not only to the West but to all those Muslim and non-Muslim peoples whom they deem expendable *kufur*, apostates and infidels. They should be vivid reminders to take these new totalitarians at their word. But when we recall the aftermath that 9/11 had opened to previously closed eyes – the dangers of proliferating WMD, the dedicated intent of jihadists to acquire and use WMD in and against the citizens of the developed world, and the utterly amoral and immoral regimes content to sell or supply Islamist forces such weapons – that terrorist attacks should be small scale and episodic is an achievement of which western governments and publics should be grateful.

That metric offers us some reason to believe that we are safer than on 9/11. But we remain far from being safe. As Posner notes, we no longer inhabit a world where the respective nuclear arsenals of the superpowers reliably inform us of our relative safety. The struggle enveloping the world is all the more complex and challenging precisely because of the elusiveness of our enemies, the potency of the weapons they seek, the vulnerability of safeguards against their obtaining such weaponry, and the technologies that now facilitate the execution of mass murder on an unprecedented scale. If we follow the advice of the former counterterrorism czar Richard Clarke and conceive of the challenge as a series of concentric circles with al Qaeda in the innermost, jihadist terrorists in the second, jihadist sympathizers in the third, and the final outer layer of the rest of the Islamic world (or 'moderate' Muslim opinion), no one can authoritatively deduce their relative numbers.[9]

If the task confronting us is relatively straightforward in terms of its ultimate goals – eliminate the central circle, reduce the proximate ones, and pacify the outer circle – no strategy has yet emerged decisively or rapidly to achieve those ends. There is a simple reason why such a strategy has proven so elusive: it seeks to achieve incompatible aims. Clarke states that 'The jihadist terrorists oppose the US not for what it believes or does, but because they see America as a barrier to their creation of theocratic nation-states or caliphates.'[10] But the US opposes such entities not only because of its interests but also because of its ideals. What they are and what they do are inseparable. Engaging in the battle of ideas, providing assistance to Islamic nations, implementing tailored strategies for key states, improving intelligence and law enforcement, eliminating terror financing, improving military organization, shoring up homeland security, countering WMD proliferation and achieving energy security are all urgent and ambitious objectives. But, as we have emphasized, defeating jihadist Islam ultimately requires nothing less than the reform of Islam to separate mosque and state, modernization of Arab and Muslim societies, and steps toward genuine self-government. Only when the glaring deficiencies of information and technology, women's empowerment, and political liberty are corrected can the stagnation and barbarity of the Middle East be transcended.

As such, whether the next president calls it by its name or not, the Second Cold War against Islamist terrorism should and, we hold, will continue apace after Bush with little reason to anticipate that it will prove to be less protracted, less punctuated by setbacks as well as successes, or less momentous than the First Cold War. Like its predecessor, it will comprise a struggle waged as much or more with political, economic, ideological, cultural, and covert means as conventional battles. But it will necessarily take as its starting point that this civilizational struggle is in its dawn, not its twilight. Those who take comfort that January 2009 will usher in the end of the Bush years must confront the reality that that date marks only the end of the beginning of an epochal struggle.

American primacy: are we all multipolar now?

Although 9/11 was the key date in the joining of the Second Cold War, it was the First's end that ushered in the 'American era' of unipolarity and primacy. Since the end of the First Cold War, as Kagan and Daalder observe:

> the United States has taken military action with greater frequency than ever before and with far greater frequency than any other nation during that time. From 1989 to 2003 the United States intervened with significant military force on nine occasions – Panama (1989), Somalia (1992), Haiti (1994), Bosnia (1995–96), Kosovo (1999), Afghanistan (2001), and Iraq (1991, 1998, 2003), an average of one large-scale military intervention every 18 months. This interventionism has been a bipartisan affair – five interventions were launched by Republican administrations, four by Democratic administrations – and regardless of often-alleged, but in fact largely mythical doctrinal distinctions.[11]

Critics who view the most recent Iraq campaign as the death-knell for militarism need to factor Washington's propensity for intervention into their predictions and prescriptions. Less than one decade after peace was reached in Korea in 1953, John F. Kennedy began committing troops to a prolonged and costly conflict in Vietnam. Five decades after the Korean War was concluded, some 30,000 US troops remained in South Korea. Five years after the final helicopters left Saigon in America's first and worst military defeat, Americans elected Ronald Reagan to the presidency to restore an assertive America and counter the ambitions of an 'evil empire.' The historical record is not one that augurs well for those who aspire to a perpetually peaceful America.

But the end of a two-term administration is a reliably propitious time for political futurology. Already, by the time of the 2006 midterms and animated by the Democrats' congressional victory, critics were contemplating life after Bush with relish and relief. A return to the realism of his father's administration or the pragmatic liberalism of the Clinton years was posited as not so much possible and desirable but inevitable. The era of 'ideology' in foreign policy, of utopian transformational ideals and neoconservative designs, was declared over. Anatol Lieven pronounced in the fall of 2006 that 'The foreign and security strategy of the Bush administration lies in ruins.'[12] Concurring, Michael Lind announced that the 'neo-conservative fantasy of unilateral global hegemony has been discredited.'[13] A re-embrace of multilateralism, a new concern for the limits on American power and utility of a multipolar world, and a renewed focus on interests over ideals were deemed to be imminent.

Even among Bush critics, however, dissident voices raised important notes of skepticism to this growing 'un-Bush' consensus. For example, the foreign editor of the London *Times*, surveying the stand-off between the US and Iran over the latter's nuclear program, noted that: 'The central question about Ahmedinejad, and Bush, is whether they are aberrations. More likely, they are the shape of the future.'[14] Arguing that 'We're all multilateralists now, but we inhabit a world that makes the Cold War seem like the good old days,' David Ignatius observed:

> The difficulty is that nobody today has any real experience with how a genuinely multilateral system might work. And the more you think about it, the more potential obstacles you begin to see in the passage from unilateral hell to multilateral heaven.[15]

Offering past examples of failed predictions of new multilateral dawns, Ignatius quoted the nuclear strategist, Herman Kahn, whose 1983 essay on 'multipolarity and stability' had prophesied that by 2000 a stable multipolar world with orderly rules would have worked itself out, comprising six economic giants (the US, Japan, the USSR, China, France, and Brazil). But the central problem Kahn had foreseen was the transition from a bipolar to a multipolar system, the moment of maximum danger and instability in world affairs. Needless to say, neither that problem nor that world arose.

Even Lieven and Lind, while decrying Bush's foreign policy, found optimism about a future alternative difficult to come by. While advancing a case for an 'ethical realism' that rejected neoconservatism, Lieven pointed to three features limiting the prospects for change. First, in his view, America lacks a formal foreign policy opposition:

> Both Democrats and moderate Republicans oppose the most extreme plans of Dick Cheney and the neo-conservatives, but on the great majority of issues – the environment being a partial exception – the Democratic establishment stands squarely behind the official line of the Bush administration.[16]

The bipartisan 'establishment' comprises American nationalists, convinced by the founding myth of America's civic nationalism and virtue. Second, this leads them to be 'American imperialists,' animated by American primacy and identifying closely with Israel. Third, a revolt against established foreign policy 'would have to enjoy huge support from ordinary Americans, and in particular the most important political constituency, the white middle classes of the "heartlands."'[17]

Lind, similarly, deemed not only neoconservatism but also neoliberalism – the preferred alternative of the 'Democratic party's complacent foreign policy establishment' – and its 'dream of a UN-led international order' to be 'an illusion as well' but one that still preoccupied the Party's mainstream.[18] Another – conservative – analyst, Andrew Sullivan, while noting the 'neo-isolationist' impulses animating elements of the left and right after Iraq, nonetheless concurred that 'It's hard to see a tectonic shift that draws the US away from its late 20th-century unipolar role.'[19]

Such skeptical voices may prove mistaken, and the more common expectation/prescription of a multilateral order may come to pass. But if a nascent multipolarity is seriously on the cards, how organized a multipolar world is likely to emerge? Is the Muslim world from Algeria to Indonesia a 'pole,' and, if so, what is its leading power? Is Russia's geo-political ambition commensurate with the reality of its powerfully constrained strategic position? Can the EU, as its widening compromises its deepening, become a consequential 'pole'? It has become fashionable (perhaps more out of hope than expectation for its proponents) to predict the end of the American era. The rise of China and India, the consolidation of the EU, the recovery of the Japanese and German economies, and the problems seemingly besetting America together conspire to make coming years an age of limits rather than ambition for Washington. But we have been here before, on more than one occasion. Indeed, the rapid shifts in the consensus of the foreign policy commentariat – that 'superpower' understated US power and 'hyperpower' was more fitting in the later 1990s, that 'hyperpower' or 'hegemon' was insufficient and 'empire' was back in vogue in the early 2000s, followed by a backtracking to 'overstretch' and 'decline' in the mid-2000s – are indicative of debates over the true extent of US power which stretch back centuries.[20]

In the context of American primacy, it is worth recalling William Wohlforth's observations on measuring power.[21] Four points argue that the days of American primacy and a unipolar world are not yet over.

First, power as a relational concept and power as resources are quite different concepts. That is, the ability to achieve certain stated international ends or global public goods need not, of itself, reveal the relative power of a state. The stalemate reached in Korea in the early 1950s, for instance, did not negate America's superpower position in the First Cold War. Similarly, America's failed counter-insurgency in Vietnam did not bring into being a multipolar world. Whether or when America 'fails' in Iraq, that intervention is equally unlikely to usher in a new multipolarity. America remains the world's leading power 'after Iraq.' It spends roughly as much on defense as the rest of the world put together. The Pentagon's budget bid for fiscal year 2008, of $578 billion, represented approximately 4 percent of GDP, a low proportion by historical standards. Of course, the ability to use those resources and the need to do so are contingent matters. American power has not been able to establish a secure constitutional democracy in Iraq any more than it could decisively quell the communist subversion of South Vietnam. But the fact of American primacy endures even in the face of a campaign that did not secure its original objectives. The cardinal indicators of a challenge to that unipolar world – a balancing of other powers against the superpower or a meaningful increase in rival powers' defense spending – have simply not occurred.

Second, shifting the goalposts – evaluating US power by its ability to resolve global problems from drug proliferation to climate change – does not offer a solid perspective. The US did not cease to be a superpower after the Bay of Pigs fiasco or on being ejected from the UN Commission on Human Rights. The failure to intervene in Darfur will come to be regarded as a global abdication of responsibility by international actors, just as Rwanda was previously. But it was not authored by Washington and it affects American power not a jot.

Third, relying on a single indicator is typically unreliable in evaluating national power. To be sure, analysis of budget and trade deficits highlights possible weaknesses in the American economy. But the economy is, on other indicators – growth, inflation, unemployment – in robust health. Moreover, even in terms of the financial position of the US, growing interdependence means that those states (notably China and Japan) that hold most in terms of dollar reserves are themselves exposed should they abandon them. There exist few states with a relationship with the US (and all developed states have one) that would not be materially disadvantaged if America suffered a serious economic downturn.

Fourth, analysts often overlook latent power – the degree to which resources can or could be mobilized by a government. Despite America waging a global campaign since 9/11, it has been the military rather than the nation as a whole that has been at war. The public has not been asked or required to make serious material sacrifices either to secure the homeland or to assist the struggle against jihadism abroad. Taxes remain low, America has an exclusively volunteer army, and fatalities in Iraq – while tragic – do not remotely brook comparison with those of Vietnam, Korea, or the Second World War. In sum, America possesses ample reserves with which to defend its global role and primacy, if needed.

Of equal importance to America's enduring strengths are its potential rivals' weaknesses. While predictions of a new multipolar era may be realized, unipolarity is more likely. As we argued in chapter 5, whatever the ultimate outcome in Iraq, the war on terror remains widely supported in the US. As its success in preventing another, or worse, 9/11 continues, dissident voices will question its worth. But the reality of the threat and the profound illiberalism of jihadist Islam are unlikely to be forgotten by most Americans. China's rise, Russian authoritarianism, rogue states, and the 'sniper power' of the EU offer important additional challenges. But, as we explained in the previous chapter, none is well placed to rival American power for decades to come.

Moreover, in contrast to simple assumptions, what much of the world will seek from Bush's successor is unlikely to be the 'un-Bush,' a demonstration of humility, self-restraint and self-abasement in the face of an anti-American world. As we saw in the aftermath of the retreat from Vietnam, America's allies – democratic and non-democratic – could take little comfort in a weak and vacillating Washington. What they seek is, rather, reassurance that America will stay strong, engaged, and committed to defending their security and prosperity. In short, an America that is engaged and capable of acting decisively is a global public good. The consequences of Iraq may make the issuance of such reassurance by Washington, and faith in it from Washington's allies, more difficult in the short term. But that does not mean that those allies will fail to seek, and the White House and Congress will be under strong pressure to grant, a credible restatement of American purpose in an increasingly dangerous world. To do otherwise would be to discard the lessons of 9/11.

It remains possible, however, that Americans themselves may turn temporarily against primacy as too costly a burden. But if the costs strike many Americans as excessive, what alternatives exist? Three appear to be the principal contenders to an American era of hegemony. Each is feasible. None is attractive.

The most immediate and – in Europe – popular alternative is a multipolar world, one that sees a configuration of great power rivals exercising a benign and prudent balance of power. On this view, security issues become the province of the key regional powers most directly concerned. But this vision has grievous problems. Previous balances of power have been anything but stable and benign. One need merely consider the consequences prior to 1914, and in the inter-war years, of such balances. Even were some new concert of major powers to be thrashed out, it is doubtful that such a set of rival powers would resolve the failed states, humanitarian crises, ethnic cleansing, genocides, and Islamism that together threaten the international order today. Perhaps, more pointedly, the rival powers are themselves inhibited by all manner of problems ranging from demographics to energy needs. The EU, for example, faces acute demographic problems that deeply complicate the still unresolved institutional and political dilemmas in its development. China's remarkable economic growth and the dynamics of Southeast Asian security constrain its prospects for constructive international intervention. Jihadist Islamism remains a threatening international force but has yet, mercifully, to achieve the garb of a nuclear state.

A second alternative, perhaps not apparent until the 2020s, envisions a return to a bipolar world of two superpowers, the US and

China. As with the First Cold War, such bipolarity might see the entire world stabilized through ties to the superpowers' respective spheres of influence. But even if such a bipolar world were to arise – a prospect vastly complicated by the possibilities of economic crisis and political turmoil in China – the likelihood of its benign character is minimal. It is worth recalling how close the world came to annihilation during the First Cold War in this regard. Moreover, China has, like Russia, shown little enthusiasm for the UN's recent endorsement of a 'responsibility to protect' against ethnic cleansing, one reason why Beijing has proven congenial to a range of tyrannies from North Korea to Sudan. Its autocracy has proven a key supplier of arms and technology to Pakistan, Iran, Sudan, and Egypt. While cooperation may be as plausible an outcome as confrontation between Beijing and Washington, the former has shown minimal interest in advancing a global balance of political and economic power that favors freedom. A rising China, as we examined in chapter 7, poses as many problems as it does potential solutions to international order.

But a third possible alternative to American primacy is an era of apolarity, where an absence – not a balance – of power gives rise to a new era of violence and economic stagnation. As Niall Ferguson has argued, the assumption that power, like nature, abhors a vacuum is not as well grounded as is often assumed:

> a world with no hegemon at all may be the real alternative to US primacy. Apolarity could turn out to be an anarchic new Dark Age: an era of waning empires and religious fanaticism; of endemic plunder and pillage in the world's forgotten regions; of economic stagnation and civilization's retreat into a few fortified enclaves.[22]

If Americans succumb to the three deficits – manpower, budgets, and attention span – that Ferguson identifies as inhibiting decisive action by Washington, while an aging Europe and Russia, a crisis-ridden China, and a warring Islamic civilization fail to act, that bleak new era has every prospect of being realized.

If these three unattractive prospects are to be avoided, Washington needs to reinvigorate its leadership ambitions and credentials. The grand strategy crafted by Bush after 9/11 married a belief in Wilsonian ideals to a conviction in realist means, a union that remains – for all its tensions – robust. This version of American internationalism provoked extensive and acrimonious criticism. But it seems to us that none of the key elements of the Bush Doctrine – primacy, prevention, coalitions of the willing and democracy promotion – will be abandoned in practice by successor administrations, whatever their rhetorical recalibrations and tactical adjustments. Part of the reason for this is the unappealing nature of alternative approaches.

Narrow realists, adjectival realists and ineffectual internationalists: 'coalitions of the unwilling and the unable'

If the end of the American era is not at hand, most foreign policy observers nonetheless take for granted the passing of the neoconservative moment. Buried in an Iraqi 'cemetery' with neither mourners nor headstone, a once ascendant movement now resembles a band of eccentric courtiers, semi-exiled by those who once trusted their advice. Most looked with relief to the re-embrace of pragmatic modes of global engagement. Even some former neoconservatives – most notably Fukuyama – recanted their former faith. 'Neo culpa' was the order of the day.[23] For apostates and implacable opponents alike, the twilight of the Bush years heralded a return to normalcy in foreign policy.

But the debate over the future of American foreign policy revolves around themes central not so much to the neoconservative world view but to the mix of realism and idealism that has always characterized such discussions. Divisions over Iraq have obscured the breadth of the consensus that exists on America's role and influence in the world. But just as the partisan divisions over Vietnam failed to

mute the much broader consensus on containing communism, so Iraq has had relatively limited effect on the wider bipartisan concurrence on the Second Cold War (even if it is known by another name). As we explain below, the salience of national security to American elections, and the impact that this has exerted on Democratic Party leaders and advisors (albeit less so rank-and-file activists), is the most telling signal of an America more unified than divided over its role and responsibilities. In many senses, and notwithstanding the bungled Iraq occupation, the shift in foreign policy thinking is one that owes its origins not to neoconservative ideas but to the combination of accident and intent that typically condition foreign policy-making in America. Despite the opposition of many of its members to American priorities and preferences, the agenda of the UN has nonetheless shifted to reflect US preoccupations. Much that was unthinkable in 2000 is more or less mainstream today. In a sense, the breadth of agreement on grand strategy is the tribute that virtue pays to vice (the 9/11 attacks).

One indication of this breadth is the degree to which analysts have labored, without significant success, to define a new paradigm for foreign policy. In essence, the task of reconciling realist and liberal approaches is the central pivot on which much of this activity tilts. The strategic alternatives to a distinctly American internationalism appear three-fold: realism; 'ethical' versions of realism; and liberal internationalism.

For some, a return to realism looms as a welcome, long overdue, and partially realized prescription. For many, this was what had already occurred in Bush's second term of office, even prior to the Democrats' 2006 midterm victory. Rice's appointment as secretary of state, Wolfowitz's departure to (and then from) the World Bank, Bolton's exit from the role of US ambassador to the UN, the partial endorsement of the Baker–Hamilton Iraq Study Group recommendations on (and euphemisms for) partial withdrawal, and the protracted multilateral efforts at diplomatic resolutions of the Iranian and North Korean nuclear threats all suggested the eclipse of the putative ideological fervor of Bush's first term.

Yet even writers who advocate a more realistic foreign policy approach cannot accept an unqualified Kissingerian realism. The adjectival catch-ups they employ are significant. Thus Fukuyama contends that:

> The United States remains too big, wealthy, and influential for it ever to abjure big ambitions in world politics. What is needed is not a return to a narrow realism but rather a *realistic* Wilsonianism that recognizes the importance to world order of what goes on *inside* states and that better matches the available tools to the achievement of democratic ends.[24]

But precisely how this realistic Wilsonianism departs from a distinctly American internationalism remains stubbornly obscure. If it means matching more closely means to ends then this is a prescription that 'neoconservatives' from Charles Krauthammer and Robert Kagan to William Kristol have consistently advocated.

Lieven and Hulsman, as we explored in chapter 3, likewise advocate an 'ethical realism' in which a sound foreign policy should focus on prudence, possible results rather than good intentions, a close study of the nature, views, and interests of other states, and a willingness to accommodate them when possible. All this plus a profound awareness of the limits on American power and goodness.[25] Policymakers should prioritize a small number of achievable goals and work more closely with Russia and China to secure them. But Lieven and Hulsman believe that, despite its expansionist leadership ambitions, Iran can be contained, that terrorist groups such as Hezbollah and Hamas should be given a wide berth, and that Middle East peace requires an independent Palestinian state and Israel joining the European Union and NATO. In short, their realism is unrealistic.

More pertinently, the stubborn fact remains that realism is neither ethical nor Wilsonian, it is amoral. Its amorality and lack of ethical prescriptions have made realism a powerful analytical tool and source of policy advice. But the most clear-cut case of realism in office – the Nixon-Kissinger era – illustrated precisely the problems that realists face operating in an environment where most Americans demand and expect that national policy be influenced by values as well as interests. Moreover, as the adjectival qualifications above suggest, the more purist forms of realism did not catch up with 9/11's lesson that an unduly narrow conception of the national interest serves that interest poorly. That does not mean that policy decisions should be made without attention to national capacities, resources, or allies. The configurations of domestic public opinion also remain key. They determine the viability of interventionism and nation-building. It does, however, entail that the national interest be conceived not merely in the short but also the longer term.

For realists, America should simply cast its conception of self-interest much more narrowly than occurred in Bush's first term, not only in geographic but also temporal terms. The prospect that a regime might, at some future date, sell or supply WMD to terrorists, that it might under a flag of convenience sail a ship into a city port and explode a nuclear device, or that it might annihilate an entire nation state that happens to be a reliable ally should not legitimate precipitate American action. Similarly, the notion that the form of government, not the unit, is what matters should be rejected. States do what states have always done in seeking to maximize their power and security, to calculate balances of probabilities, and to act prudently in the face of potentially costly consequences. It may or may not be true – at least, many if not most Americans would concur – that people universally desire freedom and certain inalienable individual rights. But however desirable that end state, it should not be confused with the more pressing priority of what their governments do in the international arena. We should not tar all non-democratic regimes with the same brush. To the extent that they have often been more successful than open societies in repressing terrorists, a return to Realpolitk commends itself.

But American presidents after Bush will confront the same reality revealed by 9/11: that the logic of First Cold War containment no longer applies as fully and adequately in the Second. Jihadi terrorist groups who actively seek martyrdom alongside mass murder are not the types of state-centric, risk-calculating entities of the First Cold War. Nor can certain state-centric threats – Saddam's Iraq, Ahmadinejad's Iran, Assad's Syria, Kim Jong Il's North Korea – be credibly seen as value-maximizing rational actors. Their continuance in power depends not on a successful dialogue and engagement with Washington but the appeasement of dissent at home by projecting the responsibility for domestic problems onto foreign powers.

If realism and ethical realism are therefore insufficient and oxymoronic, respectively, a third option presents itself. We might usefully dub it 'ineffectual internationalism.' It is advanced by that coterie of well-intentioned but ineffective left-liberal commentators for whom the nobility of multilateral pacifity invariably trumps the practical realities of unilateral action or 'coalitions of the willing.' For such putative cosmopolitans, the remedies to current ills continue to reside in forces above and beyond the nation state. Most notably, they place excessive faith in (and wrongly treat as synonymous) international law, multilateralism, and the UN, simultaneously overestimating the unilateralism of the Bush years while exaggerating the multilateralism of prior administrations. For cosmopolitans, UN approval of military interventions – whether to topple tyrannies or to prevent genocide – is usually a prerequisite (Kosovo divided them on this issue in 1999). Yet in demanding such a high standard on principle, cosmopolitans effectively preclude interventions in practice.

The peculiar embrace that characterizes critics of the Bush Doctrine is therefore one that, from markedly distinct motivations, reaches the same result – a coalition of the unwilling (and the indifferent or the unable). To be clear, neither realists nor cosmopolitans advance world views that are without merit or importance. The realist understanding of how states act remains, for all its flaws, the most persuasive. The cosmopolitan notion of how the world should look is highly attractive, even compelling. But realists' lack of a moral sense is not only an affront to all of us who recognize and wish to resolve global problems from genocide and failed states to the spread of HIV/AIDS, it is also a failing within the realists' own terms. National security cannot be assured by a retreat from international intervention, however modest or carefully calibrated. At the same time, cosmopolitan concern for the UN's imprimatur, the necessity of multilateral action, and the centrality of international law ignore the self-interest of nation states and the extent to which they remain the key units in the international arena. The message that cosmopolitans send in the face of genocides such as Rwanda in 1994 and Darfur in 2003–8 is less 'Never again' than 'Never again pronounce "never again."' It is a message that repeats the slogan of the Stop the War Coalition, 'Not In My Name,' and applies it across the board. It is a clarion call not to arms but to inaction, one whose sonorous theme is that, no matter how devastating the disaster, how pressing the threat, and how obvious the sectional interest of particular UNSC states in vetoing intervention, only concerted prior UN agreement will suffice. It renders the UN, and all of us, 'complicit with evil.'[26] As Anne Applebaum, reflecting on the shameful lethargy of the 'international community' in the face of Darfur, observed:

> when future generations look back on this era, they will judge us not only for how we responded to the most primitive and the most apolitical of horrors. They will also judge us by the consistency with which Western and international institutions battled sophisticated totalitarianism in all its forms: That is, they will judge us by the United Nations' application of its own declarations on human rights, by America's ability to live up to the rhetoric of its leaders, by Europe's willingness to stand behind its stated values.[27]

In this respect the foremost objection to the Bush Doctrine is, of course, Iraq. As we argued in chapter 5, the occupation was riddled

by failings that undermined the success of the war, failings critics are
entirely right to highlight. But only critics who are so blinded by
hatred of Bush that they ignore the instinctive nationalism of the
American people – Republican and Democrat alike – can interpret
Iraq as the end of American military interventionism. Americans
dislike weakness in their leaders, inconclusiveness in their wars, and
damage to their nation's authority. But just as Vietnam made little
difference to their anti-communism, so the failures in Iraq have made
little difference to the support for the wider war on Islamist terror. It
may be doubtful, in the short term, that a large-scale occupation will
again be mounted by the US. But the revival of the Powell Doctrine
will not negate the revolution in military affairs or the willingness of
the military and public alike to support less ambitious interventions.
American war-fighting has consistently been aggressive, geared to
decisive victory, and sought to employ the most advanced technology possible. But it has also been adaptable. Another constant has
been the propensity of the US toward great violence at times when
Americans perceive their security to be threatened. Asymmetrical or
irregular wars may not be the norm, but this does not mean that
America is likely to shy away from waging new types of conflicts with
new configurations of personnel, resources, strategies, and tactics.

Critics of the Iraq invasion are right that this illustrates with
pellucid clarity the limits of the exceptional American empire.
American primacy in the military sphere is, even after Iraq, unchal-
lenged. But however necessary the vast military resources of the US,
they are manifestly insufficient by themselves to bring about the
global order and stability – much less the end of tyranny that Bush
declared the ultimate objective of American actions – for which millions rightly and fervently hope. 9/11 provoked divergent responses
in the West, as we noted in chapter 3. America viewed it as having
changed the world while much of the rest of the world viewed it only
as having changed America. The brute reality – one that many non-
Americans have yet to recognize – is that jihadist Islam, coupled with

terrorism and weapons of mass destruction, poses a clear and present danger to all western societies. It is a folly of the first order to imagine that a separate peace can be concluded with jihadists or that Europe can somehow successfully replicate a continent-wide Swiss-style neutrality. Until and unless other capitals treat the threat with the same seriousness as Washington, adjust their internal and external policies accordingly, and confront rather than accommodate terror, American actions – however wise, judicious, and popular, or otherwise – will not in and of themselves suffice to prevail. That does not mean that Washington's dictats should be slavishly followed, much less that the US invariably identifies the correct course. But it does mean that the gravity of the global Islamist threat, and the Islamist tactic to divide and rule the West, should be strongly resisted. It is the continued relevance, not redundancy, of American internationalism that distinguishes the post-9/11 era.

Politics at the desert's edge

Politics, according to the old American adage, stops at the water's edge. But it never has. Partisanship has been a constant in foreign policy, as has debate over the most appropriate strategies, tactics, and priorities to be followed. The intensity of recent arguments over Iraq echoed those over Vietnam, and before that Korea. The First Cold War, for all its basic agreement upon containing communism, saw important divisions within and across both major parties from Truman through to George H. W. Bush. Americans are a markedly heterogeneous and opinionated people. Unanimity about America's world role is rare in its politics. But nor should we mistake the intensity and depth of contemporary divisions as somehow being of a completely different order to those of the past. It is in the interests of rivals for public office to exaggerate the extent and nature of the differences between them, and of the solutions that one president or one party can bring to the nation's problems over their rivals.

American democracy, with its multiple offices, independent sources of authority for distinct tiers and levels of government, and constant election cycle, strongly encourages this competition. The price to be paid is a public life that is noisy, quarrelsome, and at times ugly. But we should be wary of those who condemn today's politics as inferior whilst fantasizing about a golden age of comity, dialogue, and Socratic wisdom in Washington that never was.

Every era has its particular sources of friction, and the post-9/11 years have yielded wide-ranging conflicts between Democrats and Republicans on a range of issues, from homeland security and the ownership of American ports to NSA data-mining surveillance, the rights of unlawful enemy combatants, Guantanamo, and, of course, the pros and cons of military action in Iraq. Neither party wishes to be viewed by the 9/11 generation as 'weak' on fighting terrorism or combating the terrorist/WMD nexus.[28] The extent to which the Bush administration succeeded in exploiting security for electoral advantage in the 2002 and 2004 elections offered powerful evidence, if any was needed, that appeals to 'security moms' had now assumed a great salience. With partisan majorities narrow, elections increasingly expensive, and prospects for changes in partisan control of one or both houses of Congress hinging on a small number of competitive seats, attempts by both parties to ratchet up the rhetoric on security were unsurprising. Nor were they disingenuous. At times one could be forgiven for inverting Tip O'Neill's dictum about congressional politics. After 9/11, all politics are international.

But one of the many strengths of America is that neither major party has for long subscribed to radical or irresponsible policies at the national level (though neither party has lacked such advocates). One of the many facts lost in the anxious commentary on the Bush administration's policies was the extent to which they attracted, and relied upon, bipartisan support. America's national security constitution granted the presidency a set of *de jure* and *de facto* advantages that have made for presidential primacy in foreign affairs since at least 1950. But this has not usurped the roles of the Congress and courts. Rather, the other branches have actively supported or passively acquiesced in the presidency's pivotal international role. In this respect, we should be cautious about too hasty a pronouncement of constitutional *coups d'état* or vandalism committed by the conservative cabal around Bush. Opponents of Bush's policies have been anything but mute, let alone muted, since 2001.

From the perspective of partisan politics there are three reasons why, whatever the precise configuration of the White House and Congress into the 2010s and beyond, we should not anticipate major departures from the foreign policies charted by Bush.

First, none of the competing paradigms for American grand strategy has won, nor seems likely to secure, decisive support across both political parties. Both the Democrats and the Republicans are divided internally over foreign affairs. Each has a coalition of four distinct elements, according to Kurt Campbell and Michael O'Hanlon.[29] Democrats are divided among:

1. '*hard power*' advocates who see the flaw in the Bush Doctrine not as its conception but its execution;
2. '*globalists*' focused on problems caused by globalization and broader definitions of security and uneasy with force;
3. '*modest-power Democrats*' who want America to retrench and refocus at home, viewing Clinton Democrats as 'Republican-lite'; and
4. '*global rejectionists*,' old-style leftists, labor unions, and environmentalists, prevalent in the blogosphere and academy.

The GOP coalition is internally divided into:

1. '*Oldsmobile conservatives*': Wall Street Republicans and Bush Sr.-style realists;
2. *Neoconservatives*: the 'Vulcans,' journalists, and think tankers who strongly favor hard power and are skeptical of the UN;
3. '*America Firsters*': paleo-conservatives focused on immigration and protectionism; and

4. *'Faith-based interventionists'* concerned for humanitarian intervention and the moral purpose of foreign policy.

But the fact that, as ever, both parties represent coalitions of distinct tendencies should not cause us to expect a rapid realignment in US foreign policy. Mainstream Democrats and Republicans have much in common. The substantive differences between Mitt Romney, John McCain, Joe Lieberman, Hillary Clinton, Barack Obama, Fred Thompson, and Rudy Giuliani are less on foreign affairs than the partisan shrillness of Washington politics – and the inevitable dynamics of primary and general election campaigns – might suggest.

Imagine, in this regard, a likely presidential debate in 2008 (or 2012 or 2016) and a moderator asking these three questions:

- Would you, as president, repudiate the notion that the world is safer and better off with America as its major power?
- Would you, as president, reject the prosecution of the war on terror as America's number one foreign policy priority?
- Would you, as president, disagree that America is safer when more of the world's nations are mature democracies?

It is difficult to imagine a serious contender for the White House, of either party, replying 'yes' to any. As Campbell and O'Hanlon argue compellingly, national security is the essential presidential election issue for *both* Democrats *and* Republicans: 'It's the war, stupid.' 'Hard power' Democrats who see multilateralism as a means to an end, not as an end in itself, and who reject the notion that war is never the answer since it depends on the question, need to recover their mojo and to take a leaf from the neoconservative playbook on vision as well as competence if the Democrats are to regain the White House.[30]

Critics of the Bush foreign policy will of course rest their hopes firmly with the Democratic Party. But the extent to which a substantial shift in policy is likely is modest, at best. Timidity in the face of terror will not win the heartland. There are certainly aspirant Democrats – from John Edwards to Dennis Kucinich – who appeal to the party's base of global rejectionists and retrenchers who would seek a different foreign policy. But their chances of winning the Democratic nomination and reaching the White House (barring the GOP nominating Paris Hilton or Michael Jackson as its candidate) are minimal. Moreover, thoughtful Democrats intent on victory will recall that weakness on national security – from Michael Dukakis's ride in an Abrams battle tank 'looking more like Elmer Fudd than a soldier'[31] to the 'Swift Boated' John Kerry in 2004 – has been an Achilles Heel of more than one presidential contender. In this sense, Lieven and Lind are correct to argue that the broad mainstream of the American foreign policy establishment and the American people have much in common across both parties.

As the Kerry campaign also demonstrated, no mainstream Democrat who aspires to be president is likely to repudiate the central tenets of the Bush Doctrine, even in their more controversial guises. In terms of preventive war, for instance, the Democrats under Bill Clinton considered this option against North Korea in 1994 and former Clinton defense secretary William Perry criticized the Bush administration for not taking such action against Pyongyang in 2006. Hillary Clinton, among others, condemned the administration's second-term efforts to deal with Iran's nuclear ambitions by enlisting the assistance of the EU3 (the UK, France, and Germany) as 'outsourcing' American security. Kerry echoed Bush in 2004 in declaring that while he sought to re-establish 'respect' for America in the world, he would not allow other nations – in the UN Security Council and beyond – to exercise a veto over American national security. With the possible exception of Edwards (whose claim that the war on terror was a 'bumper sticker' promised to reduce his campaign to a similar status), the serious aspirant Democratic Party presidential candidates for 2008 were liberal hawks. As one assessment put it:

> The Democratic contenders for the presidency – whether it is Barack Obama promising to invade Pakistan if he deems it necessary to win

the War on Terror, or Hillary Clinton trying to sound like General Patton over Iran and other potential threats – have figured out that Americans may want a different president but they still don't want to outsource foreign policy to the United Nations or the European Union.[32]

Thus, while Democrats sought to appeal to their primary voters and to capitalize politically on the administration's particular Iraq failures, they sought simultaneously to assuage the concerns of American voters more generally that they would prove to be 'soft' on security issues.

Among Republicans, John McCain has long advocated an assertive American world role and a much greater commitment of American ground troops in Iraq, and had been supported by avowed neoconservatives such as William Kristol in 2000. Other leading Republicans – Giuliani, Romney, Thompson, Gingrich – were equally staunch supporters of the war on terror in general and the Iraq War in particular (Giuliani arguably even more so). Thus, in terms of the mainstream of both parties, the center of gravity was firmly behind the broad Second Cold War on jihadist Islam. While issues like trade and the environment might plausibly see important shifts depending on whether a Democrat or Republican occupies the White House after 2008, the war is not going to cease under either.

Second, with the exception of Iraq, most of the divisions that have occurred over the war on terror have been relatively modest and peripheral ones. This is not to diminish the significance of the concerns or the seriousness of the tactical disputes they have generated; it is to place them into a proper perspective. For example, the furor that erupted over the NSA surveillance program did not see Democrats reject the notion that the agency should be monitoring phone calls. The issue, for critics of the program, was its legality under established statutory law and the requirement of gaining FISA Court approval for its activities. That is a substantive and genuine conflict, to be sure, but it is not one that exposes a fundamental difference between Democrats and Republicans over the war on terror. Conflicts over the PATRIOT Act, Guantanamo, extraordinary rendition, and torture were of a similar nature – tactical disagreements over how best to wage the Second Cold War on Islamist terror at its margins, important without doubt, but not fundamental differences over whether to fight that war.

The third reason why we should expect more continuity than change in American foreign policy rests on the institutionalized fragmentation and competition of American government. It is worth recalling that, even in 9/11's immediate aftermath and the brief interlude of revived nationalism and bipartisanship it occasioned, the traditional features of American government and politics rapidly reasserted themselves. Thus the defense budget increased in absolute terms by margins ($48 billion) that dwarfed the entire defense budgets of most nation states in the rest of the world. In the aftermath of the 2006 results, the Democrats likewise moved to legislate an increase of $75 billion to the $500 billion Pentagon budget, an increase larger than the defense budget of the United Kingdom. Reorganization of the federal government occurred on a scale unseen since Truman's era, but the extent to which this achieved the desired ends remains a matter of debate. Congress is still a co-equal partner but one that is invariably weakened by its bicameral and co-equal nature, its complex structures and procedures, arcane devices such as the filibuster, and the ever-present threat of a presidential veto. Add to this the narrow majorities of recent congresses, pronounced partisanship, and the divisions within as well as between the congressional parties, and decisive action remains more the exception than the rule by this remarkably powerful body. As chapter 2 detailed, despite the formal constitutional provisions, American foreign policy is a matter largely of presidential primacy. Continuity, not change, is the norm in foreign policy. Congressional elections rarely influence the broad contours of foreign policy, rather than operating at its margins to mostly modest – though not unimportant – effects.

Exceptional America

Our case for continuity rests, fourthly and finally, on American exceptionalism. Like the aspects of the organization of American governing arrangements mentioned above, this is a factor that some international relations scholars tend either deliberately or unconsciously to ignore in discussions of foreign policy. That neglect is at one level perfectly understandable if one accepts the proposition that states – all states, always – do what states do, and that questions about their governing arrangements, their people's self-conception, and their particular demographics are largely irrelevant to their international conduct. Since 9/11, however, writers on American foreign policy, IR and anti-Americanism have sought to understand the elusive nature of this peculiar nation and people.[33] While the analyses have varied in their persuasiveness, that quest is a necessary part of any analysis of American foreign policy past, present or future.

It is sometimes said 9/11 shocked Americans out of their alleged innocence about the rest of the world and rendered them more like the rest of us. But America has never been unaware of dangers lurking beyond its shores. A nation that waged a fifty-years war against Soviet communism, with fronts on continents across the world with in excess of 10 percent of its GDP going on national defense, can hardly be seen as naïve about the wider world. A nation that spends so much on defense cannot be viewed as ignorant about foreigners – whose wars it quieted decisively in the last century. The four forces of geography and ideology, security and trade, have pulled America in different directions over time, their tensions played out within as well as between the two main parties and the two ends of Pennsylvania Avenue. But however seductive the temptation to

withdraw from the world's troubles that the 'coalition of the unwilling' offers, there is no prospect of a new, lasting, and truly isolationist America. A draw down of troops, even to the point of total
withdrawal, from Iraq will perhaps decrease the scenes of bloody
carnage unfolding on American television screens (not because the
carnage has ceased but because the coverage of it has). But the
threats from jihadist Islam will not recede apace with such a withdrawal, however more palatable the evening television fare. Nor will
dedicated efforts at public diplomacy somehow convince millions
who adhere to what one might term, paraphrasing Richard
Hofstadter,[34] 'the paranoid style about American politics' to revise
their view of America's malign nature, role, and intentions. It will
only, ultimately, be a deft weaving of incentives and sanctions, of
steadfast support for an Islamic reformation, and a strong American
presence in the world that will secure ultimate victory in the Second
Cold War.

Values as well as interests have been, and will remain, crucial com-
ponents of American policies to this end. In this regard, there may
well be a short-lived revival of insularity and 'exemplarism' – a sense
that America should serve as a model for others to choose to emulate
but should not actively seek to promote its ways of life to those
around the world who remain mired under tyrannies, command
economies, and corrupt regimes unable to comprehend, much less
realize, the non-negotiable demands of human dignity. It may be that
the standard national response to foreign crises becomes 'too bad, it's
their problem.' But if 9/11 taught us anything instructive it was that
not even the US could inoculate itself against global maladies and
maniacs.

We remain confident, though, that the bulk of Americans will
not retreat from engagement with the world. As Robert Kagan
noted, even in the midst of Iraq, Americans of both parties evinced
more belief in the utility and justice of military force than did other
peoples.[35] While incorporating Iraq's lessons into future policy

will be imperative, such lessons by themselves will provide no adequate response to the fanatical menaces still troubling and targeting the United States. A balance of power that favors freedom is an inescapable end. America's role in generating that balance is unavoidable.

Conclusion

The partisan attacks of recent years suggest an America divided against itself as much as against its terrorist and pariah state enemies. But this is misleading. Politics has been polarized, on both foreign and domestic policies. But the Bush years consolidated rather than gave birth to this development (one can plausibly trace it back to Reagan, even Nixon). Republicans and Democrats alike were complicit, abetted by a mass media eager for newsworthy stories, scandal, and revelations. Internet blogs and activist organizations compounded the coarser contours of an always adversarial and noisy political culture. At a time of war, with Americans sacrificing their lives to defend and advance liberty, the surprise would have been if controversy had not enveloped American politics.

Students of foreign policy, searching for a golden age of complete consensus, or a hastening of its return, are therefore likely to be disappointed. But while the need for 'change' is a regular American election mantra, too many factors exist, at home and abroad, that militate against a dramatic shift in the substance of American statecraft. The case for continuity is not a version of everyone agreeing that everything will turn out fine. This is not a Panglossian view of the past, present, or future. But the major division in US foreign policy over coming years will be between those who reject the Bush Doctrine in substance (not just style) and those who, with us, hold it still to be the most appropriate grand strategy to preserve American primacy, advance American ideals, and prevail over America's enemies. A minority of Americans may reject the Doctrine in substance, but the majority does not. Moreover, the opportunity and the need for an assertive America that continues to take seriously its global engagement, the military dimensions of the war on terror, and the political reform aspects of its forward agenda of freedom remain urgent.

Conclusion:
The case for continuity

PRESIDENT: I know there is much we can learn from each other if
  we can negotiate a truce. We can find a way to coexist. Can there
  be peace between us?
ALIEN: Peace? No peace.
PRESIDENT: What do you want us to do?
ALIEN: Die.

Independence Day, directed by Roland Emmerich (1996)

By early in Bill Clinton's first term the cabal was in place. Tony Lake,
conscientious objector to Henry Kissinger, was the new national
security assistant. His deputy, Samuel Berger, was a foreign policy
liberal and multilateralist – later found guilty of stealing classified
national security documents. Number three on the new NSC staff
was Nancy Soderberg, a young female acolyte of Senator Ted
Kennedy, a liberal relativist of impeccable credentials. At Foggy
Bottom was Warren Christopher, a secretary of state whose previous
White House service had been in the vacillating Carter administration, 1977–81. Several other ex-Carter people reappeared in the
new Democratic administration. Within weeks of their residency in
Washington these men and women were calling for and were on the
way to implementing a foreign policy of democratic enlargement,

engagement, humanitarian assistance, and international social work.

There was, in short, a liberal conspiracy at the heart of the Clinton administration. This domestically focused president – a man whose most effective campaign slogan was 'It's the economy, stupid!' – was victim to a liberal cabal who made foreign policy in its image. Gone was the cautious realism of George Bush Sr. In the new era America would 'light fires in the hearts of millions of freedom-loving people around the world.'[1]

The notion that a liberal conspiracy drove the Clinton administration is of course absurd. Yet, we are asked to believe that a conspiracy of neoconservatives lay at the heart of the George W. Bush administration. In reality, conspiracies rarely endure as the organizational principle of any democracy's foreign policy – let alone a democracy as open, separated, and noisily conflictual as the United States. A cursory glance at the Clinton foreign policy team reveals significant divisions and the absence of doctrine – conspiratorial or otherwise – despite early, but ultimately vain, attempts to create one.[2] Warren Christopher never much rated Tony Lake; Lake himself sat uneasily with a policy-making machine obsessed with political calculation and popularity. Bush's team was hardly immune to differences, of the sort that are usually ruinous of sustained intrigue. The history of his first term was marked by the recurrent battling of Powell on one side and Rumsfeld and Cheney on the other. Condoleezza Rice, as the national security advisor, too often refused to intercede in their battles. And yet it is from this complicated mixture of personalities, operating under the exceptional conditions made by 9/11, that a neoconservative conspiracy was purportedly hatched. We find the attribution of conspiracy ridiculous, the province of left-wing websites, the BBC, disgruntled conservatives, and populist rhetoricians.[3] Would that there were such an influence driving the US reaction to al Qaeda's assault.

We begin our conclusion, therefore, by rejecting the argument that the foreign policy of the Bush administration represents a neoconservative revolution. Our contention throughout has been that American foreign policy in the Bush years actually varied very little from previous eras. The fundamental utility of the Bush Doctrine, like that of the Truman, will cause subsequent presidents to change foreign policy only slightly. Whilst much wordy scholarship, from right and especially left, is expended on denouncing a 'toxic Texan foreign policy,' we enjoin in neither praise nor blame for what the forty-third president wrought. Instead, we have argued that Bush was much more in tune with his predecessors than commentators caught up in the moment have been prepared to admit. Fuller revisions of the Bush years will undoubtedly follow our own. As they appear in the coming years and decades their emphasis, we predict, will, like ours, be on the essential continuity of Bush foreign policy with what went before and what came after.

Our historical reference point has been the Truman era and the First Cold War. 'Like George W. Bush more than a half-century later, Harry Truman had to devise new strategies and join in creating new governmental entities such as the CIA and National Security Council to confront a global threat from an unexpected adversary, all the while putting his belief in freedom and democracy, as well as his religious faith, at the center of his foreign policy.'[4] Consider the similarities between then and now:

- at the beginning phase of a long war;
- the president chastised for his foreign policy failure;
- his poll numbers disastrously low;
- America's enemy appeased by liberals who would themselves suffer greatly from its victory (imagine had Henry Wallace been retained by FDR as his vice-presidential candidate in 1944 and assumed the presidency the following year);
- engaged in a bloody war far away against an existential enemy of shifting character.

Despite this unpropitious beginning, Truman crafted a foreign policy that met the various vicissitudes of the First Cold War and provided a basis for winning it. It is not unreasonable to believe Bush did the same in the Second. Perhaps all we are waiting on is a Reagan, after Bush, to complete the task. There may be a Carter or two along the way but the path is clear.

Because the enemy is like the alien in this chapter's epigraph, no president is likely to underestimate the threat it poses. The greater its capacity, the more it will be confronted with force. Appeasement is not an option.[5] Like communism, Islamism is not at war with the West in order to secure concessions from it but to replace it. An accommodation in this Second Cold War is perhaps even less likely than it was in the First. The Soviet Union and its allies wanted only material dominion. There was no heaven – nor accompanying retinue of waiting virgins – for Marxists. There were plenty of Marxist fantasies about heaven on earth but no Marxist meta-physics. The reward of class struggle can be realized only in the temporal realm – there is no other. Communist extremists, like Castro, who would sacrifice their nation for a futile war on the United States that advanced the communist cause were the exception, not the rule, in the First Cold War. The existential threat Castro hoped to pose to America was negated by Kremlin caution – who would sacrifice Moscow for Havana? But there is no such break on Islamism in the Second Cold War. In this new war, the only check on the ambitions of the enemy is an American willingness to confront and overcome it. The delicate balance of terror that kept America and the communist world at relative peace for nearly fifty years does not apply in the new situation. The powerful impediment to communist belligerence was the fear of its assured destruction. Islamists, in contrast, embrace death so long as America, Israel and the West die too.

If this is the case and if the stakes are really so high, how do we maintain the efficacy of the First Cold War strategy in fighting the Second? Aren't the opponents in each war so different that they demand different responses? Our answer is that neither war was a war of choice for the United States. The actual flexibility of US options was not nearly so great in the First Cold War as is often assumed. Presidents who tried to shift American strategy away from the Truman platform – whether in more bellicose or pacific directions – invariably fared poorly. Support for 'rollback' during the 1950s was rhetorical, not substantive, while America's attempts – under both Republicans and Democrats – to compromise with communism in the 1970s merely advanced its territorial gains and aspirations. Under Reagan, America returned the First Cold War to a more confrontational mode, allowing him to negotiate from a position of strength.[6] In the war on terror, too, America has actually very few options available to it. A policy of confrontation has no viable alternative, especially given the nature of this enemy versus the previous communist one. No US president will allow Islamism to spread in the hope that by spreading it might fracture and thus moderate its theological/ideological fervor. No US president will be slow to act when Islamist weapons technology breaches a threshold of acceptability. In the First Cold War, presidents were prepared to risk their enemy's expansion and their ambitions for nuclear parity; in the Second they will not.

For this reason, and despite the hopes of the liberal left and the predictions of realists, there is not a single mainstream US politician with serious presidential ambitions who would choose the constraints of multipolarity over the freedom of US primacy. It is inconceivable that a presidential candidate who seeks a permission slip to act on behalf of American security could win the White House; in 2004, John Kerry's reference to 'a global test' US foreign policy should pass won him very few votes. Whilst building the United Nations into the Second Cold War is fine in principle, the structural and political impediments to doing so are manifold and, we confidently predict, quite beyond the remit of even the most tactically astute, rhetorically gifted, and politically empowered American president. The European Union, likewise, offers the United States very little in terms of enhanced military or diplomatic effectiveness. The freedom of action Bush enjoyed, which included the freedom to botch disastrously the aftermath of the Iraq War, is one none of his successors will sacrifice.

Much as it pains Bush's many detractors – on the right and left – to acknowledge, a change of administration in Washington will have no measurable effect on Islamist ideology, though it might on their capacity; a sound policy will negate that capacity, a poor one will advance it. The Bin Laden camp waged war as fiercely against Bill Clinton as it did against George W. Bush and will continue to do against their successors. A jihadist suicide bomber is supposedly afforded seventy-two virgins in heaven whether he kills Democrats or Republicans. Because the frustrations and ambitions of the enemy are unlikely to change much over time we should not expect the American response to those ambitions to alter very much either. Continuity of threat will determine the continuity of American strategy. This imperative will be one few American presidents can amend without risking catastrophe. We predict the next few will not try.

The odds are also stacked against a counter-revolution in US foreign policy after Bush. Foreign policy-making in the United States is a glacial process. Rarely does a single president transform the international posture of his nation. Such a transformation is invariably generational, with important foreign policy presidents casting a shadow over their successors. The First Cold War was fought against a backdrop of institutional turf war and the checks and balances of America's separated system of government. It took several decades for it to bear fruit – and even then was capable of significant regression. The Second Cold War, despite an insistence from some quarters that it has trumped the US Constitution and ushered in a military dictatorship, will likewise be waged within a highly contested political space. Presidents of both parties will fight that war. Each is likely to face opposition from Congress, the judiciary, and the media. This state of affairs is basic to the American system of government and there is no reason to suppose the existential fears of the Islamist challenge will change them very much. Indeed, it is that challenge, like communism before it, which will reinforce an essential consensus within a political system prone to separation and internal competition. As Gerard Baker observes:

> Though they are under intense pressure from the Move On left to denounce the [Iraq] war and the broader evils and hypocrisy of US foreign policy, the Democrats' leadership has no intention of running far off the tracks the Republicans have laid down.
>
> Speak to the foreign policy people floating around the campaigns of Mark Warner or John Edwards and you will find similarly no plans to repudiate the basics of Bush foreign policy. As for Al Gore, for all his recent criticism of the war, it was, remember, the former vice-president whose embrace of an assertive foreign policy was derided by Governor George W. Bush, in their 2000 presidential debate, as lacking sufficient humility.[7]

The United States is fighting a winnable war, but the victory needs to be defined. The Second Cold War, unlike the First, does not intend primarily to convert the enemy to an American ideology. This might well be a happy consequence of waging a war against Islamic fundamentalists but it is not its central purpose. Measuring success by counting converts from Islamism is unreliable. Rather, the Second Cold War aims to contain the capacity of Islamist terrorists to wage war against western, specifically American, populations. It is, perhaps even more so than in the First Cold War, a question of containment. It seeks to keep weapons of mass destruction out of the hands of those who would use them. The First Cold War was not so premised. The war against global communism accepted that the enemy had and would retain WMD. Certainly, US presidents were sensitive to their proliferation – as the Cuban Missile Crisis of 1962 is testament – but they did not countenance military action to prevent Moscow and Beijing joining the nuclear club. The Soviets and Chinese, in turn, did not proliferate (Cuba excepted). The American defense of South Vietnam, for example, was not motivated by a need to keep Saigon nuclear-free. The war on terror, however, *is* motivated by a need to keep the Taliban, Islamist outlaw states such as Iran, and their imitators nuclear-free. We, therefore, measure success by how far the United States and its allies deny to these actors the state-level support necessary to arm themselves with such weapons.

As we have argued in this book, this imperative has so far been met by the Bush Doctrine – and for this reason the Doctrine will endure. It is not its novelty that will account for its longevity but its drawing together of the enduring features of US foreign policy. First, it means to counter terrorism by a reformation of the domestic institutions charged with homeland security. Here a consensus obtains. Second, the Doctrine seeks to enlarge the sphere of democracies – not, primarily, to shower happiness and capitalist prosperity on their citizens but in order to render unthinkable the proliferation of WMD from such states to jihadists. This branch of the Doctrine draws on a substantial and longstanding faith in the Democratic Peace theory, embraced by every successful foreign policy president since Woodrow Wilson, and, arguably, the defining characteristic of American foreign policy since the birth of the Republic.[8] Again, this international approach commands a significant domestic consensus. Whilst debate over the means to this end is apparent – over how multilateralism and unilateralism are to be balanced, for example – the end itself – a democratic peace – is sought across the political spectrum.

This argument relates to the one we have relied on throughout this book. That is, that US foreign policy in the current era is animated by a universalism which places it firmly within the American foreign policy tradition. Understanding what Bush tried to do, and what his successors will continue, depends on accepting the fundamentally ideological nature of his project – not on the caricaturing of the Bush Doctrine as a neocon conspiracy, but on the acceptance that

US foreign policy is driven by ideals and values as well as interests. For every American president, democracy has represented the only legitimate form of government. All other forms are transitory. This bedrock understanding means that setbacks do not endure for long. Self-evident truths are not easily falsified. The Vietnam–Iraq analogy is recurrently cited but for the wrong reasons. What these conflicts reveal is the continuity and resilience of values in American foreign policy. The apparently futile pursuit of democracy in Southeast Asia (1954–75) was supposed to put paid to the notion of regime change and emasculate the US military. Yet within six years of a humiliating withdrawal America embarked upon a winning First Cold War strategy that embraced regime change and military confrontation as positive moral aims. There is no reason to suppose that the ongoing travails in Iraq will negate a centuries-old reliance on such approaches, especially since there is no equivalent Soviet Bloc in the current era to check US power.

For these reasons we conclude that Bush led no foreign policy revolution. September 11 invoked precedent not transformation. He was no more capable of escaping America's enduring strategic culture and ideological imperatives after 9/11 than any of the presidents before him. Thus, by default and by design, the Bush administration imitated the foreign policy of its predecessors. His successors will do the same. The war on terror – the Second Cold War – has had its Truman. We await its Reagan.

Notes

INTRODUCTION: WINNING THE SECOND COLD WAR

1. Robert Kagan, *Dangerous Nation* (New York: Alfred A. Knopf, 2006).
2. For accounts that document these failings with depressing but humorous detail, see Richard A. Posner, *Public Intellectuals: A Study in Decline* (Cambridge, MA: Harvard University Press, 2003); and Philip E. Tetlock, *Expert Political Judgment: How Good Is It? How Can We Know?* (Princeton, NJ: Princeton University Press, 2005).
3. See Francis Fukuyama, *The End of History and the Last Man* (New York: Avon, 1992); and Samuel P. Huntington, *The Clash of Civilizations and the Remaking of World Order* (New York: Simon and Schuster, 1996).
4. See Niall Ferguson, *Colossus: The Rise and Fall of the American Empire* (London: Allen Lane, 2004); Alejandro Colás and Richard Saull, eds., *The War on Terrorism and the American 'Empire' after the Cold War* (London: Routledge, 2005); Chalmers Johnson, *Blowback: The Costs and Consequences of American Empire* (New York: Henry Holt, 2000); and John B. Judis, *The Folly of Empire: What George W. Bush Could Learn from Theodore Roosevelt and Woodrow Wilson* (New York: Lisa Drew/Scribner, 2004).
5. John J. Mearsheimer, 'Why We Will Soon Miss the Cold War,' *Atlantic Monthly* (August 1990), 35–50.
6. The LSE scholar, Fred Halliday, first coined the notion of a 'second' cold war to describe the period from 1979 to 1983 when Soviet–American relations deteriorated severely (Halliday, *The Making of the Second Cold War* [London: Verso, 1983]). While we acknowledge that generational conflicts undergo distinct periods, the term 'cold war' seems to merit a more holistic treatment.

7. This concept is explored by Philip Bobbitt, *The Shield of Achilles: War, Peace and the Course of History* (London: Penguin, 2003).

8. See Mark Bowden, *Guests of the Ayatollah: The First Battle in the West's War with Militant Islam* (London: Atlantic Books, 2006).

9. John Mueller, 'What Was the Cold War About? Evidence from Its Ending,' *Political Science Quarterly* 119, 4 (2004–5), 609–32.

10. For a strong case that sees the current struggle as 'World War IV,' see Norman Podhoretz, *World War IV: The Long Struggle Against Islamofascism* (New York: Doubleday, 2007).

11. John Lewis Gaddis, *The Long Peace: Inquiries into the History of the Cold War* (Oxford: Oxford University Press, 1987).

12. See Odd Arne Westad, *The Global Cold War: Third World Interventions and the Making of Our Times*, new edn (Cambridge: Cambridge University Press, 2007).

13. See Ian Kershaw, *Fateful Choices: Ten Decisions that Changed the World, 1940–1941* (London: Allen Lane, 2007).

1. BUSH AND THE AMERICAN FOREIGN POLICY TRADITION

1. Walter Russell Mead, *Special Providence: American Foreign Policy and How It Changed the World* (London: Routledge, 2002), xv. Mead provides a highly persuasive typology of the American foreign policy tradition in which 'four basic ways of looking at foreign policy' – Hamiltonian, Wilsonian, Jeffersonian, and Jacksonian – have interacted to produce a stable and successful strategy.

2. Noam Chomsky, *What Uncle Sam Really Wants* (Berkeley, CA: Odonian Press, 1992), 56.

3. Mead, *Special Providence*, 311.

4. The causal relationship between an evangelical religiosity and American foreign policy, tenuous at best, is an article of faith for several anti-Bush scholars. See, for example, Tariq Ali, *The Clash of Fundamentalisms: Crusades, Jihads and Modernity* (London: Verso, 2002); Kevin Phillips, *American Theocracy: The Peril and Politics of Radical Religion, Oil, and Borrowed Money in the 21st Century* (New York: Viking, 2006); and Damon Linker, *The Theocons: Secular America Under Siege* (New York and London: Doubleday, 2006). Michael Mann opens his *Incoherent Empire* (London: Verso 2005), vi, with the Benjamin Franklin quotation used by the Cheneys in their 2003 Christmas cards: 'And if a sparrow cannot fall to the ground without His notice, is it probable that an Empire can rise without His aid?'

5. The best unabridged translation is Harvey C. Mansfield and Delba Winthrop's 2000 edition (Chicago: University of Chicago Press), from which the following references are taken.

6. Ibid., 21 and 27.

7. Ibid., 27.

8. See Perry Miller, *Errand into the Wilderness* (Cambridge, MA: Belknap Press of Harvard University Press, 1956). Emphasis added.

9. See Mansfield and Winthrop introduction to Tocqueville, *Democracy*, xix.

10. See John Lewis Gaddis (who rejects this textbook reading) in his *Surprise, Security and the American Experience* (Cambridge, MA: Harvard University Press, 2004), 7–8. This description of Canada is taken from Michael Cox, 'America and the World,' in Robert Singh, ed., *Governing America: The Politics of a Divided Democracy* (Oxford: Oxford University Press, 2003), 20.

11. Tocqueville, *Democracy*, 265. See also 618.

12. Ibid., 26.

13. See Gaddis, *Surprise*, 7; and David C. Hendrickson, 'Toward Universal Empire: The Dangerous Quest for Absolute Security,' *World Policy Journal* 19, 3 (2002), 1–10.

14. John Adams to James Warren, March 20, 1783; cited in Arthur M. Schlesinger Jr., *The Cycles of American History* (Boston: Houghton Mifflin, 1986), 52.

15. Tocqueville, *Democracy*, 228.

16. 'Withdrawal' as isolationism, 'return' as interventionism (Schlesinger Jr., *The Cycles of American History*, 51).

17. George Washington, Farewell Address, 1796.

18. Tocqueville, *Democracy*, 218.

19. George Washington, cited by John Marshall, *Life of Washington*, vol. IV (Philadelphia, 1807), 705, cited in Tocqueville, *Democracy*, 218.

20. See Robert Kagan, *Paradise and Power: America and Europe in the New World Order* (London: Atlantic Books, 2003), 3–11, esp. 10–11.

21. http://xroads.virginia.edu/~Hyper/TURNER/chapter1.html#foot1. See also William Appleman Williams, 'The Frontier Thesis and American Foreign Policy,' *Pacific Historical Review* 24 (1955).

22. http://xroads.virginia.edu/~Hyper/TURNER/chapter1.html#foot1.

23. The 'how to' manual by Ziauddin Sardar and Merryl Wyn Davies, *Why Do People Hate America?* (Cambridge: Icon Books, 2002), is animated by such readings of American history.

24. Of the first fifteen US presidents (1789–1861), only one (James Polk) held no significant foreign policy position prior to his inauguration. Six were former secretaries of state. In contrast, of the last sixteen (since 1913) only two (Eisenhower and Bush Sr.) entered office with formal, high foreign policy experience (Herbert Hoover's brave relief efforts in post-First World War Belgium not withstanding). See Mead, *Special Providence*, 13; and Michael Nelson, 'Person and Office: Presidents, the Presidency, and Foreign Policy,' in Eugene R. Wittkopf and James M. McCormick, eds., *The Domestic Sources of*

American Foreign Policy: Insights and Evidence, 4th edn (Lanham, MD: Rowman and Littlefield, 2004), ch. 9.

25. The US–Canada border is, of course, longer but spans ten American states. 'Quasi' because foreign policy is the exclusive preserve of the national government (US Constitution, Art. I, Sec. 10).

26. Bush in Bob Woodward, *State of Denial* (New York: Simon and Schuster, 2006), 3. Candidate Bush also failed a foreign policy 'pop quiz' which, during the 2000 primaries, elevated the foreign policy credentials of his rival, John McCain.

27. See, for example, the October 11, 2000 presidential debate; at www.debates.org/pages/trans2000B.html.

28. See Christopher Layne, *The Peace of Illusions: American Grand Strategy from 1940 to the Present* (Ithaca, NY: Cornell University Press, 2005), 29.

29. 'Much like imperialism and liberalism, other protean concepts frequently bandied about in serious historical and political discourse, ideology is hard to pin down' (Michael H. Hunt, *Ideology and US Foreign Policy* [New Haven and London: Yale University Press, 1987], xi). See also Hunt, 'Ideology,' in Michael E. Hogan and Thomas G. Paterson, eds., *Explaining the History of American Foreign Relations*, 2nd edn (Cambridge: Cambridge University Press, 2004), ch. 14.

30. Stalin, of course, initiated this buffer zone in 1939 under the terms of his pact with Hitler.

31. Hofstadter, quoted in Hans Kohn, *American Nationalism: An Interpretive Essay* (New York: Macmillan, 1957), 13.

32. Hunt, *Ideology and US Foreign Policy*, 13.

33. Speech at Springfield, Illinois, 26 June 1857.

34. These labels are offered by Paul T. McCartney, 'American Nationalism and US Foreign Policy from September 11 to the Iraq War,' *Political Science Quarterly* 119, 3 (2004), 399–424, 401.

35. In Hunt, *Ideology and US Foreign Policy*, 92.

36. Thomas Paine, *Common Sense* (1776).

37. The American 'enjoys two pleasures at once: he dreams of his trade and gets drunk decently within the home . . . drinkers are in the majority, and temperance is unpopular' (Tocqueville, *Democracy*, 582, 215).

38. Ibid., 585.

39. See Rogers M. Smith, 'Beyond Tocqueville, Myrdal, and Hartz: The Multiple Traditions in America,' *American Political Science Review* 87, 3 (1993), 549–66; and, disputing Smith but still rejecting Hartz, Jacqueline Stevens, 'Beyond Tocqueville, Please!' *American Political Science Review* 89, 4 (1995), 987–95. The notion of a cohesive liberal tradition is also given short shrift (and Tocqueville never mentioned) in Desmond King, *The Liberty of Strangers: Making the American Nation* (Oxford: Oxford University Press, 2005).

40. Louis Hartz, *The Liberal Tradition in America: An Interpretation of American Political Thought since the Revolution* (San Diego, CA: Harvest Books, 1991; originally published 1955), 286. See also Samuel P. Huntington, 'American Ideals versus American Institutions,' *Political Science Quarterly* 97, 1 (1982), 1–37, esp. 14–37.

41. Alan Cassels, *Ideology and International Relations in the Modern World* (London: Routledge, 1996), 48.

42. See Colin Dueck, *Reluctant Crusaders: Power, Culture, and Change in American Grand Strategy* (Princeton, NJ: Princeton University Press, 2006). The Wilson and Truman examples are his.

43. Walter LaFeber, *The American Age: United States Foreign Policy at Home and Abroad since 1750* (New York: Norton, 1989), 11–12.

44. The fear that Great Britain would side with the southern confederacy, for reasons of trade, was basic to Abraham Lincoln's diplomatic maneuvering. See Howard Jones, *Abraham Lincoln and a New Birth of Freedom: The Union and Slavery in the Diplomacy of the Civil War* (Lincoln, NE: University of Nebraska Press, 1999).

45. Similarly, foreign nations cognizant of America's distance from themselves nevertheless considered the new republic a security threat to them. For an excellent tabulation of American foreign adventures see Richard F. Grimmett, 'Instances of Use of United States Armed Forces Abroad, 1798–2006,' CRS Report (RL30172), January 8, 2007.

46. On purported First Cold War exaggerations see Scott Lucas, *Freedom's War: The US Crusade Against the Soviet Union, 1945–1956* (Manchester: Manchester University Press, 1999). We do not share his interpretations. Truman's NSC-68 (1950) is often held as indicative of American paranoia in the First Cold War as Bush's National Security Strategy (2002) is in the Second.

47. Woodrow Wilson established his academic credentials in an 1885 book so named.

48. This argument is made by James M. Lindsay, 'From Deference to Activism and Back Again: Congress and the Politics of American Foreign Policy,' in Wittkopf and McCormick, eds., *Domestic Sources*, ch. 12.

49. See Tocqueville, *Democracy*, 115–19.

50. Examples of congressional activism during the Clinton administration include the House's refusal to support the bombing of Kosovo in April 1999 and the Senate's voting down of the Comprehensive Test Ban Treaty in October 1999. It is also true that as the salience of foreign policy declines, congressional activism in foreign policy rises (since it carries reduced electoral risks). See Lindsay, 'From Deference to Activism and Back Again.'

51. See Fukuyama, *End of History* and Charles Krauthammer, 'Holiday from History,' *Washington Post*, February 14, 2003.

52. Tocqueville, *Democracy*, 118.

53. Walter Russell Mead argues that 'American realism . . . won the twentieth century' because European 'Continental realism' since the nineteenth century failed to take commerce seriously: 'the shopkeepers [of Anglo-America] got [Napoleon] in the end.' See Mead, *Special Providence*, xvi and ch. 2.

54. 'Why in America, country of democracy par excellence,' asked Tocqueville, 'does no one make heard those complaints against property in general that often ring out in Europe? Is there need to say it? – it is that in America there are no proletarians. Each one, having a particular good to defend, recognizes the right of property in principle' (*Democracy*, 228; also see vol. II, pt. I, ch. 19 [526–9]).

55. When the Second World War ended the USA controlled over 50 percent of the world's total industrial output, over 90 percent of its petroleum and 75 percent of its merchant marine and aircraft. See Cox, in Singh, ed., *Governing America*, 28. Much of the British welfare state, for example, was possible only of the basis of American post-Second World War largesse. See Greg Behrman, *The Most Noble Adventure: The Marshall Plan and the Time When America Helped Save Europe* (New York: Free Press, 2007).

56. See Martin Wolf, *Why Globalization Works* (New Haven, CT: Yale University Press, 2004).

57. The Louisiana Purchase created most of the American Midwest.

58. Alaska, purchased in 1867 for $7.2 million. See Table 2 in Ferguson, *Colossus*, 40.

59. See www.whitehouse.gov/infocus/developingnations/millennium.html.

60. In Deroy Murdock, 'Giuliani's Finest Hour,' *National Review*, September 14, 2001.

61. Article 13, League of Nations Covenant; at www.yale.edu/lawweb/avalon/leagcov.htm.

62. George F. Kennan, *American Diplomacy 1900–1950*, expanded edn (Chicago and London: University of Chicago Press, 1984), 95.

63. Ibid., 95.

64. 'When [the state] accepts the responsibility of governing, implicit in that acceptance is the assumption that it is right that the state should be sovereign, that the integrity of its political life should be assured, that its people enjoy the blessings of military security, material prosperity and a reasonable opportunity for, as the Declaration of Independence put it, the pursuit of happiness. For these assumptions the government needs no moral justification, nor need it accept any moral reproach for operating on the basis of them' (Kennan, 'Morality and Foreign Policy,' *Foreign Affairs* 64, 2 [1985], 206; see also Kennan, *American Diplomacy*).

65. 'If situations are properly handled,' cabled Kennan, 'there need be no prestige-engaging showdowns.'

66. G. John Ikenberry observes the same pattern but draws different conclusions

in *After Victory: Institutions, Strategic Restraint, and the Rebuilding of Order after Major Wars* (Princeton, NJ: Princeton University Press, 2001).

67. The ship was so-named when Rice was on the Chevron board, prior to her appointment as NSA.

68. 'American Foreign Policy and the Democratic Ideal,' speech at Pabst Theater, Milwaukee, WI, October 1, 1992; reproduced in *Orbis* 37, 4 (1994), 651–60.

69. The NEC's creation is told in Bob Woodward, *The Agenda: Inside the Clinton White House* (New York: Simon and Schuster, 1994).

70. For a neat tabulation of Clinton's (generally very good) foreign economic stewardship see 'Clinton's Foreign Policy,' *Foreign Policy* 114 (2000), 18–29.

71. According to Fred I. Greenstein, Bush 'favors a corporate model of political leadership in which he avoids immersing himself in details and relies on subordinates to structure his options' ('The changing leadership of George W. Bush,' in Wittkopf and McCormick, eds., *Domestic Sources*, 359).

72. At the end of Bush's term, US investment (assuming a financial return is to be made) or spending (assuming it won't) in Iraq will be over $100 billion.

73. Clinton used Halliburton too, in the Balkans reconstruction. See Byron York, 'Halliburton: The Bush/Iraq Scandal that Wasn't,' *National Review*, July 14, 2003. This trade emphasis in foreign policy is neither new nor uniquely American. For the classic exposition see Max Weber, *The Protestant Ethic and the Spirit of Capitalism* (London: Scribner, 1958, originally published 1904). A more recent treatment is Richard Rosecrance, *The Rise of the Trading State: Commerce and Conquest in the Modern World* (New York: Basic Books, 1986).

74. He implied this as a criticism, we do not. Robert M. Perito, 'Defense Policy Panning Board Briefing, February 28, 2003: Establishing Post-conflict Security in Iraq' in Michael Gordon and Bernard Trainor, eds., *Cobra II: The Inside Story of the Invasion and Occupation of Iraq* (London: Atlantic Books, 2007), 661.

75. Carl N. Degler, *Out of Our Past: The Forces that Shaped Modern America*, 3rd edn (New York: Harper and Row, 1984), 509.

76. See Naomi Klein, *No Logo* (New York: Picador, 2000).

77. For Williams, US First Cold War strategy was a betrayal of a more legitimate tradition (hence its 'tragedy') and invited foreign competition, envy and, as in the case of Vietnam which increased the popularity of his work, war. William Appleman Williams, *The Tragedy of American Diplomacy* (New York: W. W. Norton, 1959; 1962; 1972).

78. See ibid., chs. 2, 6 and 8.

79. Not all are from academic leftists. For a more sophisticated version of economic determinism see, most recently, Layne, *Peace of Illusions*.

80. 'You must not speak of us who come over here as cousins, still less as brothers; we are neither . . . there are only two things which can establish and maintain closer relations between your country and mine: they are a community of

ideals and of interests' (cited in B. J. C. McKercher, *Anglo–American Relations in the 1920's* [Edmonton: University of Alberta Press, 1990], 212).

81. Madeleine Albright, speech in Columbus, Ohio, February 18, 1998.

82. Ibid.

83. Felix Gilbert, *To the Farewell Address: Ideas of Early American Foreign Policy* (Princeton, NJ: Princeton University Press, 1961), 17.

84. In 1776 there was no basis in international law for overthrowing the rule of a sovereign monarch.

85. Kagan, *Paradise and Power*, 146. De Villepin was French foreign minister 2002–4.

86. Cited by Norman Podhoretz, 'Is the Bush Doctrine Dead?' *Commentary*, September 2006, 17–31, 21.

87. See David M. Malone and Yuen Foong Khong, eds., *Unilateralism and US Foreign Policy: International Perspectives* (Boulder, CO, and London: Lynne Rienner, 2003); Stewart Patrick and Shepard Forman, eds., *Multilateralism and US Foreign Policy: Ambivalent Engagement* (Boulder, CO, and London: Lynne Rienner, 2002); and Michael Ignatieff, ed., *US Exceptionalism and Human Rights* (Princeton, NJ: Princeton University Press, 2005). Some of the obvious but important reasons why the CTBT has not been ratified are assessed by Christopher Jones, 'Rejection of the Comprehensive Test Ban Treaty: The Politics of Ratification,' in Ralph Carter, ed., *Contemporary Cases in US Foreign Policy: From Terrorism to Trade*, 2nd edn (Washington, DC: CQ Press, 2005), ch. 7.

88. For a qualified defense of American activism ('a model of good sense') and an indictment of EU (specifically British) inaction, see Brendan Simms, *Unfinest Hour: Britain and the Destruction of Bosnia* (London: Allen Lane, 2001), esp. 340.

89. Consider that in Bosnia between 1991 and 1994 'the Security Council . . . adopted more than 60 resolutions and experimented with almost every available form of coercion short of war in an attempt to influence Serbia and protect its victims. Diplomatic isolation, high-level conferences and prominent mediators, expulsion from multilateral organizations, loss of sporting and cultural links, arms embargoes, economic embargoes (ranging from oil products to all trade), naval blockade, air-exclusion zones, air and land humanitarian relief corridors, control of artillery pieces, ceasefire lines, traditional peacekeeping operations, preventive deployments, the establishment of "safe areas" – all [were] tried' (Lawrence Freedman, 'Why the West Failed,' *Foreign Policy* [Winter 1994], 53–69, 59).

90. See, for example, David Skidmore, 'Understanding the Unilateralist Turn in US Foreign Policy,' *Foreign Policy Analysis* 2 (2005), 207–28.

91. Locking conflicted parties into an interminable process has become an occasionally successful conflict resolution strategy. The EU's success stems from this, an interpretation offered by its supporters. See Mark Leonard, *Why Europe will run the 21st Century* (London: Fourth Estate, 2005). Northern

Ireland, one could also argue, was quieted by straitjacketing the warring sides into a peace process from which they could not easily escape.

92. Robert W. Tucker and David C. Hendrickson, 'The Sources of American Legitimacy,' *Foreign Affairs* 83, 6 (2004), 18–32; this quote is the article summary on p. 1. For similar lines of argument, see Mann, *Incoherent Empire*, and Josef Joffe, *Uberpower: The Imperial Temptation of America* (New York: W. W. Norton, 2006).

93. Tucker and Hendrickson, 'The Sources of American Legitimacy,' 19–20.

94. G. John Ikenberry takes a similar line. American primacy and hegemony has legitimacy abroad because it contributes to a 'rules-based' international order. When it breaks the rules its legitimacy is weakened. See Ikenberry, 'America's Imperial Ambition,' *Foreign Affairs* 81, 5 (2002), 44–60; and Ikenberry, 'Liberal Hegemony or Empire? American Power in the Age of Unipolarity,' in David Held and Mathias Koenig-Archibugi, eds., *American Power in the 21st Century* (Cambridge: Polity, 2004), ch. 3. Ivo H. Daalder and James M. Lindsay, *America Unbound: The Bush Revolution in Foreign Policy* (Washington, DC: Brookings Institution Press, 2003), make a similar criticism.

95. See John Yoo and Robert J. Delahunty, 'Executive Power v. International Law,' *Harvard Journal of Law & Public Policy* 30, 1 (2006).

96. Lawrence F. Kaplan, 'The Bush Doctrine Must Survive the Iraq War,' *Financial Times*, October 24, 2006.

97. Robert Kagan, 'A Matter of Record,' *Foreign Affairs* 84, 1 (2005), 170–3, 170. See also Kagan, 'America's Crisis of Legitimacy,' *Foreign Affairs*, 83, 2 (2004).

98. Ibid., Introduction.

99. State of the Union Address, January 20, 2004.

100. Obama speech at Chicago Council on Global Affairs, April 23, 2007.

101. The president's remarks can be found at www.yale.edu/lawweb/avalon/sept_11/president_015.htm. The president was not alone in calling for a crusade. US congressmen cast the conflict in these terms also; see www.yale.edu/lawweb/avalon/sept_11/house_proc_091401.htm.

102. See, for example, the April 1950 National Security Council strategy paper no. 68 (NSC-68), which warned American policy-makers of the 'perverted faith' of Soviet communism and advised a more proactive response to it.

103. On such 'modernistic prejudice' see Hans J. Morgenthau, *Politics Among Nations: The Struggle for Power and Peace*, brief edn, revised by Kenneth W. Thompson (New York: McGraw Hill, 1993), 4.

2. THE CONSTITUTION OF AMERICAN NATIONAL SECURITY

1. Tom Wolfe, 'The Intelligent Coed's Guide to America,' *The Purple Decades* (London: Picador, 1993), 297–309, 302–3.

2. See Stefan Halper and Jonathan Clarke, *America Alone: The Neo-Conservatives and the Global Order* (Cambridge: Cambridge University Press, 2004).

3. See Arthur M. Schlesinger Jr., *War and the American Presidency* (New York: W.W. Norton & Company, 2004).

4. Ira Katznelson and Martin Shefter, eds., *Shaped by War and Trade: International Influences on American Political Development* (Princeton, NJ: Princeton University Press, 2002).

5. The most persuasive treatment of the constitutional issues raised by the war on terror is Richard A. Posner, *Not a Suicide Pact: The Constitution in a Time of National Emergency* (New York: Oxford University Press, 2006).

6. The War of 1812, the Mexican War of 1846, the Spanish–American War of 1898, and World Wars I and II.

7. Samuel P. Huntington, *American Politics: The Promise of Disharmony* (Cambridge, MA: Harvard University Press, 1981).

8. Huntington's argument that a minority of Americans frequently oppose military action is reinforced by opinion surveys, which document how opinion leaders and elites are, with few exceptions, consistently more willing to use force to defend allies from attack and advance US interests than the public. See Ole R. Holsti, *Public Opinion and American Foreign Policy*, revised edn (Ann Arbor, MI: The University of Michigan Press, 2004).

9. Cass Sunstein, *Radicals in Robes: Why Extreme Right-wing Courts Are Wrong for America* (New York: Basic Books, 2005), 151.

10. The depiction of the US as an 'offshore balancer' is disputed. See the contrary positions advanced by John Mearsheimer, *The Tragedy of Great Power Politics* (New York: W. W. Norton, 2001) and, opposing the concept, Layne, *Peace of Illusions*, 23–5.

11. Albright used this phrase in a speech on 5 December 1996 and repeatedly thereafter; see Michael Dobbs and John M. Goshko, 'Albright's Personal Odyssey Shaped Foreign Policy Beliefs,' *Washington Post*, December 6, 1996, A25.

12. Turf battles and poor intelligence sharing across the US government were highlighted in the 9/11 Commission Report, chapter 13, at www.9-11commission.gov/report/index.htm. The unitary nature of the presidency does not insulate it from such endemic problems.

13. Steven Kull and Clay Ramsay, 'The Myth of the Reactive Public: American Public Attitudes on Military Fatalities in the Post-Cold War Period,' chapter 9 in Philip Everts and Pierangelo Isernia, eds., *Public Opinion and the International Use of Force* (New York: Routledge, 2001), 205–28; I. M. Destler, 'The Reasonable Public and the Polarized Policy Process,' chapter 5 in Anthony Lake and David Ochmanek, eds., *The Real and the Ideal: Essays on International Relations in Honor of Richard H. Ullman* (Lanham, MD: Rowman and Littlefield, 2001), 75–90; and Peter D. Feaver and Christopher Gelpi, *Choosing Your*

Battles: American Civil–Military Relations and the Use of Force (Princeton, NJ: Princeton University Press, 2005). For a competing set of arguments over Iraq, see John Mueller, 'The Iraq Syndrome,' *Foreign Affairs* 84, 6 (2005), 44–54; and Christopher Gelpi, 'Misdiagnosis,' *Foreign Affairs* 85, 1 (2006).

14. Niall Ferguson also advances this argument, with supporting data, in *Colossus*, 94–104.

15. This does not, however, equate to the notion that Americans have become 'seduced' by militarism and are disastrously unrealistic about the possibilities of, and limits to, military might, as argued by Andrew Bacevich, *The New American Militarism: How Americans Are Seduced by War* (New York: Oxford University Press, 2005). The only modern poll that directly asked Americans to assess their tendency toward militarism, by CBS in November 1991, saw 75 percent of those surveyed respond that they were 'peace loving' rather than 'warlike' (which just 17 percent agreed with). But in a 2005 Pew Global Attitudes Project poll, 49 percent of Americans affirmed that they were 'violent.' As one commentator noted, 'Deep down, many of us know we are both.' Carl M. Cannon, 'Why We Fight,' *National Journal*, July 1, 2006, 21–8, 21–2.

16. Karl Schonberg, 'Global Security and Legal Restraint: Reconsidering War Powers after September 11,' *Political Science Quarterly* 119, 1 (2004), 115–42, 128.

17. Louis Fisher, 'The Way We Go to War: The Iraq Resolution,' in Gary L. Gregg II and Mark Rozell, eds., *Considering the Bush Presidency* (Oxford: Oxford University Press, 2004), 107–24, 120–1.

18. Robert Byrd, 'Preserving Constitutional War Powers,' *Mediterranean Quarterly* 14, 3 (2003), 1–5, 3.

19. Louis Fisher, *Presidential War Power*, 2nd edn (Lawrence, KS: University Press of Kansas, 2004); Michael J. Glennon, *Constitutional Diplomacy* (Princeton, NJ: Princeton University Press, 1990); Harold H. Koh, *The National Security Constitution: Sharing Power After the Iran-Contra Affair* (New Haven, CT: Yale University Press, 1990).

20. In Michael J. Glennon, 'The Gulf War and the Constitution,' *Foreign Affairs* 70, 2 (1991), 84–101, 87.

21. See, for example, Fisher, *Presidential War Power*.

22. Glennon, 'The Gulf War and the Constitution,' 84.

23. Edward S. Corwin, *The President: Office and Powers, 1878–1957*, 4th revised edn (New York: New York University Press, 1957), 171.

24. It is striking, for example, that war powers merit no mention at all in such detailed treatments as Philip Bobbitt, *Constitutional Interpretation* (Oxford: Basil Blackwell, 1991); Robert H. Bork, *The Tempting of America: The Political Seduction of the Law* (New York: The Free Press, 1990); Michael J. Perry, *The Constitution in the Courts: Law or Politics?* (New York: Oxford University Press,

1994); a mere two pages in Mark Tushnet, *Taking the Constitution away from the Courts* (Princeton, NJ: Princeton University Press, 1999); and one page in Stephen M. Griffin, *American Constitutionalism: From Theory to Politics* (Princeton, NJ: Princeton University Press, 1996).

25. John Yoo, *The Powers of War and Peace: The Constitution and Foreign Affairs After 9/11* (Chicago: University of Chicago Press, 2005).

26. Ibid., 143.

27. Ibid., 160.

28. 548 US, pp. 2–3, at www.supremecourtus.gov/opinions/05pdf/05-184.pdf#search=%22Hamdan%20v%20Rumsfeld%22.

29. Yoo, *Powers of War and Peace*, 159.

30. *Terminiello v. City of Chicago* (1949), 337 US, 37.

31. Stephen Holmes, 'Liberalism in the Mirror of Transnational Terror,' *Tocqueville Review* 22, 2 (2001), 5, 6.

32. Sunstein, *Radicals in Robes*, 165–6.

33. Such as *Youngstown Sheet and Tube Co. v. Sawyer*, 343 US 579 (1952).

34. William Howell, *Power without Persuasion: The Politics of Direct Presidential Action* (Princeton, NJ: Princeton University Press, 2003), 7.

35. Ibid., 7.

36. Ibid., xvii. Emphasis added.

37. Eighteen members of Congress filed a lawsuit in the DC Federal District Court in an attempt to have Clinton's actions ruled a violation of the WPR and the Constitution. It was rejected by the court on the grounds that the plaintiffs did not have legal standing. See Richard F. Grimmett, 'The War Powers Resolution After Thirty Years,' CRS Report (RL34051), June 22, 2004.

38. Byrd, 'Preserving Constitutional War Powers,' 5.

39. Howell, *Power without Persuasion*, 13.

40. Richard A. Posner, *Law, Pragmatism and Democracy* (Cambridge, MA: Harvard University Press, 2005).

41. Al Qaeda declared war on America with Bin Laden's August 23, 1996 *Declaration of Jihad Against the Americans* and repeated in his February 23, 1998 *Jihad Against Jews and Crusaders: World Islamic Front Statement*. See Bruce Lawrence and James Howarth, eds., *Messages to the World: The Statements of Osama Bin Laden* (London: Verso, 2005), chs. 3 and 6.

42. In both the House and the Senate one independent also voted against.

43. Fisher, 'The Way We Go to War,' 120–1.

44. Fisher, *Presidential War Power*.

45. *Washington Post*, March 12, 2003.

46. In Sunstein, *Radicals in Robes*, 181.

47. See Carol K. Winkler, *In the Name of Terrorism: Presidents on Political Violence in the Post-World War II Era* (New York: State University of New York Press, 2006).

48. Posner, *Law, Pragmatism and Democracy*, 296, 298.
49. Bruce Ackerman, *Before the Next Attack: Preserving Civil Liberties in an Age of Terrorism* (New Haven, CT: Yale University Press, 2006).
50. Yoo, *Powers of War and Peace*, 172.

3. THE SECOND COLD WAR ON ISLAMIST TERROR: NEGATIVE AUDITS

1. William Greider, 'Under the Banner of the War on Terror,' *The Nation*, 21 June 2004.
2. Clive James, *Cultural Amnesia: Notes in the Margin of My Time* (London: Picador, 2007), 456.
3. Quoted in Jeffrey Goldberg, 'Breaking Ranks: What Turned Brent Scowcroft against the Bush Administration?' *New Yorker*, October 31, 2006.
4. Fareed Zakaria, 'The Reagan Strategy of Containment,' *Political Science Quarterly* 105, 3 (1990), 373–95, 392.
5. See, for example, the *National Interest*, the *American Interest*, *National Review*, the *Conservative American*, the *Weekly Standard*, the American Enterprise Institute and the Heritage Foundation.
6. Robert Kagan and William Kristol, 'Toward a Neo-Reaganite Foreign Policy,' *Foreign Affairs* 75, 4 (1996).
7. Lamont beat Lieberman in the 2006 Democratic primary but lost in the subsequent election to Lieberman, running as an independent. The war on terror commands a consensus that Lamont's fate suggests is robust.
8. There are several variations of realism. Classical realists see states as power maximizers, which leads them into competition with opponent states. The paradigm's chief architects are Thucydides (c. 460–400 BC), *History of the Peloponnesian War*; E. H. Carr, *The Twenty Years' Crisis: 1919–1939: An Introduction to the Study of International Relations*, 2nd edn (London: Macmillan, 1969; first published 1939); and Morgenthau, *Politics Among Nations*. Structural or *defensive* realism, because its development followed classical realism, is also referred to as neo-realism. The seminal work is Kenneth N. Waltz, *Man, the State, and War: A Theoretical Analysis* (New York: Columbia University Press, 1959; reprint 2001) refined in his *Theory of International Politics* (New York: McGraw Hill, 1979). Structural/defensive realists argue that the anarchic *structure* of international relations makes states security maximizers, that states want 'not much more power than what they have' and will settle for a security that can be attained rather than absolute power which cannot. *Offensive realists*, in contrast, contend that states want all the power they can get. The seminal work is Mearsheimer, *The Tragedy of Great Power Politics*.
9. John J. Mearsheimer, 'Hans Morgenthau and the Iraq War: Realism vs. Neoconservatism,' *Open Democracy*, April 21, 2005; at www.opendemocracy.net/content/articles/PDF/2522.pdf.

10. George Will concurs but on the basis that Bush's faith in the war on terror to deliver up cultural change is misplaced (Will, 'Time for Bush to See the Realities of Iraq,' in Gary Rosen, ed., *The Right War? The Conservative Debate on Iraq* [New York: Cambridge University Press, 2005], ch. 8).

11. Paul Kennedy, *The Rise and Fall of the Great Powers: Economic Change and Military Conflict from 1500 to 2000* (London: Unwin Hyman, 1988).

12. Graham E. Fuller, 'Strategic Fatigue,' *National Interest* (Summer 2006).

13. In Stephen M. Walt, *Taming American Power: The Global Response to US Primacy* (New York: W. W. Norton & Co., 2005), 10.

14. Mearsheimer, 'Hans Morgenthau,' 4.

15. Anatol Lieven and John Hulsman, *Ethical Realism: A Vision for America's Role in the World* (London: Pantheon Books, 2006).

16. George Packer, 'Unrealistic,' *New Yorker*, November 27, 2006. Also cited in Bret Stephens, 'Realists to the Rescue?' *Commentary* (February 2007), 27–34, 28.

17. Lieven and Hulsman, *Ethical Realism*, xii.

18. Ibid., 53.

19. 'We come to you for one reason only, to enable the starving to be fed.' In Robert C. DiPrizio, *Armed Humanitarians: US Interventions from Northern Iraq to Kosovo* (Baltimore, MD: Johns Hopkins University Press, 2002), 53.

20. Ivo H. Daalder and Robert Kagan, 'America and the Use of Force: Sources of Legitimacy,' Stanley Foundation (June 2007), 1; at www3.brookings.edu/views/articles/daalder/2007june_kagan.pdf.

21. Lieber, *American Era*, 200. Also see Keir Lieber and Gerard Alexander, 'Waiting for Balancing: Why the World Isn't Pushing Back,' *International Security* 30, 1 (2005).

22. Michael Mandelbaum, *The Case for Goliath: How America acts as the World's Government in the Twenty-First Century* (New York: Public Affairs, 2005), xvi.

23. Robert Kagan, 'End of Dreams, Return of History,' *Policy Review* 143 (2007).

24. Mark L. Haas, 'A Geriatric Peace? The Future of US Power in a World of Aging Populations,' *International Security* 31, 2 (2007), 112–47, 112.

25. Tariq Ali, *Pirates of the Caribbean: Axis of Hope* (London: Verso, 2006).

26. Walter Laqueur, 'After the Cold War,' *E-Journal USA* (US Dept. of State), Foreign Policy Agenda (April 2006), 41–3; at http://usinfo.state.gov/journals/itps/0406/ijpe/ijpe0406.pdf.

27. Daalder and Kagan, 'America and the Use of Force,' 1. Emphasis added.

28. 'The peculiar qualities of the statesman's mind are not always likely to find a favourable response in the popular mind . . . The popular mind wants quick results; it will sacrifice tomorrow's real benefit for today's apparent advantage' (Morgenthau, *Politics Among Nations*, 160, 161).

29. See, for example, Henry Kissinger, *Diplomacy* (New York: Touchstone, 1995), 161, 163–4. Whereas receptivity to public opinion did not ruin the 'extra-

ordinary consistency' of nineteenth-century British foreign policy (*Diplomacy*, 100), in Germany, Russia and Austria-Hungary popular passions regularly superseded Realpolitik. Kissinger's estimation runs counter to Tocqueville's, who argued that democracies – too smitten with domestic 'ease' – were not as able in foreign policy as aristocracies. See *Democracy*, vol. I, pt. 2, ch. 5, 219. Morgenthau quotes this passage from Tocqueville approvingly and at some length (*Politics Among Nations*, 160–1).

30. John Mearsheimer and Stephen Walt, 'The Israel Lobby,' *London Review of Books* 28, 6 (2006) and their later book *The Israel Lobby and US Foreign Policy* (New York: Allen Lane, 2007).

31. Mearsheimer and Walt, 'The Israel Lobby.'

32. For reactions to it, see *Foreign Policy* (July/August 2006) and www.scribemedia. org/2006/10/11/israel-lobby/. For a comprehensive rebuttal see Abraham H. Foxman, *The Deadliest Lies: The Israel Lobby and the Myth of Jewish Control* (New York: Palgrave Macmillan, 2007).

33. See Brendon O'Connor and Martin Griffiths, eds., *The Rise of Anti-Americanism* (London: Routledge, 2005); and Peter J. Katzenstein and Robert O. Keohane, eds., *Anti-Americanisms in World Politics* (New York: Cornell University Press, 2006).

34. See, for example, Chalmers Johnson, *Blowback: The Costs and Consequences of American Empire* (New York: Henry Holt, 2000).

35. Stephen Walt argues this in *Taming American Power*, 230.

36. Michael Vlahos, 'Losing Mythic Authority,' *National Interest* 89 (2007), 87–91, 87.

37. Halper and Clarke, *America Alone*, 260–2.

38. 'Historian Bernard Lewis has pointed out that compared to prisons throughout the Arab world, Guantánamo Bay and Abu Ghraib are like Disneyland. Certainly, in terms of cleanliness, food, and amenities, America's prisons are comparable to the accommodations in midlevel Middle Eastern hotels.' Dinesh D'Souza, *The Enemy at Home: The Cultural Left and its Responsibility for 9/11* (New York: Doubleday, 2007), 84.

39. Cited in *Weekly Standard*, August 21, 2006.

40. Walt (*Taming American Power*, 229–31) puts great store in the efficacy of public diplomacy to secure US interests.

41. Brendan Simms, 'Why British Muslims Give the US No Credit for Bosnia or Kosovo,' *Bosnian Institute*, August 24, 2005; at www.bosnia.org.uk/news/news_body.cfm?newsid=2104.

42. Richard K. Betts, 'The Soft Underbelly of American Primacy: Tactical Advantages of Terror,' *Political Science Quarterly* 117, 1 (2002), 19–36, 34.

43. Richard Clarke, *Against All Enemies: Inside America's War on Terror* (New York: Free Press, 2004), 6.

44. In Mark Steyn, 'Insight,' *Jewish World Review*, September 27, 2002.

45. See Nick Cohen, *What's Left? How Liberals Lost Their Way* (London: Fourth Estate, 2007).
46. Ali, *Clash of Fundamentalisms*.
47. Ibid., xiii. Variations on this theme are offered by Zhiyuan Cui, 'The Bush Doctrine: A Chinese Perspective,' and Abdelwahab El Affendi, 'Waiting for Armageddon: The "Mother of All Empires" and its Middle East Quagmire,' in Held and Koenig-Archibugi, eds., *American Power in the 21st Century*.
48. Christopher Hitchens in Hitchens and Michael Gove, 'All Hail the New Anti-Islamist Intelligentsia,' *Spectator* 27 (2007), 16.
49. G. John Ikenberry, Bryce Lecture at the Institute for the Study of the Americas, University of London, June 5, 2005.
50. Osama Bin Laden, taped speech, February 12, 2003; see http://news.bbc.co.uk/1/hi/world/middle_east/2753751.stm.
51. Cohen, *What's Left?*, 9.
52. Though environmentalism comes a close second, especially given its increasingly anti-American sub-text.
53. See www.democrats.org/pdfs/2004platform.pdf.
54. Few politicians and mainstream commentators decry the threat of terrorism. They divide on how toppling Saddam advanced that effort. '[T]he [Iraq] war was, at best, a distraction from the struggle against Al Qaeda' (Robert Jervis, 'Why the Bush Doctrine Cannot Be Sustained,' *Political Science Quarterly* 120, 3 [2005], 351–77, 353).
55. See, for example, Keith Spence, 'World Risk Society and War Against Terror,' *Political Studies* 53, 2 (2005), 284–302, which recycles the old leftist argument that America exaggerates ('constructs') risk to justify its hegemony.
56. Claus Christian Malzahn, 'Evil Americans, Poor Mullahs,' *Spiegel* Online, March 29, 2007.
57. Arthur M. Schlesinger Jr., *The Vital Center: The Politics of Freedom* (Boston: Houghton Mifflin, 1949).
58. One of the most influential works of political science, Graham Allison's *Essence of Decision: Explaining the Cuban Missile Crisis* (Boston: Little, Brown, 1971), contended that values don't shape foreign policy. A receptive academic audience concurred and mostly still does.
59. None of the top ten 'most influential' IR scholars in the US – constructed by *Foreign Policy* (November/December 2005), 62, and including liberals and realists – can be categorized as sympathetic to Bush foreign policy. They are, in order: Robert Keohane, Kenneth Waltz, Alexander Wendt, Samuel Huntington, John Mearsheimer, Joseph Nye, Robert Jervis, Bruce Bueno de Mesquita, Bruce Russett, and Robert Gilpin. Only Stephen Krasner, ranked at number twelve, can claim Bush sympathies. He has been Director for Policy Planning at the State Department since 2005.

60. See Timothy J. Lynch, 'Whither American Power?: A Review Essay,' *British Journal of Politics and International Relations* 9, 3 (2007), 535–44; Lieber, *American Era* (2005), 32–7; and Robert G. Kaufman, *In Defense of the Bush Doctrine* (Lexington, KY: Univeristy of Kentucky Press, 2007), 63–86.

61. William Watson, 'Quodlibets of Religion and State' (1602).

62. Michael Ignatieff, *The Lesser Evil: Political Ethics in an Age of Terror* (Princeton: Princeton University Press, 2004), 32.

63. See Simon Jeffery, 'Lord Goldsmith's Legal Advice and the Iraq War,' *Guardian*, April 27, 2005.

64. George H. W. Bush and Brent Scowcroft, *A World Transformed* (New York: Alfred A. Knopf, 1998), 489.

65. See Judis, *Folly of Empire*, 154.

66. Jonathan Freedland, 'Bush's Amazing Achievement,' *New York Review of Books*, June 14, 2007.

67. Richard Falk, *The Great Terror War* (New York: Olive Branch Press, 2003), 82, 83.

68. Ibid., 82.

69. George W. Bush, radio address, July 29, 2006.

70. The 'fetid swamp' metaphor is from Mark Steyn, 'Realists Have It Wrong,' *Washington Times*, January 31, 2005.

71. This debate is explored by Michael Ignatieff (in dialogue with Robert Skidelsky) in Ignatieff, *Virtual War: Kosovo and Beyond* (London: Vintage 2001), 71–87.

72. www.un.org/aboutun/charter/.

73. Clinton did not remove the Serb leader from office, but it is hard to imagine Milošević would have fallen without NATO intervention in Kosovo in 1999.

74. Mann, *Incoherent Empire*, 189.

75. Ibid., xxv. Similar arguments are offered in Stephen Holmes, *The Matador's Cape: America's Reckless Response to Terror* (New York: Cambridge University Press, 2007).

76. Eric Hobsbawm, *Globalisation, Democracy and Terrorism* (New York: Little, Brown, 2007).

77. Cohen, *What's Left?*, 280–1.

78. This was affirmed at the EU's fiftieth birthday celebrations in March 2007. See http://europa.eu/50/future/index_en.htm. The number of French who considered the environment the 'top global threat' rose from 29 percent in 2002 to 52 percent in 2007. See the Pew Global Attitudes Project Report (June 2007), 2; at http://pewglobal.org/reports/pdf/256.pdf.

79. The request was made by US General Bantz Craddock, Supreme Allied Commander of NATO, at a meeting of NATO defense ministers in Seville, Spain. See Gerard Baker, 'Continental Drift: Europe Gets Even Less Serious,' *Weekly Standard*, March 19, 2007.

80. Robert Kagan, 'Power and Weakness,' *Policy Review* 113 (2002) and Kagan, *Of Paradise and Power*, 3.

81. Timothy Garton Ash, 'The New Anti-Europeanism in America,' in Tod Lindberg, ed., *Beyond Paradise and Power: Europe, America and the Future of a Troubled Partnership* (New York: Routledge, 2005), 122.

82. This rationale is described well, though we dispute his wider thesis, in Leonard, *Why Europe Will Run the 21st Century*, ch. 1.

83. Lincoln in Carl Sandburg, *Abraham Lincoln: The War Years*, vol. I (New York: Harcourt Brace and World, 1939), 90.

84. Jean-Marie Colombani, '*Nous sommes tous américains*,' *Le Monde*, September 13, 2001.

85. On the supposed superiority of cosmopolitanism over 'compellance' see Mary Kaldor, 'American Power: From "Compellance" to Cosmopolitanism,' in Held and Koenig-Archibugi, eds., *American Power in the 21st Century*, ch. 7.

86. See Paul Arthur, ' "Quiet Diplomacy and Personal Conversation," Track Two Diplomacy and the Search for a Settlement in Northern Ireland,' in Joseph Ruane and Jennifer Todd, eds., *After the Good Friday Agreement: Analysing Political Change in Northern Ireland* (Dublin: University College Dublin Press, 1999), 71–95; Timothy J. Lynch, *Turf War: The Clinton Administration and Northern Ireland* (Aldershot: Ashgate, 2004), 123; and, in another context, Hussein Agha *et al.*, *Track-II Diplomacy: Lessons from the Middle East* (Cambridge, MA: MIT Press, 2004).

87. See Peter Taylor, 'Al Qaeda: Time To Talk?' BBC series, 2006.

88. Al Qaeda attacked the Madrid metro on March 11, 2004, killing 191. The war-on-terror-supporting PM, José María Aznar, lost the ensuing election, three days later, to the socialist candidate, José Luis Rodríguez Zapatero, who moved quickly (on April 19, 2004) to withdraw Spain's 1,300 troops from Iraq. According to Mark Steyn, 'the Spanish knowingly made polling day a victory for appeasement and dishonored their own dead' (*America Alone: The End of the World as We Know It* [Washington, DC: Regnery Publishing, 2006], 37).

89. Frederick Kagan made this argument with clarity in a talk, attended by the authors, at the International Institute for Strategic Studies, London, July 23, 2007.

90. July 30, 2007; see http://news.bbc.co.uk/1/hi/world/americas/6922840.stm.

91. David Livingstone, Associate Fellow, International Security Programme, Chatham House, in interview on the BBC Radio 4 *Today* Programme, July 26, 2007. He was explaining why five British Muslim students chose to download bomb-making instructions ('The Terrorist Handbook') and videos of beheadings from the internet. They were jailed for between two and three years. See http://news.bbc.co.uk/1/hi/uk/6916654.stm.

92. See, for example, progressives who 'get it' such as Peter Beinart, Paul Berman, Christopher Hitchens, Nick Cohen, David Aaronovitch, Michael Ignatieff,

Robert Lieber, Michael O'Hanlon, and the signatories of the Euston Manifesto at www.eustonmanifesto.org/, and the Henry Jackson Society at www.henryjacksonsociety.org/.

4. THE SECOND COLD WAR ON ISLAMIST TERROR: A POSITIVE AUDIT

1. John Stuart Mill, 'The Contest in America,' *Harper's New Monthly Magazine* 24, 143 (1862), 677–84, 683.
2. In Rick Maze, 'No More GWOT, House Committee Decrees,' *Military Times*, April 4, 2007.
3. Rod Liddle, 'The Public Know How These Attacks Happen – Unlike the Politicians,' *Spectator*, July 7, 2007, 14–15, 14.
4. See www.whitehouse.gov/nsc/nss.pdf and www.whitehouse.gov/nsc/nss/2006/nss2006.pdf.
5. Address to Congress, September 20, 2001. Bush's speech in Whitehall, London, November 19, 2003 also offers a powerful restatement of this strategic approach.
6. See www.9-11commission.gov/report/911Report.pdf (published July 22, 2004).
7. On the redundancies of renaming attempts see 'The GWOT No More,' *Weekly Standard* 10, 44 (August 8, 2005). On the name's unpopularity see Maze, 'No more GWOT.' The British Foreign Office was never convinced of the title and urged it to be dropped by the British government. See Jason Burke, 'Britain Stops Talk of "War on Terror,"' *Observer*, 10 December 2006.
8. Daniel Maliniak, Amy Oakes, Susan Peterson, and Michael J. Tierney, 'Inside the Ivory Tower,' *Foreign Policy* 151 (2007), 62–8, 64. The full survey appears at www.wm.edu/irtheoryandpractice/trip/surveyreport06-07.pdf.
9. Citizens from approximately eighty countries were killed on 9/11.
10. See data presented in Anna Sabasteanski, ed., US Department of State, *Patterns of Global Terrorism Report, 1985–2005* (Great Barrington, MA: Berkshire Publishing Group, 2005).
11. Robert J. Lieber, 'Foreign-Policy "Realists" Are Unrealistic on Iraq,' *Chronicle of Higher Education* 49, 8 (2002).
12. For concurrence see Peter W. Singer, *The 9-11 War Plus 5, Looking Back and Looking Forward at US–Islamic World Relations*, Brookings Institution (September 2006), esp. 5–8; and David P. Auerswald, 'Deterring Non-state WMD Attacks,' *Political Science Quarterly* 121, 4 (2006), 543–68. According to Lieven and Hulsman (*Ethical Realism*, xiii), 'The threat from Islamist terrorism has to be taken very seriously indeed – more seriously than any other security issue now facing the United States.'
13. Ourselves excepted, we would not make the same contention on behalf of British or European academics.

14. Bush speech at Czernin Palace, Prague, June 5, 2007.

15. Terrorist finances have certainly been disrupted by internal American measures, suggesting safety has augmented. See, though she questions the permanent effects of such measures, Anne L. Clunan, 'The Fight against Terrorist Financing,' *Political Science Quarterly* 121, 4 (2006), 569–96.

16. See Mike McConnell, 'Overhauling Intelligence,' *Foreign Affairs*, 86, 4 (2007).

17. The Japanese attack is brilliantly retold in Walter Lord, *Day of Infamy* (New York: Henry Holt, 1957; Owl Books, 2001). Intelligence failings, substantially those of the FBI and CIA, are described in the 9/11 Commission Report, ch. 8 ('The system was blinking red'); the Phoenix Memo is discussed at 272.

18. See the top secret 'Office of Inspector General Report on CIA Accountability with Respect to the 9/11 Attacks, June 2005,' made public August 21, 2007, at http://graphics8.nytimes.com/packages/pdf/national/CIA_SUMMARY. pdf.

19. See Anne M. Khademian, 'Homeland (In)Security,' in Robert Maranto, Douglas M. Brattebo, and Tom Lansford, eds., *The Second Term of George W. Bush: Prospects and Perils*. The Evolving American Presidency Series (New York: Macmillan, 2006), 179–99, note 2.

20. See Tom Lansford, 'Homeland Security from Clinton to Bush: An Assessment,' *White House Studies* 3, 4 (2003).

21. Department of Homeland Security, at www.dhs.gov/xabout/history/publication_ 0005.shtm.

22. The DNI's role is explored by Bush's second DNI, Mike McConnell, 'Overhauling Intelligence.' See also Jeffrey T. Richelson, *The US Intelligence Community*, 5th edn (Boulder, CO: Westview Press, 2007).

23. Martin Wolf observes that 'Only in a market economy would the wealthy give large sums of money to universities that provide comfortable homes to those who despise the wealthy and the system that made them so. The market economy does not merely support its critics, it embraces them' (*Why Globalization Works*, 55).

24. See Abraham D. Sofaer, 'Presidential Power and National Security,' *Presidential Studies Quarterly* 37, 1 (2007), 101–23.

25. See James Risen, 'White House Is Subpoenaed on Wiretapping,' *New York Times*, June 28, 2007.

26. In *Hamdan*, the Court reaffirmed *Youngstown Sheet and Tube Co. v. Sawyer* (1952) that 'Whether or not the President has independent power, absent congressional authorization, to convene military commissions, he may not disregard limitations that Congress has, in proper exercise of its own war powers, placed on his powers.'

27. Michael C. Dorf, 'The Detention and Trial of Enemy Combatants: A Drama in Three Branches,' *Political Science Quarterly* 122, 1 (2007), 47–58, 58.

28. *Al-Marri v. Wright* (2007).

29. See William Glaberson, 'Military Judges Dismiss Charges for 2 Detainees,' *New York Times*, 5 June 2007.

30. In 2005, 62 percent of Americans believed the PATRIOT Act was 'about right' and/or that it 'does not go far enough' (versus 34 percent who thought it 'goes too far'). See www.galluppoll.com/content/default.aspx?ci=5263.

31. See 'Muslim Americans: Middle-class and Mostly Mainstream,' Pew Research Center, May 22, 2007, 3; at http://pewresearch.org/assets/pdf/muslim-americans.pdf.

32. Migration from Egypt and Saudi Arabia, the nations from which sixteen of the nineteen 9/11 hijackers came, increased from 7,350 in 1996 to 12,042 in 2006. See www.dhs.gov/xlibrary/assets/statistics/yearbook/2006/table03d.xls.

33. The Pew Global Attitudes Project Report (June 2007), 105, provides significant evidence that Arabs in the Middle East think they would have 'better' lives in America; at http://pewglobal.org/reports/pdf/256.pdf.

34. David Davis, 'We Must Fight Terror the American Way,' *Sunday Telegraph*, March 25, 2007.

35. See, respectively, www.9-11commission.gov/report/911Report.pdf, www.gpoaccess.gov/serialset/creports/911.html, and www.whitehouse.gov/homeland/ book/.

36. Both were released in 2004. Hutton dealt specifically with the suicide of the British weapons inspector Dr David Kelly, Butler with British intelligence on WMD in Iraq. See www.butlerreview.org.uk/ and www.the-hutton-inquiry.org.uk/.

37. Davis, 'We Must Fight Terror the American Way.'

38. Andrew Marr, 'If "Islamist" Is Out, What Do We Call Them?' *Daily Telegraph*, July 4, 2007.

39. See, for example, his speech to London Muslims, July 15, 2005; at http://news.bbc.co.uk/1/hi/england/4686519.stm; and, for a denunciation of his approach, Charles Moore, 'Where Is the Gandhi of Islam?' *Daily Telegraph*, July 9, 2005.

40. Steven Simon, cited in Steve Coll and Susan B. Glasser, 'In London, Islamic Radicals Found a Haven,' *Washington Post*, July 10, 2005. See also Christopher Hitchens, 'Londonistan Calling,' *Vanity Fair* (June 2007); and Melanie Phillips, *Londonistan: How Britain Is Creating a Terror State Within* (London: Gibson Square Books, 2006).

41. Speech in Tipp City, Ohio, April 19, 2007.

42. Joseph S. Nye Jr., *The Paradox of American Power: Why the World's Only Superpower Can't Go It Alone* (Oxford: Oxford University Press, 2003), 9. His terms 'hard' and 'soft power' have become basic to the discourse surrounding American foreign policy. See Nye, *Soft Power: The Means to Success in World Politics* (New York: Public Affairs, 2005).

43. His remarks were contained in a October 18, 2003 leaked memo from

Rumsfeld to Dick Myers, Paul Wolfowitz, Peter Pace, and Douglas Feith; reproduced in full at www.globalsecurity.org/military/library/policy/dod/d20031016sdmemo.pdf.

44. See Bruce W. Jentleson, 'Jordan Bombings and the Rumsfeld Terrorism Metric,' America Abroad: notes on foreign affairs (November 16, 2005); at http://americaabroad.tpmcafe.com/story/2005/11/16/95918/444. Richard Clarke, former White House counterterrorism official, interpreted the memo as an admission of defeat (Clarke, *Against All Enemies*, 246).

45. Jervis, 'Why the Bush Doctrine Cannot Be Sustained,' 353.

46. This difficulty is acknowledged by John L. Esposito and Dalia Mogahed, 'What Makes a Muslim Radical?' *Foreign Policy* (November/December 2006).

47. James Fallows, 'Declaring Victory,' *Atlantic Monthly* (September 2006), 60–73. For a contrary assessment see Mark Mazzetti, 'Qaeda Is Seen as Restoring Leadership,' *New York Times*, April 2, 2007.

48. See James Fallows, 'Can We Still Declare Victory?' *Atlantic Unbound*, August 11, 2006.

49. See Gilles Kepel, *Jihad: The Trail of Political Islam* (Cambridge, MA: Belknap Press, 2003).

50. See Fukuyama, *End of History*, 45–6 and 235–7.

51. For contrasting assessments of al Qaeda's intent and the impact of America's war against them, see Richard J. Harknett, 'Barbarians at and behind the Gates: The Loss of Contingency and the Search for Homeland Security,' *The Forum* 1, 2 (2002); Bruce Riedel, 'Al Qaeda Strikes Back,' *Foreign Affairs* 86, 3 (2007); Max Abrahms, 'Why Terrorism Does Not Work,' *International Security* 31, 2 (2006); Robert A. Pape, *Dying to Win: The Strategic Logic of Suicide Terrorism* (New York: Random House, 2005); Michael Doran, 'The Pragmatic Fanaticism of al Qaeda: An Anatomy of Extremism in Middle Eastern Politics,' *Political Science Quarterly* 117, 2 (2002); and Martin D. Libicki, Peter Chalk, and Melanie Sisson, *Exploring Terrorist Targeting Preferences* (Santa Monica, CA: Rand Corporation, 2007).

52. John Mueller, 'Is There Still a Terrorist Threat?: The Myth of the Omnipresent Enemy,' *Foreign Affairs* 85, 5 (2006). See also John Mueller, *Overblown: How Politicians and the Terrorism Industry Inflate National Security Threats, and Why We Believe Them* (New York: The Free Press, 2006).

53. In John Mueller, 'Is There Still a Terrorist Threat?'

54. In Ron Suskind, 'The Untold Story of al-Qaeda's Plot to Attack the Subway,' *Time*, June 19, 2006.

55. Robert Kagan, 'More Leaks Please,' *Washington Post*, September 26, 2006. He continues: 'the question of what actions make us safer cannot be answered simply by counting the number of new terrorist recruits those actions may inspire, even if we could make such a count with any confidence. I would worry about an American foreign policy driven only by fear of how our actions

might inspire anger, radicalism and violence in others. As in the past, that should be only one calculation in our judgment of what does and does not make us, and the world, safer.'

56. See http://news.bbc.co.uk/1/hi/uk/6261899.stm. In April 2007, five British jihadists – linked to the July 7, 2005 terrorists – were convicted for conspiring in a bomb plot that relied on ammonium nitrate, an over-the-counter agricultural fertilizer. See http://news.bbc.co.uk/1/hi/uk/6195914.stm.

57. Rod Liddle's fictitious headline after these failed attacks appears in this chapter's epigraph. The *Sun's* headline (July 10, 2007) was 'MORON TERROR'.

58. The attraction of transportation disruption is common to many terrorists. For example, on March 9 and 11, 1994, the IRA fired mortars into Heathrow airport to increase British concessions in the emergent peace process. The religious sect Aum killed twelve people in a sarin gas attack on the Tokyo subway on March 12, 1995. Jihadists have extended their targeting to night clubs (in London and Bali) and weddings (in Jordan).

59. See Daniel L. Byman, 'After the Storm: US Policy toward Iraq since 1991,' *Political Science Quarterly* 115, 4 (2000), 493–516; and the 9/11 Commission Report, pt. 4.

60. Speech at West Point, New York, June 1, 2002.

61. State of the Union Address, January 29, 2002.

62. Donald Rumsfeld, Congressional testimony, July 9, 2003. On the impact of 9/11 on the decision to invade Iraq see Christopher Hemmer, 'The Lessons of September 11, Iraq, and the American Pendulum,' *Political Science Quarterly* 122, 2 (2007), 207–38.

63. In Suskind, 'The Untold Story of al-Qaeda's Plot to Attack the Subway.'

64. George Tenet, *At the Center of the Storm: My Years at the CIA* (New York: HarperCollins, 2007, p. 265). This is not the interpretation Ron Suskind applies to Cheney's doctrine. Rather, he uses the vice-president's words to conclude that evidence that negated war-mongering was discouraged in the Bush administration. See Suskind, *The One Percent Doctrine: Deep Inside America's Pursuit of its Enemies since 9/11* (New York: Simon and Schuster, 2006), p. 62; and William Kristol, 'Inadvertent Truths: George Tenet's Revealing Memoir,' *Weekly Standard*, 5 May 2007.

65. The Democratic foreign policy primer by Kurt M. Campbell and Michael E. O'Hanlon, *Hard Power: The New Politics of National Security* (New York: Basic Books, 2006), makes this point: see ch. 8.

66. University of Miami, September 30, 2004. Also cited in Robert S. Litwak, *Regime Change: US Strategy through the Prism of 9/11* (Baltimore, MD: Johns Hopkins University Press, 2007), 292.

67. Barack Obama, 'Renewing America's Leadership,' *Foreign Affairs* 86, 4 (2007), 2–16.

68. Max Boot, 'The Paradox of Military Technology,' *The New Atlantis* 14 (2006). The problems and opportunities that nuclear terrorists face are explored in William Langewiesche, *The Atomic Bazaar: The Rise of the Nuclear Poor* (New York: Farrar, Straus and Giroux, 2007). See also Daniel Byman, *Deadly Connections: States that Sponsor Terrorism* (Cambridge: Cambridge University Press, 2007); and *Nuclear Black Markets: Pakistan, A. Q. Khan and the Rise of Proliferation Networks: A Net Assessment*, IISS (May 2007); at ww.iiss.org/publications/strategic-dossiers/nbm.

69. Graham Allison, *Nuclear Terrorism: The Ultimate Preventable Catastrophe* (New York: Henry Holt, 2004), 4. See also the website that accompanies this book, which gives nuclear 'blast maps' for various US cities, at www.nuclearterror.org/.

70. Cited in Joshua Micah Marshall, 'Remaking the World: Bush and the Neoconservatives,' *Foreign Affairs* 82, 6 (2003).

71. Madeleine Albright, Graham Allison, Samuel Berger, and James Steinberg, among other Democrats, were part of the National Security Advisory Group, chaired by William Perry, that produced the report 'Worst Weapons in Worst Hands: US Inaction on the Nuclear Terror Threat since 9/11' (2005); at http://democrats.senate.gov/pdfs/NSAG_WorstWeaponsinWorstHands_July2005.pdf.

72. 'Preemption' does not occupy a large place in the NSS 2002 (variations of the word preemption are used on only seven occasions in the 12,600-word text; in two of these the notion is disparaged as a guide to force deployment and in another preemption is defined as an option 'long maintained'. See pp. 6 (pt. III), 15 and 16 (pt. V). The British, for example, have an almost exclusive modern history of preemptive war, rarely attacking a nation that has actually attacked their territory. In 1914 they went to war when Germany invaded Belgium and in 1939 when Germany invaded Poland. The Falklands War (1982) is the only major example of a non-preemptive British war: Margaret Thatcher responded to an actual Argentinian attack not an anticipated one.

73. See Nye, *Soft Power*.

74. See Amy Belasco, 'The Cost of Iraq, Afghanistan, and Other Global War on Terror Operations since 9/11,' CRS Report (RL33110), 28 June 2007 ('summary'); at ww.fas.org/sgp/crs/natsec/RL33110.pdf.

75. James Dobbins, 'Nation-Building: The Inescapable Responsibility of the World's Only Superpower,' *RAND Review* 27, 2 (2003), 17–27, 23. Staying, he argues, does not guarantee success, leaving guarantees failure. No effort at democratization, he concludes, has taken less than seven years.

76. In David Ignatius, 'Beirut's Berlin Wall,' *Washington Post*, February 23, 2005, A19.

77. See Neil MacFarquhar, 'Mubarak Proposes a Freer Vote,' *New York Times*, February 28, 2005.

78. See http://news.bbc.co.uk/1/hi/world/middle_east/6689025.stm.

79. Edward Walker, ambassador to Egypt 1994–8, in Charles Levinson, '$50 Billion Later, Taking Stock of US Aid to Egypt,' *Christian Science Monitor*, April 12, 2004.

80. See Bruce W. Jentleson and Christopher A. Whytock, 'Who "Won" Libya? The Force–Diplomacy Debate and Its Implications for Theory and Policy,' *International Security* 30, 3 (2005/6), 47–86. They 'enclose "won" in quotes both to account for the success achieved and to acknowledge that the full extent and definitiveness of Libya's policy changes are not yet clear' (47, note 2).

81. Tony Blair, statement on Libya, December 19, 2003; in Jentleson and Whytock, 'Who "Won" Libya?' 48. Emphasis added.

82. Seif al-Islam Gaddafi in Litwak, *Regime Change*, 194.

83. See http://news.bbc.co.uk/1/hi/world/africa/4911434.stm.

84. This is argued by Robert Kagan and William Kristol, 'The Right War for the Right Reasons,' *Weekly Standard*, February 23, 2004, reprinted in Rosen, ed., *The Right War?* ch. 18.

85. Cheney, vice-presidential debate with John Edwards, October 5, 2004; in Jentleson and Whytock, 'Who "Won" Libya?' 48.

86. Charles Krauthammer, 'The Doggedness of War,' *Washington Post*, December 26, 2003, A35; in Litwak, *Regime Change*, 170.

87. White House, Office of the Press Secretary, December 19, 2003; in Litwak, *Regime Change*, 169.

88. Jentleson and Whytock, 'Who "Won" Libya?' 81.

89. See Kagan, *Paradise and Power*.

90. See, for example, Andrei Lankov's argument in favor of a soft policy of regime change, 'Memorandum,' *Foreign Policy* (March/April 2007), 70–4, and the counter-response by Haksoon Paik, 'Kim Can Survive [Letter],' *Foreign Policy* (May/June 2007), 12–13.

91. See Sheena Chestnut, 'Illicit Activity and Proliferation: North Korean Smuggling Networks,' *International Security* 32, 1 (2007), 80–111.

92. 'Everything in Zimbabwe,' declared Robert Mugabe, 'is associated with the exploits of President Kim Il Sung'! See [North] Korean Central News Agency, May 27, 2007; at www.kcna.co.jp/index-e.htm.

93. Colin Dueck, 'Doctrinal Faith,' *National Interest* (May/June 2007), 82–7, 84.

94. Kaufman, *In Defense of the Bush Doctrine*, 97.

95. Norman Podhoretz, 'Is the Bush Doctrine Dead?' *Commentary* (September 2006), 17–31, 30.

96. The US, in effect, pays Pakistan to police its borders, with limited results. See David E. Sanger and David Rohde, 'US Pays Pakistan to Fight Terror, but Patrols Ebb,' *New York Times*, May 20, 2007; and Jane Perlez, 'Aid to Pakistan in Tribal Areas Raises Concerns,' *New York Times*, July 16, 2007. According

to Nye, somewhat paradoxically, 'payments' don't count as soft power but economic might does; see Nye, *Soft Power*, x. The problems posed by Pakistan for the three Ts nexus are considered by Daniel L. Byman, 'Do Counterproliferation and Counterterrorism Go Together?', *Political Science Quarterly* 122, 1 (2007), 25–46.

97. The 2007 National Intelligence Estimate was scathing about the poor progress made in Pakistan. We concur but diagnose the failure as one of soft, not hard, power.

98. In an August 2007 campaign speech, Obama warned that 'If we have actionable intelligence about high-value terrorist targets and President Musharraf won't act, we will.' See Jeff Zeleny, 'Obama Calls for US to Shift Focus on Terrorism,' *New York Times*, August 1, 2007.

99. According to Pervez Musharraf, in 9/11's wake, US Deputy Secretary of State Richard Armitage (Colin Powell's closest ally in the administration) told the Pakistan intelligence director to 'Be prepared to be bombed. Be prepared to go back to the Stone Age.' In Pervez Musharraf, *In the Line of Fire: A Memoir* (London: Simon and Schuster, 2006), 201.

100. See, for example, Joseba Zulaika, 'The Self-Fulfilling Prophesies of Counterterrorism,' *Radical History Review* 85 (2003), 191–9.

101. Jeane Kirkpatrick, 'Dictatorship and Double Standards,' *Commentary* (November 1979), 34–45, 34. A similar argument is made by Norman Podhoretz, 'Is the Bush Doctrine Dead?' 29–30.

102. Reagan, it should be recalled, funded Bin Laden's Mujahadeen not because he shared their vision of the caliphate but because this temporary alliance would negate Soviet power. Holding hands with the devil, as FDR described it, is a common expedient in American diplomacy.

103. See White House, *Historical Tables, Budget of the United States Government, Fiscal Year 2008*, 8 and 126 (table 8.4); at www.whitehouse.gov/omb/budget/fy2008/pdf/hist.pdf.

104. In FY 2006, spending on defense was $551.5 billion vs. $924.5 billion on social security and Medicare. See *Historical Tables FY 2008*, 319 (table 15.4). Figures in 1968, for comparison, were, respectively, $87.2 billion vs. $28.4 billion; in 1948, $13.7 billion vs. $0.5 billion.

105. From 61.7 and 19.6, respectively, in 2006. See *Historical Tables FY 2008*, 135 (table 8.3). By 2040, according to one analyst, Medicare and social security 'will require nearly two out of every three federal income tax dollars. Eventually, the deficits in these two programs will absorb the entire federal budget' (Thomas R. Saving, 'Medicare Meltdown,' *Wall Street Journal*, May 9, 2007).

106. Or $245,370 per minute. The US spent $10 billion on Iraq in 2007. See Gordon Adams, 'Iraq's Sticker Shock,' *Foreign Policy* (March/April 2007), 34–5. According to the State Department: 'Nearly 97 percent of the requested 2008 counterterrorism funding – $285.1 billion – would go to the Defense

Department to pay for ongoing military operations in Iraq and Afghanistan, which the Bush administration considers to be key fronts in the global war on terrorism'; at http://london.usembassy.gov/terror723.html.

107. The US does not face an either/or decision. Social insurance programs are funded by special taxes not general revenues (from which defense comes), i.e., they do not compete for fiscal resources with the DOD.

108. The 1991 Gulf War left Saddam in power, presaging thirteen years of crippling sanctions and a far more problematic and costly war to remove and replace him.

109. These figures are for discretionary defense spending as a proportion of GDP. They include the total defense bill, not just operation, bases etc. in Vietnam, and are taken from the White House's *Historical Tables, FY 2008*, 8 and 126 (table 8.4)

110. Department of Defense and Brookings Institution Iraq Index via NationMaster; at www.nationmaster.com/graph/mil_ira_ple_of_rec_aid_pergdp-pledges-re-construction-aid-per-gdp.

111. White House, 2008 Budget Fact Sheets, February 2007; at www.whitehouse.gov/infocus/budget/BudgetFY2008.pdf. For an independent breakdown of defense spending see Anthony H. Cordesman, 'The Changing Challenges of US Defense Spending,' CSIS Report, February 12, 2007.

112. CIA World Fact Book via NationMaster; at www.nationmaster.com/graph/mil_exp_per_of_gdp-military-expenditures-percent-of-gdp.

113. Cordesman, 'The Changing Challenges of US Defense Spending,' 8.

114. Mackubin Thomas Owens, 'A Balanced Force Structure to Achieve a Liberal World Order,' *Orbis* 50, 2 (2006), 307–25, 307.

115. Ibid., 324.

116. Ibid., 325.

117. 'Motor vehicle crashes' are the leading cause of death among Americans aged 4–34. See www-nrd.nhtsa.dot.gov/pdf/nrd-30/NCSA/RNotes/2006/810568.pdf. In the 1990s, some 30,000 Americans died from gun violence every year, the majority suicides.

118. See Sean Rayment, 'British Death Rate in Iraq Now Worse than America's,' *Sunday Telegraph*, July 15, 2007, 1, 6. His report details the findings of Sheila Bird at the Royal Statistical Society. See also Glenn Kutler, 'US Military Fatalities in Iraq in Perspective: Year 4,' *Orbis* 51, 3 (2007).

119. James Moody, 'In Box: War Bonds,' *Foreign Policy* (May/June 2007), 18. The calculations cited are made by James Moody, a Duke University sociologist.

120. As of summer 2007, nearly 3,500 US personnel have been killed in Iraq, or 875 per year since 2003. See also Kutler, 'US Military Fatalities in Iraq in Perspective: Year 4.'

121. The Pentagon's Quadrennial Defense Review (February 2006, 9–18) referred to the struggle as 'The Long War.'

122. See Cass R. Sunstein, 'The Case for Fear,' *New Republic*, December 11, 2006, 29–33; and (reviewed by Sunstein) Mueller, *Overblown*.

123. George Bush, remarks at a dinner for Senatorial candidate Elizabeth Dole, Greensboro, NC, July 25, 2002.

124. Congressional Budget Office; at www.cbo.gov/budget/historical.xls (table 13).

125. See his national radio address on welfare reform, February 15, 1986.

126. Kaplan, 'The Bush Doctrine Must Survive the Iraq War.' The foregoing Carter example is Kaplan's.

5. IRAQ: VIETNAM IN THE SAND?

1. Gerard Baker, 'The Wisdom of Ronald Reagan Speaks Down the Years,' *Times*, May 4, 2007, 23. The reference is to the senior military planning briefing Reagan was given in 1983 prior to the US invasion of Grenada.

2. In Henry Kissinger, *Years of Renewal* (New York: Touchstone, 1999), 518–19.

3. Melvin P. Laird, 'Iraq: Learning the Lessons of Vietnam,' *Foreign Affairs* 84, 6 (2005) 22–43.

4. It is notable how often Reagan refers to his belief that Armageddon may be imminent in the Middle East in the first three years of his diaries. See Ronald Reagan, *The Reagan Diaries*, ed. Douglas Brinkley (New York: HarperCollins, 2007).

5. http://edition.cnn.com/2004/ALLPOLITICS/08/30/gop.mccain.transcript/index.html

6. See Edward Luttwak, 'The Middle of Nowhere,' *Prospect* 134 (2007), 26–9.

7. See Ali A. Allawi, *The Occupation of Iraq: Winning the War, Losing the Peace* (New Haven, CT: Yale University Press, 2007); Peter W. Galbraith, *The End of Iraq: How American Incompetence Created a War Without End* (New York: Simon and Schuster, 2006); Gordon and Trainor, *Cobra II*; George Packer, *The Assassin's Gate: America in Iraq* (New York: Farrar, Straus and Giroux, 2005). David L. Phillips, *Losing Iraq: Inside the Postwar Reconstruction Fiasco* (Boulder, CO: Westview Press, 2005); and Thomas E. Ricks, *Fiasco: The American Military Adventure in Iraq* (New York: Penguin Press, 2006).

8. Harold Meyerson, 'The Korean Analogy,' *Washington Post*, June 6, 2007, A23.

9. Robert Litwak, *Rogue States and US Foreign Policy: Containment after the Cold War* (Baltimore, MD: Johns Hopkins University Press, 2000), 123.

10. Quoted in ibid., 128.

11. Ibid., 128.

12. Lawrence F. Kaplan and William Kristol, *The War over Iraq: Saddam's Tyranny and America's Mission* (San Francisco: Encounter Books, 2003), 63.

13. Lawrence Freedman, 'Iraq, Liberal Wars and Illiberal Containment,' *Survival* 48, 4 (2006–7), 51–66, 64.

14. Daalder and Lindsay, *America Unbound*.

15. See Steven Hurst, 'Myths of Neoconservatism: George W. Bush's "Neo-conservative" Foreign Policy Revisited,' *International Politics* 42 (2005), 75–96.

16. See Peter Riddell, *Hug Them Close: Blair, Clinton, Bush and the 'Special Relationship'* (London: Politico's, 2003).

17. Kenneth M. Pollack, *The Threatening Storm: The Case for Invading Iraq* (New York: Random House, 2002). He remains very opposed to any invasion of Iran; see Pollack, *The Persian Puzzle: The Conflict between Iran and America* (New York: Random House, 2005).

18. Zbigniew Brzezinski, for example, has written that the Iraq War's 'only saving grace is that it made Iraq the cemetery of neo-con dreams' (*Second Chance: Three Presidents and the Crisis of American Superpower* [New York: Basic Books, 2007], 157).

19. See Timothy J. Lynch, 'Kristol Balls: Neoconservative Visions of the Middle East and Political Islam,' *International Politics* (forthcoming).

20. Frederick W. Kagan, paper at IISS, London, July 23, 2007.

21. See Frederick W. Kagan, paper at IISS, and 'Cheap Hawks Can't Fly,' *Weekly Standard*, November 4, 2002.

22. Frederick W. Kagan, 'New Thinking, Old Realities,' *AEI National Security Outlook* (October 2006), 1–4, 3.

23. Interview with Frederick W. Kagan, PBS Frontline, January 29, 2004; at www.pbs.org/wgbh/pages/frontline/shows/invasion/interviews/kagan.html.

24. Walt, *Taming American Power*, 118–19.

25. Witness, for example, the 2006 admission of Hassan Nasrallah, leader of Hezbollah, that had he accurately anticipated the scale of the Israeli military response, he would never have approved the kidnapping of two Israeli soldiers in June 2006, despite his simultaneously claiming 'victory' in the subsequent Lebanon War.

26. See 9/11 Commission Report (2004), 61, 66; at www.9-11commission.gov/report/9-11Report.pdf.

27. See Kevin Woods, James Lacey and Williamson Murray, 'Saddam's Delusions: The View From the Inside,' *Foreign Affairs* 85, 3 (2006).

28. See David E. Murphy, *What Stalin Knew: The Enigma of Barbarossa* (New Haven, CT: Yale University Press, 2006).

29. Woods, Lacey, and Murray, 'Saddam's Delusions.'

30. Stanley A. Renshon, 'Premature Obituary: The Future of the Bush Doctrine,' in Stanley A. Renshon and Peter Suedfeld, eds., *Understanding the Bush Doctrine: Psychology and Strategy in an Age of Terrorism* (New York: Routledge, 2007), 296.

31. Litwak, *Rogue States*.

32. Cited in Lieber, *American Era*, 211.

33. White House, Commission on the Intelligence Capabilities of the United States Regarding Weapons of Mass Destruction, March 31, 2005; at www.wmd. gov/report/.

34. Author's original emphasis in italics. Richard A. Posner, *Uncertain Shield: The US Intelligence System in the Throes of Reform* (Lanham, MD: Rowman and Littlefield, 2006), 22–3.

35. Ibid., 24.

36. Cited in Lieber, *American Era*, 135.

37. Laird, 'Iraq: Learning the Lessons of Vietnam,' 31–2. By comparison, one might recall JFK's conviction during the initial days of the Cuban Missile Crisis that, if he did not act to ensure the missiles were removed or destroyed, he would be impeached by Congress. As Renshon notes in 'Premature Obituary,' the powerful difference between the pristine clarity of international relations theory and the muddy reality of the political world confronting the White House is too often forgotten in analyses of presidential decision-making.

38. Posner, *Uncertain Shield*, 35.

39. Quoted in Charles Krauthammer, "Rewriting History," *Washington Post*, May 4, 2007.

40. Renshon, 'Premature Obituary.'

41. Gaddis, *Surprise*.

42. Lieber, *American Era*, 141.

43. Fouad Ajami, *The Foreigner's Gift: The Americans, the Arabs and the Iraqis in Iraq* (New York: The Free Press, 2006).

44. Toby Dodge, 'The Causes of Failure in Iraq,' *Survival* 49, 1 (2007), 85–106.

45. Cohen, *What's Left?*, 286.

46. Dodge, 'The Causes of Failure in Iraq,' 94.

47. Cohen, *What's Left?*, 288.

48. Ferguson, *Colossus*.

49. On the Vietnam/Iraq comparison, see Robert K. Brigham, *Is Iraq Another Vietnam?* (New York: Public Affairs, 2006); John Dumbrell and David Ryan, eds., *Vietnam in Iraq: Lessons, Legacies and Ghosts* (New York: Routledge, 2006); Lloyd Gardner and Marilyn B. Young, eds., *Iraq and the Lessons of Vietnam: Or, How Not to Learn From the Past* (New York: New Press, 2007); and Kenneth J. Campbell, *Tale of Two Quagmires: Iraq, Vietnam, and the Hard Lessons of War* (New York: Paradigm Publishers, 2007).

50. Brigham, *Is Iraq Another Vietnam?*, 90.

51. John Mueller, 'The Iraq Syndrome,' *Foreign Affairs* 84, 6 (2005), 44–54, 45.

52. Brigham, *Is Iraq Another Vietnam?*, 134.

53. Steven Miller, 'The Iraq Experiment and US National Security,' *Survival* 48, 4 (2006–7), 17–50, 29.

54. See Christopher Coker, *The Warrior Ethos: Military Culture and the War on Terror*, revised edn (London: Routledge, 2007).

55. See, for example, Ed Husain, *The Islamist: Why I Joined Radical Islam in Britain, What I Saw Inside and Why I Left* (London: Penguin, 2007); and Mohamed Sifaoui, *Inside Al Qaeda: How I Infiltrated the World's Deadliest Terrorist Organization* (London: Granta Books, 2003).

56. Brigham, *Is Iraq Another Vietnam?*, 36.

57. See Matthew Continetti, 'Hands off My Analogy: Liberals Object When Bush Discusses Vietnam,' *Weekly Standard*, September 3, 2007.

58. Freedman, 'Iraq, Liberal Wars and Illiberal Containment,' 55.

59. Brigham, *Is Iraq Another Vietnam?*, 139.

60. NSS 2006, p. 18.

61. Laird, 'Iraq: Learning the Lessons of Vietnam,' 24.

62. Brigham, *Is Iraq Another Vietnam?*, 156.

63. See, for example, the National Military Strategy of the United States of America 2005 and the DOD Quadrennial Defense Review Report 2006.

64. See Michael O'Hanlon, *Defense Strategy for the Post-Saddam Era* (Washington, DC: Brookings Institution Press, 2005).

65. In a 2000 Gallup poll, the US military outscored every other branch of the American polity in terms of public confidence (64 percent); Congress was ranked thirteenth (24 percent). See *National Journal*, July 15, 2000, 2329.

66. See Eliot A. Cohen, *Supreme Command: Soldiers, Statesmen and Leadership in Wartime* (New York: Anchor, 2003) and Charles A. Stevenson, *Warriors and Politicians: US Civil–Military Relations Under Stress* (New York: Routledge, 2006).

67. Arthur Herman, 'How to Win in Iraq – and How to Lose,' *Commentary* 123, 4 (2007), 23–8.

68. Michael O'Hanlon and Kenneth Pollack, 'A War We Just Might Win,' *New York Times*, July 30, 2007.

69. Steven Simon, 'America and Iraq: The Case for Disengagement,' *Survival* 49, 1 (2007), 61–84, 80–1.

70. See Max Boot, 'How Not to Get Out of Iraq,' *Commentary* (September 2007), 19–26.

71. James Kitfield and Brian Friel, 'The Clock Winds Down,' *National Journal*, April 21, 2007, 26–32, 32.

72. Daniel L. Byman, and Kenneth M. Pollack, 'Things Fall Apart: Containing the Spillover from an Iraqi Civil War,' *Saban Center Analysis* 11 (January 2007).

73. Kitfield and Friel, 'The Clock Winds Down,' 32.

74. David Rothkopf, *Running the World: The Inside Story of the National Security Council and the Architects of American Power* (New York: Public Affairs, 2006), 446.

75. Tocqueville, *Democracy in America*, 621.

76. Michael Lind, *Vietnam – the Necessary War: A Reinterpretation of America's Most Disastrous Military Conflict* (New York: Free Press, 2002).

77. Campbell and O'Hanlon, *Hard Power*, 53. Like us, Campbell and O'Hanlon argue 'there was a real case for overthrowing Saddam, even with the benefit of crystalline hindsight' (48).

78. Kaufman, *In Defense of the Bush Doctrine*, 140.

79. See Campbell and O'Hanlon, *Hard Power*; and Lieber, *American Era*.

80. Reuel Marc Gerecht, 'On Democracy in Iraq,' *Weekly Standard*, 30 April 2007, 10.

81. Miller, 'The Iraq Experiment and US National Security,' 33.

6. THE MIDDLE EAST: REFORMATION OR ARMAGEDDON

1. The song was inspired by Philip Habib, Middle East envoy under Carter and Reagan.

2. Clive James, 'A Nightclub in Bali,' in *The Meaning of Recognition: New Essays 2001–2005* (London: Picador, 2005), 210–15, 213.

3. Cited in Peter J. Boyer, 'Mayberry Man,' *New Yorker*, August 20, 2007, 44–61, 57.

4. Michael Burleigh, 'Lawyers Sap Our Will to Combat Terrorism,' *Times*, July 27, 2007, 17.

5. Richard Haass, *The Opportunity: America's Moment to Alter History's Course* (New York: Public Affairs, 2006), 219.

6. Dennis Ross, 'The Middle East Predicament,' *Foreign Affairs* 84, 1 (2005), 61–74, 72.

7. Zbigniew Brzezinski, *The Grand Chessboard: American Primacy and Its Geostrategic Imperatives* (New York: Basic Books, 1998); Nye Jr., *The Paradox of American Power*.

8. Michael B. Oren, *Power, Faith and Fantasy: America in the Middle East: 1776 to the Present* (New York: W. W. Norton, 2007).

9. See Joseph Wheelan, *Jefferson's War: America's First War on Terror, 1801–1805* (New York: Carroll & Graf Publishers, 2003); and Robert Kagan, *Dangerous Nation*, 93–103.

10. Rachel Bronson, *Thicker than Oil: America's Uneasy Partnership with Saudi Arabia* (New York: Oxford University Press, 2006).

11. Ian Buruma and Avishai Margalit, *Occidentalism: A Short History of Anti-Westernism* (London: Atlantic Books, 2004).

12. John Lewis Gaddis, *Strategies of Containment: A Critical Appraisal of Postwar American National Security Policy* (Oxford: Oxford University Press, 1982), 180.

13. See in particular Bob Woodward, *Bush at War* (New York: Simon and Schuster, 2002) and, *Plan of Attack* (New York: Simon and Schuster, 2004).

14. George W. Bush, speech at Whitehall, London, November 19, 2003.

15. Glenn P. Aga, Roger W. Cressey, and Richard Clarke, *Defeating the Jihadists: A Blueprint for Action* (New York: Century Foundation Press, 2004), 100.

16. Jonathan Stevenson, *Counter-Terrorism: Containment and Beyond*, IISS Adelphi Paper 367 (Oxford: Oxford University Press, 2004), 82–3.

17. Barry Rubin, 'The Real Roots of Arab Anti-Americanism,' *Foreign Affairs* 81, 6 (2002), 73–85.

18. Bernard Lewis, *From Babel to Dragomans: Interpreting the Middle East* (London: Phoenix, 2005), 395–6.

19. UN Development Program, Arab Human Development Report (2002); see www.undp.org/arabstates/ahdr2002.shtml.

20. UN Development Program, Arab Human Development Report (2003); see www.undp.org/arabstates/ahdr2003.shtml.

21. 'Muslim bellicosity and violence are late-twentieth-century facts which neither Muslims nor non-Muslims can deny' (Huntington, *Clash of Civilizations*, 258).

22. In Elaine Sciolino and Ariane Bernard, 'Sarkozy Lists Foreign Priorities, with Iran First,' *New York Times*, August 28, 2007.

23. Litwak, *Regime Change*, 294.

24. Ibid., 98.

25. Mandelbaum, *The Case for Goliath*, 24–5.

26. Robert S. Leiken and Steven Brooke, 'The Moderate Muslim Brotherhood,' *Foreign Affairs* 86, 2 (2007), 107–21.

27. Lieven and Hulsman, *Ethical Realism*, 125.

28. Sam Harris, *The End of Faith: Religion, Terror, and the Future of Reason* (London: Free Press, 2006), 109–10.

29. Litwak, *Regime Change*, 74.

30. Haass, *The Opportunity*, 218.

31. Natan Sharansky, *The Case for Democracy: The Power of Freedom to Overcome Tyranny and Terror* (New York: Public Affairs, 2004), 23.

32. See Pape, *Dying to Win*.

33. Bruno Tertrais, *War without End: The View from Abroad* (New York: New Press, 2005), 113.

34. Josef Joffe, 'A World Without Israel,' *Foreign Policy* (January/February 2005), 36–42.

35. Campbell and O'Hanlon, *Hard Power*, 154.

36. Martin Indyk, 'Israel–Palestine: A US Perspective,' in Ivo H. Daalder, Nicole Gnesotto, and Philip Gordon, eds., *Crescent of Crisis: US–European Strategy for the Greater Middle East* (Washington, DC: Brookings Institution Press, 2006), 43–54, 53.

37. Geoffrey Kemp, 'Iran: The Next Hegemon?' *Survival* 49, 1 (2007), 213–20, 213.

38. Quoted in Ignatius, 'Talk Boldly with Iran,' A25.

39. Litwak, *Regime Change*, 240.

40. Daniel L. Byman, 'What Iran Is Really Up To,' *Washington Post*, February 18, 2007, B01.

41. Bowden, *Guests of the Ayatollah*, 596.

42. Byman, 'What Iran Is Really Up To.'

43. Therese Delpech, *Iran and the Bomb: The Abdication of International Responsibility* (London: Hurst and Company, 2007), 95.

44. Haass, *The Opportunity*, 160.

45. Delpech, *Iran and the Bomb*, 95.

46. George Walden, 'So, Henry, How Would You Handle It? George Walden Meets Henry Kissinger,' *Sunday Times* (News Review), April 1, 2007, 5.

47. Ray Takeyh, 'Time for Detente with Iran,' *Foreign Affairs* 86, 2 (2007), 17–32; Ray Takeyh, *Hidden Iran: Paradox and Power in the Islamic Republic* (New York: Times Books, 2006); Ali Ansari, *Confronting Iran* (London: Hurst and Company, 2006); Alireza Jafarzadeh, *The Iran Threat: President Ahmadinejad and the Coming Nuclear Crisis* (New York: Palgrave Macmillan, 2007).

48. Bruce W. Jentleson, 'Preventive Diplomacy: Analytical Conclusions and Policy Lessons,' in Jentleson, ed., *Opportunities Missed, Opportunities Seized: Preventive Diplomacy in the Post-Cold War World* (Lanham: Rowman and Littlefield, 2000), 342, 344.

49. Mort Zuckerman, editor of *US News and World Report*, argues this. ('The Mullah Menace,' December 11, 2006, 86.)

50. Delpech, *Iran and the Bomb*, 105.

51. Mandelbaum, *The Case for Goliath*, 56.

52. See Barry Rubin, *The Truth about Syria* (New York: Palgrave Macmillan, 2007).

53. Eva Goes and Reinoud Leenders, 'Promoting Democracy and Human Rights in Lebanon and Syria,' in Daalder, Gnesotto, and Gordon, eds., *Crescent of Crisis*, 94–109, 107.

54. Volker Perthes, *Syria Under Bashar al-Asad: Modernisation and the Limits of Change*, IISS Adelphi Paper 366 (Oxford: Oxford University Press, 2004), 67.

55. See Daniel Pipes, 'God and Mammon: Does Poverty Cause Militant Islam?' *National Interest* 66 (2001/2), 14–21.

56. Jackson Diehl, 'Mideast Relations 101,' *Washington Post*, April 16, 2007.

57. Seth Jones, 'Pakistan's Dangerous Game,' *Survival* 49, 1 (2007), 15–32.

58. Ibid., 28–9.

59. Bowden, *Guests of the Ayatollah*, 597.

60. Harris, *End of Faith*, 147, 152.

61. Indyk, 'Israel–Palestine: A US Perspective,' 53.

7. FRIENDS AND FOES AFTER BUSH

1. Washington, Farewell Address.
2. White House, 'A National Security Strategy for a Global Age,' National Security Strategy of the United States, December 2000.
3. Andrew Roberts, A History of the English-Speaking Peoples since 1900 (London: Weidenfeld and Nicolson, 2006), 1.
4. Expanding and fading since the political palatability of enlargement into Eastern Europe in the 1990s was owed to the declining strategic imperatives that compelled the creation of NATO in the first place.
5. See NSS 2002, pt. VIII ('Develop Agendas for Cooperative Action with the Other Main Centers of Global Power'); and Colin Powell, 'A Strategy of Partnerships,' Foreign Affairs 83, 1 (2004), 22–34.
6. On this see F. Stephen Larrabee, 'Old Europe and the New NATO,' San Diego Union-Tribune, February 18, 2003.
7. Realists argued that without an external enemy, like the Soviet Union, NATO had no reason to exist. See John Mearsheimer, 'Back to the Future: Instability in Europe after the Cold War,' International Security 15, 1 (1990); and Kenneth N. Waltz, 'The Emerging Structure of International Politics,' International Security 18, 2 (1993), 44–79. Left-liberals were never keen on NATO, viewing it as a provocation to America's enemies; it was the wrong kind of international organization, founded on power and American dominance. Both interpretations are faulty.
8. US Defense Secretary Donald Rumsfeld infamously differentiated between an 'old' and a 'new Europe'; see Keith B. Richburg, '"Old Europe" Reacts to Rumsfeld's Label,' Washington Post, January 24, 2003, A1.
9. The following nations have had troops in Iraq since 2003 (those emphasized have withdrawn or are in the process of doing so): Albania, Armenia, Australia, Azerbaijan, Bosnia-Herzegovina, Bulgaria, Czech Republic, Denmark, Dominican Republic, El Salvador, Estonia, Fiji (with UN mission), Georgia, Honduras, Hungary, Italy, Japan (withdrew its 200 troops to Kuwait), Kazakhstan, Latvia, Lithuania, Macedonia, Moldova, Mongolia, Netherlands, New Zealand, Nicaragua, Norway, Philippines, Poland, Portugal, Romania, Slovakia, South Korea, Spain, Thailand, Tonga, Ukraine, and the United Kingdom (though the timetable is unclear). See Jeremy M. Sharp and Christopher M. Blanchard, 'Post-War Iraq: Foreign Contributions to Training, Peacekeeping, and Reconstruction,' CRS Report, June 18, 2007, 20–2; at http://fpc.state.gov/documents/organization/87085.pdf.
10. Patrick Keller, 'The Future of NATO: Between Overstretch and Irrelevance,' American Foreign Policy Interests (May 2007).
11. France withdrew from NATO's integrated military command from 1966 to 1993. It remained part of its political structure. As of time of writing, the

following countries have NATO membership as a declared goal: Albania, Bosnia-Herzegovina, Croatia, FYR Macedonia, Georgia, Montenegro, Serbia, and Ukraine.

12. See Ryan C. Hendrickson, 'The Miscalculation of NATO's Death,' *Parameters* (Spring 2007), 98–114.

13. On the RMA see Frederick Kagan, *Finding The Target: The Transformation of American Military Policy* (San Francisco: Encounter Books, 2006).

14. See Hendrickson, 'The Miscalculation of NATO's Death,' 99.

15. The planned deployment, at time of writing, was for ten interceptor missiles to be based in Poland and a radar installation to be built in the Czech Republic.

16. NSS 2002 recognized several NATO weaknesses, capable of remedy, in the war on terror. See pt. VIII, 25–6.

17. See Renée de Nevers, 'NATO's International Security Role in the Terrorist Era,' *International Security* 31, 4 (2007), 34–66.

18. Preamble to the North Atlantic Treaty, April 4, 1949; at www.nato.int/docu/basictxt/treaty.htm.

19. Zimbabwe was voted chair of the CSD in May 2007. Saudi Arabia was a member of the UN Commission on Human Rights, 2003–6, and will become a member of the Human Rights Council, which replaced it, in 2009. The US was denied membership of the UNCHR from 2001 to 2003 (for its refusal to join the International Criminal Court). Russia and China, governments with a long list of human rights violations against their own people, are permanent members of the UNSC.

20. This was apparent as early as the 1970s. See '[Daniel Patrick] Moynihan on Democracy,' CQ Electronic Library, CQ Historic Documents Series Online Edition. Originally published in *Historic Documents of 1975* (Washington, DC: CQ Press, 1976); at http://library.cqpress.com/historicdocuments/hsdc75-0001221793; and Moynihan, 'The United States in Opposition,' *Commentary* (March 1975).

21. Jacques Chirac, interview with the BBC, November 19, 2004; at http://news.bbc.co.uk/1/hi/programmes/newsnight/4020663.stm.

22. Toby Dodge has proposed a UN solution ('Iraq: The Only Solution Left,' *Times*, October 5, 2006).

23. See Edward P. Joseph, 'Bystanders to a Massacre: How the U.N. Failed Srebrenica,' *Washington Post*, July 10, 2005; and Adam Lebor, '*Complicity with Evil': The United Nations in the Age of Modern Genocide* (New Haven, CT: Yale University Press, 2006).

24. Anne Marie Slaughter in Michael Hirsh, 'No Time to Go Wobbly, Barack,' *Washington Monthly* (April 2007).

25. Campbell and O'Hanlon, *Hard Power*, 246–7.

26. Kagan, 'End of Dreams'; Slaughter in Hirsh, 'No Time to Go Wobbly'; see also Slaughter, *A New World Order* (Princeton, NJ: Princeton University Press,

2004); and Slaughter, *The Idea That Is America: Keeping Faith with Our Values in a Dangerous World* (New York: Basic Books, 2007).

27. Pew Global Attitudes Project Report (June 2007), 104.

28. See Transatlantic Trends 2004, 11; at www.transatlantictrends.org/.

29. See Gary L. Guertner, 'European Views of Preemption in US National Security Strategy,' *Parameters* 37, 2 (2007), 31–44; and Baker, 'Continental Drift.'

30. See Simms, *Unfinest Hour*.

31. This feature of both campaigns questions the thesis propounded by Kagan (in *Paradise and Power*) that the US perennially opts for hard-power options and that Europeans consistently oppose them.

32. See Keith B. Richburg, 'France's Influence Wanes in Ivory Coast,' *Washington Post*, February 4, 2003, A21.

33. Walter Russell Mead, *Power, Terror, Peace, and War: America's Grand Strategy in a World at Risk* (New York: Random House, 2005), 121.

34. In Fredrik Logevall, *The Origins of the Vietnam War*, Seminar Studies in History (Harlow: Longman, 2001), 21. Ike was condemning French failure in Indochina in 1954.

35. US Major Don Fichthorn, Marine Corps (ret.), April 2003, in Halper and Clarke, *America Alone*, 254.

36. The two men were among a group of East European leaders who persuaded President Clinton, during a meeting in the Oval Office, to expand NATO. See James M. Goldgeier, *Not Whether but When: The US Decision to Enlarge NATO* (Washington, DC: Brookings Institution, 1999), 20.

37. Europe's on-going propensity to power competition and thus to war is explored in Adrian Hyde-Price, *European Security in the Twenty-First Century: The Challenge of Multipolarity* (London: Routledge, 2007).

38. See Christophe Jakubyszyn, 'L'opposition s'interroge sur le montant des vacances de M. Sarkozy, de sa femme et de leur fils aux Etats-Unis,' *Le Monde*, August 4, 2007. Sarkozy was similarly mocked for jogging in the style of any number of US presidents (including Carter, Bush Sr., Clinton, and Bush Jr.). See Joel Garreau, 'In France, Jogging Is a Running Joke: President's Exercise Regime Has Critics in a Lather,' *Washington Post*, July 7, 2007, C01.

39. Azerbaijan is considered too close to Iran and the Middle East – the likely source of an attack on Europe or the US – to make siting the shield there feasible, aside from the political issues accepting such an offer would entail. See Steven A. Hildreth and Carl Ek, 'Long-Range Ballistic Missile Defense in Europe,' CRS Report (RL34051), June 22, 2007; at www.fas.org/sgp/crs/weapons/RL34051.pdf.

40. Center for Defense Information, *Russia Weekly* no. 245, 21 (February 2003); at www.cdi.org/russia/245-14.cfm. The Russian government's official casualty statistics vary. Some 50–100,000 Chechen rebels and civilians have been killed.

41. In February 2003, Bush added three Chechen terrorist groups to the US black-list of proscribed groups – to Russian approval. See http://news.bbc.co.uk/1/hi/world/europe/2786725.stm.

42. See Mueller, 'What Was the Cold War About?'.

43. 9/11 Commission Report, p. 330; at www.9-11commission.gov/report/911Report.pdf.

44. Putin told Bush 'I am prepared to tell the heads of government of the Central Asian states that we have good relations with and that we have no objection to a U.S. role in Central Asia as long as it has the object of fighting the war on terror and is temporary and is not permanent' (cited in Woodward, *Bush at War*, 116, 118–20).

45. Condoleezza Rice, 'The West Needs a Defence System That Works,' *Daily Telegraph*, April 27, 2007.

46. Two children per woman is generally considered the minimum population replenishment level. For comparison, America's is 2.1 (2007 est.), China's 1.8, and Iran's 1.7. See CIA World Fact Book at www.cia.gov/library/publications/the-world-factbook/. See also Mark Steyn, *America Alone*.

47. In Haas, 'A Geriatric Peace?' 112.

48. Dmitri Trenin, 'Russia Redefines Itself and Its Relations with the West,' *Washington Quarterly* 30, 2 (2007), 95–105, 95.

49. Kagan, 'End of Dreams.'

50. See David Blair, 'Why Bush Is Unlikely to Sign Any G8 Pledges on Climate Change,' *Daily Telegraph*, June 7, 2007, 16.

51. This metaphor (but not argument) is Charles W. Freeman's, cited in Jim Mann, 'China Emerges as Clinton's Knottiest Foreign Problem,' *LA Times*, September 9, 1996, A3; cited by Peter W. Rodman, 'Russia: The Challenge of a Failing Power,' in Robert Kagan and William Kristol (eds.), *Present Dangers: Crisis and Opportunity in American Foreign and Defense Policy* (San Francisco: Encounter Books, 2000), 75–97, 87.

52. Trenin, 'Russia Redefines Itself,' 95.

53. Richard Bernstein and Ross H. Munro, 'China I: The Coming Conflict with America,' *Foreign Affairs* 76, 2 (1997), 18–32, 27 and 29.

54. Richard C. Bush and Michael E. O'Hanlon, *A War Like No Other: The Truth About China's Challenge to America* (Washington, DC: Brookings Institution, 2007). See also Ted Galen Carpenter, *America's Coming War with China: A Collision Course over Taiwan* (New York: Palgrave Macmillan, 2006).

55. The essentially defensive nature of Chinese foreign policy is observed in Andrew J. Nathan and Robert S. Ross, *The Great Wall and the Empty Fortress: China's Search for Security* (New York: W. W. Norton, 1997); and Zheng Bijian, 'China's "Peaceful Rise" to Great-Power Status,' *Foreign Affairs* 84, 5 (2005).

56. Dimitri Simes argues that Bush reaped the whirlwind of Clinton's folly. In the war on terror, China was less inclined to use its influence on, for example,

Pakistan. See Simes, 'Protecting Kosovo at the Expense of New York,' *National Interest* Online, September 9, 2006.

57. The 1994 showdown, which Clinton described as his Cuban missile crisis (see Scott Snyder, 'The Fire Last Time,' *Foreign Affairs* 83, 4 [2004]), is examined in Joel S. Wit, Daniel B. Poneman, and Robert L. Gallucci, *Going Critical: The First North Korean Nuclear Crisis* (Washington, DC: Brookings Institution, 2004).

58. In Tim Curry, 'Democrats Quick to Pounce on N. Korean Test,' MSNBC, October 9, 2006.

59. See Llewelyn Hughes, 'Why Japan Will Not Go Nuclear (Yet): International and Domestic Constraints on the Nuclearization of Japan,' *International Security* 31, 4 (2007), 67–96.

60. See Robert S. Ross, 'Comparative Deterrence: The Taiwan Strait and the Korean Peninsula,' in Alastair Iain Johnston and Robert S. Ross, eds., *New Directions in the Study of China's Foreign Policy* (Stanford, CA: Stanford University Press, 2006), ch. 2.

61. See Lieber, *American Era*, ch. 6.

62. For a neo-conservative critique see Tom Donnelly, 'China's Strategy,' *Weekly Standard*, March 16, 2005. For a liberal indictment see James Mann, *The China Fantasy: How Our Leaders Explain Away Chinese Repression* (New York: Viking Books, 2007).

63. Compare, for example, the Amnesty International Reports for 2001 and 2007; at www.amnesty.org/.

64. Peter Brookes and Ji Hye Shin, 'China's Influence in Africa: Implications for the United States,' *Backgrounder* no. 1916 (Heritage Foundation), February 22, 2006, 5–6.

65. See Mure Dickie and John Reed, 'China Hails Mugabe's "Brilliant Diplomacy,"' *Financial Times*, July 27, 2005. For an argument on behalf of the effectiveness of Chinese soft power see Joshua Kurlantzick, *Charm Offensive: How China's Soft Power Is Transforming the World* (New Haven, CT: Yale University Press, 2007).

66. See John J. Tkacik Jr., 'The Arsenal of the Iraq Insurgency: It's Made in China,' *Weekly Standard*, 12, 45 (August 13, 2007).

67. Arthur Herman, 'Getting Serious about Iran: A Military Option,' *Commentary* (November 2006), 28–32, 32.

68. George H. W. Bush was US envoy to China 1974–5. As Tom Wicker notes, in Bush Sr.'s 1987 autobiography, *Looking Forward*, 'the pages that describe Bush's time in China are filled primarily with the trivia of his day-to-day personal life' (Tom Wicker, *George Herbert Walker Bush* [New York: Viking, 2004], 39).

69. This ambiguity is reflected among the American public. Twenty-nine percent see China as an economic threat; 35 as a military threat; and 21 as no threat. See Transatlantic Trends 2006, 13, chart 11.

70. The phrase is from Robert S. Ross, 'Beijing as a Conservative Power,' *Foreign Affairs* 76, 2 (1997), 33–44, 35.

71. In *U.S.-China Relations: An Affirmative Agenda, A Responsible Course*, Report of an Independent Task Force, Council of Foreign Relations (2007), p. 101; at www.cfr.org/content/publications/.attachments/ChinaTaskForce.pdf. Robert McGeehan advances what he admits is an 'outrageously simplistic observation . . . that the United States has from its beginnings been disinclined to have diplomatic relations, or direct dealings . . . with states or governments of which it strongly disapproves' (McGeehan, 'American Diplomacy and Adversarial Relationships: US Practices in Historical Perspective,' *RUSI* 152, 2 [2007], 46–51, 51).

72. Roberts, *A History of the English-Speaking Peoples*. Also see Andrew Roberts, 'The English-Speaking Peoples and Their World Role Since 1900,' *Orbis* 51, 3 (2007), 381–96.

73. Lieven and Hulsman, *Ethical Realism*, 88. They contend not for an English-speaking alliance but for a 'great capitalist peace' led by the United States (ch. 4). The two concepts differ only in degree.

74. Case studies in this estrangement are examined in Lynch, *Turf War*, esp. ch. 3; and Simms, *Unfinest Hour*, 49–134.

75. Tony Blair, speech at the Economic Club, Chicago, 24 April 1999.

76. Simon Jenkins, 'Blair Is Going, but Thatcherism Still Rules,' *Spectator*, June 23, 2007, 18–19, 19.

77. FDR and Churchill shared a remarkable intimacy with one another – not repeated until the Reagan–Thatcher years – though, of course, their ideologies did not mesh when it came to the British Empire: Roosevelt was keen on its demise, Churchill for its resurrection. FDR won.

78. Harold Wilson, of course, was geo-strategically in tune with LBJ over Vietnam; he balked at the economic costs of direct British military involvement. See Peter Busch, *All the Way with JFK?: Britain, the US and the Vietnam War* (Oxford: Oxford University Press, 2003).

79. Christopher Hubbard, *Australian and US Military Cooperation: Fighting Common Enemies* (Aldershot: Ashgate, 2005), 1.

80. See www.icasualties.org/oif/.

81. Brendon O'Connor, 'Australasia,' in Mary Buckley and Robert Singh, eds., *The Bush Doctrine and the War on Terrorism* (Abingdon: Routledge, 2006), 136–49, 136.

82. See BBC World Service/GlobeScanPoll, 'World Public Says Iraq War Has Increased Global Terrorist Threat,' February 28, 2006; at www.globescan.com/news_archives/bbcpoll06-4.html.

83. Mark Steyn, 'World Is Watching as Iraq War Tests US Mettle,' *Chicago Sun-Times*, August 20, 2006.

84. In Hubbard, *Australian and US Military Cooperation*, 3.

85. On the role of 'core values' in US foreign policy see Melvyn P. Leffler, 'National Security,' in Michael E. Hogan and Thomas G. Paterson (eds.), *Explaining the History of American Foreign Relations*, 2nd edn (Cambridge: Cambridge University Press, 2004), 123–36.

86. Robert D. Blackwill, 'A Friend Indeed,' *National Interest* 89 (May/June 2007), 16–19, 16.

87. Singh speech on awarding of his honorary doctorate at Oxford University, July 8, 2005; in Lieven and Hulsman, *Ethical Realism*, 88.

88. United States–India Peaceful Atomic Energy Cooperation Act, passed in December 2006.

89. Blackwill, 'A Friend Indeed,' 17.

90. See Bill Emmott, 'India: Bush's Forgotten Success,' *Sunday Times*, February 25, 2007, 19.

91. Al Qaeda military commander, Sayf al Adl, cited in Christopher M. Blanchard, 'Al Qaeda: Statements and Evolving Ideology,' CRS Report (RL32759), July 9, 2007.

8. THE EMERGING CONSENSUS AT HOME AND ABROAD

1. David Aaronovitch, 'The Lessons of History? That's a Lot of Bunk,' *Times*, August 7, 2007, 19.

2. Hendrik Hertzberg, 'Sparring Partners,' *New Yorker*, August 20, 2007, 23–4, 24.

3. Kershaw, *Fateful Choices*.

4. See, respectively, Lawrence and Howarth, eds., *Messages to the World*; Bowden, *Guests of the Ayatollah*; and David Selbourne, *The Losing Battle with Islam* (London: Prometheus Books, 2005).

5. One of the most prominent proponents of this case is Barry Buzan. See his 'Will the "Global War on Terrorism" Be the New Cold War?' *International Affairs* 82, 6 (2006), 1101–18.

6. Robert Lieber quotes a US Senate Foreign Relations Study of June 2005 (Lugar Survey on Non-Proliferation) to this effect in the postscript to his *American Era*, 214–15. The study can be accessed at http://lugar.senate.gov/reports/ NPSurvey.pdf. See also Allison, *Nuclear Terrorism*.

7. Obama, 'Renewing American Leadership,' 9.

8. Posner, *Not a Suicide Pact*, 5.

9. Although Clarke himself estimated these in 2004 as, respectively, 400–2,000 in al Qaeda, 50,000–200,000 jihadists, 200–500 million sympathizers, and 1.5 billion Muslims (Aga, Cressey, and Clarke, *Defeating the Jihadists*, 17).

10. Ibid., 6.

11. Daalder and Kagan, 'America and the Use of Force,' 1.

12. Anatol Lieven, 'Bipartisan Disaster,' *Prospect* (September 2006), 11–13, 11.

13. Michael Lind, 'The World after Bush,' *Prospect* (November 2006), 36–40, 40.

14. Bronwen Maddox, 'The Power Is Real – but so Are the Fears,' *Times*, August 24, 2006, 38.

15. David Ignatius, 'New World Disorder,' *Washington Post*, May 4, 2007, A23.

16. Lieven, 'Bipartisan Disaster,' 12.

17. Ibid., 13.

18. Lind, 'The World after Bush,' 39–40.

19. Andrew Sullivan, 'The Isolationist Beast Stirs in America Again,' *Sunday Times* (News Review), July 29, 2007, 4.

20. Michael Cox, 'Is the United States in Decline – Again?,' *International Affairs* 83, 4 (2007), 643–53.

21. William Wohlforth, 'Unipolar Stability: The Rules of Power Analysis,' *Harvard International Review* 29, 1 (2007), 44–8.

22. Niall Ferguson, 'A World without Power,' *Foreign Policy* 143 (2004), 32–9, 34.

23. See David Rose, 'Neo Culpa,' *Vanity Fair*, November 3, 2006; and the neocon response in 'Vanity Unfair,' *National Review*, November 5, 2006.

24. Francis Fukuyama, *After the Neocons: America at the Crossroads* (London: Profile Books, 2006), 183–4.

25. Lieven and Hulsman, *Ethical Realism*.

26. See Lebor, '*Complicity with Evil*'.

27. Anne Applebaum, 'Why Only Darfur?' *Washington Post*, November 21, 2006, A27.

28. For a contrary view on this see Continetti, 'The Peace Party vs. the Power Party,' 17–24.

29. Campbell and O'Hanlon, *Hard Power*, 241–5.

30. Ibid., 1–45.

31. Ibid., 23.

32. Gerard Baker, 'Monty Python is a Poor Guide to Diplomacy,' *Times*, August 10, 2007, 17. Hillary Clinton had responded to Obama's statement that 'I think it would be a profound mistake for us to use nuclear weapons in any circumstances involving civilians' by noting that 'I don't believe that any President should make any blanket statements with respect to the use or non-use of nuclear weapons' (cited in Hertzberg, 'Sparring Partners,' 23–4).

33. See, especially, Richard Crockatt, *America Embattled: September 11, Anti-Americanism and the Global Order* (London: Routledge, 2003); Anatol Lieven, *America Right or Wrong: An Anatomy of American Nationalism* (London: HarperCollins, 2004); and John Micklethwait and Adrian Wooldridge, *The Right Nation: Why America is Different* (London: Allen Lane, 2004).

34. Richard Hofstadter, *The Paranoid Style in American Politics* (Chicago: University of Chicago Press, 1979).

35. Robert Kagan, 'Staying the Course, Win or Lose,' *Washington Post*, November 2, 2006, A17.

CONCLUSION: THE CASE FOR CONTINUITY

1. Clinton, 'American Foreign Policy and the Democratic Ideal.'
2. See Douglas Brinkley, 'The Clinton Doctrine,' *Foreign Policy* 106 (1997).
3. See, respectively, Moveon.org, BBC's *The Power of Nightmares* (2004), Halper and Clarke's *America Alone*, and everything by Michael Moore.
4. J. Garry Clifford, Review of *The First Cold Warrior: Harry Truman, Containment, and the Remaking of Liberal Internationalism*, by Elizabeth Edwards Spaulding, *Presidential Studies Quarterly* 37, 1 (2007), 167–9, 167.
5. In the movie, President Whitmore, realizing the enemy is beyond reason and thus beyond appeasement, orders a nuclear attack – ultimately futile – to save the world.
6. See John Arquilla, *The Reagan Imprint: Ideas in American Foreign Policy from the Collapse of Communism to the War on Terror* (Chicago: Ivan R. Dee, 2007).
7. www.realclearpolitics.com/articles/2006/05/bushs_foreign_policy_legacy_is.html.
8. See Michael E. Brown, Sean M. Lynn-Jones and Steven E. Miller, eds., *Debating the Democratic Peace: An International Security Reader* (Cambridge, MA: MIT Press, 1996); and Michael Cox, G. John Ikenberry, and Takashi Inoguchi, eds., *American Democracy Promotion: Impulses, Strategies, and Impacts* (Oxford: Oxford University Press, 2000).

Bibliography

1. BOOKS

Ackerman, Bruce, *Before The Next Attack: Preserving Civil Liberties in an Age of Terrorism*, New Haven, CT: Yale University Press, 2006.

Aga, Glenn P., Roger W. Cressey, and Richard Clarke, *Defeating the Jihadists: A Blueprint for Action*, New York: Century Foundation Press, 2004.

Agha, Hussein, Shai Feldman, Ahmad Khalidi, and Zeev Schiff, *Track-II Diplomacy: Lessons from the Middle East*, Cambridge, MA: MIT Press, 2004.

Ajami, Fouad, *The Foreigner's Gift: The Americans, the Arabs and the Iraqis in Iraq*, New York: Free Press, 2006.

Ali, Tariq, *The Clash of Fundamentalisms: Crusades, Jihads and Modernity*, London: Verso, 2002.

Pirates of the Caribbean: Axis of Hope, London: Verso, 2006.

Allawi, Ali A., *The Occupation of Iraq: Winning the War, Losing the Peace*, New Haven CT: Yale University Press, 2007.

Allison, Graham, *Essence of Decision: Explaining the Cuban Missile Crisis*, Boston: Little, Brown, 1971.

Nuclear Terrorism: The Ultimate Preventable Catastrophe, New York: Henry Holt, 2004.

Ansari, Ali, *Confronting Iran*, London: Hurst and Company, 2006.

Arquilla, John, *The Reagan Imprint: Ideas in American Foreign Policy from the Collapse of Communism to the War on Terror*, Chicago: Ivan R. Dee, 2007.

Bacevich, Andrew, *The New American Militarism: How Americans Are Seduced by War*, New York: Oxford University Press, 2005.

Barkawi, Tarak and Mark Laffey, eds., *Democracy, Liberalism, and War: Rethinking the Democratic Peace Debate*, Boulder, CO: Lynne Rienner, 2001.

Behrman, Greg, *The Most Noble Adventure: The Marshall Plan and the Time When America Helped Save Europe*, New York: Free Press, 2007.

Bobbitt, Philip, *Constitutional Interpretation*, Oxford: Basil Blackwell, 1991.
   The Shield of Achilles: War, Peace and the Course of History, London: Penguin, 2003.

Bork, Robert H., *The Tempting of America: The Political Seduction of the Law*, New York: Free Press, 1990.

Bowden, Mark, *Guests of the Ayatollah: The First Battle in the West's War with Militant Islam*, London: Atlantic Books, 2006.

Brigham, Robert K., *Is Iraq Another Vietnam?* New York: Public Affairs, 2006.

Bronson, Rachel, *Thicker than Oil: America's Uneasy Partnership with Saudi Arabia*, New York: Oxford University Press, 2006.

Brown, Michael E., Sean M. Lynn-Jones, and Steven E. Miller, eds., *Debating the Democratic Peace: An International Security Reader*, Cambridge, MA: MIT Press, 1996.

Brzezinski, Zbigniew, *The Grand Chessboard: American Primacy and Its Geostrategic Imperatives*, New York: Basic Books, 1998.
   Second Chance: Three Presidents and the Crisis of American Superpower, New York: Basic Books, 2007.

Buckley, Mary and Robert Singh, eds., *The Bush Doctrine and the War on Terrorism*, Abingdon: Routledge, 2006.

Buruma, Ian and Avishai Margalit, *Occidentalism: A Short History of Anti-Westernism*, London: Atlantic Books, 2004.

Busch, Peter, *All the Way with JFK?: Britain, the US and the Vietnam War*, Oxford: Oxford University Press, 2003.

Bush, George H. W. and Brent Scowcroft, *A World Transformed*, New York: Alfred A. Knopf, 1998.

Bush, Richard C. and Michael E. O'Hanlon, *A War Like No Other: The Truth About China's Challenge to America*, Washington, DC: Brookings Institution, 2007.

Byman, Daniel, *Deadly Connections: States that Sponsor Terrorism*, Cambridge: Cambridge University Press, 2007.

Campbell, Alastair, *The Blair Years*, London: Hutchinson, 2007.

Campbell, Kenneth J., *A Tale of Two Quagmires: Iraq, Vietnam, and the Hard Lessons of War*, New York: Paradigm Publishers, 2007.

Campbell, Kurt M. and Michael E. O'Hanlon, *Hard Power: The New Politics of National Security*, New York: Basic Books, 2006.

Carpenter, Ted Galen, *America's Coming War with China: A Collision Course over Taiwan*, New York: Palgrave Macmillan, 2006.

Carr, E. H., *The Twenty Years' Crisis: 1919–1939: An Introduction to the Study of International Relations*, London: Macmillan, 1969; first published 1939.

Carter, Ralph, ed, *Contemporary Cases in US Foreign Policy: From Terrorism to Trade*, 2nd edn, Washington, DC: CQ Press, 2005.

Cassels, Alan, *Ideology and International Relations in the Modern World*, London: Routledge, 1996.

Chomsky, Noam, *What Uncle Sam Really Wants*, Berkeley, CA: Odonian Press, 1992. *Hegemony or Survival: America's Quest for Global Dominance*, New York: Metropolitan Books, 2003.

Clarke, Richard, *Against All Enemies: Inside America's War on Terror*, New York: Free Press, 2004.

Cohen, Eliot A., *Supreme Command: Soldiers, Statesmen and Leadership in Wartime*, New York: Anchor, 2003.

Cohen, Nick, *What's Left? How Liberals Lost Their Way*, London: Fourth Estate, 2007.

Coker, Christopher, *The Warrior Ethos: Military Culture and the War on Terror*, revised edn, London: Routledge, 2007.

Colás, Alejandro and Richard Saull, eds., *The War on Terrorism and the American 'Empire' after the Cold War*, London: Routledge, 2005.

Collier, Peter and David Horowitz, eds., *The Anti-Chomsky Reader*, New York: Encounter Books, 2004.

Corwin, Edward S., *The President: Office and Powers, 1787–1957*, 4th revised edn, New York: New York University Press, 1957.

Cox, Michael, G. John Ikenberry, and Takashi Inoguchi, eds., *American Democracy Promotion: Impulses, Strategies, and Impacts*, Oxford: Oxford University Press, 2000.

Craig, Gordon A. and Francis L. Loewenheim, *The Diplomats, 1939–1979*, Princeton, NJ: Princeton University Press, 1994.

Crockatt, Richard, *America Embattled: September 11, Anti-Americanism and the Global Order*, London: Routledge, 2003.

D'Souza, Dinesh, *The Enemy at Home: The Cultural Left and its Responsibility for 9/11*, New York: Doubleday, 2007.

Daalder, Ivo H. and James M. Lindsay, *America Unbound: The Bush Revolution in Foreign Policy*, Washington DC: Brookings Institution Press, 2003.

Daalder, Ivo H., Nicole Gnesotto, and Philip Gordon, eds., *Crescent of Crisis: US-European Strategy for the Greater Middle East*, Washington, DC: Brookings Institution Press, 2006.

Dean, John W., *Worse Than Watergate: The Secret Presidency of George W. Bush*, New York: Little, Brown and Company, 2004.

Degler, Carl N., *Out of Our Past: The Forces that Shaped Modern America*, 3rd edn, New York: Harper and Row, 1984.

Delpech, Therese, *Iran and the Bomb: The Abdication of International Responsibility*, London: Hurst and Company, 2007.

DiPrizio, Robert C., *Armed Humanitarians: US Interventions from Northern Iraq to Kosovo*, Baltimore, MD: Johns Hopkins University Press, 2002.

Dueck, Colin, *Reluctant Crusaders: Power, Culture, and Change in American Grand Strategy*, Princeton, NJ: Princeton University Press, 2006.

Dumbrell, John, *A Special Relationship: Anglo-American Relations in the Cold War and After*, Basingstoke: Palgrave, 2001.

Dumbrell, John and David Ryan, eds., *Vietnam in Iraq: Lessons, Legacies and Ghosts*, New York: Routledge, 2006.

Eastland, Terry, *Energy in the Executive: The Case for the Strong Presidency*, New York: The Free Press, 1994.

Evangelista, Matthew. *The Chechen Wars: Will Russia Go the Way of the Soviet Union?* Washington, DC: Brookings Institution Press, 2003.

Everts, Philip and Pierangelo Isernia, eds., *Public Opinion and the International Use of Force*, New York: Routledge, 2001.

Falk, Richard, *The Great Terror War*, New York: Olive Branch Press, 2003.

Feaver, Peter D. and Christopher Gelpi, *Choosing Your Battles: American Civil–Military Relations and the Use of Force*, Princeton, NJ: Princeton University Press, 2005.

Ferguson, Niall, *Colossus: The Rise and Fall of the American Empire*, London: Allen Lane, 2004.

Fisher, Louis, *Presidential War Power*, 2nd edn, Lawrence, KS: University Press of Kansas, 2004.

Foxman, Abraham H., *The Deadliest Lies: The Israel Lobby and the Myth of Jewish Control*, New York: Palgrave Macmillan, 2007.

Fukuyama, Francis, *The End of History and the Last Man*, New York: Avon, 1992.

After the Neocons: America at the Crossroads, London: Profile Books, 2006.

Gaddis, John Lewis, *The Long Peace: Inquiries into the History of the Cold War*, Oxford: Oxford University Press, 1987.

Strategies of Containment: A Critical Appraisal of Postwar American National Security Policy, Oxford: Oxford University Press, 1982.

Surprise, Security and the American Experience, Cambridge, MA: Harvard University Press, 2004.

The United States and the Origins of the Cold War, 1941–1947, New York: Columbia University Press, 1972.

Galbraith, Peter W., *The End of Iraq: How American Incompetence Created a War Without End*, New York: Simon and Schuster, 2006.

Gardner, Lloyd and Marilyn B. Young, eds., *Iraq and the Lessons of Vietnam: Or, How Not To Learn From the Past*, New York: New Press, 2007.

Gilbert, Felix, *To the Farewell Address: Ideas of Early American Foreign Policy*, Princeton, NJ: Princeton University Press, 1961.

Glennon, Michael J., *Constitutional Diplomacy*, Princeton, NJ: Princeton University Press, 1990.

Goldgeier, James M., *Not Whether but When: The US Decision to Enlarge NATO*, Washington, DC: Brookings Institution Press, 1999.

Gordon, Michael and Bernard Trainor, *Cobra II: The Inside Story of the Invasion and Occupation of Iraq*, London: Atlantic Books, 2007.

Gregg II, Gary L. and Mark Rozell, eds., *Considering the Bush Presidency*, Oxford: Oxford University Press, 2004.

Griffin, Stephen M., *American Constitutionalism: From Theory to Politics*, Princeton, NJ: Princeton University Press, 1996.

Haass, Richard, *The Opportunity: America's Moment to Alter History's Course*, New York: Public Affairs, 2006.

Halliday, Fred, *The Making of the Second Cold War*, London: Verso, 1983.

Halper, Stefan and Jonathan Clarke, *America Alone: The Neo-Conservatives and the Global Order*, Cambridge: Cambridge University Press, 2004.

The Silence of the Rational Center, New York: Basic Books, 2007.

Handler, Edward, *America and Europe in the Political Thought of John Adams*, Cambridge, MA: Harvard University Press, 1964.

Harris, Sam, *The End of Faith: Religion, Terror, and the Future of Reason*, London: The Free Press, 2006.

Hartz, Louis, *The Liberal Tradition in America: An Interpretation of American Political Thought since the Revolution*, San Diego, CA: Harvest Books, 1991; originally published 1955.

Held, David and Mathias Koenig-Archibugi, eds., *American Power in the 21st Century*, Cambridge: Polity 2004.

Historic Documents of 1975, Washington, DC: CQ Press, 1976.

Hitchens, Christopher, *Regime Change*, London: Penguin Books, 2003.

Hobsbawm, Eric, *Globalisation, Democracy and Terrorism*, New York: Little, Brown, 2007.

Hofstadter, Richard, *The Paranoid Style in American Politics*, Chicago: University of Chicago Press, 1979.

Hogan, Michael E. and Thomas G. Paterson, eds., *Explaining the History of American Foreign Relations*, 2nd edn, Cambridge: Cambridge University Press, 2004.

Holmes, Stephen, *The Matador's Cape: America's Reckless Response to Terror*, New York: Cambridge University Press, 2007.

Holsti, Ole R., *Public Opinion and American Foreign Policy*, revised edn, Ann Arbor, MI: The University of Michigan Press, 2004.

Howell, William, *Power without Persuasion: The Politics of Direct Presidential Action*, Princeton, NJ: Princeton University Press, 2003.

Hubbard, Christopher, *Australian and US Military Cooperation: Fighting Common Enemies*, Aldershot: Ashgate, 2005.

Hunt, Michael H., *Ideology and US Foreign Policy*, New Haven, CT and London: Yale University Press, 1987.

Hunter, Shireen T., *Islam in Russia: The Politics of Identity and Security*, Armonk: M. E. Sharpe, 2004.

Huntington, Samuel P., *American Politics: The Promise of Disharmony*, Cambridge, MA: Harvard University Press, 1981.

   The Clash of Civilizations and the Remaking of World Order, New York: Simon and Schuster, 1996.

Husain, Ed, *The Islamist: Why I Joined Radical Islam in Britain, What I Saw Inside and Why I Left*, London: Penguin, 2007.

Hyde-Price, Adrian, *European Security in the Twenty-first Century: The Challenge of Multipolarity*, London: Routledge, 2007.

Ignatieff, Michael, *Virtual War: Kosovo and Beyond*, London: Vintage 2001.

   The Lesser Evil: Political Ethics in an Age of Terror, Princeton, NJ: Princeton University Press, 2004.

   ed., *US Exceptionalism and Human Rights*, Princeton, NJ: Princeton University Press, 2005.

Ikenberry, G. John, *After Victory: Institutions, Strategic Restraint, and the Rebuilding of Order after Major Wars*, Princeton, NJ: Princeton University Press, 2001.

Jafarzadeh, Alireza, *The Iran Threat: President Ahmadinejad and the Coming Nuclear Crisis*, New York: Palgrave Macmillan, 2007.

James, Clive, *The Meaning of Recognition: New Essays 2001–2005*, London: Picador, 2005.

   Cultural Amnesia: Notes in the Margin of My Time, London: Picador, 2007.

Jentleson, Bruce W., ed, *Opportunities Missed, Opportunities Seized: Preventive Diplomacy in the Post-Cold War World*, Lanham, MD: Rowman and Littlefield, 2000.

Joffe, Josef, *Uberpower: The Imperial Temptation of America*, New York: W. W. Norton, 2006.

Johnson, Chalmers, *Blowback: The Costs and Consequences of American Empire*, New York: Henry Holt, 2000.

Johnston, Alastair Iain, and Robert S. Ross, eds., *New Directions in the Study of China's Foreign Policy*, Stanford, CA: Stanford University Press, 2006.

Jones, Howard, *Abraham Lincoln and a New Birth of Freedom: The Union and Slavery in the Diplomacy of the Civil War*, Lincoln, NE: University of Nebraska Press, 1999.

Judis, John B., *The Folly of Empire: What George W. Bush Could Learn from Theodore Roosevelt and Woodrow Wilson*, New York: Lisa Drew/Scribner, 2004.

Kagan, Frederick, *Finding the Target: The Transformation of American Military Policy*, San Francisco: Encounter Books, 2006.

Kagan, Robert, *Paradise and Power: America and Europe in the New World Order*, London: Atlantic Books, 2003.

Dangerous Nation, New York: Alfred A. Knopf, 2006.

Kagan, Robert and William Kristol, eds., *Present Dangers: Crisis and Opportunity in American Foreign and Defense Policy*, San Francisco: Encounter Books, 2000.

Kaplan, Lawrence F. and William Kristol, *The War over Iraq: Saddam's Tyranny and America's Mission*, San Francisco: Encounter Books, 2003.

Katzenstein, Peter J., and Robert O. Keohane, eds., *Anti-Americanisms in World Politics*, New York: Cornell University Press, 2006.

Katznelson, Ira and Martin Shefter, eds., *Shaped by War and Trade: International Influences on American Political Development*, Princeton, NJ: Princeton University Press, 2002.

Kaufman, Robert G., *In Defense of the Bush Doctrine*, Lexington, KY: University of Kentucky Press, 2007.

Kennan, George F., *American Diplomacy: 1900–1950*, expanded edn, Chicago and London: University of Chicago Press, 1984.

Kennedy, Paul, *The Rise and Fall of the Great Powers: Economic Change and Military Conflict from 1500 to 2000*, London: Unwin Hyman, 1988.

Kepel, Gilles, *Jihad: The Trail of Political Islam*, Cambridge, MA: Belknap Press, 2003.

Kershaw, Ian, *Fateful Choices: Ten Decisions that Changed the World, 1940–1941*, London: Allen Lane, 2007.

King, Desmond, *The Liberty of Strangers: Making the American Nation*, Oxford: Oxford University Press, 2005.

Kissinger, Henry, *Diplomacy*, New York: Touchstone, 1995.

Years of Renewal, New York: Touchstone, 1999.

Klein, Naomi, *No Logo*, New York: Picador, 2000.

Koh, Harold H., *The National Security Constitution: Sharing Power After the Iran-Contra Affair*, New Haven, CT: Yale University Press, 1990.

Kohn, Hars, *American Nationalism: An Interpretive Essay*, New York: Macmillan, 1957.

Kurlantzick, Joshua, *Charm Offensive: How China's Soft Power Is Transforming the World*, New Haven, CT: Yale University Press, 2007.

LaFeber, Walter, *The American Age: United States Foreign Policy at Home and Abroad since 1750*, New York: Norton, 1989.

Lake, Anthony and David Ochmanek, eds., *The Real and the Ideal: Essays on International Relations in Honor of Richard H. Ullman*, Lanham, MD: Rowman and Littlefield, 2001.

Landy, Marc and Sidney M. Milkis, *Presidential Greatness*, Lawrence: University of Kansas Press, 2000.

Langewiesche, William, *The Atomic Bazaar: The Rise of the Nuclear Poor*, New York: Farrar, Straus, and Giroux, 2007.

Lawrence, Bruce and James Howarth, eds., *Messages to the World: The Statements of Osama Bin Laden*, London: Verso, 2005.

Layne, Christopher, *The Peace of Illusions: American Grand Strategy from 1940 to the Present*, Ithaca, NY: Cornell University Press, 2005.

Lebor, Adam, *'Complicity with Evil': The United Nations in the Age of Modern Genocide*, New Haven, CT: Yale University Press, 2006.

Leonard, Mark, *Why Europe Will Run the 21st Century*, London: Fourth Estate, 2005.

Lewis, Bernard, *From Babel to Dragomans: Interpreting the Middle East*, London: Phoenix, 2005.

Libicki, Martin D., Peter Chalk, and Melanie Sisson, *Exploring Terrorist Targeting Preferences*, Santa Monica, CA: Rand Corporation, 2007.

Lieber, Robert J., *The American Era: Power and Strategy for the 21st Century*, 2nd edn, Cambridge: Cambridge University Press, 2007.

Lieven, Anatol, *America Right or Wrong: An Anatomy of American Nationalism*, London: HarperCollins, 2004.

Lieven, Anatol and John Hulsman, *Ethical Realism: A Vision for America's Role in the World*, London: Pantheon Books, 2006.

Lind, Michael, *Vietnam – the Necessary War: A Reinterpretation of America's Most Disastrous Military Conflict*, New York: Free Press, 2002.

Lindberg, Tod, ed., *Beyond Paradise and Power: Europe, America and the Future of a Troubled Partnership*, New York: Routledge, 2005.

Linker, Damon, *The Theocons: Secular America Under Siege*, New York and London: Doubleday, 2006.

Litwak, Robert S., *Rogue States and US Foreign Policy: Containment after the Cold War*, Baltimore, MD: Johns Hopkins University Press, 2000.

Regime Change: US Strategy through the Prism of 9/11, Baltimore, MD: Johns Hopkins University Press, 2007.

Logevall, Fredrik, *The Origins of the Vietnam War*, Harlow: Longman, 2001.

Lord, Walter, *Day of Infamy*, New York: Henry Holt, 1957; Owl Books, 2001.

Lucas, Scott, *Freedom's War: The US Crusade Against the Soviet Union, 1945–1956*, Manchester: Manchester University Press, 1999.

Lynch, Timothy J., *Turf War: The Clinton Administration and Northern Ireland*, Aldershot: Ashgate, 2004.

Malone, David M. and Yuen Foong Khong, eds., *Unilateralism and US Foreign Policy: International Perspectives*, Boulder, CO, and London: Lynne Rienner, 2003.

Mandelbaum, Michael, *The Case for Goliath: How America Acts as the World's Government in the Twenty-First Century*, New York: Public Affairs, 2005.

Mann, James, *The China Fantasy: How Our Leaders Explain Away Chinese Repression*, New York: Viking Books, 2007.

Mann, Michael, *The Dark Side of Democracy: Explaining Ethnic Cleansing*, Cambridge: Cambridge University Press, 2004.

  Incoherent Empire, London: Verso, 2005.

Maranto, Robert, Douglas M. Brattebo, and Tom Lansford, eds., *The Second Term of George W. Bush: Prospects and Perils*, New York: Macmillan, 2006.

Marshall, John, *Life of Washington*, volume IV, Philadelphia, 1807.

McKercher, B. J. C., *Anglo–American Relations in the 1920s*, Edmonton: University of Alberta Press, 1990.

Mead, Walter Russell, *Special Providence: American Foreign Policy and How It Changed the World*, London: Routledge, 2002.

  Power, Terror, Peace, and War: America's Grand Strategy in a World at Risk, New York: Random House, 2005.

Mearsheimer, John J., *The Tragedy of Great Power Politics*, New York: W. W. Norton, 2001.

Mearsheimer, John J. and Stephen M. Walt, *The Israel Lobby and US Foreign Policy*, New York: Allen Lane, 2007.

Micklethwait, John and Adrian Wooldridge, *The Right Nation: Why America Is Different*, London: Allen Lane, 2004.

Miller, Perry, *Errand into the Wilderness*, Cambridge, MA: Belknap Press of Harvard University Press, 1956.

Morgenthau, Hans J., *Politics Among Nations: The Struggle for Power and Peace*, brief edn, revised by Kenneth W. Thompson, New York: McGraw Hill, 1993.

Mueller, John, *Overblown: How Politicians and the Terrorism Industry Inflate National Security Threats, and Why We Believe Them*, New York: The Free Press, 2006.

Murphy, David E., *What Stalin Knew: The Enigma of Barbarossa*, New Haven, CT: Yale University Press, 2006.

Musharraf, Pervez, *In the Line of Fire: A Memoir*, London: Simon and Schuster, 2006.

Nathan, Andrew J. and Robert S. Ross, *The Great Wall and the Empty Fortress: China's Search for Security*, New York: W. W. Norton, 1997.

Nye Jr., Joseph S., *The Paradox of American Power: Why the World's Only Superpower Can't Go It Alone*, Oxford: Oxford University Press, 2002.

Soft Power: The Means to Success in World Politics, New York: Public Affairs, 2005.

O'Connor, Brendon and Martin Griffiths, eds., *The Rise of Anti-Americanism*, London: Routledge, 2005.

O'Hanlon, Michael, *Defense Strategy for the Post-Saddam Era*, Washington, DC: Brookings Institution Press, 2005.

Oren, Michael B., *Power, Faith and Fantasy: America in the Middle East: 1776 to the Present*, New York: W. W. Norton, 2007.

Packer, George, *The Assassin's Gate: America in Iraq*, New York: Farrar, Straus and Giroux, 2005.

Paine, Thomas, *Common Sense*, 1776.

Pape, Robert A., *Dying to Win: The Strategic Logic of Suicide Terrorism*, New York: Random House, 2005.

Patrick, Stewart and Shepard Forman, eds., *Multilateralism and US Foreign Policy: Ambivalent Engagement*, Boulder, CO, and London: Lynne Rienner, 2002.

Perry, Michael J., *The Constitution in the Courts: Law or Politics?*, New York: Oxford University Press, 1994.

Perthes, Volker, *Syria Under Bashar al-Asad: Modernisation and the Limits of Change*, IISS Adelphi Paper 366, Oxford: Oxford University Press, 2004.

Phillips, David L., *Losing Iraq: Inside the Postwar Reconstruction Fiasco*, Boulder, CO: Westview Press, 2005.

Phillips, Kevin, *American Theocracy: The Peril and Politics of Radical Religion, Oil, and Borrowed Money in the 21st Century*, New York: Viking, 2006.

Phillips, Melanie, *Londonistan: How Britain is Creating a Terror State Within*, London: Gibson Square Books, 2006.

Pillar, Paul R., *Terrorism and US Foreign Policy*, Washington, DC: Brookings Institution Press, 2002.

Podhoretz, Norman, *World War IV: The Long Struggle Against Islamofascism*, New York: Doubleday, 2007.

Pollack, Kenneth, M., *The Persian Puzzle: The Conflict between Iran and America*, New York: Random House, 2005.

The Threatening Storm: The Case for Invading Iraq, New York: Random House, 2002.

Posner, Richard A., *Public Intellectuals: A Study of Decline*, Cambridge, MA: Harvard University Press, 2003.

Law, Pragmatism and Democracy, Cambridge, MA: Harvard University Press, 2005.

Not a Suicide Pact: The Constitution in a Time of National Emergency, New York: Oxford University Press, 2006.

Uncertain Shield: The US Intelligence System in the Throes of Reform, Lanham, MD: Rowman and Littlefield, 2006.

Reagan, Ronald, *The Reagan Diaries*, ed. Douglas Brinkley, New York: HarperCollins, 2007.

Renshon, Stanley A. and Peter Suedfeld, eds., *Understanding the Bush Doctrine: Psychology and Strategy in an Age of Terrorism*, New York: Routledge, 2007.

Richelson, Jeffrey T., *The US Intelligence Community*, 5th edn, Boulder, CO: Westview Press, 2007.

Ricks, Thomas E., *Fiasco: The American Military Adventure in Iraq*, New York: Penguin Press, 2006.

Riddell, Peter, *Hug Them Close: Blair, Clinton, Bush and the 'Special Relationship,'* London: Politico's, 2003.

Roberts, Andrew, *A History of the English-Speaking Peoples since 1900*, London: Weidenfeld and Nicolson, 2006.

Rosecrance, Richard, *The Rise of the Trading State: Commerce and Conquest in the Modern World*, New York: Basic Books, 1986.

Rosen, Gary, ed., *The Right War? The Conservative Debate on Iraq*, New York: Cambridge University Press, 2005.

Rothkopf, David, *Running The World: The Inside Story of the National Security Council and the Architects of American Power*, New York: Public Affairs, 2006.

Ruane, Joseph and Jennifer Todd, eds., *After the Good Friday Agreement: Analysing Political Change in Northern Ireland*, Dublin: University College Dublin Press, 1999.

Rubin, Barry, *The Truth about Syria*, New York: Palgrave Macmillan, 2007.

Ryan, David, *Frustrated Empire: US Foreign Policy, 9/11 to Iraq*, London: Pluto Press, 2007.

Sandburg, Carl, *Abraham Lincoln: The War Years*, vol. I, New York: Harcourt Brace and World, 1939.

Sardar, Ziauddin and Merryl Wyn Davies, *Why Do People Hate America?*, Cambridge: Icon Books, 2002.

Schlesinger Jr., Arthur M., *The Vital Center: The Politics of Freedom*, Boston: Houghton Mifflin, 1949.

The Cycles of American History, Boston: Houghton Mifflin, 1986.

War and the American Presidency, New York: W. W. Norton & Company, 2004.

Selbourne, David, *The Losing Battle with Islam*, London: Prometheus Books, 2005.

Sharansky, Natan, *The Case for Democracy: The Power of Freedom to Overcome Tyranny and Terror*, New York: Public Affairs, 2004.

Shawcross, William, *Allies: The US, Britain, Europe, and the War in Iraq*, New York: Public Affairs, 2004.

Sick, Gary, *All Fall Down: America's Tragic Encounter with Iran*, New York: Random House, 1985.

Sifaoui, Mohamed, *Inside Al Qaeda: How I Infiltrated the World's Deadliest Terrorist Organization*, London: Granta Books, 2003.

Simms, Brendan, *Unfinest Hour: Britain and the Destruction of Bosnia*, London: Allen Lane, 2001.

Singh, Robert, ed., *Governing America: The Politics of a Divided Democracy*, Oxford: Oxford University Press, 2003.

Slaughter, Anne-Marie, *A New World Order*, Princeton, NJ: Princeton University Press, 2004.

   The Idea That Is America: Keeping Faith with Our Values in a Dangerous World, New York: Basic Books, 2007.

Steel, Ronald, *Pax Americana*, London: Hamish Hamilton, 1967.

Stevenson, Charles A., *Warriors and Politicians: US Civil–Military Relations Under Stress*, New York: Routledge, 2006.

Stevenson, Jonathan, *Counter-Terrorism: Containment and Beyond*, IISS Adelphi Paper 367, Oxford: Oxford University Press, 2004.

Steyn, Mark, *America Alone: The End of the World as We Know It*, Washington, DC: Regnery Publishing, 2006.

Sunstein, Cass, *Radicals in Robes: Why Extreme Right-wing Courts Are Wrong for America*, New York: Basic Books, 2005.

Suskind, Ron, *The One Percent Doctrine: Deep Inside America's Pursuit of its Enemies since 9/11*, New York: Simon and Schuster, 2006.

Takeyh, Ray, *Hidden Iran: Paradox and Power in the Islamic Republic*, New York: Times Books, 2006.

Tannenwald, Nina, *The Nuclear Taboo: The United States and the Non-use of Nuclear Weapons since 1945*, Cambridge: Cambridge University Press, 2007.

Tenet, George, *At the Center of the Storm: My Years at the CIA*, New York: HarperCollins, 2007.

Tertrais, Bruno, *War without End: The View from Abroad*, New York: New Press, 2005.

Tetlock, Philip E., *Expert Political Judgment: How Good Is It? How Can We Know?* Princeton, NJ: Princeton University Press, 2005.

Tocqueville, Alexis de, *Democracy in America*, trans. Harvey C. Mansfield and Delba Winthrop, Chicago: University of Chicago Press, 2000.

Tushnet, Mark, *Taking the Constitution away from the Courts*, Princeton, NJ: Princeton University Press, 1999.

Walt, Stephen M., *Taming American Power: The Global Response to US Primacy*, New York: W. W. Norton & Co., 2005.

Waltz, Kenneth N., *Man, the State, and War: A Theoretical Analysis*, New York: Columbia University Press, 1959; reprint 2001.

Theory of International Politics, New York: McGraw Hill, 1979.

Weber, Max, *The Protestant Ethic and the Spirit of Capitalism*, London: Scribner, 1958; originally published 1904.

Westad, Odd Arne, *The Global Cold War: Third World Interventions and the Making of Our Times*, new edn, Cambridge: Cambridge University Press, 2007.

Wheelan, Joseph, *Jefferson's War: America's First War on Terror, 1801–1805*, New York: Carroll & Graf Publishers, 2003.

Wicker, Tom, *George Herbert Walker Bush*, New York: Viking, 2004.

Williams, William Appleman, *The Tragedy of American Diplomacy*, New York: W. W. Norton, 1959; 1962; 1972.

Winkler, Carol K., *In the Name of Terrorism: Presidents on Political Violence in the Post-World War II Era*, New York: State University of New York Press, 2006.

Wit, Joel S., Daniel B. Poneman, and Robert L. Gallucci, *Going Critical: The First North Korean Nuclear Crisis*, Washington, DC: Brookings Institution, 2004.

Wittkopf, Eugene R. and James M. McCormick, eds., *The Domestic Sources of American Foreign Policy: Insights and Evidence*, 4th edn, Lanham, MD: Rowman and Littlefield, 2004.

Wolf, Martin, *Why Globalization Works*, New Haven, CT: Yale University Press, 2004.

Wolfe, Tom, *The Purple Decades*, London: Picador, 1993.

Woodward, Bob, *The Agenda: Inside the Clinton White House*, New York: Simon and Schuster, 1994.

Bush at War, New York: Simon and Schuster, 2002.

Plan of Attack, New York: Simon and Schuster, 2004.

State of Denial, New York: Simon and Schuster, 2006.

Yoo, John, *The Powers of War and Peace: The Constitution and Foreign Affairs After 9/11*, Chicago: University of Chicago Press, 2005.

2. JOURNALS AND NEWSPAPERS

Where no page numbers are given, material was accessed electronically.

Aaronovitch, David, 'The Lessons of History? That's a Lot of Bunk,' *Times*, August 7, 2007, 19.

Abrahms, Max, 'Why Terrorism Does Not Work,' *International Security* 31, 2 (2006).

Adams, Gordon, 'Iraq's Sticker Shock,' *Foreign Policy* 159 (2007), 34–5.

Applebaum, Anne, 'Why Only Darfur?' *Washington Post*, November 21, 2006, A27.

Auessuard, David P., 'Deterring Non-state WMD Attacks,' *Political Science Quarterly* 121, 4 (2006), 543–68.

Baker, Gerard, 'Continental Drift: Europe Gets Even Less Serious,' *Weekly Standard*, March 19, 2007.

'The Wisdom of Ronald Reagan Speaks Down the Years,' *Times*, May 4, 2007, 23.

'Monty Python is a Poor Guide to Diplomacy,' *Times*, August 10, 2007, 17.

Berggren, D. Jason and Nicol C. Rae, 'Jimmy Carter and George W. Bush: Faith, Foreign Policy, and an Evangelical Presidential Style,' *Presidential Studies Quarterly* 36, 3 (2006), 606–32.

Bernstein, Richard and Ross H., Munro, 'China I: The Coming Conflict with America,' *Foreign Affairs* 76, 2 (1997), 18–32.

Betts, Richard K., 'The Soft Underbelly of American Primacy: Tactical Advantages of Terror,' *Political Science Quarterly* 117, 1 (2002), 19–36.

Bijian, Zheng, 'China's "Peaceful Rise" to Great-Power Status,' *Foreign Affairs* 84, 5 (2005).

Blackwill, Robert D., 'A Friend Indeed,' *National Interest* 89 (2007), 16–19.

Blair, David, 'Why Bush Is Unlikely to Sign Any G8 Pledges on Climate Change,' *Daily Telegraph*, June 7, 2007, 16.

Boot, Max, 'The Paradox of Military Technology,' *New Atlantis* 14 (2006).

'How Not to Get Out of Iraq,' *Commentary* (September 2007), 19–26.

Boyer, Peter J., 'Mayberry Man,' *New Yorker*, August 20, 2007, 44–61.

Brinkley, Douglas, 'The Clinton Doctrine,' *Foreign Policy* 106 (1997).

Brookes, Peter and Ji Hye Shin, 'China's Influence in Africa: Implications for the United States,' *Backgrounder* 1916 (Heritage Foundation), February 22, 2006, 5–6.

Burke, Jason, 'Britain Stops Talk of "War on Terror,"' *Observer*, December 10, 2006.

Burleigh, Michael, 'Lawyers Sap Our Will to Combat Terrorism,' *Times*, July 27, 2007, 17.

Buzan, Barry, 'Will the "Global War on Terrorism" be the New Cold War?' *International Affairs* 82, 6 (2006), 1101–18.

Byman, Daniel L., 'After the Storm: US Policy toward Iraq since 1991,' *Political Science Quarterly* 115, 4 (2000), 493–516.

'Do Counterproliferation and Counterterrorism Go Together?' *Political Science Quarterly* 122, 1 (2007), 25–46.

'What Iran Is Really Up To,' *Washington Post*, February 18, 2007, B01.

Byman, Daniel L. and Kenneth M. Pollack, 'Things Fall Apart: Containing the

Spillover from an Iraqi Civil War,' *Saban Center Analysis* 11 (January 2007).

Byrd, Robert, 'Preserving Constitutional War Powers,' *Mediterranean Quarterly* 14, 3 (2003), 1–5.

Cameron, Fraser, 'Utilitarian Multilateralism: The Implications of 11 September 2001 for US Foreign Policy,' *Politics* 22, 2 (2002), 68–75.

Cannon, Carl M., 'Why We Fight,' *National Journal*, July 1, 2006, 21–8.

Chestnut, Sheena, 'Illicit Activity and Proliferation: North Korean Smuggling Networks,' *International Security* 32, 1 (2007), 80–111.

Clifford, J. Garry, Review of *The First Cold Warrior: Harry Truman, Containment, and the Remaking of Liberal Internationalism*, by Elizabeth Edwards Spalding, *Presidential Studies Quarterly* 37, 1 (2007), 167–9.

Clinton, Bill, 'American Foreign Policy and the Democratic Ideal,' *Orbis* 37, 4 (1994), 651–60.

'Clinton's Foreign Policy,' *Foreign Policy* 114 (2000), 18–29.

Clunan, Anne L., 'The Fight against Terrorist Financing,' *Political Science Quarterly* 121, 4 (2006), 569–96.

Coll, Steve and Susan B. Glasser, 'In London, Islamic Radicals Found a Haven,' *Washington Post*, July 10, 2005.

Colombani, Jean-Marie, '*Nous sommes tous américains*,' *Le Monde*, September 13, 2001.

Continetti, Matthew, 'The Peace Party vs. the Power Party: The Real Divide in American Politics,' *Weekly Standard*, January 1, 2007.

'Hands off My Analogy: Liberals Object when Bush Discusses Vietnam,' *Weekly Standard*, September 3, 2007.

Cox, Michael, 'Is the United States in Decline – Again?' *International Affairs* 83, 4 (2007), 643–53.

Curry, Tim, 'Democrats Quick to Pounce on N. Korean Test,' MSNBC, October 9, 2006.

Daalder, Ivo H. and Robert Kagan, 'America and the Use of Force: Sources of Legitimacy,' Stanley Foundation, June 2007.

Daalder, Ivo H. and James M. Lindsay, 'The Bush Revolution: The Remaking of America's Foreign Policy,' Brookings Institution, April 2003.

Davis, David, 'We Must Fight Terror the American Way,' *Sunday Telegraph*, March 25, 2007.

Dickie, Mure and John Reed, 'China Hails Mugabe's "Brilliant Diplomacy,"' *Financial Times*, July 27, 2005.

Diehl, Jackson, 'The Accidental Imperialist,' *Washington Post*, December 30, 2002, A17.

'Mideast Relations 101,' *Washington Post*, April 16, 2007.

Dobbins, James, 'Nation-Building: The Inescapable Responsibility of the World's Only Superpower,' *RAND Review* 27, 2 (2003), 17–27.

Dobbs, Michael and John M. Goshko, 'Albright's Personal Odyssey Shaped Foreign Policy Beliefs,' *Washington Post*, December 6, 1996, A25.

Dodge, Toby, 'Iraq: The Only Solution Left,' *Times*, October 5, 2006.
   'The Causes of Failure in Iraq,' *Survival* 49, 1 (2007), 85–106.

Donnelly, Tom, 'China's Strategy,' *Weekly Standard*, March 16, 2005.

Doran, Michael, 'The Pragmatic Fanaticism of al Qaeda: An Anatomy of Extremism in Middle Eastern Politics,' *Political Science Quarterly* 117, 2 (2002).

Dorf, Michael C., 'The Detention and Trial of Enemy Combatants: A Drama in Three Branches,' *Political Science Quarterly* 122, 1 (2007), 47–58.

Dueck, Colin, 'Doctrinal Faith,' *National Interest* 89 (2007), 82–7.
   'Ideas and Alternatives in American Grand Strategy, 2000–2004,' *Review of International Studies* 30, 4 (2004), 511–35.

Dumbrell, John, 'The US–UK "Special Relationship" in a World Twice Transformed,' *Cambridge Review of International Affairs* 17, 3, (2004), 43–50.

Emmott, Bill, 'India: Bush's Forgotten Success,' *Sunday Times*, February 25, 2007, 19.

Esposito, John L. and Dalia Mogahed, 'What Makes a Muslim Radical?' *Foreign Policy* (November/December 2006).

Fallows, James, 'Can We Still Declare Victory?' *Atlantic Unbound*, August 11, 2006.
   'Declaring Victory,' *Atlantic Monthly* (September 2006), 60–73.

Ferguson, Niall, 'A World without Power,' *Foreign Policy* 143 (2004), 32–9.

Freedland, Jonathan, 'Bush's Amazing Achievement,' *New York Review of Books*, June 14, 2007.

Freedman, Lawrence, 'Why the West Failed,' *Foreign Policy* (Winter 1994), 53–69.
   'Iraq, Liberal Wars and Illiberal Containment,' *Survival* 48, 4 (2006–7), 51–66.

Fuller, Graham E., 'Strategic Fatigue,' *National Interest* (Summer 2006).

Gardiner, Nile, 'The Myth of US Isolation: Why America Is Not Alone in the War on Terror,' Heritage Foundation Web Memo #558, September 7, 2004.

Garreau, Joel, 'In France, Jogging Is a Running Joke: President's Exercise Regime Has Critics in a Lather,' *Washington Post*, July 7, 2007, C01.

Gat, Azar, 'Is Democracy Genocidal?' *Times Online*, March 21, 2007.

Gelpi, Christopher, 'Misdiagnosis,' *Foreign Affairs* 85, 1 (2006).

Gerecht, Reuel Marc, 'On Democracy in Iraq,' *Weekly Standard*, April 30, 2007, 10.

Giuliani, Rudolph, 'Toward a Realistic Peace,' *Foreign Affairs* 86, 5 (2007).

Glaberson, William, 'Military Judges Dismiss Charges for 2 Detainees,' *New York Times*, June 5, 2007.

Glennon, Michael J., 'The Gulf War and the Constitution,' *Foreign Affairs* 70, 2 (1991), 84–101.

Gluckman, Ron, 'Strangers in Their Own Land,' *Time's Asiaweek*, December 7, 2001.

Goldberg, Jeffrey, 'Breaking Ranks: What Turned Brent Scowcroft against the Bush Administration?', *New Yorker*, October 31, 2006.

Gove, Michael, 'All Hail the Anti-Islamist Intelligentsia,' *Spectator*, January 24, 2007, 16.

Greider, William, 'Under the Banner of the War on Terror,' *The Nation*, June 21, 2004.

Guertner, Gary L., 'European Views of Preemption in US National Security Strategy,' *Parameters* 37, 2 (2007), 31–44.

Hass, Mark L., 'A Geriatric Peace? The Future of US Power in a World of Aging Populations,' *International Security* 31, 2 (2007), 112–47.

Harknett, Richard J., 'Barbarians at and behind the Gates: The Loss of Contingency and the Search for Homeland Security,' *The Forum* 1, 2 (2002).

Hemmer, Christopher, 'The Lessons of September 11, Iraq, and the American Pendulum,' *Political Science Quarterly* 122, 2 (2007), 207–38.

Hendrickson, David C., 'Toward Universal Empire: The Dangerous Quest for Absolute Security,' *World Policy Journal* 19, 3 (2002), 1–10.

Hendrickson, Ryan C., 'The Miscalculation of NATO's Death,' *Parameters* (Spring 2007), 98–114.

Herman, Arthur, 'Getting Serious about Iran: A Military Option,' *Commentary* (November 2006), 28–32.

'How to Win in Iraq – and How to Lose,' *Commentary* (April 2007), 23–8.

Hertzberg, Hendrik, 'Sparring Partners,' *New Yorker*, August 20, 2007, 23–4.

Hirsh, Michael, 'No Time to Go Wobbly, Barack,' *Washington Monthly* (April 2007).

Hitchens, Christopher, 'Londonistan Calling,' *Vanity Fair* (June 2007).

Holmes, Stephen, 'Liberalism in the Mirror of Transnational Terror,' *Tocqueville Review* 22, 2 (2001).

Hughes, Llewelyn, 'Why Japan Will Not Go Nuclear (Yet): International and Domestic Constraints on the Nuclearization of Japan,' *International Security* 31, 4 (2007), 67–96.

Huntington, Samuel P., 'American Ideals versus American Institutions,' *Political Science Quarterly* 97, 1 (1982), 1–37.

Hurst, Steven, 'Myths of Neoconservatism: George W. Bush's "Neo-conservative" Foreign Policy Revisited,' *International Politics* 42 (2005), 75–96.

Ignatius, David, 'Beirut's Berlin Wall,' *Washington Post*, February 23, 2005, A19.

'Talk Boldly with Iran,' *Washington Post*, June 23, 2006, A25.

'New World Disorder,' *Washington Post*, May 4, 2007, A23.

Ikenberry, G. John, 'America's Imperial Ambition,' *Foreign Affairs* 81, 5 (2002), 44–60.

Isaacson, Walter, 'The Return of the Realists,' *Time* 168, 22 (2006).

Jakubyszyn, Christophe, 'L'opposition s'interroge sur le montant des vacances de M. Sarkozy, de sa femme et de leur fils aux Etats-Unis,' *Le Monde*, August 4, 2007.

Jeffery, Simon, 'Lord Goldsmith's Legal Advice and the Iraq War,' *Guardian*, April 27, 2005.

Jenkins, Simon, 'Blair Is Going, but Thatcherism Still Rules,' *Spectator*, June 23, 2007, 18–19.

Jentleson, Bruce W., 'Jordan Bombings and the Rumsfeld Terrorism Metric,' *America Abroad: Notes on Foreign Affairs*, 16 November 2005.

Jentleson, Bruce W. and Christopher A. Whytock, 'Who "Won" Libya? The Force–Diplomacy Debate and Its Implications for Theory and Policy,' *International Security* 30, 3 (2005/6), 47–86.

Jervis, Robert, 'Why the Bush Doctrine Cannot Be Sustained,' *Political Science Quarterly* 120, 3 (2005), 351–77.

Joffe, Josef, 'A World Without Israel,' *Foreign Policy* (January/February 2005), 36–42.

Jones, Seth, 'Pakistan's Dangerous Game,' *Survival* 49, 1 (2007), 15–32.

Joseph, Edward P., 'Bystanders to a Massacre: How the U.N. Failed Srebrenica,' *Washington Post*, July 10, 2005.

Kagan, Frederick W., 'Cheap Hawks Can't Fly,' *Weekly Standard*, November 4, 2002.

'New Thinking, Old Realities,' *AEI National Security Outlook* (October 2006), 1–4.

Kagan, Robert, 'America's Crisis of Legitimacy,' *Foreign Affairs* 83, 2 (2004).

'The Biggest Issue of All,' *Washington Post*, February 15, 2000.

'End of Dreams, Return of History,' *Policy Review* 143 (June-July) 2007.

'A Matter of Record,' *Foreign Affairs* 84, 1 (2005), 170–3.

'More Leaks Please,' *Washington Post*, September 26, 2006.

'Power and Weakness,' *Policy Review* 113 (2002).

'Staying the Course, Win or Lose,' *Washington Post*, November 2, 2006, A17.

Kagan, Robert and William Kristol, 'Toward a Neo-Reaganite Foreign Policy,' *Foreign Affairs* 75, 4 (1996).

Kakutani, Michiko, 'A Portrait of Bush as a Victim of His Own Certitude,' *New York Times*, September 30, 2006.

Kaplan, Lawrence F., 'The Bush Doctrine Must Survive the Iraq War,' *Financial Times*, October 24, 2006.

Keller, Patrick, 'The Future of NATO: Between Overstretch and Irrelevance,' *American Foreign Policy Interests* (May 2007).

Kemp, Geoffrey, 'Iran: The Next Hegemon?' *Survival* 49, 1 (2007), 213–20.

Kennan, George F., 'Morality and Foreign Policy,' *Foreign Affairs* 64, 2 (1985).

Kirkpatrick, Jeane, 'Dictatorships and Double Standards,' *Commentary* (November 1979), 34–45.

Kitfield, James and Brian Friel, 'The Clock Winds Down,' *National Journal*, April 21, 2007, 26–32.

Kohn, Hans, 'American Nationalism: An Interpretive Essay,' *Political Science Quarterly* 72, 4 (1957), 628–30.

Krauthammer, Charles, 'Holiday from History,' *Washington Post*, February 14, 2003.

'Rewriting History,' *Washington Post*, 4 May 2007, A23.

Kristol, William, 'Inadvertent Truths: George Tenet's Revealing Memoir,' *Weekly Standard*, May 5, 2007.

Kutler, Glenn, 'US Military Fatalities in Iraq in Perspective: Year 4,' *Orbis* 51, 3 (2007).

Laird, Melvin R., 'Iraq: Learning the Lessons of Vietnam,' *Foreign Affairs* 84, 6 (2005), 22–43.

Lankov, Andrei, 'Memorandum,' *Foreign Policy* (March/April 2007), 70–4.

Lansford, Tom, 'Homeland Security from Clinton to Bush: An Assessment,' *White House Studies* 3, 4 (2003).

Laqueur, Walter, 'After the Cold War,' *E-Journal USA* (US Dept. of State), Foreign Policy Agenda (April 2006), 41–3.

Larrabee, F. Stephen, 'Old Europe and the New NATO,' *San Diego Union-Tribune*, February 18, 2003.

Leiken, Robert S. and Steven Brooke, 'The Moderate Muslim Brotherhood,' *Foreign Affairs* 86, 2 (2007), 107–21.

Levinson, Charles, '$50 Billion Later, Taking Stock of US Aid to Egypt,' *Christian Science Monitor*, April 12, 2004.

Liddle, Rod, 'The Public Know How These Attacks Happen – Unlike the Politicians,' *Spectator*, July 7, 2007, 14–15.

Lieber, Keir and Gerard Alexander, 'Waiting for Balancing: Why the World Isn't Pushing Back,' *International Security* 30, 1 (2005).

Lieber, Robert J., 'Foreign-Policy "Realists" Are Unrealistic on Iraq,' *Chronicle of Higher Education* 49, 8 (2002).

Lieven, Anatol, 'Bipartisan Disaster,' *Prospect* (September 2006), 11–13.

Lind, Michael, 'The World after Bush,' *Prospect* (November 2006), 36–40.

Luttwak, Edward, 'The Middle of Nowhere,' *Prospect* 134 (2007), 26–9.

Lynch, Timothy J., 'Kristol Balls: Neoconservative Visions of the Middle East and Political Islam,' *International Politics* (forthcoming).

'Whither American Power?: A Review Essay,' *British Journal of Politics and International Relations* 9, 3 (2007), 535–44.

MacFarquhar, Neil, 'Mubarak Proposes a Freer Vote,' *New York Times*, February 28, 2005.

Maddox, Bronwen, 'The Power Is Real – but so Are the Fears,' *Times*, August 24, 2006, 38.

Maliniak, Daniel, Amy Oakes, Susan Peterson, and Michael J. Tierney, 'Inside the Ivory Tower,' *Foreign Policy* 151 (2005), 62–8.

Malzahn, Claus Christian, 'Evil Americans, Poor Mullahs,' *Spiegel* Online, March 29, 2007.

Mandelbaum, Michael, 'Foreign Policy as Social Work,' *Foreign Affairs* 75, 1 (1996).

Mann, Jim, 'China Emerges as Clinton's Knottiest Foreign Problem,' *LA Times*, September 9, 1996, A3.

Marr, Andrew, 'If "Islamist" Is Out, What Do We Call Them?' *Daily Telegraph*, July 4, 2007.

Marshall, Joshua Micah, 'Remaking the World: Bush and the Neoconservatives,' *Foreign Affairs* 82, 6 (2003).

Maze, Rick, 'No more GWOT, House Committee Decrees,' *Military Times*, April 4, 2007.

Mazzetti, Mark, 'Qaeda Is Seen as Restoring Leadership,' *New York Times*, April 2, 2007.

McCartney, Paul T., 'American Nationalism and US Foreign Policy from September 11 to the Iraq War,' *Political Science Quarterly* 119, 3 (2004), 399–424.

McConnell, Mike, 'Overhauling Intelligence,' *Foreign Affairs* 86, 4 (2007).

McGeehan, Robert, 'American Diplomacy and Adversarial Relationships: US Practices in Historical Perspectives,' *RUSI* 152, 2 (2007), 46–51.

Mearsheimer, John J., 'Back to the Future: Instability in Europe after the Cold War,' *International Security* 15, 1 (1990), 5–56.

'Hans Morgenthau and the Iraq War: Realism vs. Neo-conservatism,' *Open Democracy*, April 21, 2005; at www.opendemocracy.net/content/articles/PDF/2522.pdf.

'Why We Will Soon Miss the Cold War,' *Atlantic Monthly* (August 1990), 35–50.

Mearsheimer, John J. and Stephen Walt, 'The Israel Lobby,' *London Review of Books* 28, 6 (2006).

Meyerson, Harold, 'The Korean Analogy,' *Washington Post*, June 6, 2007, A23.

Mill, John Stuart, 'The Contest in America,' *Harper's New Monthly Magazine* 24, 143 (1862), 677–84.

Miller, Steven, 'The Iraq Experiment and US National Security,' *Survival* 48, 4 (2006–7), 17–50.

Moody, James, 'In Box: War Bonds,' *Foreign Policy* (May/June 2007).

Moore, Charles, 'Where Is the Gandhi of Islam?' *Daily Telegraph*, July 9, 2005.

Moynihan, Daniel Patrick, 'The United States in Opposition,' *Commentary* (March 1975).

Mueller, John, 'What Was the Cold War About? Evidence from Its Ending,' *Political Science Quarterly* 119, 4 (2004–5), 609–32.

'Is There Still a Terrorist Threat?: The Myth of the Omnipresent Enemy,' *Foreign Affairs* 85, 5 (2006).

'The Iraq Syndrome,' *Foreign Affairs* 84, 6 (2005), 44–54.

Murdock Deroy, 'Giuliani's Finest Hour,' *National Review*, September 14, 2001.

Nevers, Renée de, 'NATO's International Security Role in the Terrorist Era,' *International Security* 31, 4 (2007), 34–66.

O'Hanlon, Michael and Kenneth Pollack, 'A War We Just Might Win,' *New York Times*, July 30, 2007.

Obama, Barack, 'Renewing America's Leadership,' *Foreign Affairs* 86, 4 (2007), 2–16.

Owens, Mackubin Thomas, 'A Balanced Force Structure to Achieve a Liberal World Order,' *Orbis* 50, 2 (2006), 307–25.

Packer, George, 'Unrealistic,' *New Yorker*, November 27, 2006.

Paik, Haksoon, 'Kim Can Survive [letter],' *Foreign Policy* (May/June 2007), 12–13.

Perlez, Jane, 'Aid to Pakistan in Tribal Areas Raises Concerns,' *New York Times*, July 16, 2007.

Perry, William J. and Ashton B. Carter, 'If Necessary, Strike and Destroy: North Korea Cannot be Allowed to Test this Missile,' *Washington Post*, June 22, 2006.

Pipes, Daniel, 'God and Mammon: Does Poverty Cause Militant Islam?', *National Interest* 66 (2001/2),14–21.

Podhoretz, Norman, 'In Praise of the Bush Doctrine,' *Commentary* (September 2002), 19–29.

'Is the Bush Doctrine Dead?' *Commentary* (September 2006), 17–31.

Powell, Colin, 'A Strategy of Partnerships,' *Foreign Affairs* 83, 1 (2004), 22–34.

Powell, Michael, 'Appeals Court Weighs Bush's War Powers,' *Washington Post*, March 12, 2003.

Rayment, Sean, 'British Death Rate in Iraq Now Worse than America's,' *Sunday Telegraph*, July 15, 2007.

Rice, Condoleezza, 'The West Needs a Defence System That Works,' *Daily Telegraph*, April 27, 2007.

Richburg, Keith B., ' "Old Europe" Reacts to Rumsfeld's Label,' *Washington Post*, January 24, 2003.

'France's Influence Wanes in Ivory Coast,' *Washington Post*, February 4, 2003, A21.

Riedel, Bruce, 'Al Qaeda Strikes Back,' *Foreign Affairs* 86, 3 (2007).

Risen, James, 'White House is Subpoenaed on Wiretapping,' *New York Times*, June 28, 2007.

Roberts, Andrew, 'The English-Speaking Peoples and their World Role Since 1900,' *Orbis* 51, 3 (2007), 381–96.

Rose, David, 'Neo Culpa,' *Vanity Fair*, November 3, 2006.

Ross, Dennis, 'The Middle East Predicament,' *Foreign Affairs* 84, 1 (2005), 61–74.

Ross, Robert S., 'Beijing as a Conservative Power,' *Foreign Affairs* 76, 2 (1997), 33–44.

Rubin, Barry, 'The Real Roots of Arab Anti-Americanism,' *Foreign Affairs* 81, 6 (2002).

Safire, William, 'Language: Islamofascism Anyone?' *New York Times Magazine*, October 1, 2006.

Sanger, David E. and David Rohde, 'US Pays Pakistan to Fight Terror, but Patrols Ebb,' *New York Times*, May 20, 2007.

Saving, Thomas R., 'Medicare Meltdown,' *Wall Street Journal*, May 9, 2007.

Schonberg, Karl, 'Global Security and Legal Restraint: Reconsidering War Powers after September 11,' *Political Science Quarterly* 119, 1 (2004), 115–42.

Sciolino, Elaine and Ariane Bernard, 'Sarkozy Lists Foreign Priorities, with Iran First,' *New York Times*, August 28, 2007.

Shawcross, William, 'Abandon Iraq and See a Vietnam Horror Show,' *Sunday Times* (News Review), August 26, 2007.

Simes, Dimitri, 'Protecting Kosovo at the Expense of New York,' *National Interest* Online, September 9, 2006.

Simms, Brendan, 'Why British Muslims Give the US No Credit for Bosnia or Kosovo,' *Bosnian Institute*, August 24, 2005.

Simon, Steven, 'America and Iraq: The Case for Disengagement,' *Survival* 49, 1 (2007), 61–84.

Skidmore, David, 'Understanding the Unilateralist Turn in US Foreign Policy,' *Foreign Policy Analysis* 2 (2005), 207–28.

Smith, Rogers M., 'Beyond Tocqueville, Myrdal, and Hartz: The Multiple

Traditions in America,' *American Political Science Review* 87, 3 (1993), 549–66.

Snyder, Jack, 'The Crusade of Illusions,' *Foreign Affairs* 85, 4 (2006), 183–9.

Snyder, Scott, 'The Fire Last Time,' *Foreign Affairs* 83, 4 (2004).

Sofaer, Abraham D., 'Presidential Power and National Security,' *Presidential Studies Quarterly* 37, 1 (2007), 101–23.

Spence, Keith, 'World Risk Society and War Against Terror,' *Political Studies* 53, 2 (2005), 284–302.

Stephens, Bret, 'Realists to the Rescue?' *Commentary* (February 2007), 27–34.

Stevens, Jacqueline, 'Beyond Tocqueville, Please!' *American Political Science Review* 89, 4 (1995), 987–95.

Steyn, Mark, 'Insight,' *Jewish World Review*, September 27, 2002.

'Realists Have It Wrong,' *Washington Times*, January 31, 2005.

'World is Watching as Iraq War Tests US Mettle,' *Chicago Sun-Times*, August 20, 2006.

Sullivan, Andrew, 'The Isolationist Beast Stirs in America Again,' *Sunday Times* (News Review), July 29, 2007, 4.

Sunstein, Cass R., 'The Case for Fear,' *New Republic*, December 11, 2006, 29–33.

Suskind, Ron, 'The Untold Story of al-Qaeda's Plot to Attack the Subway,' *Time*, June 19, 2006.

Takeyh, Ray, 'Time for Detente with Iran,' *Foreign Affairs* 86, 2 (2007), 17–32.

'The GWOT No More,' *Weekly Standard* 10, 44 (August 8, 2005).

Tkacik Jr., John J., 'The Arsenal of the Iraq Insurgency: It's Made in China,' *Weekly Standard*, 12, 45 (August 13, 2007).

Trenin, Dmitri, 'Russia Redefines Itself and Its Relations with the West,' *Washington Quarterly* 30, 2 (2007), 95–105.

Tucker, Robert W. and David C. Hendrickson, 'The Sources of American Legitimacy,' *Foreign Affairs* 83, 6 (2004), 18–32.

'Vanity Unfair,' *National Review*, November 5, 2006.

Vlahos, Michael, 'Losing Mythic Authority,' *National Interest* 89 (2007), 87–91.

Walden, George, '"So, Henry, How Would You Handle It?" George Walden Meets Henry Kissinger,' *Sunday Times* (News Review), April 1, 2007, 5.

Waltz, Kenneth N., 'The Emerging Structure of International Politics,' *International Security* 18, 2 (1993), 44–79.

Wedgwood, Ruth and Kenneth Roth, 'Combatants or Criminals?' *Foreign Affairs* 83, 3 (2004), 126–9.

Williams, William Appleman, 'The Frontier Thesis and American Foreign Policy,' *Pacific Historical Review* 24 (1955).

Wohlforth, William, 'Unipolar Stability: The Rules of Power Analysis,' *Harvard International Review* 29, 1 (2007), 44–8.

Woods, Kevin, James Lacey and Williamson Murray, 'Saddam's Delusions: The View from the Inside,' *Foreign Affairs* 85, 3 (2006).

Yoo, John and Robert J. Delahunty, 'Executive Power v. International Law,' *Harvard Journal of Law & Public Policy* 30, 1 (2006).

York, Byron, 'Halliburton: The Bush/Iraq Scandal That Wasn't,' *National Review*, July 14, 2003.

Zakaria, Fareed, 'The Reagan Strategy of Containment,' *Political Science Quarterly* 105, 3 (1990), 373–95.

Zeleny, Jeff, 'Obama Calls for US to Shift Focus on Terrorism,' *New York Times*, August 1, 2007.

Zuckerman, Mort, 'The Mullah Menace,' *US News and World Report*, December 11, 2006, 86.

Zulaika, Joseba, 'The Self-fulfilling Prophesies of Counterterrorism,' *Radical History Review* 85 (2003), 191–9.

3. SPEECHES

Albright, Madeleine, speech in Columbus, Ohio, February 18, 1998.

Blair, Ian, speech to London Muslims, July 15, 2005.

Blair, Tony, speech at the Economic Club, Chicago, April 24, 1999.

Bush, George W., remarks by the president, September 16, 2001.

speech to joint session of Congress, September 20, 2001.

State of the Union Address, January 29, 2002.

speech at West Point, New York, June 1, 2002.

remarks at a dinner for Senatorial candidate Elizabeth Dole, Greensboro, North Carolina, July 25, 2002.

speech at Whitehall, London, November 19, 2003.

State of the Union Address, January 20, 2004.

radio address, July 29, 2006.

speech in Tipp City, Ohio, April 19, 2007.

speech at Czernin Palace, Prague, June 5, 2007.

Clinton, Bill, 'American Foreign Policy and the Democratic Ideal,' speech at Pabst Theater, Milwaukee, Wisconsin, October 1, 1992.

Clinton, Hillary, Democratic presidential candidate debate, New Hampshire, June 3, 2007.

Ikenberry, G. John, Bryce Lecture at the Institute for the Study of the Americas, University of London, June 5, 2005.

Kagan, Frederick, paper at the International Institute for Strategic Studies, London, July 23, 2007.

Lieber, Robert J., 'The American Era,' paper at Institute for the Study of the Americas, University of London, November 10, 2006.

Lincoln, Abraham, speech at Springfield, Illinois, June 26, 1857.

McCain, John, Republican convention address, 2004.

Obama, Barack, speech at Chicago Council on Global Affairs, April 23, 2007.

Reagan, Ronald, national radio address on welfare reform, February 15, 1986.

Roosevelt, Franklin Delano, speech at Chautauqua, New York, August 14, 1936.

Rumsfeld, Donald, congressional testimony, July 9, 2003.

Washington, George, Farewell Address, 1796.

4. COURT CASES

Al-Marri v. Wright (2007)
Campbell v. Clinton (1999)
Crockett v. Reagan (1982)
DaCosta v. Laird (1973)
Dellums v. Bush (1990)
Dennis v. United States (1951)
Doe v. Bolton (2003)
Hamdan v. Rumsfeld (2006)
Hamdi v. Rumsfeld (2004)
Holtzman v. Schlesinger (1973)
Lowry v. Reagan (1987)
Prize Cases (1863)
Rasul v. Bush (2004)
Schenck v. US (1919)
Terminiello v. City of Chicago (1949)
Trop v. Dulles (1958)
US v. Curtiss-Wright Export Corporation (1936)
US v. Nixon (1974)
Youngstown Sheet and Tube Co. v. Sawyer (1952)

5. DOCUMENTS, REPORTS, AND OTHER MEDIA

Belasco, Amy, 'The Cost of Iraq, Afghanistan, and Other Global War on Terror Operations since 9/11,' CRS Report (RL33110), June 28, 2007; at www.fas.org/sgp/crs/natsec/RL33110.pdf.

Blarchard, Christopher M., 'Al Qaeda: Statements and Evolving Ideology,' CRS Report (RL32759), July 9, 2007.

Butler Review of Intelligence on Weapons of Mass Destruction; at www.butlerreview.org.uk/.

Center for Defense Information, *Russia Weekly* no. 245, 21 (February 2003), at www.cdi.org/russia/245-14.cfm.

Chomsky, Noam, Interview on BBC *Newsnight*, May 20, 2004.

Cordesman, Anthony, 'The Changing Challenges of US Defense Spending,' CSIS Report, February 12, 2007.

Council of Foreign Relations, 'US–China Relations: An Affirmative Agenda, A Responsible Course,' Report of an Independent Task Force, (2007); at www.cfr.org/content/publications/.attachments/ChinaTaskForce.pdf.

Gallup Poll on Patriot Act, 2005, at www.galluppoll.com/content/default.aspx?ci=5263.

Grimmett, Richard F., 'The War Powers Resolution after Thirty Years,' CRS Report (RL32267), March 11, 2004.

'Instances of Use of United States Armed Forces Abroad, 1798–2006,' CRS Report (RL30172), January 8, 2007.

Hildreth, Steven A. and Carl Ek, 'Long-Range Ballistic Missile Defense in Europe,' CRS Report (RL34051), June 22, 2007; at www.fas.org/sgp/crs/weapons/RL340514.pdf.

Hutton Inquiry: Investigation into the Circumstances Surrounding the Death of Dr. David Kelly; at www.the-hutton-inquiry.org.uk/.

Iraq Study Group Report (2006); at www.usip.org/isg/iraq_study_group_report/report/1206/.

Lugar, Richard, The Lugar Survey on Proliferation Threats and Responses, June 2005; at http://lugar.senate.gov/reports/NPSurvey.pdf.

'Muslim Americans: Middle-class and Mostly Mainstream,' Pew Research Center, May 22, 2007; at http://pewresearch.org/assests/pdf/muslim- american.pdf.

National Intelligence Council, Trends in Global Terrorism: Implications for the United States, National Intelligence Estimate, April 2006.

Prospects for Iraq's Stability: A Challenging Road Ahead, National Intelligence Estimate, January 2007.

The Terrorist Threat to the US Homeland, National Intelligence Estimate, July 2007.

Prospects for Iraq's Stability: Some Security Progress but Political Reconciliation Elusive, National Intelligence Estimate, August 2007.

National Security Advisory Group Report, 'Worst Weapons in Worst Hands: US Inaction on the Nuclear Terror Threat since 9/11' (2005); at http://democrats.senate.gov/pdfs/NSAG_WorstWeaponsinWorstHands_July2005.pdf.

National Security Council strategy paper no. 68 (NSC-68), April 1950.

9/11 Commission Report (2004); at www.9-11commission.gov/report/911Report.pdf. Amnesty International Reports for 2001 and 2007; at www.Amnesty.org.

Nuclear Black Markets: Pakistan, A. Q. Khan and the Rise of Proliferation Networks: A Net Assessment, IISS, May 2007; at www.iiss.org/publications/strategic-dossiers/nbm.

Office of Homeland Security, National Strategy for Homeland Security (2002).

Office of Inspector General Report on CIA Accountability with Respect to the 9/11 Attacks, June 2005; made public August 21, 2007; at http://graphics8.nytimes.com/packages/pdf/national/CIA_SUMMARY.pdf

PBS, Frontline: The Invasion of Iraq, broadcast 2004; at www.pbs.org/wgbh/pages/frontline/shows/invasion/.

Pew Global Attitudes Project Report, June 2007.

Presidential Debate, University of Miami, September 30, 2004; at http://www.debates.org/pages/trans2004a.html.

Rumsfeld, Donald, memorandum to Dick Myers, Paul Wolfowitz, Peter Pace, and Douglas Feith, October 18, 2003; reproduced at www.globalsecurity.org/military/library/policy/dod/d20031016sdmemo.pdf.

Sabasteanski, Anna, ed., US Department of State, 'Patterns of Global Terrorism Report, 1985–2005', Great Barrington, MA: Berkshire Publishing Group, 2005.

Sharp, Jeremy M. and Christopher M. Blanchard, 'Post-war Iraq: Foreign Contributions to Training, Peacekeeping, and Reconstruction,' CRS Report (RL32105), June 18, 2007.

Singer, Peter W., *The 9–11 War Plus 5, Looking Back and Looking Forward at US–Islamic Relations*, Bookings Institution, September 2006.

Taylor, Peter, *Al Qaeda: Time To Talk?*, BBC series, 2006.

The National Military Strategy of the United States of America 2005.

Transatlantic Trends 2004, 2005, 2006, German Marshall Fund of the United States; at www.transatlantictrends.org/.

UN Development Program, Arab Human Development Report, 2002; at www.undp.org/arabstates/ahdr2002.shtml.

Arab Human Development Report, 2003; at www.undp.org/arabstates/ahdr2003.shtml.

US Congress, Joint Inquiry into Intelligence Community Activities before and after the Terrorist Attacks of September 11, 2001 (2002).

US Department of Defense, Principal Wars Table; at http://siadapp.dmdc.osd.mil/personnel/CASUALTY/castop.htm.

The Quadrennial Defense Review Report, February 2006.

US Department of Homeland Security, *Yearbook of Immigration Statistics 2006*; at http://www.dhs.gov/ximgtn/statistics/publications/LPR06.shtm.

US Office of Management and Budget, *The Budget for Fiscal Year 2005, Historical Series*, 45–50.

White House, 'A National Security Strategy for a Global Age,' National Security Strategy of the United States, December 2000.

National Security Strategy of the United States, September 2002.

Commission on the Intelligence Capabilities of the United States Regarding Weapons of Mass Destruction, March 31, 2005; at www.wmd.gov/report/.

National Security Strategy of the United States, March 2006.

2008 Budget Fact Sheets, February 2007; at www.whitehouse. gov/infocus/budget/BudgetFY2008.pdf.

Historical Tables, Budget of the United States Government, Fiscal Year 2008; at www.whitehouse.gov/omb/budget/fy2008/pdf/hist.pdf.

Index